GROUP COUNSELING IN K–12 SCHOOLS

A Handbook for School Counselors

KENNETH R. GREENBERG

University of Maryland at College Park

Boston   New York   San Francisco
Mexico City   Montreal   Toronto   London   Madrid   Munich   Paris
Hong Kong   Singapore   Tokyo   Cape Town   Sydney

To my precious wife, Betty, whom I love very much; to George, our highly intelligent and very special Bichon Frise who was under my chair as I wrote every page of the book; and to the hundreds of my students who taught me as much as they learned from me.

Executive Editor: *Virginia Lanigan*
Editorial Assistant: *Robert Champagne*
Production Administrator: *Marissa Falco*
Electronic Composition: *Galley Graphics, Ltd.*
Composition and Prepress Buyer: *Linda Cox*
Manufacturing Buyer: *JoAnne Sweeney*
Cover Administrator: *Kristina Mose-Libon*

For related titles and support materials, visit our online catalog at www.ablongman.com.

Library of Congress Cataloging-in-Publication Data

CIP Data not available at time of publication

ISBN 0-205-32195-x

Printed in the United States of America

10 9 8 7 6   RRD-IN   09 08 07

CONTENTS

standardized tests yet is getting Ds or is doing failing work; a student who is engaging in delinquent behaviors; a young adolescent whose problems relate to having begun experimentation with drugs and sex; a student who is truant, refuses to do school work, and insults and defies teachers; or a young adolescent who is showing signs of oppositional and defiant behaviors. Although the early warning signs of aggressive and hostile behavior can often be identified in the elementary grades, it is during the middle and junior high school years that hostile and antisocial behavior becomes apparent. Middle and junior high school counselors will also try to intervene with students who have been identified as being "at risk" of dropping out of school.

The high school counselor must be prepared to work with many of the problems seen in elementary, middle, and junior high schools. Inasmuch as academic and social problems that begin in the elementary school years often continue into middle and junior high school and high school, the problems that have been ignored or not adequately dealt with earlier will persist into the high school years.

On any given day, a high school counselor could see an adolescent who threatens to commit suicide, an adolescent who drinks alcohol to excess or uses illicit drugs, a girl who is pregnant and does not want her parents to know, or an adolescent who displays violent behavior toward classmates. The high school counselor must also focus on college counseling for the college-bound student and school-to-work transitions for those students who will enter the workforce. High school counselors see students who have a history of a negative attitude toward school and who will either drop out of school or graduate lacking basic academic skills. These are the students who leave school unprepared for work and without a vocational direction.

In addition to these issues, all school counselors are prepared to face crisis situations that involve the total school community. Most schools experience one or more crisis situations every year. A crisis situation could result from a shooting or killing of a student, a racial incident, a traffic accident resulting in serious injury or death to one or more students, a bomb threat that disrupts the school and upsets students and their parents, the death of a student or member of the school's faculty, or a national crisis, such as a war or military action that takes parents and/or siblings away from the home.

With increased diversity in our society, schools face multicultural issues resulting in language and teaching problems. Interactions between the school and home are difficult when teachers or counselors are unable to communicate with either the student or the student's parents. There has been a steady increase of non-English-speaking children at all school levels, and most school counselors are not bilingual. The school counselor, functioning in a pluralistic society and working with a diverse student population, must be culturally sensitive to ethnic and racial groups.

School counseling, whether it is done individually or in groups, is directed at the child who does not present severe emotional problems or clinical disorders and whose behavior and/or attitude concerns fall within the training and scope of the counselor. School counselors are not expected to function as if they had the therapeutic training of a clinical psychologist, psychiatrist, or psychiatric social worker. School counselors' training allows them to work with students in a K–12 school setting who are having academic, social, behavioral, coping, career, and certain personal adjustment problems. School counselors will often, however, encounter a student whose attitude or behavior deviates from what is considered *normal* and whose problems exceed the boundaries of the school counselor's professional competency based on the counselor's training. Children who frequently and seriously talk about committing suicide, who threaten to harm themselves or others, who present what would appear to be a serious eating problem, who seem to be extremely sad or highly agitated, or who demonstrate behavior that is viewed by the counselor to be bizarre or unusual are examples of this deviation. The ethical professional school counselor would be prepared to refer such children to an appropriate out-of-school source.

In order to meet the many challenges of their profession, school counselors must be able to select from a variety of counseling approaches and utilize multiple strategies. Colleges and universities that train graduate students to become school counselors emphasize the importance of developing and maintaining a *comprehensive guidance and counseling program* that includes individual and group counseling, consultation with teachers and parents, coordination of pupil services, and classroom guidance activities. This book will examine one of the strategies that is utilized by almost all elementary school counselors, most middle and junior high school counselors, and many high school counselors, namely, group counseling.

Many sources refer to a child who is seen by the school counselor as a *client.* Although this is a valid term that can be used to describe the recipient of counseling, this writer feels the term *client* may not be appropriate for describing the child seen by a school counselor in a K–12 setting. Some school-aged children are not comfortable being referred to as a client. For this reason, the words *student, child,* or *counselee* will be used to refer to the person seen by the counselor in a school setting. *Group member* or *member* will be used to refer to students who are in a group counseling situation.

A COUNSELING POINT OF VIEW: ACTIVE COUNSELING

Before discussing the establishment of a group counseling program in K–12 schools, an overview of the author's approach to counseling that underlies both individual and group counseling as described in this text will be presented. School counselors have the opportunity to exert a major impact on the life of a child. Whether conducting individual or group counseling, what a counselor says, or fails to say, to a counselee can mean the difference between effective and ineffective counseling. School counselors *listen carefully* to what students are saying and they talk *with* a child. The counselor often represents the only adult with whom a child or adolescent can comfortably interact and feel safe. Counselors should be cognizant of the responsibility they undertake each time they interact with a child. What a school counselor says and how it is said can either encourage or discourage a child, reduce or exacerbate angry and negative feelings, succeed or fail to motivate a child to improve academic performance, or develop a reputation in the school that is either appealing or unappealing to students.

School counselors are aware that counseling services are for all students and that change is not easily achieved. They should also realize that for change to occur, the counselor must be prepared to either do something *for* or say something *to* the counselee. Inviting a child to become a member of a group or helping a child develop more effective study habits is something the counselor can do *for* a child. Praising a student who has low self-esteem when the child has successfully completed an assigned task or offering an interpretation that enables a counselee to acquire insight into a problem are examples of something the counselor can *say to* a child. In order for counseling to be successful, a counselee must be sufficiently motivated to make changes and be willing to do what is necessary in order to bring about change. Active counseling places responsibility on both the counselor and counselee to work together to develop a *game plan* that looks at what needs to be done and how to go about doing it most efficiently. Whereas some problems are best met through individual counseling, other problems would suggest that group counseling might be the strategy of choice. When feedback from a peer group is important or when a student is in need of a peer support system, the preferred approach would be to use group counseling. When confidentiality is necessary or when environmental and family matters are involved, individual counseling would be preferred. Both individual and group counseling should be goal directed and both should utilize an active approach on the part of the counselor.

The primary tool that school counselors use to help children is *words*. Words help the counselor establish the counseling relationship. Words are used to communicate to students that the counselor accepts them as they are and regards their concerns as important. Words are used to help students feel that their counselor is understanding, empathic, and caring. Words are what the counselor uses to help students develop insights, anticipate consequences, learn to problem solve, or encourage change. Appropriate words can encourage and help to motivate a child. The words that are used are a reflection of the counselor's training, experience, knowledge, and the skill needed in order for counseling to make a difference in the child's life.

Words that children hear can also explain why children have negative feelings about themselves and have acquired certain problems. Children who have been insulted by being referred to as lazy, stupid, clumsy, fat, or other negative words can be expected to react to the labels others have placed on them. Whether the words come from parents, peers, or teachers, children react to the implied meaning of the words that have been directed toward them. Children also label themselves and act in accordance with the label. A girl who has labeled herself shy will probably act shy in social situations. People are inclined to either live up to or down to their labels. The label frequently becomes a self-fulfilling prophecy. Our self-esteem is determined largely on the basis of the words we have heard ascribed to us and the words we use to describe ourselves. It is also determined by our perception of how people have reacted to us. For example, if Steve is called a liar by his father, he could feel justified in continuing to lie to his father since he could view the label as a license to lie. The opposite is likewise true. A counselor who says to a student who is underachieving, "Your teachers and the results of your achievement test scores indicate that there is very good reason to feel that you are bright enough to get higher grades in all of your subjects. Why don't we find a way to help you get better grades?" could be using words to correct a misperception and possibly motivate a child to begin to succeed.

SKILLS FOR EFFECTIVE SCHOOL COUNSELING

There is no single strategy that can be used for all students or all problems. Counselors need to be knowledgeable and feel comfortable with a variety of intervention strategies and know when each could be used. When a counselor sees a student four or more times as part of a sustaining relationship, favorable outcomes are more predictable when some discernible strategy and counseling plan has been used. Counseling is not just saying whatever comes to the counselor's mind. Counselors who do not employ a strategy or do not counsel from a plan are less effective. A counseling plan should be tailor-made according to the uniqueness of each student and developed with goals that are realistic.

A counseling game plan would start with trying to understand the problem through an examination of the behavior and symptoms presented by the counselee. It would tentatively identify a counseling goal and would take into consideration specific characteristics of the counselee, such as the attitude toward the presenting problem, the strength of motivation for change, the counselee's basic ability, and how much of the solution lies within or outside the control of the counselee. It would look at the things that need to be done in order for the counselee to move in the direction of the goal or subgoals. It would identify what might be anticipated as barriers to reaching the goal, the history and severity of the problem, the counselee's success with problem solving, and what specific strategies could be tried.

Essentially, a counselor's approach in either individual or group counseling can be active, passive, or a combination of both. Passive counselors are genuine, empathic, and attentive to what the counselee says. They reflect feelings, pose questions, avoid offering suggestions, and are careful not to reveal their values. The focus of passive counseling is on the client as a person, rather than on the specific problem the client is experiencing. The counseling relationship seeks to create a climate that is conducive to self-exploration. Although the words used by the counselor in passive counseling might ultimately encourage the client to do problem solving, emphasis is placed on the relationship that develops between the counselee and the counselor, which is directed toward the growth of the person.

In active counseling, the focus is on change, the acquisition of insights into the reasons for specific behaviors, the actions the student will need to take, or the attitudes the student will need to alter in order to achieve the counseling objectives. The words the counselee hears from the counselor are the vehicle whereby changes can occur. This writer does not feel that using a passive approach exclusively is appropriate with children in a K–12 setting. Children at these ages need greater structure, specific direction, clearly defined goals, and two-way interaction with the counselor. Because the school counselor does not have the luxury of seeing children many times, school counseling should be thought of as being short-term and, therefore, more direct and goal-oriented.

Active counselors are encouraged to speculate about what could be causing a child's behavior. They evaluate how motivated their counselees' are to make changes and what words or actions could move them in the direction of mutually agreed-on counseling goals. Active counselors also try to differentiate *symptoms* from *problems*. Underachievement is a symptom. Lying, bullying, aggressiveness, and what teachers refer to as conduct problems are also symptoms. A lack of self-esteem or a feeling of inadequacy would be an example of a problem. *Symptoms* address overt and observable behaviors. *Problems* relate more to attitudes and the underlying feelings that bring about the symptoms. Symptoms identify *what* the child is doing; the problem looks at *the reason* the child is doing it. If a counselor is successful in helping a student elevate low self-esteem, many symptoms might be reduced or even disappear.

Thirteen-year-old John has been identified by students as being a bully. He uses his strength to intimidate weaker students and claims to enjoy the reputation of being tough.

Over the years, John has done poorly in school, despite having average ability as measured by a standardized test of intelligence. John is also in constant conflict with his parents and is, admittedly, not a happy child. At school he is known and feared, but he is not popular. He is aware of this and shows a seemingly unconcerned I-don't-care attitude. John's bullying behavior gets him the attention and status he is seeking. He feels powerful when he is able to control others and appears indifferent to the effect his bullying has on those whom he torments. If, through counseling, John can be shown that he could be liked and respected for his strength and that he does not have to resort to bullying in order to feel powerful, helping John to elevate his self-esteem might reduce his need to be a bully. From a counselor's perspective, focusing on symptoms might offer immediate relief to a situation, but if the underlying reason for the behavior is not identified, counseling goals will be limited and symptoms could reappear.

There will be times when a counselor can easily relate a symptom to the underlying problem. Identifying Katie's unhappiness in school as a function of her lack of social skills would be an example of this. Only knowing that Katie lacks social skills may not accurately define the problem and, consequently, it may not identify the most effective way for the counselor to help Katie reduce or overcome her problem. Knowing whatever has prevented Katie from acquiring appropriate social skills would focus on the problem. Knowing something about the antecedents of her problem would be necessary if the counselor is to formulate a strategy for helping her learn effective social skills. If, for example, the problem relates to a lack of social experiences due to parental prohibitions, the counselor may feel it is necessary to consult with Katie's parents. Likewise, learning *why* Adam underachieves addresses Adam's problem of underachievement. The active counselor tries to identify the problem.

School counselors have large case loads and are responsible for doing many things in addition to counseling. Consequently, the number of sustaining cases they can work with at a given time is restricted. For this reason, and also because their training limits them to school-related problems, school counselors are forced to focus primarily on symptoms. Even so, by talking with a child and through careful fact-finding, counselors should be able to come close to defining the underlying problem. Using Jason as an example, let us suppose Jason's third-grade teacher refers him to the school counselor. Jason is disobedient, distracts the class with attention-getting behaviors, rejects the teacher's authority, and refuses to turn in his homework. The teacher feels that Jason has a serious conduct problem. Through interacting with Jason, the school counselor determines that Jason's problem is related to the way his parents treat him. The counselor feels that Jason appears to be rebelling against strict parental control, which seems to carry over to the interactions he has with his teacher. Unfortunately, the school counselor will feel frustrated because the counselor will probably not be able to address the parental issue; the counselor is neither trained nor expected to do family counseling. The school counselor, who will work with Jason to help him to acquire better self-control, should realize that Jason's behavior is probably symptomatic of an underlying problem that was caused by events that occurred, or are still occurring, in his home and must be content to work on Jason's symptoms because dealing with the problem goes beyond the counselor's scope. If addressing the symptoms is successful in helping Jason reduce or overcome his conduct problem, a significant change could occur that would have an impact on how he interacts with his teacher and could effect both his school attitude and academic progress. The school counselor would probably make contact with Jason's parents and encourage them to seek help in resolving a family problem. Even though the counselor is dealing with symptoms, the active school counselor never loses sight of the source of the problem.

In the context of counseling, it is important to differentiate two uses of the word *problem.* There is the *basic problem,* which is the underlying cause of the behavior that is seen, and the *presenting problem,* which is used to describe the behavior that brings a student into the counselor's office. Jason's teacher identifies his problem as one of refusing to follow class rules and disrupting the class. This would be the presenting problem. A counselor could view not following class rules and disrupting the class as a symptom of some underlying basic problem. Jason's behavior signals resistance toward the teacher. Resistance toward the teacher could be due to the teacher's authoritative way of speaking to Jason. This could be an unconscious reminder of the way his parents speak to him, and if Jason is inclined to resist parental authority, he might also resist the teacher's authority. The basic problem could reflect the anger that Jason is building up toward people with authority. It could also indicate an autonomy problem that conceivably could plague Jason throughout his life. An active counselor is not content to just identify the source of a problem and then do nothing. If the source lies in parental or environmental issues, the counselor would work with the child but would also attempt to consult with parents, once or twice, to discuss the options that could resolve or reduce the problem. If this is not possible, or if this fails, the ethical thing to do would be to refer the parents to an out-of-school source.

In active counseling, counselees are asked to assume responsibility for their own progress and, when the counselor feels that counselees are ready, they are encouraged to show a willingness to take the risks necessary for change to occur. Risk-taking is accomplished through specific homework assignments directed toward the counseling goals. Homework assignments enable the counselee to practice what is being addressed in counseling. Active school counseling, conducted either individually or within a group, requires counselors to do creative thinking through asking purposeful questions, making meaningful statements, and interpreting responses that will encourage counselees to acquire insights into the reasons for their behavior.

It is important for the counselor to understand what motivates a counselee to engage in specific behaviors and the basis for attitudes that could underlie the problem. This often requires the counselor to ask a variation of *why* questions: "What makes you think it's so difficult for you to make friends?" or, "Your teacher says that you often refuse to do what she asks you to do. Is there a reason that you aren't willing to cooperate with her?" When good rapport has been established, even a question beginning with *why* can be appropriate. It will be viewed by the counselee as a way for the counselor to obtain important information that could be helpful and need not put the child in a defensive mode. For example, assuming there is good rapport, asking "Why do you think you are picked on by your classmates?" would be seen as probing for information and an opportunity for children to realize that their opinions and explanations are valued. *How* the question is asked is important because our tone of voice and the words we emphasize can make a difference in the way a question is interpreted.

Active counselors speculate as to *why* students might have certain problems. In order to move from speculation to feeling more confident of the reasons for the behavior, counselors need to hear their counselees talk about what *they* think the cause of the problem to be. Knowing *why* something occurs removes much of the speculation. It also yields information as to the dynamics, or the cause–effect relationship of the basic problem. Counselee insight often starts with the counselor's awareness of the basic problem. Once the counselor acquires an understanding of the problem, it is possible to help the counselee gain the insights that are needed to understand *why* the problem exists and persists. Information learned by the counselor should facilitate counselor interpretations, which are often followed by counselee insights. Insights can determine the specific things the counselee could start or stop doing in order to reduce or eliminate the problem. Because there is often more than one way to interpret behavior, the counselor should examine each interpretation to determine which explanation seems to be the most valid for a particular counselee.

Tony says to his counselor, "I don't like my teacher." When asked why, Tony responds, "Because she's mean."

Counselor: Explain what you mean by "she's mean."

Tony: Oh, she hollers at me all the time.

Counselor: Do you really mean all of the time . . . or is it just some of the time?

Tony: Well, most of the time.

Counselor: Are you the only one she hollers at?

Tony: (pause) No, but she hollers at me a lot.

Counselor: Who else hollers at you?

Tony: Nobody.

Counselor: Nobody? You mean no one else ever gets mad and hollers at you?

Tony: Well, sometimes my father hollers at me.

Counselor: Do you think that your father is mean?

Tony: (pause) Sometimes.

Counselor: When does your father get mad at you?

Tony: When he tells me to do something . . . and I don't do it right away.

Counselor: What else does he do when you don't do something right away?

Tony: He makes me go to my room and won't let me watch television.

Counselor: Is that the only way he punishes you?

Tony: Well, he used to spank me, but he hasn't done that lately.

Counselor: I have the impression that you don't like to be told what to do.

Tony: (pause) I guess so.

Counselor: And it sounds like your teacher often tells you what to do.

Tony: Yeh. She's always telling me what to do.

The counselor may be starting to identify the problem although further probing would be necessary. The initial impression is that Tony could be rebelling against authority and does not like to be told what to do. He could be displacing the occasional anger he feels toward his father on to his teacher, knowing she cannot punish him the way his father does. The active counselor tries to understand why we do what we do and attempts to interpret what the symptoms could mean.

Active counselors know when and how to probe for more information. They also *use* the information they obtain in order to understand and help their counselee. They are not just collecting unnecessary information to engage the counselee in conversation. Every question should have a purpose. Active counselors encourage their counselees to reflect on their behavior by responding to questions that seek answers to *why* they might be doing certain things. In talking with Tony, the active counselor might ask, "What makes it difficult for you to do what your father asks you to do?" or, "Help me to understand why you would do something that you know will upset your teacher?" They also try to motivate their counselees to learn to do effective problem solving. Active counselors believe that change is possible and they understand that one of the functions of a counselor *is to do and say what is necessary to facilitate change.* They know that a counselor cannot *make* a counselee change; only the counselee can bring about change. They also never forget that *it is the counselee who owns the problem.* The mission of the active school counselor is to develop and implement a plan, agreed to by the counselee, that would encourage the counselee to engage in behaviors that would make the counseling goals attainable.

The scope of the school counselor also limits what they can do. They are not in a position to deal with the problem of dysfunctional parents or negative environmental conditions that may be impacting on the student and, ultimately, the counseling goals. To illustrate how parental factors influence counseling goals, let us suppose a school counselor is seeing Nancy, a self-referred, withdrawn 12-year-old girl who lacks social skills and says she has no friends. Nancy's self-esteem is low and she states that she is very unhappy. Counseling goals, or the game plan, could be to help her to acquire one or two friends and to elevate her self-esteem. Before Nancy can be happy and feel good about herself, she must begin to like and respect herself. The counselor learns from Nancy that her parents have always been highly critical and verbally abusive to her. They have called her an "airhead" and have told her repeatedly that she "never does anything right." They also criticize her for letting people take advantage of her. She has frequently heard her father say, "You just don't have common sense." Her parents refer to her classmates as being stupid, silly, and only interested in using her. Both of her parents have given Nancy reasons to feel that no matter what she does she cannot please them. They seldom, if ever, praise her and are quick to point out her shortcomings. Nancy is not able to play or interact with her peers after school because she is expected to come home directly from school and do her homework, while baby-sitting her 4-year-old brother. When she is not in school, Nancy is responsible for her brother. Both of her parents are employed and neither will miss work in order to meet with the counselor. Her mother has also told Nancy that the time she spends talking with the counselor is a waste of time. Her mother's message to Nancy is, "You've got to help yourself. No one can do it for you." Under these circumstances, the school counselor would feel that the initial counseling goals, as stated earlier, will be difficult to achieve.

Until Nancy's parents are able to be comprehend the level of their daughter's unhappiness and be willing to examine the strong impact their comments have had on her, the school counselor can only deal with the symptoms of her problem. Nancy has been programmed to dislike herself and to doubt her ability. Until her parents stop their verbal abuse, Nancy will continue to be unhappy. Nancy has been labeled by her parents and she is living down to the label. The counselor might be able to help Nancy acquire school friendships, but the prognosis for helping her elevate her self-concept is contingent upon changes in her home environment.

Being aware of the unobtainable goals for Nancy, subgoals would need to be established by the counselor that are realistically attainable. For example, encouraging Nancy to say "Hi" to a girl in her class would be a subgoal. Sitting next to someone at lunch who appears to be friendly would be another subgoal. Making a point of saying something to that person in the lunchroom is yet another subgoal. When the counselor feels that Nancy is ready, she would be encouraged to try to join in with two or three girls on the playground or talk with girls on the school bus. This represents a significant subgoal. All subgoals are directed toward the final goal, which, unfortunately, is being thwarted by parental attitudes and lack of cooperation.

The counselor would encourage Nancy to take an active role in solving her presenting problems, yet if she were unable to initiate ideas for overcoming or reducing them, the active counselor would be prepared to suggest activities. "Tell me what would you like to try to do?" is the type of question the active counselor would ask. Nancy will never be asked to do something that the counselor feels she is not able or ready to do. Setting an unrealistic goal would set up Nancy for another failure, which she does not need. Many school counselors develop contracts with their counselees that are beyond what the counselee is willing or able to do. The result is often another negative experience for the counselee and disappointment for the counselor.

The active counselor would also keep trying to make contact with Nancy's parents and stress to them why it is in Nancy's best interest that they meet with the counselor. At a parental meeting the counselor would attempt to tactfully discourage their verbal abuse and encourage them to allow Nancy to develop peer relationships. They would also be asked to examine the consequences of their attitude toward their daughter. Parents can be reluctant to change until they are shown that their parenting practices are harming their child. Unless otherwise informed, the counselor should believe that parents want to help their children and want to see them succeed. The statement her parents would hear from the counselor might be, "I want Nancy to become a happy child and enjoy her life and also feel confident about herself. I'm sure you want the same things for her and, with your help, there's a good chance this can happen."

All counselor trainees are expected to learn about such things as the role of the school counselor, what a comprehensive guidance and counseling program tries to accomplish, and the principles of developmental and responsive counseling. They should be able to recognize the symptoms of common school problems such as separation anxiety, school phobia, academic underachievement, conduct disorders, low self-esteem, shyness, passivity, nonassertiveness, bullyness, and the signs of an attention deficit disorder with and without hyperactivity. Active school counselors would be expected to be able to offer reasons that could explain why children have these specific problems and practice intervention strategies for dealing with each of these issues.

Counseling is more than cognitive awareness of problems. Counseling is the skill of developing a good rapport with the counselee. Counseling is a method of interacting. Counseling encourages problem solving. Effective counselors are perceptive, incisive, and highly communicative. Counseling is as much an art as it is a skill. The key word in defining counseling objectives is *change.* For this reason, school counselors could properly refer to themselves as being *change agents.* Counseling that does not produce any noticeable change in attitude or behavior has not been successful. If the relationship between the child and counselor only results in the child feeling comfortable with the counselor, but the presenting problems that brought the child into counseling remain, the effectiveness of the counseling is questionable. In individual counseling, changes that occur can be attributed, in part, to the relationship that is established between the child and counselor. In group counseling, changes occur as a result of the impact that the group interactions have had on the child, aided by the skillful leadership of the counselor, who functions as the group leader.

Counseling for children in K–12 schools must be more than asking a series of questions and reflecting back to the counselee the feelings that were just expressed. School counseling must be more than giving a child a piece of candy to reinforce good behavior, or developing a behavior chart in hopes that a child will not tire of complying in order to earn a gold star. School counseling must be more than just listening to what a counselee says and responding with an "uh huh." Children who are referred to the counselor need help; children who self-refer to the counselor are asking for help. The counselor who is committed to becoming an active counselor will try to do more than just *"band-aid" counseling,* which focuses primarily on symptoms and ignores the problem. The active counselor seeks the causes that could explain the symptoms.

The school counselor in the twenty-first century can expect to see children with multiple problems who need to acquire insights and learn how to do problem solving in order to overcome or reduce those things that are troubling them. Counselors must feel that they possess the skills needed to help their counselees work toward obtaining solutions to their problems. School counselors must believe that given the opportunity, they can make a difference in the life of a child.

A model for brief counseling using an active approach can be found in Appendix A. It is recommended for use when the counselor feels that short-term counseling, involving six or more sessions, is appropriate and when the counselee is or can be motivated to make changes. The model does not make reference to parental involvement, although contact with parents is often necessary. The school counselor can certainly see parents once, and perhaps twice, but because the counselor's function is primarily to work with students, the counselor should be prepared to refer parents to outside professional resources when it is felt that parental or family counseling is needed. Seeing both parents can be important. Despite the fact that both parents may be employed and that meeting with the counselor may be inconvenient for them, the active counselor views parental participation as an indication of parental priorities involving the welfare of their child. If Donna had a toothache, her parent would find a way to take her to a dentist. If a physician were giving a report to parents about a serious medical problem their child was experiencing, in all probability both parents would attend that consultation. The counselor should expect the same cooperation and interest from parents when it is felt that parental involvement is necessary in order to attain the counseling goals. A favorable prognosis is often dependent on the degree to which parents become actively involved in the game plan.

CAPITAL-C AND SMALL-c COUNSELORS

School counselors should realize that some teachers feel that in comparison to what they do as teachers, the work of the counselor is less demanding, less important, and has less value. These are the teachers who view school counselors as members of the faculty who do not have to prepare lesson plans, do not have to teach 25 or more students at one time, spend hours grading papers, deal with discipline problems in a classroom, concern themselves over low standardized test scores, attempt to teach resistant children, experience the frustration of classroom management problems, face hostile or demanding parents, or account to parents and the principal for why Johnny can't read or pass algebra. Some teachers feel that the counselor has an easy job. After all, counselors have a private office with a telephone, furniture that is more comfortable than what teachers have in their classrooms, often a carpet on their office floor, a computer and printer, and in most secondary school programs, a secretary. They believe that counselors are free to set their own schedules, do what they want, and seem to have an abundance of free time. These teachers are often unaware of what the counselor actually does during the day.

Unfortunately, this negative image of counselors can be valid for what this writer refers to as the *small-c counselor.* In contrast to what can be called the *capital-C counselor,* small-c counselors manage to keep very busy doing many things . . . other than counseling. The reputation of many school counselors in secondary schools is such that a student would see a counselor only when a class schedule needed to be developed or altered or when a change is wanted from one class to another. Students in high schools would see a counselor when a letter of recommendation to a college or work situation is needed. Unfortunately, many students in secondary schools who could benefit from counseling do not view the counselor as the person to see if they are facing a personal problem that is having an impact on their school attitude, schoolwork, or life in general. In some schools, the counselor's role is viewed primarily as a guidance function, rather than a counseling function. This is due, in part, to what counselors have been assigned to do by the principal, rather than what their training has expected or encouraged them to do or what they really want to do.

It is unfortunate when the role of the counselor includes a number of noncounseling activities. Any activity whether before, during, or after school that places the counselor in a potentially authoritative role, involves the counselor in an administrative function within the school, or prevents the counselor from doing guidance or counseling tasks would be an inappropriate activity. Counselors who routinely perform lunch duty, hall duty, or bus duty, or function as substitute teachers, or, in the case of some elementary school counselors, serve as the acting principal when the principal must be out of the building, could conceivably find themselves being forced to assume a dual role should it become necessary to assume the role of a disciplinarian. When counselors, who strive to be perceived as being nonthreatening, nonpunitive, and nonconfrontational, are forced to become authoritative in order to control unruly students, they have compromised their primary role. Engaging in a dual role runs contrary to the ethical standards established by the American Counseling Association (ACA) and the American School Counselors Association (ASCA).

Middle, junior, and high school counselors who spend enormous amounts of time working out class schedules for students throughout the school year or doing work that a competent secretary might be expected to do are not available to deliver needed guidance or counseling services. Small-c counselors infrequently engage in the practice of individual or group counseling; they seldom do classroom guidance. They spend considerable time consulting with teachers and parents even though their contact with the student they are discussing is minimal. They keep busy performing guidance functions instead of performing counseling services. Guidance functions *are* important, and they need to be done. School counselors should not see guidance versus counseling as a choice. If a school is to have a comprehensive guidance and counseling program, the school counselor *must* find a way to do both guidance and counseling that includes seeing students individually and in groups. Nevertheless, counseling should be considered an essential part of a school's guidance and counseling program, and these services need to be available at all school levels.

Capital-C counselors view their work as a challenge. They show a genuine interest in wanting to help children overcome, reduce, or cope with their problems. They have acquired the ability to actively listen and they try to remember most of what they hear. They are realistic and realize that the resolution of many problems is beyond the scope of what they can do to bring about change. They respect the strong influence the environment has on a child. However, they seek to overcome certain environmental problems by involving parents. Capital-C counselors work to establish a strong rapport with their counselee. They strive to increase their counselee's motivation to change and teach and encourage their counselees to do problem solving. They want their counselees to be responsible for their own progress. They often develop a written *game plan* with the counselee that outlines the counseling goals and determines the specific tasks that are needed to accomplish these goals. The counselee is made aware of the problem being addressed and the importance of cooperation. It is unfortunate and also unethical when counselees are not aware of the reason they are seeing a counselor and what it is they should be working on that could reduce or resolve their problem. Capital-C counselors view themselves as *change agents*.

GROUP COUNSELING: AN INTEGRAL PART OF THE PROGRAM

Counseling young children in groups has been shown to be an effective technique for encouraging change in school-aged children (Ehly & Dustin, 1991; Nims, 1998; Hutchinson, Freeman, & Quick, 1996; Yalom, 1975; Kreig, 1988). A successful guidance and counseling program is built around the needs of the school community and the cooperation of the administrator, faculty, and parents. Group counseling is only one aspect of the total comprehensive guidance and counseling program. Working with students in groups can only be successful when the overall guidance and counseling program is effective. For this to happen, the counselor must have acquired a reputation for being effective with students and helpful to teachers. It is essential that the comprehensive program is respected by the faculty. Respect, however, does not happen automatically; it must be earned over time. Counselors must continually work to prove their value to the faculty. They do this by successful outcomes with students, through their consultations and involvement with teachers and parents, by building a good relationship with the principal, and through the reputation they have earned in the school community. When teachers realize that spending time with the counselor is time well spent, they are not reluctant to release students for counseling purposes.

A Rationale for Group Counseling

We live in a highly socialized society that encourages both large- and small-group activities. Most children enjoy themselves more when they are playing with a group of children than when they are playing alone. Birthdays and other party occasions are fun because they involve peer groups. Groups help us form common bonds, encourage peer interaction, provide us with a sense of belonging, and encourage us to share experiences. Peer groups form naturally in schools. Students who feel they are part of a group of friends, even if the group consists of only two or three children, enjoy school more than the child who is isolated and feels alone. For many children being a member of a group is the *fun* of going to school. Membership and participation in certain groups also has the potential of helping children achieve specific goals. Being selected to be on an athletic team or being elected to membership on the student council is a large boost to a child's developing self-esteem. Peer recognition is very important to children.

When used in counseling, small groups serve many purposes. When children are upset or troubled they are inclined to feel that their problem is unique. Intellectually they might realize that other children have similar problems, but children tend to think about their own feelings and dwell on their own problems. Preoccupied with themselves and thinking that no one is faced with an identical problem, troubled children often feel that no one can understand the emotions they are experiencing. They are also inclined to seek solitude in their misery and often have difficulty sharing their feelings with someone. "No one understands me, and no one can help me," is a common feeling of children and adolescents who are troubled.

A 10-year-old girl in the fifth grade whose parents are divorcing might feel devastated and unable to imagine how she will be able to cope without having both a father and mother in her home. She could feel a deep sense of loss, be overwhelmed with sadness and self-pity, embarrassed to face her friends, and have the feeling of being alone in the world. However, if this girl were to be put in a group with other fifth-grade students whose parents are divorcing or have already divorced, she could experience an immediate awareness that she is with peers who can understand what she is feeling because *they have been there*. In a group of fifth-grade students who are currently having or who have experienced this problem, this girl could overcome much of her embarrassment and begin to form a bond with the group members who share her thoughts. *Universality*, or the awareness that others face similar problems, can be comforting to her even though it may not lessen her sadness. Misery does love company, especially when one has perceived that the misery was unique. Groups enable us to feel that our problems are not as unique as we believed.

Effective groups encourage peer interaction. Children often find it easier to talk with their peers than to talk with an adult even when the adult is a counselor in the school. It is more meaningful for a child to listen to a peer with a similar problem say, "You'll get used to not seeing your father every day," than it would be for the counselor to say the same thing. We know that when it comes to listening to advice, older children and adolescents are inclined to relate better to what their peers say than what an adult tells them.

Effective group counseling provides students with a valuable learning experience. Group counseling affords children the potential both to see group members as role models and to become a role model for others in the group. Group members are encouraged to offer support and help other members of the group. As a result, a positive sense of self can occur when children perceive they have said something that has been meaningful and helpful to a group member. An ideal attitude of a group member could be expressed as, "I hope that being in this group can help me, and I'd like to feel that maybe I can be helpful to someone in this group."

Perhaps the strongest rationale for doing group counseling is that it *can* be effective. When the counselor has done what needs to be done in order to start and run a group, the objectives of the group *can* be accomplished to a significant degree. This presumes that the group members and goals for the group have been selected realistically and that the counselor, who is the group leader, possesses the necessary skills to lead the group toward the stated objective.

Disadvantages of Group Counseling

Although group counseling can be successful in effecting change, there are some disadvantages to group counseling. One of the critical components that is mandatory in any counseling relationship is trust. It is not easy for some school-aged children to trust the counselor to treat everything that is said as confidential. In fact, in accordance with informed consent, the counselor must tell the student what can and what cannot be kept confidential.

When it is difficult for a child to trust the counselor, who is an adult and viewed as an ally, the matter of trust is even more difficult when it comes to trusting peers in a group situation. Despite establishing a group rule to protect confidentiality and frequently referring to the importance of keeping everything that is said within the group, it should be assumed that all group members cannot or will not respect confidentiality. When something that is said by a group member comes across as *good gossip* or as something that a group member feels a need to share with someone, trust has been destroyed. A child who cannot trust the group will not be open with the group. One danger a lack of trust creates occurs when a group member has said something that is very personal and perhaps shocking to the group. The group member might regret what was inadvertently said and fear possible repercussions. This might make the group member feel guilty and could create a situation in which the member no longer feels comfortable with the group.

The counselor should be able to recognize when the potential for this has happened and say something to prevent the repercussions. If Jim, a group member in a high school setting, were to say, "I'm a bit upset. Yesterday, when I got home from school, I saw a man whom I had never seen before, come out of my mother's bedroom. When my mother saw me I know she was embarrassed," the counselor needs to anticipate what effect this statement could have on the group and take steps to protect the group member and prevent gossip. The counselor could say to the group, "Let's be sure that we don't tell anyone what we just heard

Jim say," or, "Jim has just shared something very personal that bothered him. I'm sure that Jim needs to know that what he said will be kept confidential. Does anyone have a problem with this?"

Another disadvantage of group counseling is that membership in a group can pose a problem for some students because they will have to miss a certain number of classes. Although some students look forward to missing class, conscientious students might be reluctant to commit to being absent from class six or eight times. This is especially true at the high school level where there is pressure to get high grades. The fact that students will be required to miss classes can be a disadvantage unless the counselor develops a way to address this problem. A suggestion that can reduce the problem of missing class is discussed in the next chapter.

Group Counseling at Different Grade Levels

Needless to say, there are significant differences between doing group counseling with third-grade youngsters and group counseling with high school adolescents. In order to differentiate school levels, children who are in grades kindergarten through 2 will be referred to as the *introductory level* grouping. Children in grades 3 through 5 will be referred to as the *primary level* grouping. Students who are in grades 6 through 8 will be referred to as the *intermediate level* grouping, and high school students will be referred to as the *secondary level* grouping. In school districts that have junior high schools, there is a ninth grade. Ninth-grade students are included in the intermediate level grouping.

The effectiveness of group counseling at the kindergarten and first-grade introductory level grouping is controversial. Although many elementary school counselors feel group counseling at these grade levels can be meaningful, this writer's experience is that most children in kindergarten and first grade should not be expected to interact effectively with members of a group. The changes that are seen in a group member occur because of the interaction between the child and the counselor rather than because of the impact the group has had on the group member. On the other hand, children in the second grade have a good potential for functioning the way group members should respond. This writer is not saying that group counseling should not be attempted with children who are in kindergarten and first grade, only that the goals and expectations for children at these grade levels need to be realistic and should be based on the maturity of each child in the group. Many 5- and 6-year-old children lack the verbal skills to express their feelings, and communication problems involving language development are common. Children under the age of 8 are usually unable to analyze their behaviors or be critical of themselves. They are not expected to be able to acquire insights, and they have difficulty with problem solving.

The goals of group counseling at the introductory level must be minimal and based more on what the counselor can accomplish with each child rather than what the child can derive from the group experience. At the introductory level, the counselor should arrange for short, weekly, individual visits with each of the group members to discuss what occurred during group because children at this age have difficulty internalizing what is said by group members. At an individual meeting with Mike, a first-grade child who had a brief temper outburst in a group meeting, the counselor might say, "The other day, in group, when Tracy said that she thought you were acting like a baby, you didn't say anything. What were you thinking?" Mike might have difficulty remembering what he was thinking at that time, and even if he remembered, he might not be able to express what he was feeling. But Tracy's comment opened a door for the counselor to probe into Mike's level of maturity.

Goals, at the introductory level, can include helping the child to feel more comfortable in school and encourage the development of social skills through group interaction. Group discussion can address a child's fears, insecurities, and adjustment to school. The friendly counselor encourages a child to feel that school is a safe place to be and lets the child know that the counselor is a safe person with whom to talk. Group counseling utilizing play media is a way to encourage expression of feelings and is also used to promote group interaction. Children can draw, build with play-dough, act out roles with puppets, and play simple board games as a way of interacting and expressing themselves. Friendship, divorce, grief, and social skills groups can serve useful purposes with very young children.

At the primary level, for children in grades 3, 4, and 5, we can expect the child to be capable of interacting with the counselor both one-on-one and in groups. At this level, children are beginning to understand basic cause–effect relationships and are able to develop minimal insights. They are also able to do simple problem solving. Goal-directed counseling can focus on methods of problem solving through practice in simulated situations. For example, in a friendship group a counselor might say, "Suppose Billy is your friend. Last week you told the teacher that it was Billy who threw chewing gum on the playground. The teacher punished Billy and now Billy won't play with you. If you wanted Billy to be your friend again, what would you do?"

Communication skills have improved in the child at this age level. Children in grades 3 to 5 can express their feelings and identify their emotions. However, children at this level have not acquired the self-presence to respond to the needs of others in their group. This somewhat lowers the counselor's expectations for group member responses and reduces the potential effectiveness of group interaction. Nevertheless, children at the primary level enjoy group experiences and can benefit from the interaction. Membership in a group can enhance their social awareness and give them a feeling of importance and a sense of belonging.

Group counseling with children who are at the intermediate level, grades 6 though 8 in a middle school or grades 7 through 9 in a junior high school, is always a challenge for the school counselor. At this age level, children are at an in-between stage of development. They do not want to be considered children, nor are they always ready to be called adolescents. Many children at the intermediate level want to hold on to certain advantages of being a child, but they also want to be seen as preadolescents who are ready for more autonomy and greater freedom. Middle and junior high school counselors feel that groups can be beneficial. When the group leader has carefully and modestly defined the purpose of the group and feels comfortable that students are ready to be in a group, movement toward the goals of the group can be achieved. Holding the group's attention can be a problem because it is difficult for students at the intermediate level to maintain a focus on the topic, especially if the group is too large. Students at this grade level tend to be restless and like to socialize. For this reason, the group leader needs to maintain control of the group. Preadolescents are able to acquire insights and are interested in speculating about their futures. Peer groups are important to them, so group counseling becomes a comfortable experience. They are quick to offer suggestions to their fellow group members, yet they often become defensive when they perceive they are being criticized by a group member.

High school counselors face many obstacles that prevent them from doing much counseling, whether individually or in a group. Unfortunately, many high school counselors are bogged down with so many counseling-related, but noncounseling, activities, they do not allow themselves much time to do responsive counseling or make the commitment to run groups. The difficulties high school counselors encounter when doing group counseling can be viewed as more a problem of logistics than of student needs. In high schools it is not easy for students to be excused from class on a regular basis. Gaining cooperation can be a problem because both parents and teachers often feel that time spent in the classroom is more important for a student than time spent with the counselor, whether it be for individual or group counseling. This is unfortunate because of all school levels, high-school-aged students have the most maturity to benefit from counseling and, because of academic, social, and parental pressures, they also have the greatest need for individual and group counseling. High school students are faced with a multitude of issues that are stressful.

Groups in a high school setting can be very effective because group members have the ability to understand both the purpose of groups and their responsibility as a member of a group. Adolescents are interested in talking with their peers and have many concerns that would lend themselves to group interaction. They feel many pressures and are not always comfortable talking with their parents. Sharing their feelings and knowing how their peers feel about a topic of common interest could, in a group situation, have a significant impact on them. For adolescents who are preparing to leave high school to face either college or the world of work, group topics that are career oriented can be meaningful for their future. Adolescents often have a problem establishing priorities for what they should be doing. This can affect their academic achievement when, for example, schoolwork is viewed as being important, but less important then their social life. High school students need counselors who are prepared to help them cope with their problems and guide them in making serious decisions. The high school student who feels estranged or uncomfortable talking with parents about a problem and seeks input from a professional and caring adult should be able to turn to a counselor.

A strong message is sent when, as a counselor educator, this writer has met for the first time with a class of prospective school counselors and asked the question, "When you were in high school, how many of you would have made an appointment to speak to your high school counselor if you had a personal problem?" On numerous occasions, no hands have been raised. The response of class members was usually silence, a smile, or a snicker, which conveys how beginning graduate students who are training to become school counselors viewed their high school counselor. The message from the class illustrates a problem that needs to be solved, a void that needs to be filled. A goal for counselor trainees who are interested in becoming high school counselors should be to fill that void by changing the situation. It *can* be done, but it will probably require counselor assertiveness and a proactive position.

Group Counseling versus Individual Counseling

Whether a student is placed in a group or receives individual counseling should not be an either/or decision, but one based upon a professional decision as to which setting would best meet the needs of the student. Group counseling tends to be less personal, more confrontational, and students tend to be more guarded than when they are receiving individual counseling. Group members are not inclined to self-disclose in front of their peers when what they say might be embarrassing or too revealing. This explains why group members often restrain or hide their feelings and emotions. For example, students are often reluctant and embarrassed to cry in front of their group. They will not, however, hesitate to express their feelings and emotions during an individual counseling session once good rapport has been established and the counselor is considered to be a safe person they can talk with freely. Confidentiality being a major concern in group counseling, children in the primary, intermediate, and secondary grade levels are inclined to censor their expressions in order to guard or protect their image. Young children at the introductory grade level are not as image conscious and not as worried about confidentiality.

Group counseling is not a substitute or replacement for individual counseling. Individual counseling has many advantages. It involves a private relationship and tends to be more confidential, more individually focused, and highly sensitive to the needs of the student. One-on-one counseling makes it easier for the student to talk about sensitive areas and to discuss feelings that might not be appropriate or safe to express in front of a group. Individual counseling can, however, be difficult for the child who feels pressure in a one-on-one situation. Children who are not comfortable talking about themselves, or those who are not used to discussing personal matters, often will find it easier to talk in a group setting. Interacting with a counselor one-on-one for 40 minutes puts pressure on counselees if they feel they are expected to do most of the talking. In a group where there are four or five students talking and interacting, the pressure is reduced.

Cultural factors also make it difficult for some students to interact with a counselor. Many children are uncomfortable discussing problems with a "stranger," or someone outside of the family. In some homes, children are discouraged, and even ordered, not to discuss problems with the school counselor. In a home environment that teaches its members that it is not appropriate to discuss family matters outside of the family, putting a child in a counseling relationship can create conflict and frustration for the student. The multiculturally sensitive school counselor should be able to know when such a situation has occurred.

It is tempting for a school counselor with a large case load to utilize group counseling in order to see more students. However, the justification for doing group counseling should not be based on a "numbers game" and the fact that more students can be seen using groups than can be seen individually. In looking at the issue of quality versus quantity, the criteria for counselor effectiveness cannot be measured solely on the basis of the number of students who are seen by the counselor. Inviting a child to become a member of a group is a decision the counselor makes. The decision to put a child into a group, rather than into individual counseling, should be based on such factors as the presenting problem, the needs of the student, the predicted ability of the youngster to handle a group situation, and the welfare of the student.

There are a number of reasons why a school counselor would prefer seeing a student for individual counseling. They would include, but are not limited to, a child who is extremely shy, a child who cannot or does not comfortably relate with peers, a youngster whose problems are due largely to environmental issues, a student who would be uncomfortable in a group situation, a student who the counselor feels presents a problem that is very personal and requires greater privacy and confidentiality, or a child whose problem is such that it would be embarrassing to be in a group (e.g., a student who has been diagnosed as HIV positive, or a stutterer who is not ready to be exposed to the pressure of having to speak in a group). However, many of these issues could also be dealt with in a group situation when the counselor feels that individual counseling with a youngster has enabled the counselee to be ready for placement in a group.

Every student who comes into the counselor's office with a concern is not a potential counselee for individual or group counseling. Many students come to the counselor's office for guidance information and/or scheduling assistance and are not in need of personal counseling. Counselors are often able to resolve the concerns of many students in one or two visits when the problem relates to an interpersonal issue between students or when the concerns do not involve the need for a change in behavior. Examples of these situations would be when seventh-grader Karen is unhappy because yesterday Suzanne and Jennifer wouldn't interact with her. Today Suzanne is the one who is unhappy because Karen and Jennifer won't interact with her. Or, Ashley is very unhappy with her teacher and wants to be moved to a different fifth-grade section in order to be with her friend Amy. The school counselor should also be aware that some children manufacture problems just to get out of class. There are also students who make weekly visits to the counselor's office just because they like talking with the counselor.

Even when a counselor feels there is a need to see a student on a sustained basis, the number of times a student will see a counselor is usually five or six. This number will vary according to the student's presenting problem, grade level, the size of the counselor's case load, the amount of time the counselor is permitted to devote to counseling, and the individual practices of the school counselor. School counselors cannot be expected to accomplish, in their short-term counseling, what mental health counselors in private or agency settings could accomplish.

Group counseling can be viewed as a valuable adjunct to individual counseling. This does not mean that all children who are in a group should also be seen individually, but that a counselor is exposed to a different dimension of the child when the child is interacting with a peer group. Frequently a student will say something in group that would prompt a counselor to further exploration in the safety of an individual counseling situation. It is not unusual for a counselor to see personality characteristics in a child revealed in a group that were not seen during individual counseling. Our personality is not always consistent from one situation to another. Group counseling also provides a way for counselees' to rehearse or try out behaviors that have been discussed or suggested during individual counseling.

Group Counseling versus Group Psychotherapy

David, an eighth grader, seems to have undergone a major transformation. When he was in the seventh grade, David was a B student. He attended school regularly and was not viewed as a problem for any of his teachers. When David returned to school the following fall, David's teachers felt they were seeing a belligerent and angry young adolescent. He was often truant, refused to do his homework, and was defiant to all of his teachers. David offered no explanation to the school counselor for the change in his behavior or why he now disliked school. David's parents saw the change in their son and knew there was a need to do something in order to understand the problem and help David. The parent's question was, should David get individual counseling from the school counselor, be put in a counseling group in his school with students who have similar problems, or should they take him to someone for individual or group psychotherapy?

The basic question being posed is whether there are significant differences between counseling and psychotherapy. Are the differences only a matter of semantics? Could David get the help he needs in a school situation from the counselor, or should his parents take him to a clinical psychologist, psychiatrist, or psychiatric social worker? To a great extent, the answer to this question lies in the nature of the basic problem and the approach that is needed to help David gain insights and solutions to his problem. As it should be practiced, counseling focuses on helping children attain their potential by encouraging them to make needed changes in their attitude and/or behavior that might enable them to deal more effectively with the concerns or problems they are having. Counseling that takes place in a group setting utilizes the input of peers to facilitate these changes.

Psychotherapy should be viewed as a concept rather than a specific technique. Psychoanalysis is a form of psychotherapy, but so is the technique called behavior modification, and they differ significantly. As conceived by Sigmund Freud and those theoreticians who adhere to his principles, psychotherapy should be concerned with unconscious awareness; but psychotherapy as practiced by Alfred Adler and others regards nothing as unconscious. Psychotherapy has been identified with depth therapy, but cognitive behavior therapy, or reality therapy, along with a growing number of brief or short-term therapies that are seen in practice today, remove depth therapy as a term that would differentiate psychotherapy from other treatment modalities. For some time, the only unique aspect of psychotherapy that differentiated it from other treatment methods was that it did not employ chemical or physical methods as a way of effecting change (Stedman, 1987). Today, since the treatment of moderate or severe emotional problems usually involves both verbal interaction and medications, the concept of psychotherapy has become more difficult to define. Counselors, however, do not prescribe medications, nor do clinical psychologists or psychiatric social workers.

The psychotherapeutic strategies used today are as numerous as the number of individuals who have developed a system that helps us understand human behavior, suggests ways to modify behavior, or teaches us ways to cope with life. Indeed, inasmuch as there are many eclectic clinicians and few "purists" whose approach to psychotherapy devoutly mimics the philosophy and principles of a published theorist, there are as many types of counseling and psychotherapy as there are clinical psychologists, psychiatrists, psychiatric social workers, and academicians who have published psychotherapeutic or counseling strategies. Although research supports a number of these psychotherapeutic and counseling approaches, the principles and techniques of counseling and psychotherapy are based on theory, hypotheses, and probability, rather than scientific laws or proven facts.

Psychotherapy is usually the term of choice in specific disciplines. Clinical psychologists, psychiatrists, and psychiatric social workers usually refer to what they do as psychotherapy. Their training, whether it is at the doctoral level, in the case of clinical psychologists or psychiatrists, or at the masters level, for psychiatric social workers, even encourages the use of the term. There is no universal agreement as to whether counseling can be considered a form of psychotherapy. If the term *treatment* is inherent in the definition of psychotherapy, then school counselors do not do psychotherapy; most school counselors do not view themselves as *treating* counselees. On the other hand, if treatment can be interpreted as implying helping, assisting, guiding, or directing a person in order to effect change, then counseling is a form of psychotherapy. Even if school counselors feel they are practicing a form of psychotherapy, they should never refer to what they do as psychotherapy. Parents would not be comfortable thinking of their child as seeing a psychotherapist in a school setting, nor do most school counselors view what they do as psychotherapy. Although the issue may be purely an exercise in semantics, school counselors counsel. Let the other mental health practitioners call what they do anything they want, but it is imperative for counselors to use the term *counseling* in a school setting.

Returning to David and the question of who could best help him, the answer depends on such factors as determining the cause of the basic problem, the severity of the problem, David's motivation to cooperate, the length of time it could be expected to take in order to effect change, the amount of parental involvement needed, and the training and skills of the person who works with him. Until we have knowledge of these factors, it is conceivable that either the school counselor or the person who practices psychotherapy could be effective with David. At face value, the problem that David presents is one that could be handled by the school counselor in a school setting utilizing both individual and group counseling. However, should it be determined that David is rebelling against a pending divorce, responding to deep-seated and unidentified problems, heavily involved with alcohol or drugs, suicidal, dealing with sibling rivalry, facing serious home problems that would necessitate parental or family involvement, or that David could benefit from medication, David's problem would best be handled in an out-of-school clinical setting.

Group Counseling versus Group Dynamics

Group counseling can be defined as a setting in which several persons having a common goal interact with each other and a group leader or co-leader in order to facilitate attitude or behavioral changes within group members. Group dynamics, on the other hand, looks at what goes on *within* the group, *between* group members, and *how* the group interacts with the group leader. For the group leader, it is important to know if a particular group member emerges as a person who has influence over the group and who the active or more vocal members are. The group leader needs to know which members say the least, who tries to dominate the group, who tends to argue, who is defensive, who does and who does not share personal information, whether members seem to like being in the group, whether the group is becoming cohesive, and other intragroup feelings and behaviors. The group leader in the K–12 setting is often directing the flow of discussion. For this reason, the group leader's knowledge of the dynamics of the group enables the group leader to know such things as which members need to be encouraged to interact, which group member is distracting the group, and how much control of the group the leader needs to maintain. The group leader is expected to hear what each of the group members is saying but also should be aware of the dynamics going on within the group.

The dynamics of a group will vary in accordance with the topic of the group, the age and personality of the group members, and the size of the group. Pregroup friendships are important to consider since there can be *subgroups* within the group. A subgroup occurs when two or more group members were good friends prior to coming into the group. Because group members in a school setting are usually from the same grade, the group leader can anticipate that there will often be subgroups within the group. Having a friend in the group can be advantageous for the member who may have doubts about being included in the group or the member who is not initially comfortable in the group. When students are talking in front of their friends, there is less danger of feeling intimidated by the group. Subgroups, however, can create problems for the group leader. When one group member is not part of a subgroup and senses that the other members are a subgroup, that member can feel isolated from the group. Problems can also occur if the subgroup "gangs up" on a nonsubgroup member. The group leader needs to be aware of subgroups and take steps to prevent members from feeling isolated or intimidated. It may be necessary for the group leader to make a point of inserting a member who is not part of a subgroup into group discussions.

An effective way for the group leader to anticipate the dynamics of a group can be through the screening interview. One of the reasons that screening interviews are important as a requirement for acceptance into a group is to enable the leader to get a feeling about the composition and compatibility of the group prior to the first session. The counselor, being aware of group dynamics, tries to put together a group that has the potential to become cohesive and to move in the direction of the group objectives. There will, however, be instances when the counselor is working with an involuntary group or a group whose composition suggests that the members may not be compatible. The group leader in an anger management group might have problems with group dynamics, as could the leader of a group of at-risk students who are not motivated to stay in school or of an ADHD group. When working with difficult groups it is important to keep the groups small and set limited and realistic goals.

K–12 Group Counseling versus Adult Group Counseling

Counseling with a school-aged population is very different from counseling with older adolescents or adults. This is especially true when it comes to group counseling. An adult group tends to become more cohesive and more focused. It is also more confronting and its responses to group interaction reveal more emotions than will be seen in a child or adolescent group. Adult groups are also inclined to be goal-directed and often put pressure on the group leader to bring issues to closure. Even the group dynamics of an older group are not the same as those of adolescents and younger children. Adult group members are more aware of their feelings and offer more help to members of the group. There is usually more disagreement between adult members, and the group leader must be prepared to quickly intervene in a dispute. Due to their maturity, adult groups may not need the same type of leadership that is necessary when working with groups in a K–12 setting. Adult groups are often self-governing, with the group leader providing more of a stabilizing influence than serving in a leadership role. Adult groups are inclined to remember much of what was said in group from week to week, and, although it is discouraged, they often have discussions among themselves outside of the group sessions.

In the K–12 setting, when a group session ends, the group leader should not assume that all group members will remember what was discussed in a session or what they were talking about when the session ended. Beginning each session with a review of the previous session serves to refresh their memories and refocuses them on the group's objectives. A review is also a good practice with adult groups even though adult groups tend to remember more about what was discussed in a session. In both adult and K–12 groups, the group leader has the responsibility of keeping the group on task and discouraging inappropriate laughter, sarcasm, or other distractions. The group leader should encourage all members to participate in the discussion and protect the feelings of group members. Confrontations between members are more dangerous in the K–12 groups and should be avoided because children and adolescents are inclined to overreact to a confrontation, which could affect their interpersonal behavior outside the group. Adult groups usually see each other only on the day the group meets, but in a school setting the members have the potential for frequent contacts throughout the school day.

CONCLUDING REMARKS

School counseling is an integral part of the total education process. The school counselor holds a significant and unique position within a school. It is significant because school counselors, working in conjunction with administrators, teachers, and parents, function to help students achieve their academic potential and assist them in making school a meaningful growth experience. It is unique in that they are viewed by students as being nonjudgmental, nonthreatening, empathic advocates who are also members of the faculty. However, counseling, whether it is done individually or in groups, is not always effective. Counselors cannot be expected to bring about change in every student. Nevertheless, school-aged children who make contact with a school counselor should be able to feel they are interacting with a professional who is committed to helping them find ways to reduce or resolve their concerns.

REFERENCES

Ehly, S., & Dustin, D. (1991). *Individual and group counseling in the schools*. New York: Guilford.

Hutchinson, N. L., Freeman, J. G., & Quick, V. E. (1996). Group counseling intervention for solving problems on the job. *Journal of Employment Counseling, 33*, 2–19.

Kreig, E. J. (1988). *Group leadership training and supervision manual for adolescent group counseling in schools* (3rd ed.). Muncie, IN: Accelerated Development.

Nims, D. R. (1998). Searching for self: A theoretical model for applying family systems to adolescent group work. *Journal for Specialists in Group Work,* 133–144.

Stedman (1987). *Webster's concise medical dictionary*. New York: Prentice Hall General Reference.

Yalom, I. D. (1975). *The theory of practice of group psychotherapy* (2nd ed.). New York: Basic Books.

CHAPTER TWO

GETTING STARTED

It is 10 A.M. on a Tuesday morning. The school counselor has just greeted a group of five fifth-grade students for the first time. They are seated around a table and the topic for the group to discuss is how to deal with a bully. Each of the group members has been or is currently the victim of a bully. Both the counselor and group members are feeling some anxiety about the first meeting and both have unanswered questions. For the counselor, who will be the group leader, this moment represents the culmination of many hours of planning and preparation. The counselor is hopeful that all of the time and work that went into planning for this group will result in a successful experience for each of the group members. For the group members, this first meeting represents a hope that somehow, and in some way, they will be able to resolve a problem that has made going to school an unpleasant experience and one that has plagued them for some time.

The counselor has many questions that will soon be answered. "Will each of the group members be willing to share experiences with the group?" "How will group members react to what they hear from each other?" "Will the members be compatible?" "Will the group become cohesive?" "To what extent will the group attain its objective?" "Over the next eight weeks, will each of the members gain something that will be helpful to them?" "Will the group plan for each session produce the results that are being sought?"

Each member also has questions that will soon be answered. "Now that I'm in this group, what is expected of me?" "Will I be embarrassed to tell about my experiences of being bullied?" "Does anyone really want to hear what I say?" "Is it safe to talk in front of this group or will the other kids in this group tell their friends what I say?" "I'm here to learn what to do the next time I am being bullied. Will this be a successful experience?" "Does everyone feel the way I do?" "I'm missing class. Should I be here or in my classroom?" "What am I missing that my teacher will expect me to know?"

By 10:40 on this Tuesday morning, both the counselor and group members will have some answers to their questions. The key word in this scenario is *planning*. Groups do not form by themselves nor should they be put together in a haphazard manner. Successful groups require planning down to the last detail. Planning begins when the counselor makes the decision that group counseling is the proper strategy to use in order to deal with a specific problem. Planning continues when the group leader decides who should be in the group and the most expedient way of obtaining parental permission. Planning includes the number of group sessions there should be and the best time of day for each session. Group plans, prepared in advance, for each group meeting need to be developed. A place to meet must be found. The role of the group leader needs to be determined. Without careful planning, many things can go wrong and group counseling will not succeed.

PROMOTING THE OVERALL COMPREHENSIVE PROGRAM

Group counseling is a part of the school's overall guidance and counseling program. A group counseling program cannot be successful unless the overall program is effective and respected. Anyone who has a product to sell or a service to offer knows that *it pays to advertise*. This is certainly true for a school's guidance and counseling program. In many ways, a school counselor needs to *sell* the faculty and administration on the fact that the guidance and counseling program aids and facilitates the mission of the school and the work of the teacher. *Visibility* is the key word when it comes to promoting the program, and *educating* is necessary in order to gain the cooperation and respect from teachers, parents, and administrators. It is critical that both the activities of the guidance and counseling program and the school counselor be seen frequently throughout the school.

There are many ways to *advertise* or promote a guidance and counseling program within a school. In a strong comprehensive guidance and counseling program, administrators, teachers, students, and parents must be made aware of the services that are available. Some of the ways to increase visibility would be to

■ Develop a monthly counselor's newsletter that will be sent home to parents.

■ Use bulletin boards throughout the school to post information on current and upcoming programs and activities.

■ Present an overview of the guidance and counseling program to the faculty at the first faculty meeting.

■ Introduce the guidance and counseling program to parents through an orientation at the first PTA or PTSA meeting.

■ Distribute needs assessment surveys to faculty, students, and parents on suggested topics for group counseling; suggestions for a schoolwide counseling focus; student, teacher, or parental concerns; or ideas to improve the school community.

■ If there is a school newspaper, devote a regular column to what is happening related to the guidance and counseling program, what is being planned, and what has already happened.

■ Encourage teachers to become involved in the program. For example, the art teacher could be asked to have students draw things that relate to careers or the activities the counselor is covering in classroom guidance units. These drawings can be placed on the bulletin boards throughout the school. The English teacher could be asked to have students write themes related to topics about school or social issues (e.g., cultivating a positive school attitude, diversity issues, anger management, planning for the future, making friends, etc.).

■ Initiate a peer mediation program and assist in training students to become peer mediators.

■ Distribute handouts to students and parents on a variety of topics relevant to student welfare (e.g., suggestions for developing good study habits, ways of dealing with test anxiety, tips on selecting a college, preparing for a job interview, improving social skills, and topics related to mental health issues).

■ Visit classrooms as a way of introducing yourself to students and to inform them about all of the services offered by the program. This encourages students to make an appointment to see the counselor for academic or personal reasons and, if the teacher remains in the room, defines the guidance and counseling program to the teacher.

■ Promote an active classroom guidance program covering topics of interest to students.

■ Consult with teachers frequently and encourage them to refer students to the counselor.

■ Arrange to have specified times to meet with the principal to discuss program concerns and goals. Keep the principal informed of the activities taking place within the program, including the groups that are planned.

■ Coordinate, with the principal, the development of in-service programs for parents and/or teachers.

■ Take snapshots of students doing various things around the school and place the photos in or around the counseling office (e.g., a group of students coming off of the bus, eating lunch, playing in the all-purpose room, walking in the hall, playing sports). When students see the counselor taking pictures that could be displayed, it gives the counselor visibility and creates student interest.

■ Conduct frequent lunch bunches involving the counselor and selected students. Lunch could be combined with a brief group counseling session in the counselor's office or, at times, lunch could be just a social contact with students.

■ Send memos to faculty announcing such things as the topics for groups that are being formed, dates of standardized testing, plans for a career day, and the general activities of the program.

■ When there is a school crisis, assume an active leadership role in the resolution of the problem.

The primary function of a school counselor is to help students learn. Essentially, a school counselor seeks to remove or reduce the problems that serve to detract or prevent students from doing their best work in school. Whether the issue is one of poor study habits, a lack of social skills, unhappiness for a variety of reasons, succumbing to distractions, negative attitudes, or personal problems that interfere with or take priority over learning, the counselor's objectives are directed at helping the child become more receptive to learning and able to focus on what is being taught. For this reason, much of what the counselor attempts to accomplish with a student will ultimately assist teachers. Anything that is done to help the student helps the teacher.

PREPARING THE ADMINISTRATION FOR GROUP COUNSELING

The principal, or in the case of a large school, the principal and assistant principals, need to be knowledgeable about the role of the counselor and the objectives of the guidance and counseling program. Because some administrators at the secondary school level do not utilize the services of the counselor properly, it is often necessary for the school counselor or counseling staff to educate administrators about the services that counselors are trained to deliver. Too often, administrators will assign duties to a counselor that are neither ethically nor professionally appropriate. School counselors often need to become proactive and tactfully assertive when it comes to defining their role to the principal. Administrators must be made aware of the training the school counselor received and how that training can best be utilized.

The most expedient way to accomplish this objective is for the counselor to arrange for a weekly 30-minute conference with the principal. During this meeting the counselor can discuss professional issues without violating confidentiality and inform the administrator about upcoming activities, which would include the type of counseling groups that are being planned. Because the cooperation of the school's administrator is essential to a successful program, having a regularly scheduled dialogue with the principal would encourage the principal to become involved in the program. Through the development of a cooperative relationship, the principal would be encouraged to offer suggestions that would enable the program to meet the needs of students, teachers, and the school community more effectively. The principal should be made aware of the counselor's weekly planned activities and any logistical problems the program is having. In order to establish a strong guidance and counseling program that includes group counseling, the school counselor must have the full cooperation and support of the principal. When the school counselor is in conflict with the school's administrator, the entire program is in jeopardy.

PREPARING THE FACULTY FOR GROUP COUNSELING

In order for a school counselor to have a successful program of either individual or group counseling, a good professional relationship needs to be established with teachers. Counselors should not forget that they are members of the school's faculty, and consulting with teachers should be viewed as an important part of the counselor's work. Consulting with teachers serves both a professional and a public relations function. Professionally, it provides counselors with important information about a student they are seeing. This would include teacher concerns, anecdotal information related to the student's attitude and behavior, and the academic progress the student is making. It allows teachers to express their feelings and/or frustrations about a child in a confidential and safe setting. Consultation also enables the counselor to gain insights into the teacher and the teacher–student relationship, and, based on what the counselor learns about the teacher from the consultation, it could possibly validate or invalidate the feelings a counselee may have expressed about a teacher. From a public relations point of view, consultation gives the counselor visibility and communicates to teachers that the counselor is both prepared and able to offer assistance to teachers in order to facilitate their work. Consultation fosters a team approach to resolving or reducing the concerns of the teacher.

Several students, independently of each other, speak with the counselor about a common problem. All say they are unhappy in school because they have no friends. They feel very lonely but lack the know-how to start a friendship. These students feel ignored and rejected by their classmates. They envy their classmates when they see them interacting with friends and believe they are enjoying their lives. For the unhappy students, however, school is an unpleasant experience because school, which is a major part of their lives, is not fun. Their dislike of school probably impacts on their academic achievement despite their academic potential. Starting a group that deals with social skills and how to establish friendships would be an appropriate activity for the counselor to initiate. To accomplish this, the counselor will need to meet with the group six or eight times, and this requires the cooperation of teachers. The counselor must be comfortable with asking teachers to release these students from their classes that many times.

Unless the counselor has prepared the faculty, in advance, for its role in the guidance and counseling program, teacher resistance can be anticipated. Even with preparation, the counselor could experience resistance on the part of some members of the faculty. Yet if the counselor had previously met with the teachers and had discussed the important role they play in a comprehensive guidance and counseling program, the resistance should be lessened.

The first few weeks in September are very busy times for counselors. Nevertheless, during the first few weeks at the beginning of a school year, the counselor should arrange to meet with individual teachers, small groups of the faculty, or team leaders to explain the objectives of the guidance and counseling program and the teachers' role in the program. This can be done at lunchtime, during a planning period, or after school. Collegiality should be stressed as well as the importance of teamwork. Teachers should be encouraged to view themselves as integral members of a team whose goal is to help students learn. The school counselor is a member of that team. The message that should come across is that the counselor is committed to helping teachers but needs help *from* teachers in order to make the program successful. Even though there are no guarantees that counseling will produce the results that teachers want, there is always hope that an intervention, whether done individually or through a group, can be helpful to some degree.

Meeting with all of the teachers is easier to do in elementary schools than it is in middle, junior high, and high schools. In secondary schools, where there are multiple counselors, the task is more difficult, but not impossible. It requires meeting with small groups of teachers, rather than meeting individually with one teacher. Unfortunately, secondary school counselors are usually very involved with the scheduling problems of students in the first few weeks in September and might not be as free to meet with the faculty. Arranging to meet during the week before school begins might be better for both counselors and teachers. When the success of a program is so dependent on faculty cooperation, it is recommended that counselors set aside time as early in the school year as possible to meet with the teachers who are new to the school and would not be expected to know much about the guidance and counseling program. Gaining faculty cooperation should be a high priority for the counseling staff.

Defining the Teacher's Role in the Guidance and Counseling Program

There are at least a dozen things that define the role of a teacher in the guidance and counseling program. Teachers help the counselor when they are willing to

- Be a source for referring students to the counselor.
- Consult with the counselor about a student the counselor is or should be seeing.
- Offer feedback to the counselor about the progress a counselee is making.
- Allow the counselor to come into their classroom to present a group guidance unit.
- Permit the counselor to observe a counselee in the classroom.
- Meet with the counselor and parents of a student when necessary.
- Meet with the counselor and a student when necessary.
- Serve on the faculty guidance committee, if asked by the principal.
- Assist the counselor by enhancing the guidance curriculum (e.g., teachers can discuss careers in their academic fields with students, they can share their method of studying, they can serve as role models, assist in coordinating a career day, etc.).
- Suggest topics for group counseling.
- Offer suggestions for the improvement of the guidance and counseling program.
- Excuse students from class so that they can participate in either individual or group counseling.

Consulting with Teachers

Consulting with teachers is a very important function of the school counselor. When done properly, consultation can be helpful to both the counselor and the teacher. When done improperly, it can be harmful to the welfare of the student. School counselors must be very careful not to breech the confidentiality that the counselee expects from the counselor. Teachers will often ask the counselor specific questions about a student they have referred and expect specific answers. The counselor needs to learn how to respond to the questions posed by an interested teacher without compromising what the counselee has said in confidence. "No wonder Lisa is flunking. I hear that her father is a drunk and her mother is never home. Has Lisa told you this?" asks a teacher about a child she had referred to the counselor. Assuming the counselor were able to answer this question based on what Lisa had told the counselor in confidence, answering "Yes" to that question would violate confidentiality. "Let's just say that Lisa has some problems she needs to deal with," would be a more appropriate counselor's response. The counselor can hope that the teacher gets the message that the counselor has responded ethically to the question and would respect the counselor's way of responding.

When interacting with teachers, counselors need to be aware of the professional problems that confront teachers. Teaching is a difficult and stressful job. Teachers are faced with high expectations from administrators and parents. As a result of having to deal with large class size and reticent students for whom education is not a high priority, they often work under very unfavorable conditions. The work of the teacher can be further complicated by disruptive students who detract from the time the teacher could spend with more motivated students. This forces teachers to become both teacher and disciplinarian, and most teachers resent the time they are forced to spend being a disciplinarian. When students fail to learn, the teacher is often the person who is blamed. Many teachers feel a lack of respect from students and parents. They feel overly criticized, unappreciated, and are often accused of not doing their job properly. Counselors who show respect to teachers communicate their empathic awareness of how frustrated some teachers feel about the way their work is viewed. Of course, it is nice when the teacher can show empathy for the work of the counselor, but the counselor is wise not to expect this.

Prior to meeting with teachers, the counselor should have met with and informed the principal that individual and group counseling will be a part of the comprehensive program. It may be necessary to explain the rationale for doing group counseling to the principal. Essentially, the counselor wants to inform the principal what teachers will be asked to do, specifically, to allow students to be excused from class for counseling purposes. Assuming the principal shows support for the counseling program, when meeting with faculty members early in the school year the message the counselor wants the faculty to hear is, "I've just discussed our program with the principal, and she feels that doing both individual and group counseling is important. We'll probably run several groups throughout the year and the principal knows this means you will be asked to allow some of your students to be excused from class in order to be a part of these groups. Do you have a problem with this?" If a teacher has a problem with excusing students, this is the time to discuss it. It is very important to get the principal's sanction to do what you have to do in order to run groups and then inform the faculty of this sanction.

Teacher Resistance

As previously mentioned, not all teachers feel good about the school counselor or the counseling program. It becomes a challenge for a counselor when a teacher is not supportive of what the counselor is trying to do. What is required to meet this challenge is a combination of some good public relations and teacher education. A teacher's negative attitude will not change until the counselor says or does something that encourages the teacher to rethink attitudes toward the counselor or counseling program.

One way to educate a resistant teacher is by involving that teacher in the guidance and counseling program. Asking the principal to invite a teacher who has negative feelings about the program to become a member of the faculty guidance committee would start to educate this teacher about the importance of the program and the role of the counselor. As a member of this committee, the teacher would learn about the program through being involved in program decisions that are unrelated to the counseling process. Another way to educate this teacher would be to develop a professional relationship with that teacher and gradually introduce the teacher to the kind of work being done in the program by arranging to have a series of informal consultations. If teacher resistance is to be overcome, the counselor must know and understand the reasons for the resistance. Some of the possible explanations for teacher resistance would include

- A lack of respect for the field of counseling.
- A lack of respect for the counselor.
- A negative experience with the counselor.

- Resentment of the role of a school counselor.
- Questioning the effectiveness of the counselor.
- Questioning the effectiveness of counseling.
- A lack of respect for the previous counselor that carries over to the present counselor.
- A negative experience with a previous counselor.
- Something the counselor said or did that offended the teacher.
- Misconceptions about the role of the counselor.
- The feeling that the counselor is "not pulling their weight" in the school.
- The belief that missing classes would be detrimental to the student.
- The view by a teacher who has been in psychotherapy that the counselor is someone who poses a threat.

The best way to overcome resistance either in a counselee or a teacher is to confront it directly and try to understand the basis for it. If, through direct communication, the reason for teacher resistance can be discovered, the counselor should explain to the teacher that they both share common educational goals for students and that working together benefits the teacher, student, and counselor. The reason should motivate the counselor to do something that would lessen the resistance. Although resistance can often be overcome, there may be times when teacher resistance is so great that the counselor is forced to accept the fact that a teacher's negative feelings should not be expected to change.

Cooperation is a two-way street. The counselor must cooperate with teachers. Teachers should be informed that they will not be asked to excuse students when a test is being given or when excusing a student creates a problem for the teacher. For scheduling purposes, it is helpful for the counselor to know the dates, in advance, that teachers plan to give tests. Teachers should also be informed that group members are told repeatedly that they are responsible for making up any work that is missed and that being in counseling is not an excuse for not doing the work that is required. Teachers should be asked to tell the counselor when someone who is involved in counseling is not doing what is expected or if the student's attitude toward school or performance level has changed. One reason the counselor will consult with teachers periodically is to track the progress of counselees.

PREPARING PARENTS FOR GROUP COUNSELING

Despite the fact that counseling can be very helpful for a student, some parents are threatened when the school counselor seeks parental permission to see their child individually or in a group situation. Some parents will permit their child to talk with a counselor individually but will admonish their child not to say anything about what goes on inside the home. Knowing that their child is being considered for group counseling can be more threatening to parents because they do not know what their child will share with the group and have no reason to feel what their child says will be held in confidence by the group. Inasmuch as written parental permission is usually required by a school system before a child can be included in a group, it is imperative that good communication be established between the school counselor and parents. In some school districts, counselors are also required to notify parents when their child has been seen three times for individual counseling and there are plans to continue counseling. School districts differ in this requirement. The school counselor, who is often the liaison between school and home, should do those things that are needed to gain parental confidence and be seen as a professional who can be trusted.

Parental preparation begins in the fall when the counselor sends home materials that address the planned activities of the program. A brief but detailed letter to parents should inform them about the school counselor's role and what they can expect from the counseling program. This letter should be written in all the languages found in the school since it is important that all parents be informed about the services they can expect from the counseling program. The letter should also include reference to group counseling, the requirement of parental permission if their child is selected to become a member of a group, and how a student can be referred to the counselor. This letter could accompany the parental needs assessment survey (see Appendix B).

School counselors who encourage parental involvement will seek frequent contact with them. Through back-to-school nights, PTA meetings, parent in-service programs, newsletters, and communications that are sent home with the child, parents can be kept informed of what is happening with the guidance and counseling program. Parents who have made contact with the counselor will be less inclined to feel threatened when they are asked to allow their child to become involved in a counseling relationship.

In accordance with informed consent, when a student is being considered for placement in a group and parental permission is requested, the parent is entitled to know the purpose of the group, the number of times the group will meet, how long each session will last, how many students will be in the group, who will lead the group, and how their child was selected to be in the group. They should also be informed that confidentiality within the group is stressed at every group session and of the ethical and legal exceptions to confidentiality (e.g., Tarasoff). The school counselor is required to inform parents any time the child talks about doing harm to self or others.

SELECTING GROUP COUNSELING TOPICS

Groups are formed according to the needs of the students and the school community. Learning that several students share a concern could prompt the counselor to begin a group. A school crisis can also suggest a need for forming one or more groups (e.g., a racial incident, an act of violence, or a drug bust in the school). Although certain counseling groups are routinely formed in a school, early in the school year the counselor should develop needs assessment surveys that enable the parents, faculty, and students to indicate what groups they feel are needed (see Appendices B, C, and D). Topic selection can be determined on the basis of what the counselor perceives as being needed; the results of the needs assessment surveys given to the faculty, parents, and students; and the special needs of the school community.

The topics for groups will vary according to grade level and circumstances. For logistical reasons, more group counseling takes place in the elementary school. Nevertheless, middle, junior, and high school counselors who want to do group counseling can certainly have very active groups running throughout the school year.

TYPES OF GROUPS

Groups can be categorized as *remedial, support,* or *preventive,* although there is a fine line between the objectives of remedial and support groups. Remedial groups tend to focus on problems faced by most students, whereas support groups look more at personal problems or circumstances beyond the student's control. Remedial groups focus on correcting a problem; support groups strengthen the person's resolve to cope more effectively with problems being faced. Examples of topics remedial groups would address are

1. Improving grades through study skills.
2. Developing better study habits.
3. Becoming more assertive.
4. Raising self-esteem.
5. Improving social skills.
6. Developing and maintaining friendships.
7. Overcoming shyness and passivity.
8. Learning to do effective problem solving.
9. Learning how to organize schoolwork efficiently.
10. Overcoming test-taking anxiety.
11. Learning to control anger/aggressive/hostile behavior.
12. Becoming more sensitive to the feelings of others.
13. Learning to deal with frustrations.
14. Improving punctuality and school attendance.
15. Overcoming a fear of speaking in class.
16. Changing a negative attitude toward school.
17. Making better adjustments to school and/or life situations.
18. Dealing effectively with stress.
19. Overcoming a fear of new situations.
20. Acquiring better listening skills.

Support groups, dealing with more personal issues, help students to realize that some of their peers are faced with similar problems. This has been referred to as *universality.* By sharing experiences with each other, support groups provide a setting that makes it safe for a child or adolescent to express feelings without fear of being embarrassed or criticized. A goal for support groups, as well as remedial groups, is to encourage members to learn from each other. When one member of the group tells how he or she has coped with prejudice or discrimination, other members of the group can be encouraged to experiment with this student's method in the hope that they, too, can handle the problem of prejudice more effectively. Examples of support group issues are

1. Parental separation or divorce.
2. Grief resulting from the death of someone close.
3. ADD or ADHD.
4. Problems due to multicultural/diversity issues.

   5. Substance abuse/alcohol problems.

   6. Being at risk of dropping out of school.

   7. Bullying.

   8. Sharing a common medical problem in conjunction with the school nurse (e.g., diabetes, eating disorders, a physical impairment).

   9. Pregnancy.

10. In-school mothers.

11. Preparing for college.

12. Vocational direction for students who are not going to college.

13. Problems involving career selection.

14. Single-parented families.

15. Grandparent-raised families.

16. Stopping a bad habit (e.g., smoking, lying, stealing).

17. Being new to the school.

18. English as a second language.

19. "Blended" families (stepparent's children).

20. Parent or sibling problems.

Support groups pose the least threat to members. They also promote the greatest amount of empathy among members and make it easy for the group to share feelings. Alcoholics Anonymous is a prototype of a support group. Support groups can be gender-specific. All-male or all-female groups can be effective when they are dealing with topics that could be embarrassing to discuss in a heterogeneous group. Support groups can also be racially or ethnically specific when it seems to be appropriate. Regardless of the type of group being run, the school counselor, either as group leader or co-leader in a K–12 setting, must be prepared to assume an active role.

Preventive groups focus on avoiding problems. Prevention is usually carried out through classroom guidance, or what is also called *group guidance*. Group guidance refers to a planned program of information presented to a class by the counselor that focuses on the academic, social, personal, career, and/or educational development of students. A list of classroom guidance topics that a counselor can present would parallel the topics that could also be used in small group counseling. Classroom guidance presentations could be on such topics as

   1. Character education.

   2. Conflict resolution.

   3. Problem-solving methods.

   4. Dealing with frustrations.

   5. Anger management.

   6. Being sensitive to the feelings of others.

   7. Handling stress.

   8. Coping with peer pressure.

   9. Cultivating good health habits (presented in conjunction with the school nurse).

10. Friendship skills.

11. Assertiveness training.

12. Controlling temper.
13. Getting along with parents.
14. Showing empathy.
15. Career planning.
16. Controlling moods.
17. Use of leisure time.
18. Getting organized.
19. Dealing with jealousy.
20. Effective study methods.
21. Overcoming test anxiety.
22. Overcoming shyness.
23. Learning to anticipate consequences.
24. Increasing motivation to succeed in school.
25. The importance of getting good grades.

SELECTING GROUP MEMBERS

Group members are selected through the needs assessment surveys given to teachers, parents, and students. In the absence of such surveys, they are selected by referrals from teachers, parents, administrators, self-referrals, and by the counselor. Effective groups should be small, which can make the selection of group members difficult. Problems can result when the number of students who would like to be in a group exceeds the number that the counselor feels is appropriate. When this occurs, the counselor has several options. The counselor can (1) run two or more groups simultaneously, if the counselor's schedule permits; (2) create a waiting list consisting of students who qualify for a group and run that group at a designated date; (3) consider increasing the size of the group if only one or two students are on the waiting list, unless the counselor feels a larger group might jeopardize the success of the group; (4) seek help from a community mental health agency by requesting that someone who is competent to lead a group come to the school and run one or more groups on the same topic; or (5) if eight weekly sessions had been planned, reduce this number to six in order to shorten the waiting time for a second group, again unless the counselor feels this would jeopardize the success of the group. The counselor should resist pressure to form a group that is larger than the counselor feels is appropriate.

When parents have requested that their child be included in a group through a needs assessment survey, there can be a problem with angry and disappointed parents whose child is not placed in a group. For this reason, the needs assessment survey they receive should indicate that the counselor will make every effort to accommodate parental requests, but it may not always be possible to do so. However, when the group counseling program is initiated early in the school year, the counselor should be able to accommodate every child at some time during the academic year.

Criteria for Selection of Group Members

Randomly assigning students with similar concerns to a group is risky and tends to reduce the potential effectiveness of a group. Although there are no perfectly matched groups, to the extent that it is possible a group should be selected on the basis of specific criteria. This criteria should be based on the needs of students, the severity of the problem, the duration of the problem, and the readiness of the student to become a group member. Need can be determined by the observations of the counselor and/or teachers, by the expressed needs and interest of the student, or by a parental referral. The child's current behavior and a history of the problem would let the counselor know if a child is experiencing mild, moderate, or severe reactions to a problem situation. Teacher input also defines severity. Students who are felt to be experiencing severe reactions to their problem might need to be referred to outside professional care because a severe reaction could be indicative of a student whose needs cannot be met within a school setting. The duration of the student's problem is another important variable to consider in determining selection. The child who was just informed that parents plan to separate might be in greater need of a support group than the child whose parents separated several months ago. The duration of the problem can also be a determinant of readiness. The longer a child has lived with an upsetting problem, the more ready that child might be for counseling. Readiness is often ascertained by the counselor through the initial interview with the prospective member. Readiness, which indicates that a person is prepared and willing to take an action or do something to effect change, is actually the second step necessary for change to occur. The first step is the desire to make a change.

Screening Prospective Group Members

Conducting a brief individual interview for each prospective group member is a time commitment, but this writer feels that it is necessary in order for the group leader to form an effective group. Screening prospective group members is also a standard of practice cited in the Code of Ethics of the American Counseling Association (A.9.a). The individual interview, which takes about 20 minutes, should provide the counselor with a basis for determining if a student meets the criteria for admission into a group. It also informs the prospective group member of the counselor's expectations for group membership. When a student who is either not willing or not ready to be in a group is placed in a group, not only will the group's effectiveness be reduced but serious and possibly long-lasting emotional harm could be done to the student. An unexpected embarrassment or an insult from a group member are examples of an unfortunate experience that could harm a child and may not be easily forgotten.

Group counseling is not for all students. The ideal criteria for being a group member are (1) possession of the necessary language skills to communicate with the group, (2) willingness and ability to speak in a small group, (3) willingness to participate in group interactions, (4) willingness to share personal feelings and experiences, (5) willingness to accept and be governed by the rules of the group, (6) desire to be helpful to the other group members, and (7) commitment to attending all group sessions and being on time.

An individual interview with an elementary-aged child who is being considered for membership in a friendship group could begin with the counselor's question, "I am planning to begin a small group for students who would like to have more friends. Is this a group you might want to join?" If the answer is yes, the counselor could ask other questions:

1. "In a group, all members are expected to talk and share their experiences. Is this something you would be willing to do?"

2. "Everything that you hear in a group is private and you must promise not to share what you hear from a group member with anyone. You could tell your parents what *you* said, but you should not tell them what another group member said. Would you have a problem with this?"

3. "A member of a group is expected to try to help the other members of the group. Would you be willing to help others who are in the group?"

4. "The group will meet eight times and you will be expected to be present and on time at all of the group meetings. Is this something you would be willing to do?"

5. "In a group, everyone is expected to talk and not interrupt someone who is talking. Can you agree to this?"

6. "There are rules in a group that everyone is expected to follow. I will recommend some of these rules and other rules will be developed by the group. Do you think you'll be able to follow the rules of the group?"

7. " If you are a member of the group, you may have to miss some classes. Of course you would be excused from class by your teacher, but you will be expected to make up any work you miss and turn in all of your assignments. Would you agree to do all of your homework and make up any work that you miss?"

8. "In order to be in a group, your parents have to allow you to be in the group. You would have to take a permission slip home and ask your parent to sign it. Do you think this would be a problem?"

9. "If you agree to be in a group, and your parents say it's all right with them, you will be expected to sign a contract that says you will not break any of the rules set by the group. Are you willing to do this?" (assuming the child can write; otherwise, the contract would be verbal).

Since this is to be a friendship group, the counselor might want to do some preliminary fact-finding about the prospective member's experiences with friendship issues. Has the student ever had a friend? Why has it been difficult to make friends? How is the student treated by peers? How motivated does the child seem to be to develop friendships? Does the student seem to be willing to actively do something in order to have a friend? In other words, the counselor should know some things about each member of the group before the first group meeting. Consulting with teachers often provides the counselor with much of the information that is needed.

The counselor should inform the prospective member the date that the group will begin, how many sessions there will be, how long each session will last, and the day and times when the group will meet. When the counselor decides that a student would be a good member of the group and parents have signed and returned a permission statement, the student can be asked to sign a contract in which the student agrees to abide by those items that were listed as the criteria for selection. The purpose of the contract is to impress upon the student the commitment being made and that being in a group should be taken seriously. A sample of a contract can be found in the self-esteem group plan in Chapter Nine.

Involuntary Groups

The preceding criteria for group selection would not be used if the group is comprised of involuntary members who, instead of being recommended for a group, are assigned or ordered to be in a group by the principal, the courts, or teacher recommendation. Involuntary groups are difficult to work with because the motivation of the group members to be involved in a counseling group can be low. Involuntary groups could be formed for students involved in a racial incident for whom sensitivity training would be appropriate; for students who reject the rules of the school and disrupt classes; for students who are showing hostile or aggressive behavior that endangers the school community; for students who act out or misbehave in class, which could indicate a need to acquire greater self-control; or for students who are under a court-ordered sentence for certain juvenile crimes.

Groups comprised of involuntary members are less likely to achieve the intended goals. For this reason, *movement toward improvement,* rather than attaining the group goal, would be a more realistic objective. Involuntary groups are not always time-limited. They could meet for several weeks, one semester, or sporadically throughout the school year. These groups should be small—possibly as small as three or four members—and will require the group leader to be more active and prepared to exert greater control. Even with an involuntary group, however, the school counselor needs to feel that, in some way, each member could benefit from the group experience and would not pose a problem for other members in the group. In those instances where the counselor feels a student cannot be part of an involuntary group, an out-of-school referral might be appropriate because such a child's problem is probably more severe than can be handled in a school setting.

Matched Groups

The better a group is matched, the greater the potential will be for running a successful group. For example, let us say that a counselor is running a five-member divorce group for fifth-grade students. Ann, Julie, Angie, Jeff, and Michael are the group members. One night, six months ago and without an explanation, Ann's mother left her house and never returned. Her leaving was a complete shock to Ann and her father. Her mother is now legally separated from her father and a divorce is pending. Ann is still traumatized by what she perceives to be a rejection and abandonment by her mother. Ann lives with her father and rarely sees her mother, who is living with another man. She is still deeply hurt and feels the loss of her mother. Ann is an only child.

Julie's parents just separated four weeks ago and her father sees or talks with her daily. Each of her parents has told her that they love her, and her father tells her that there could be a reconciliation. However, Julie's mother has told her that this won't happen because her father is still seeing another woman. Julie is very upset and confused by her father's behavior. She cannot believe what her father tells her. Julie is the youngest of three children.

Angie lived with parents who were constantly bickering, arguing, and shouting at each other. This went on for so many years that Angie cannot recall a time when her parents did not fight. A year ago her father left the house and now he rarely sees her. He forgot her birthday this year and a Christmas present came three days after Christmas. Angie had been close to her father and misses him. She often clashes with her mother and at those times would like to be able to live with her father. Her parents are still legally married but both show hostility when they have any contact with each other. Angie frequently hears her mother putting her father down and tells her what a terrible father she has since he is not prompt with child-support payments. Angie is confused.

Jeff witnessed a lot of physical violence between his parents before they divorced and, on several occasions, police had to be called to intervene. Jeff blames his father, who is an alcoholic, and feels protective of his mother. His parents are divorced and he doesn't want to see his father. He resents the fact that his father has visiting privileges and dreads the time he and his younger sister must spend with him.

Michael's parents divorced two years ago and although they have both remarried, they are still friends and have joint custody of Michael. He misses the family he used to have. He feels that he has two homes and is tired of traveling back and forth from one home to the other. He often makes excuses for why he cannot visit with his father. Michael is frustrated with the court-ordered joint custody, feeling that going back and forth from one parent to the other has disrupted his life.

Although all the group members are feeling the effects of divorce, this would not be a well-matched group. Each member is reacting to a different situation caused by separation or divorce. Michael could have difficulty relating to what Angie is feeling since he was never exposed to what she experienced. Ann might not be able to relate to what Jeff has experienced, and Angie could even be feeling a sense of relief knowing that the shouting and bickering are over. Julie could feel isolated in this group because she feels that she has only a father problem. Her frustration relates to the fact that the words of her father are contradictory to his actions.

In a well-matched group, the members can easily share and identify with the feelings and emotions of the other members. A counselor who is trying to put together a group that is well matched would try to find common ground, including similar experiences and comparable reactions to the problem. Gender need not be a factor, although some topics would suggest that a group of the same sex would be advisable. Diversity in group membership would also not necessarily be a factor when member experiences and reactions are similar. Failure to develop a well-matched group can result in a group in which some members feel superior to others while other members feel inferior. This is seen when members ridicule or are highly critical of the feelings of other members because they cannot respect or relate to their feelings.

Well-matched groups are ideal, but not always possible. The divorce group just described could still be beneficial to the members, although finding a common goal would be difficult. Perhaps what Michael could contribute might help Ann and Julie adjust to living without one parent. Angie and Jeff might console each other and acquire some insights about their parents. A common goal might be to find ways for them to adjust to their home situation as it is, rather than as they would like it to be. It is almost certain that each of the members would feel better if they were given an opportunity to express their feelings, frustrations, and disappointments.

GROUP SIZE

The number of students who form a group should be determined on the basis of what the counselor feels is a workable number. Age is an important variable because attention span is a major consideration. Younger children, who have a short attention span, will be more easily distracted in a large group and lose interest in listening to what is being said or what is happening. The nature of the topic can be a variable. A group of youngsters with ADHD or students with conduct problems would require the group leader to exert more control than would be needed in a grief group. The size of the room where the group will meet is also a variable. It would be inappropriate to put too many children in a small room. Finally, the level of experience of the group leader is a variable. Until the leader gains confidence in running a group, the size should be small.

Although school counselors often run groups of seven or more at all grade levels, this writer would limit groups from the introductory level to three members with a maximum of four, primary level groups could have four members with a maximum of five, intermediate level groups could have up to five members with a maximum of six, and a secondary level group could have up to six members with a maximum of seven. The larger the group, the fewer opportunities all group members will have to speak and the greater the potential is for group distractions. In large groups the leader has less control of the group and the possibility of group cohesiveness is reduced. Logistically, fewer children in a group means that fewer students will have to be excused from class, resulting in less classroom disruption for teachers. This is especially true when a majority of members are from the same teacher's class, which is not uncommon in the elementary grades. Although small groups will not serve as many students, the emphasis should be on quality, not quantity.

GRADE LEVEL AND AGE OF GROUP MEMBERS

Seniors in a high school tend to look upon freshmen or sophomores as being young and less mature; they often feel superior to them. The same is true for the way eighth-grade students often feel toward sixth graders, and how fifth-grade students might feel about third graders. In group counseling with a K–12 population, grade levels need to be considered. A fifth-grade student would be reluctant to take the advice of a third grader, and a second-grade student could be intimidated by the presence of a fifth-grade student. In the composition of a group, age is not as important as grade level.

It is advantageous for all members to be in the same grade. When, for some reason, this cannot happen, the experience of this writer is that a one-grade difference within the group is still workable. This would mean that if a counselor wanted six students to form a seventh-grade grief group but only four seventh graders were selected, the counselor could bring in two students from either the sixth or eighth grade. It would not be appropriate to include one sixth- and one eighth-grade student because this would create a two-year difference from the majority of the members.

TIME OF GROUP SESSIONS

The length of time for each session is also a variable that is affected by the size of a group. A counseling session should be long enough to enable all members of the group to frequently take part in the discussion without feeling the pressure of time. The leader needs time in the beginning of the session to briefly review the previous session and indicate where the group left off at the last meeting. The leader also needs time at the end of the session to summarize the group's discussion prior to ending the session. Groups in a school setting should always start and end at a predetermined time and should meet once a week.

As a rule of thumb in primary, intermediate, and secondary groups, the counselor should allow a minimum of 5 minutes per member plus 10 minutes for the leader. This would mean that a group of four should meet for a minimum of 30 minutes, a group of five should meet for at least 35 minutes, a group of six should meet for 40 minutes, and so on. These are minimum times and the grade level and group's responsiveness are important factors. Nevertheless, the maximum time for a group in a high school setting should not be longer than 45 minutes. In many high schools this represents one class period. Time must be calculated to allow sufficient time for the members to come from and return to class. In kindergarten and first grade, the counselor might have to collect the students. This would mean walking the children from their classroom to the counselor's office and walking them back to their classrooms at the conclusion of the session. Groups from kindergarten and first grade might not go for 30 minutes. Although play media will be used at these grade levels, the group leader would have to judge the length of time for a session on the basis of the group's attention span and activity level. When several of the group members become restless, seem bored, or lose interest in the activities, the session should be terminated. The group's behavior, not the clock, is the indicator of how long a session would be for children at the introductory level.

Taking into consideration the attention span at various ages, introductory level groups, including planned activities, should try to meet for 20 to 25 minutes, and primary level groups could meet for 25 to 30 minutes. At these grade levels the group leader may not need 10 minutes for reviewing and summarizing the session. Intermediate level groups could meet for 30 to 40 minutes, and secondary groups could meet for 45 minutes. Teachers need to be informed of the planned time for a group meeting. An important group rule should require the members to come directly from a classroom to the counselor's office and also return directly. This rule must be reiterated and verbally rewarded when members arrive on time. The counselor should have a supply of time cards that inform a teacher when the student arrived at the counselor's office and when the student left the counselor's office. A time card should be given to each group member when leaving the counselor's office to give to the teacher (see Appendix E).

Some counselors try to hold a group session during lunch. This is often a convenient time to see students. However, if lunchtime is only 25 minutes, the counselor should consider the time it takes for students to go to the cafeteria, wait in line for lunch, and then go to the counselor's office. It is doubtful that the session would last more than 15 minutes because students would also have to be back in their classrooms when the lunch period ends. For this reason, lunchtime would seem to be appropriate for a group of no more than three members. Middle and high schools that utilize block times of 85-minute periods pose fewer time problems. Even so, the maximum time would be 45 minutes for a weekly group session.

In elementary schools, whether a counselor should use the recess period for group counseling is controversial. Children look forward to recess and need this time for a change of pace or to interact with their friends. Recess allows relief from the structure of classes. The writer's view is that if fourth- or fifth-grade students are willing to forgo one recess period a week and not resent it, and if parents support this, group counseling can be held at that time. It should be the members' unanimous choice, and the counselor would accommodate their decision. Using recess as a time to meet is similar to using the lunchtime. Recess is usually only 30 minutes and this restricts the number of students who could be in a group. Whether to use lunch or recess time for groups is the type of issue that could come before the counselor's faculty advisory committee. This writer is reluctant to see lunch or recess time used for groups, although there can be exceptions to this that are dictated by circumstances.

OPEN VERSUS CLOSED GROUPS

Open groups allow new members to enter the group at any time, or at least after the first session. In a closed group, no new members are allowed after the first group session. In the K–12 setting, it is recommended that groups be closed. The exception to this would be ongoing groups for students who are new to the school. Groups for new students can meet throughout the school year on such topics as getting to know the school. In this group, students would come and go according to their needs, and the content would be repeated as often as necessary. Because this is a vehicle for introducing students to each other, group cohesiveness is not something that would be expected, nor is getting to know the school a topic that lends itself to confidentiality problems. Screening would be based solely on the students' needs. Such a group is more like a guidance group than a counseling group.

Ordinarily at the first group session, members meet each other, rules are discussed and agreed on, goals are established, and the group leader orients members to what is expected of them. Because this orientation covers important issues, students who miss the first session would either have to meet with the counselor privately to go over what was missed, or the counselor could ask the student to wait for the next group that forms on that topic. Closed groups are time-limited, and the members should know how many times the group will meet. Six-session groups can be planned for students who are in the introductory or primary grade level. Groups who are at the intermediate and secondary grade levels could follow an eight-session format.

GROUPS TO AVOID

The school counselor needs to be careful not to run a group that could result in either emotional harm to a child or serious concern for a parent. If there is a potential for a negative stigma to be attached to the group, running the group might pose a danger to the members because it should be presumed that the group topic would become known within the school community. Ethical standards require that groups protect and respect the privacy of the all of the members. This is not to say that any specific topic should be categorically avoided, yet dealing with some topics requires careful consideration due to the implications of the topic. For example, in a high school setting a group for gay and lesbian students might be very appropriate, but this topic could create problems for the members and/or parents. The counselor would need to anticipate the consequences of the group topic and identify the potential harm that could come to group members from students in the school community.

In some schools this topic might be appropriate; in other schools it would not be advisable. The same could be said for running a group for students who have tested positive for HIV. Such a group, run in conjunction with the school's nurse and a team of medical experts, could be very important for its members. However, depending on the school community, the topic might be inappropriate. On the other hand, both topics could be appropriate for a group guidance unit in a classroom. When the counselor has doubts about running a specific group, the faculty advisory committee and principal can be asked for their input. The counselor can also confer with colleagues.

WORKING WITH TEACHERS

As mentioned, the most common problem teachers have with counseling, whether it be individual or group, is excusing students from their classes six or eight times. It is understandable that teachers will be reluctant to release a child from class who is doing poor academic work. Even if a teacher respects the potential positive impact a group can have on a student, the teacher is under pressure to follow a designated curriculum and to do something to improve a student's grades and test scores. Parents often feel the same way and view membership in a group as being less important than what their child could derive from being in the classroom.

On the other hand, if the student's problem is one for which group membership offers potential for improving the student's attitude toward learning, such as a study skills group or a group that looks at negative attitudes toward school, there is justification for asking the teacher to excuse a student for membership in the group. The impact of the group experience might be the incentive that is needed to produce a major change in the student's attitude and academic performance.

Groups involving academic underachievers can pose a dilemma for teachers because they feel these students need class time to overcome their academic deficiencies. Underachievement is a common and serious problem that does not go away by itself, as evidenced by the fact that students frequently present a history of underachieving year after year. The fact that underachievement has persisted would indicate that unless there is some intervention, there is little reason to expect change. For this reason, students who underachieve *should* be seen by the school counselor either for individual and/or group counseling. Students should not be denied the opportunity to overcome their scholastic problem.

One solution to the problem of missing classes in order to participate in group counseling is a staggered schedule in which the group would meet weekly at different times. A two-tier schedule would involve meeting at two different times, such as meeting during the second period the first week, the fourth period the second week, the second period the third week, the fourth period the fourth week and so on. In elementary schools, where there are no designated class periods, a two-tier schedule would mean meeting one week at 10:00, the next week at 11:30, the third week at 10:00, and so on. A three-tier schedule would utilize three different times; a four-tier schedule would involve four different times. The major problem with staggering is that members can forget the times that groups meet from week to week. To solve this problem, the counselor can devise methods of reminding students about group times. The easiest method for reminding students when their group meets is to arrange to send a note to both the group members and their teachers the day before the group meets and also ask each member to remind the other members of the meeting time. When the counselor knows the schedules of all of the teachers the task is easier. It is this writer's preference not to take students out of math or English classes because most homework centers around these subjects. Nevertheless, counselors must respect the nonacademic subjects, such as gym and art, just as much as science, foreign languages, and social studies. It would offend the faculty who teach music, art, or physical education if they felt that their class times were the only ones that were being used for counseling times.

Another problem created for teachers as a result of group counseling relates to the work missed by students, especially tests. Even when group sessions are staggered, students will miss some class instruction and class activities. The counselor should frequently remind the group members of their responsibility for making up any work that is missed. When the counselor knows, in advance, the dates and times when teachers will do testing, provisions should be made to meet at different times during that week. Group members are also responsible for obtaining and turning in their homework assignments. On days when the group meets, members should plan to meet with their teachers during the day if they did not receive their homework assignment prior to coming to group. They could plan to see the teacher in the morning before school begins, at lunchtime, during a free period, or even after school.

Teachers need to know the counselor's policies when it comes to expectations for students and should realize that the school counselor views classwork and homework as a very high priority. The school counselor and teacher are not working at cross purposes; the counseling program is attempting to facilitate learning, not interfere with it. The counselor needs to periodically check with teachers to see that the group members are meeting their classroom obligations. In the event that a student has neglected to make arrangements to make up assignments or has not turned in homework, the counselor would have to put pressure on the group member to comply with the teacher's expectations. Failure of a member to meet academic responsibilities could result in a request to leave the group. Although it is very important that members attend all group meetings, it is also important that group membership not interfere with the member's academic responsibilities.

SHARING INFORMATION WITH TEACHERS

Reference has already been made to a common problem for the counselor, namely, deciding what information can be shared with the referring teacher. This issue poses both a professional and ethical dilemma. On the one hand, the counselor is responsible for protecting each member's privacy and maintaining confidentiality. The counselor is not a spy for teachers or parents. On the other hand, it can be important for the referring teacher to receive input from the group leader. The critical issue is one of trust, and the question is, should the school counselor, as the group leader, be bound by the same rules that govern the group, namely, to keep what is said in the group confidential?

The answer to the dilemma of what a counselor can tell teachers could be based on three principles. The first would relate to Kitchener's term (1984) *nonmaleficence.* In essence this means *never say or do anything to anyone that could be harmful to your counselee.* The second principle involves informed consent. When the counselor feels it is necessary to say something to the referring teacher, *the counselor should inform the group member that a conference with the teacher is being planned and what will be said to the teacher.* The group member should be told that the counselor will not repeat anything that was said in the group and would only offer impressions and opinions. In the conference with the teacher, the counselor should also let the teacher know that what is being told to the teacher is to be considered confidential.

For example, Mark was referred to the school counselor by his fourth-grade teacher. The referral stated that Mark appeared to be very timid, always looked like he was frightened, and appeared to be isolated from his classmates. The teacher commented that she had never seen a student interact with Mark either in class or on the playground. In the classroom, Mark was noticeably silent and only spoke when the teacher asked him a direct question. Even then, Mark gave one-word answers or an "I don't know" response. When the teacher attempted to talk with him, he shrugged his shoulders, said nothing, looking as if he were about to cry. Mark usually turned in his homework, but it was often incomplete and there were frequent mistakes. His grades were mostly Cs and Ds with a B in art. The teacher had checked with his third-grade teacher and learned that Mark's behavior had been consistent.

The counselor met with Mark and she heard similar nonenthusiastic, one-word responses. The counselor learned that Mark spent a lot of time with the family canary. The counselor decided to use birds as a vehicle to encourage Mark to talk. At the second session, the counselor brought in two picture storybooks about birds, and they took turns reading from the books. Mark was willing to talk about what they read. In the third session, Mark started to talk about personal things. The counselor learned that Mark, who is an only child, described his parents as being "very old." He said that his father was "always tired" and didn't talk much. His mother talked to Mark, but when his father came home, not much was said in the house. Watching television was a nightly ritual for his parents. His father usually fell asleep watching television while his mother was sewing and making clothes for herself. School was almost never discussed, and he was on his own to do homework and get himself to bed. His mother woke up early every morning and saw to it that Mark got up in time to catch the school bus. Neither Mark's academic progress nor social interactions were ever mentioned by his parents. The family seldom left the house; on rare occasions they would eat at a fast-food restaurant. This was one of Mark's few treats.

Mark was not sure what kind of work his father did. Some days his father was home all day. There was almost no interaction between Mark and his father, and although Mark's mother frequently talked to him, he seldom asked her questions and knew very little about the childhood of either of his parents. His father did not comment on his report card, and the mother's response was usually, "Just do your best." Mark heard his father make an occasional reference to seeing a doctor, but he did not know anything about his father's medical condition. The counselor saw Mark weekly for individual counseling and noted that Mark had never asked her a question.

The counselor's impression of Mark was that there were a number of significant voids in his life. His basic needs were being minimally met. Largely through television, Mark was aware that there is an outside world where people communicate, interact, experience satisfaction, and do interesting things, but he was unable to relate to this world because he was not a part of it. School was Mark's primary source of social interaction, but lacking the social skills to develop friends, Mark was an observer rather than a participant. During the summer months, or when there was no school, Mark spent his time playing with "Petey," the family's canary, engaging in fantasy and solitary play with toy soldiers, listening to his radio, and watching television with his parents. He never had a friend and had to struggle to recall an experience that he called fun. Mark looked and acted like a sad 9-year-old boy who might have been depressed.

After five individual counseling sessions, the counselor asked Mark if he would like to be in a group that would talk about how to make friends. Mark quickly agreed, and the counselor noted that this was the most excited response she had ever seen Mark make. The counselor phoned Mark's mother and explained that she would like Mark to be included in a social skills group and that she was sending a permission slip home for her or her husband to sign. The permission slip was signed and returned the following day.

If the referring teacher makes contact with the counselor to inquire about Mark's progress, the counselor should tell Mark that she will be talking with his teacher. She could ask Mark what he would like her to say to his teacher. The details of what Mark said to the counselor either during individual counseling or in the group would not be divulged to the teacher unless Mark knew and agreed to it. Mark would know that the counselor would tell the teacher that Mark had some family issues that were being worked on and that he needs to learn how to make friends. The specific family issues would not be cited. She could tell the teacher that Mark is a very unhappy boy who has not had much social contact and wants to improve his interpersonal skills. If the counselor plans to make suggestions to his teacher, Mark should also know what these suggestions are. The counselor might ask his teacher to try to spend some private time with Mark and encourage him to talk with her. Mark should become aware of some things he could do that would please her, such as answering questions in class, talking with a classmate during lunchtime, or saying "good morning" to the teacher when he enters the classroom. The teacher might also ask him to help her to do things in the classroom from time to time. The counselor should explain that Mark needs to feel important and begin to value himself. He needs to improve his social skills through greater participation and a willingness to try new things.

The third principle that governs what is told to the referring teacher could be summed up as *the teacher's need to know.* This addresses the information that the teacher needs that would enable the teacher to help the child. Although, as mentioned, the details of what a group member says in group remain confidential, the counselor's impressions of what the student has said could offer the teacher valuable insights into the child's reactions. If, however, the counselor perceives that the request for information is based on the teacher's curiosity and would not benefit the counselee, a vague response would be sufficient. "What's Ann saying in the group?" asks a teacher out of curiosity. "Oh, Ann is doing very well in group. She's a very active member of the group. How is she doing in your class?" sends the message that you are not going to share confidential material.

The time to talk about confidentiality with teachers is during the fall orientation presentation to the faculty. Teachers need to understand that school counselors ascribe to a code of ethical conduct. They also need to know the reasons that confidentiality is important and when the duty to warn must be invoked, thus breaking confidentiality.

There may be times when a group leader feels it is necessary to consult with a colleague about a counselee or professional concern that may necessitate citing specific comments made in the group. This might occur if a situation involving a questionable ethical situation has arisen. Discussing matters pertaining to the group with another counselor is ethical and should be encouraged. Sharing information with a professional colleague for the purpose of getting a second opinion on an issue is not the same as sharing information with the referring teacher. A professional colleague is bound by the same code of ethics that deals with confidentiality, whereas teachers are not. However, even when discussing a counselee or group member with a colleague, the name of the member should never be used. It is not even safe to refer to a counselee by first name. If a name has to be used, a substitution for the counselee's real name should be made.

GROUP PLANS

Preparations for conducting group counseling requires attention to details. This should include developing a plan for each of the group sessions. Such a plan should address such things as the "icebreaker" that would be used at the first session, any planned activities that would be used at each of the sessions, the materials that will be needed for each session such as visual aids or media-related materials, and discussion questions, prepared in advance, for each session. Working from an organized plan will give new counselors a sense of confidence and reduce the anxiety over what to do and when to do it. Even experienced counselors do better with a prepared *game plan*. Needless to say, the amount of structure needed for group sessions can be reduced as the group leader gains more experience. Sample group plans for group counseling are presented in Chapter Nine. It is a good idea to develop a checklist of the things to do prior to the first group meeting to avoid forgetting to do what is necessary. After running several groups, the counselor might dispense with the checklist, although it is always nice to know that all of the important details have been covered.

TRAINING GROUP MEMBERS

The counselor should realize that being a member of a group will be a new experience for most students. Students who are participating in their first group experience should not be expected to know what is expected of members in a counseling group. It is the responsibility of the group leader to train the group members. Member training extends into the first few group meetings through constructive comments.

A list of what it means to be a good group member would be similar to that used as part of the screening interview, including the rules that govern the group. If the group is old enough to be expected to read, the list should be distributed. At the first group meeting the counselor could review this list. Emphasis should be placed on being a good listener, participating in the group, sharing experiences and feelings, helping others, not interrupting, showing respect for members, and the importance of confidentiality. Positive reinforcement from the group leader is important when a member or the group demonstrates praiseworthy behavior.

PHASES OF GROUP COUNSELING

Although the literature on group counseling makes reference to various stages, this writer does not feel that, in practice, group leaders in a school setting are aware of or concerned with discrete stages of the group counseling process. At the initial or introductory group counseling session, logistical issues that have been previously cited would be covered. Group interaction does not always take place during the first session because getting to know each other and feeling comfortable in the group are goals for the first session. The second session is often seen as the beginning of discussion among group members. The first two sessions could be viewed as the introductory period, but when a group plan outlining each proposed session is followed, the group process is more continuous than discrete. It would be difficult to discern when a second or middle counseling stage starts and when a third stage begins. Inasmuch as group counseling in schools is limited to six or eight sessions, planning sessions in accordance with specific stages would not be appropriate. Termination of the group, however, should be planned in advanced. In an eight-session group, starting at the sixth session the group leader should remind the group that there are only two more sessions after this one. At the seventh session, the group should be told there will be only one more session. This information is not meant to imply, however, that a middle counseling stage is about to end and the final stage is about to begin. Announcing the terminal session in advance is a way of preparing the group for the ending of the group experience. It has the potential of encouraging discussion and opening up members who might be holding back. Stages in group counseling might be appropriate for adult groups when time is not necessarily limited and the group meets for a longer time than groups meet in a school setting.

SUMMARY OF THE DOZEN STEPS FOR SETTING UP A GROUP

Reviewing what has been said,

1. Group counseling actually begins when the counselor meets with the principal to discuss the guidance and counseling program and the plan for running groups.

2. Arrange to orient the faculty to the guidance and counseling program. This can occur at the first faculty meeting, at meetings with small groups of faculty, or at intermediate and secondary school levels, in talks with team or department leaders.

3. Early in the new school year, the counselor should distribute needs assessment surveys to teachers, administrators, and parents in order to learn what groups the school community is interested in starting. Friendship, grief, and divorce groups will usually be selected. A separate survey should be given to students to learn in which groups they would like to participate. Self-referrals should be encouraged.

4. From the results of these surveys, the counselor decides on the group topic, the size of the group, the number of sessions the group will meet, the grade level of the group, and the prospective group members.

5. The process of interviewing prospective group members begins and the date of the first group session is established.

6. The counselor identifies the names of an appropriate number of students to invite for a screening interview. All students would be from the same grade, although allowing a one-grade difference is acceptable. For most groups, gender is not an issue and diversity should be encouraged.

7. A request should be forwarded to each student's teacher(s) indicating the names of the students who are being considered for a group that is being formed and requesting that they be excused to meet with the counselor for a 15-minute screening interview. Although it is not a good practice to reject a child who has been referred or is self-referred, it is also not a good practice to admit a student to a group who the counselor feels is either not ready to be in a group or appears likely to have an adverse impact on the group. In the event the counselor feels a student is not ready to be in a group, individual counseling should be initiated. One of the goals for the individual counseling might be to get the student ready to become a member of a group.

8. If the counselor feels that a student would benefit from a group experience and also would be a good member of a group, and if the student is willing to be considered for placement in a group, the counselor would ask the student to take a permission statement home for a parental signature. It will probably take several days to interview the students who are being considered and another two or three days to get a signed parental permission statement returned. The date for beginning the group would be at least five days from the day the last prospective group member was interviewed. The prospective members should be told the approximate date of the first group meeting and have impressed on them that they cannot be in the group until the parental permission statement has been signed and returned.

9. When permission slips are returned, the student would be asked to sign a contract in which the student agrees to abide by certain group expectations. The importance of confidentiality should be emphasized. The counselor retains a copy of this contract, and a copy is given to the student. If the student is unable to read or write, the contract would be read to the student and a handshake would suffice for a signature. The reason for a contract is to impress on group members that the group has a serious purpose and that certain things will be expected of them. Members should understand that a contract is binding and needs to honored (see Appendix F).

10. Meet with the teacher(s) whose students will be members of the group. Coordinate the days, times, and number of group sessions. This coordination can be facilitated if the counselor has previously obtained the schedule of each member of the faculty. Groups should meet weekly for either six or eight sessions, depending on the grade level and topic. Teachers should know that group members will be expected to do all assigned schoolwork, and the importance of their communicating with the group leader in the event a student is not meeting academic responsibilities should be stressed.

11. The group leader should develop a session-by-session group plan with open-ended stimulus questions for each session.

12. The last thing a counselor needs to do is find a room that would be appropriate for the group to meet and determine the seating arrangement for the group. Sitting on chairs in a full circle and allowing for proper space between chairs would make the sessions conducive to good group interaction. With primary and elementary groups, the chair that the group leader uses should be the same size as the chairs used by the group members. Although sitting on the floor might be more comfortable, it is not recommended because it encourages sprawling, frequent body movements that can be distracting, lying down, accidental kicking, occasional touching, and restless behaviors. Small groups could meet around a table.

Students should know that attendance at the first meeting is mandatory. This might encourage the student to get the permission statement signed and returned quickly. The signature of one parent is sufficient, provided that the parent who signs the contract has custodial rights. In the event there is joint custody and both parents are required, by law, to grant permission, both signatures are necessary. Be sure that groups start and end on time.

GROUP GUIDANCE

There are significant differences between classroom guidance and group counseling. When doing group guidance in the classroom, the counselor functions more as an educator, informing and presenting information to a large group. Although there is some group interaction and sharing of ideas in group guidance, not all students are active in the discussion unless the class is involved in a group activity. Also, whereas there are a number of rules in group counseling, only rules that pertain to common courtesy are expected in group guidance. Classroom guidance can result in two or three meetings with the class, although a single presentation is more common. The role of the counselor in classroom guidance is also different from the role of the group leader in group counseling. The leader in group counseling may elect to be passive and allow the group members to function somewhat independently. In group guidance, the counselor makes a presentation on the topic and then encourages class discussion.

It is essential that counselors in training who have not been classroom teachers acquire effective classroom management skills. The counselor who does not have control of the class will be ineffective in presenting a topic to the class. When a school counselor trainee has not been a classroom teacher, the practicum or internship experience must provide the trainee with many opportunities to make presentations to classes. Observing the field supervisor conducting a group guidance session during the field experience is important. The field supervisor should serve as a role model for demonstrating classroom management skills. Classroom observations of teachers will also help the trainee learn techniques that are effective in managing a class. It is strongly recommended that the inexperienced counselor trainee ask the classroom teacher to remain in the classroom during the guidance presentation in order to maintain discipline in the classroom, to offer a critique to the counselor trainee, and to conduct any follow-up activities that might be suggested in the presentation. Guidelines for classroom guidance and effective classroom management skills should be emphasized in all academic programs that prepare school counselors. Suggested guidelines for the counselor doing classroom guidance would include

1. Preparing a detailed plan that outlines what you plan to do and how you will do it.

2. Knowing your subject. Ideally, you should feel that you are an expert on your subject.

3. Asking the classroom teacher to remain in the room throughout the entire presentation.

4. Approaching the class with confidence. Expect some initial anxiety, but also expect that this initial feeling of discomfort will pass in a short while. If you feel a lack of confidence, talk to yourself in constructive and positive ways. Focus on your strengths, what you *can* do, what you know about the topic, and do not negate the fact that *you have successfully completed a graduate program and are a certified school counselor.* Confidence relates to the attitude you have about yourself, so *think positively.*

5. Establishing a few ground rules for the class (e.g., raise your hand before you speak, do not interrupt someone who is talking, stay on the subject, etc.).

6. Planning activities that will encourage class participation and will hold the interest of the class.

7. Staying on target. Don't allow yourself to be distracted from the topic.

8. Involving the entire class in discussion or activities.

9. Not attempting to cover too much in one session. It is better to thoroughly cover one or two points than rush over three or four points.

10. Watching your time. Pace yourself and try to cover what you planned to cover.

11. Encouraging student participation through positive verbal reinforcement.

12. Preparing questions in advance that could elicit class reaction. Allow the students sufficient time to think and reflect on what is being asked.

13. Maintaining good eye contact with the class. Look at every student from time to time.

14. Maintaining the necessary control of the class from the beginning. If the class perceives that you are lax on discipline, it will probably take advantage of your inexperience. Should this happen, your presentation would be rendered ineffective. Although the classroom teacher may be in the room to maintain discipline, a counselor does not want to get a reputation for being a "pushover" on discipline.

15. Taking into consideration the age level of your class and its expected attention span. Watch for signs of inattentiveness (e.g., restlessness, talking to classmates, yawning,

facial expressions showing boredom, etc.). Should you perceive the class has "turned you off," switch to an activity that involves the entire group.

16. Talking to the level of the class. Use words and concepts that the class can comprehend.

17. Avoiding lecturing. Cite examples, ask questions, encourage group interaction and class discussion.

18. Paying attention to *how* you deliver your message. Your voice will communicate your enthusiasm for the topic. Speak loud enough but neither too fast nor too slow. Avoid using a monotone. It is a good idea to tape a partial practice session and listen for ways to improve your delivery.

19. Using visual aids, such as videos, posters, overhead projector templates, etc., to help make a presentation more interesting. Use what is appropriate, not what just takes up time.

20. Develop follow-up activities, if appropriate, that the teacher would be willing to do. A follow-up activity for the topic of showing empathy could be to ask the class to report to the teacher any incidents in which empathy was shown.

21. Asking the classroom teacher to give you feedback on your presentation.

22. Critiquing and evaluating yourself on the presentation. Identify your strengths and what you might do the next time to improve your presentation.

23. If follow-up activities are recommended, checking with the teacher to ascertain how the activities went.

Regardless of the experiential level of the counselor, classroom presentations should follow a group plan. The group plan could include

1. The title of the unit (e.g., "Controlling Anger and Aggression").

2. An explanation of the rationale for presenting this unit (why this unit is important).

3. The goals/objectives of the unit (what the counselor seeks to accomplish).

4. Time required (number of classroom visits and time for each visit).

5. Media/materials to be used (visual aids, audio equipment, posters, overhead projector, handouts, pamphlets, etc.).

6. Format for the presentation (group discussion, small group interaction, reading to the class, questions to the class, etc.).

7. Activities planned (seatwork, sharing experiences, watching a video).

8. Student involvement (individual participation, hands-on approach, completing a survey, etc.).

9. Suggested follow-up activities (assignments that would be discussed at the counselor's second session with the class or something the classroom teacher would be asked to implement).

In preparation for presenting a guidance unit to a class, the counselor should confer with the teacher to determine the day and time that is convenient for the teacher as well as the number of visits that will be needed. The recommended time for a presenting a guidance unit to kindergarten through first grade would be about 20 to 25 minutes; for grades 2 through 4, 25 to 30 minutes; for grades 5 and 6, 30 to 35 minutes; grades 7 and 8, 40 to 45 minutes; and grades 9 through 12, 45 minutes or a class period. These times can vary according to the particular class and the interest that is shown for the topic. The counselor should develop specific questions on the topic to stimulate discussion and keep the group involved. In kindergarten through second grade, it is wise to include a project that would actively involve the class in order to accommodate their short attention span. A project could be coloring, using puppets, or drawing. Keeping a log or record of what happens in the group is also recommended. A self-critique can be used for future presentations. It is also a good practice to seek the critique of the classroom teacher. Constructive criticism results in improvement.

Inasmuch as the appearance of a counselor in a classroom could be the introduction of the counselor to the students, it is important that the presentation made by the counselor be one that will encourage students to visit the counselor. An effective way to begin the presentation is to say a few things about the counseling and guidance program (e.g., what services the counselor is prepared to offer and how students can arrange to see the counselor). A warm-up activity, or "icebreaker," involving the entire class is also a good way to begin a classroom guidance unit. In secondary school settings, this can be done by asking the class to complete a questionnaire, relate personal experiences relative to the topic, or do role playing.

A list of classroom guidance topics that a counselor can present would parallel the topics that could also be used in small group counseling. For a list of these topics, see pages 35–36.

Each of the next three chapters was written by an experienced school counselor who works in either an elementary, middle, or high school setting. All are graduates of the Department of Counseling and Personnel Services and the school counseling program at the University of Maryland's College of Education. These school counselors are reporting on what they have found to be effective when they do group counseling. Just as no two counselors will counsel the same way, we can expect to see individual differences and preferences when it comes to doing group counseling. School counselors acquire comfort with the procedures they use frequently and feel are effective. The methods and practices used by one counselor may not be exactly the same as the methods and practices used by another counselor, so as the three experienced counselors discuss their methods of doing group counseling at different grade levels, the reader should expect to see what might appear to be inconsistent or even contradictory statements on certain issues. For example, what this writer has found to be a workable number of third-grade students in a divorce group may not be the same number that another counselor elects to use with a similar group. School counselors do not always agree on every aspect of group counseling. This writer strongly recommends individual screening with prospective group members, whereas other counselors feel the time needed for this activity is not warranted. Although there is not universal agreement on what *is* appropriate, there is a consensus on what is inappropriate and ineffective.

The basic process for setting up groups will not vary much from one grade level to another. For this reason, the reader will note a similarity in the way the counselors describe what they do in preparation for group counseling. For example, each counselor addresses the selection of group members, the importance of confidentiality, setting up rules for the group, the need to gain the cooperation of teachers, and the tasks that must be accomplished in order to run a successful group. Although certain tasks are repeated at different grade levels, this should be viewed as an indication that there is commonality in doing group counseling across grade levels.

REFERENCES

Kitchener, K. S. (1984). Intuition, critical evaluation and ethical principles: The foundation for ethical decisions in counseling psychology. *The Counseling Psychologist,* 12 (3): 43–55.

Tarasoff v. Regents at University of California, 529 P.2d 553, 118 Cal. Rptr. 129 (1974), *vacated,* 17 Cal. 3d 425, 551 P.2d 334, 131 Cal. Rptr. 14 (1976).

CHAPTER THREE

GROUP COUNSELING IN AN ELEMENTARY SCHOOL

ARIELLA GILBERT

Binks Forest Elementary School, Palm Beach County Schools, Florida

The elementary school is an ideal setting for group counseling. Elementary schools have single-teacher, contained classrooms with essentially one teacher working with an average of 30 children for the entire year. The intimacy of this setting allows teachers to become familiar with each child's strengths, weaknesses, and needs. Inasmuch as there are fewer students in elementary schools than there are in middle and high schools, the elementary school counselor is able to know all of the teachers and almost every child in the school. In elementary schools, counselors have frequent contact with the principal and also regular contact with teachers and parents. All of these factors pave the way for the elementary school counselor to have easy access to a wealth of information that can be used to provide counseling services to all students. Elementary school counselors are not encumbered with the scheduling duties frequently assigned to middle and high school counselors, and teachers are usually willing to excuse a child for counseling purposes, which makes group counseling in an elementary school something that can be accomplished with relative ease.

The focus of the elementary school counselor is more on prevention and identification of problems than on remedies. Nevertheless, elementary school counselors attempt to help children who present problems that impact severely on the academic, social, and emotional aspects of their lives. In almost all middle and high schools, there will be multiple counselors. In most elementary schools that offer a counseling program, there is only one counselor. As a result, the pupil-counselor ratio can range from 300 to upwards of 1,000 students. Being the only counselor in the school can leave the counselor feeling somewhat isolated and overwhelmed with the lone responsibility for developing and implementing a comprehensive guidance and counseling program.

There is, however, a remedy for elementary school counselors who do not have a colleague in the building and feel professionally isolated. It is recommended that elementary school counselors form teams with three or four other elementary school counselors within the school system. This team could meet for a Saturday lunch or after school to discuss problem cases and situations requiring consultation or collaboration. They could also meet alternately in each of the counselors' schools. Teams can communicate through e-mail and by telephone. Knowing that there is help when it is needed is comforting and professionally sound. In contrast to middle and high school counselors, elementary school counselors will do more individual counseling, more classroom guidance, and more group counseling. They are also very involved in consulting with teachers, meeting with parents, and coordinating pupil services for children with special educational needs.

Academically and socially, the years between ages 5 and 10 are the most formative years in the life of a child. Attitudes toward school are formed long before a student enters a middle or junior high school. Helping to shape a positive attitude toward learning is one of the important reasons that elementary school counselors can be vital to the academic success of a child. It is during the elementary school years that socialization skills are formed. The elementary school counselor monitors the social development of children and attempts to help young children acquire good social skills. It is unfortunate that all elementary schools do not employ at least one full-time elementary school counselor.

RATIONALE FOR CONDUCTING GROUP COUNSELING IN ELEMENTARY SCHOOLS

One reason that group counseling can be a powerful influence on a child is that students in grades 1 through 5 are easily influenced by their peers. The child who may be completely rejecting or marginally responsive to adult input will often accept suggestions from peers. When the needs of the child can best be met through peer interaction, it is more efficient to work with a group of five to seven students in a 30- to 45-minute period than seeing one or two children in the same time frame.

The concept of universality, in which the group member becomes aware that others have the same problem, is very important even with elementary-school-aged children. Students who are experiencing divorce or separation or those who are grieving the loss of a loved one can receive needed support by being in group counseling. The relief they report on learning that there are other children in their school who share the same feelings and experiences is enlightening and can reduce a student's sense of isolation and frustration. Group counseling also provides a forum for children to receive factual information about life events like divorce and death and can dispel myths and false beliefs that they may be harboring. For example, a common belief of some children who are in a divorce group is that they may have been the reason their parents got divorced. Based on the misconception that they caused the problem, these children feel that they should have the power to bring about a reconciliation between the parents. When they realize that they cannot effect a reconciliation, they often experience feelings of guilt. Group counseling works to correct faulty perceptions.

Group counseling should occur in a supportive and nonjudgmental environment in which students are encouraged to voice their feelings and opinions. Group counseling offers relief to students who are distracted by their inner turmoil and are having difficulty coping with the stresses they are feeling. As a result of stress, students are often unable to devote the necessary time or energy to their school performance, and consequently, their achievement level is not commensurate with their abilities. When students have had an opportunity to express their feelings about something that is happening in their lives that they find to be all-consuming or disrupting, they often return to the classroom feeling better and more able to focus on their schoolwork. Teachers report that as a result of participating in group counseling, their students find it easier to concentrate and, when group counseling has been successful, they even have a more positive attitude toward learning. Teachers frequently comment on a student's improved interpersonal relationship skills that developed through group counseling.

FREQUENTLY USED TOPICS

Although there are many topics that would be appropriate for children in the elementary school, this writer feels there are several group topics that should be offered routinely because they represent issues that confront so many children.

With the divorce rate in the United States now exceeding 50 percent, a group to help students cope with this very disruptive emotional experience should be a must in every elementary school. The increasing number of children who have been diagnosed with ADD or ADHD would certainly point to a need for a group to assist students to understand the diagnosis and to develop helpful coping strategies. Most students diagnosed with ADD or ADHD have difficulty with study skills, social interactions, organizing their work, and classroom behavior management. Group goals would focus on these issues. Because children with ADD and ADHD frequently have friendship problems, they could also be invited to participate in a friendship or social skills group.

Friendship, or social skills groups, are another must in every elementary school. From a developmental point of view, friendship skills are a primary focus for children from pre-kindergarten through the fifth grade. These children are just beginning to learn how to interact with peers in positive, constructive, and helpful ways. For example, if children have been taught that in sharing their opinion "honesty is the best policy," they would need to learn when and how to temper their remarks with tact and appropriateness. Empathy and the importance of being sensitive to others are concepts that could be new to some young children. How empathy and sensitivity are shown can be incorporated into a social skills group.

Loss due to the death of loved ones or friends is becoming a very common experience for young children as the rate of cancer and death due to heart attacks increases. In large cities and inner-city schools, television and newspapers report daily murders, incidents involving random killings, and road rage. The victims of these crimes can be children who are students or members of a family who are in the counselor's school. Many couples are postponing marriage and parenting is often delayed. This results in an increased number of parents of elementary aged children who are in their forties. Their children are more frequently exposed to the death of grandparents. Death is a very confusing and difficult concept for young children to understand. It often results in a temporary disruption of the child's normal functioning, which can impact on school life, peer relationships, and personal feelings. A child who is reacting to grief may experience fear, anxiety, or doubts or become easily distracted. Grief groups can utilize activities that allow children to express their feelings and realize that they are not alone in their concerns. For children who have experienced a loss, this can be extremely important by helping them to achieve closure.

Most schools emphasize excellence in education. There is pressure to achieve academic success and schools focus on the need for students at all grade levels to develop study skills. Study skills groups are welcomed by teachers and parents.

Single-parent homes, hectic home schedules, involvement in numerous after-school activities, divorce and/or separation, and daily exposure to violence on television have been identified as contributing factors that could explain the increase in angry, frustrated, and overly stressed children in today's society. Cognitively, these children are too young to comprehend a cause-effect relationship between these factors and hostile or dysfunctional behavior. Young children are still in the process of learning how to verbalize their feelings. They often rely on their tears, fists, temper tantrums, and hurtful words to release the feelings that underlie their emotions. Participation in an anger management group can help children sort out their feelings and identify what triggers their explosive reactions. Through anger management groups the student is able to learn and practice effective coping skills. The increase in school violence has forced school administrators and teachers to focus on training students to deal with conflict resolution. Anger management groups can also provide relief to those students who have been identified as being at high risk for violent and aggressive behavior.

TEACHER COOPERATION

Obtaining cooperation from teachers is critical to a counseling program and is best accomplished with a multifaceted approach. Asking teachers to complete a needs assessment survey at the beginning of the school year in order to identify the groups that are needed will directly involve teachers in group counseling. Attending team meetings, such as Educational Management Teams (EMT), Individual Educational Program (IEP) meetings, or student review meetings, provides an opportunity for teachers to view the counselor as a member of the faculty with whom they can share common concerns involving students. A counselor should treat teachers as partners and seek their input on students they have referred for counseling. The classroom teacher is a valuable source of information about a student's academic performance, classroom behaviors, peer relationships, and specific emotional reactions. When a counselor communicates respect for a teacher's input, the teacher will usually reciprocate. Teachers should be consulted about the days and times that are convenient for their students to be excused from class in order to attend counseling sessions. Counselors should also seek teacher input as to the group topics that seem to be most relevant to their students. A sample of a needs assessment survey for teachers follows.

GROUP COUNSELING NEEDS ASSESSMENT

Dear Teachers,

I will be conducting small group counseling during the academic year. I would like your suggestions for topics that should be considered so that I can best meet your needs and the needs of your students. Please help me to plan my counseling groups by identifying those areas where you believe your students may have special needs. Also, if you feel your class may benefit from a particular classroom guidance lesson, please indicate this below.

Thank you for completing this survey. Please return it to me or place it in my mailbox by _____ date _____ .

_____ Social skills/Friendship skills (Making and keeping friends and being a friend).

_____ Divorce/Separation (Assisting a child to cope with the trauma and emotions that accompany a current, recent, or past family breakup).

_____ Study skills (Students who you feel are underachieving or not working up to their potential).

_____ Organizational concerns (Helping students organize their work and daily schedules more efficiently).

_____ Anger management (For children who you feel have temper or anger problems or have shown aggression that could become a problem for you or the school community).

_____ Death, dying, and loss issues (For children who are experiencing grief).

_____ Worry and/or stress management (For children who you feel are preoccupied and are feeling pressure that is creating a problem for them).

_____ Other. Please specify _____

Request for a specific guidance lesson(s) on _____

Teacher's name _____ Grade _____ Date _____

Counselor's name, Counselor

A similar needs assessment survey should be distributed to students. With children who are unable to read, the teacher can read the items to the class. A sample follows on page 61.

GATHERING YOUR GROUP

Gathering students for group counseling can occur with relative ease if the counselor has planned well. One week prior to beginning the group, each member's teacher should receive an announcement indicating the names of students from the class who will be participating in a counseling group. Teachers should also be informed of the day of the week, the beginning and ending times for each session, the number of sessions that are planned, and the dates

STUDENT NEEDS SURVEY

Name _____ Age _____ Today's date _____

Teacher _____ Grade _____

I have put a check in front of all of the things that concern me. I would like to join a group with other kids in the school who share these concerns.

_____ *Friendship.* I have trouble making and keeping friends. I would like to learn to get along better with others.

_____ *Banana Splits.* My parents are separated, divorced, or they don't live together. I am having a hard time with this.

_____ *Study and organizational skills.* It is sometimes difficult for me to concentrate or focus on my work. I would like to get help to do better in school.

_____ *Attention problems.* I have a hard time sitting in my seat and paying attention to what the teacher is saying. Some people have said that I have an attention deficit disorder.

_____ *Sadness and loss.* Someone in my family or someone who was very close to me died. I feel very sad. Sometimes I might even feel mad. I would like some help with these feelings.

_____ *Worry.* I worry about things a lot. I would like to worry less.

_____ *Fears.* I am afraid of something and this bothers me. I would like to get rid of my fears.

_____ *Anger management.* I feel angry a lot. Sometimes it is hard for me to control my temper.

_____ *Other concerns.* On the following line, indicate any other concerns for which you would like help. _____

When you have finished, please give this to your teacher or put it in the counselor's box in front of her office.

that the group will start and end. Teachers are asked to notify the counselor immediately of any schedule conflicts.

Appointment slips reminding students of the day and time to come to the counselor's office for group counseling should be delivered to the appropriate classroom teachers on the morning of each group meeting. This serves as an additional reminder to both the teacher and student. There may be times when the counselor might have to ask group members who are present to go to classrooms and round up those who are not present. Students are almost always eager to help in this way. For students who are in the first and second grades, it is often necessary for the counselor to personally gather the group members. It is recommended that the counselor begins at the classroom that is furthest from the counselor's office. This minimizes the amount of time that children will be in the hallways.

SCHEDULING

Scheduling the group's meeting time is often seen as the most challenging aspect of group counseling. It is essential that the counselor be aware of students' math and reading times as well as when they attend art, music, and physical education. Media center, lunch, and recess schedules should also be obtained. Meeting with students during math and reading periods should be avoided.

Although some counselors choose to meet with students during their lunch and/or recess times, a counselor may want to consider the difficulty encountered when students are trying to eat and participate in a group. It is difficult to engage students in arts and crafts activities when there is food on the table. A counselor would also have to consider the benefits that students would miss from the physical activity and the socializing that occurs during recess. Students are rarely enthusiastic about forfeiting their recess.

It is not feasible to schedule groups during the time that students are taking standardized tests. Teachers may also be reluctant to release students the week or two prior to standardized testing due to intensive preparations that take place in the classroom.

GROUP SIZE

In forming groups, counselors need to weigh the issue of quality versus quantity. For elementary-aged students, six seems to be an ideal number for maximum effectiveness in a group. It is a sufficient number for students to experience the power of universality while allowing each student ample opportunity to actively share in discussions. Group size could range from five to seven students. It is best to balance the number of boys and girls as equally as possible. On the other hand, homogeneous groups of all boys or all girls can also be very effective.

If it becomes necessary to form multigrade groups, it is best to combine first graders with second graders, or third graders with fourth graders, and fourth graders with fifth graders. The cognitive levels of students in these grade combinations are similar enough to produce a stimulating interchange. This counselor feels that groups involving kindergarten students should be discouraged. Children at this age are just becoming acclimated to the elementary school setting and are usually anxious about their new surroundings. Removing them from the safety and security of their classroom, their peers, and teacher, can be counterproductive and could create additional anxiety for them. Another reason for not including kindergarten children in group counseling is that 5-year-olds can learn friendship skills and appropriate classroom behaviors best by just being in the classroom. Classroom guidance, however, is very appropriate for students at the kindergarten level and can provide information and activities similar to those in the group counseling sessions.

The ideal number of group counseling sessions would be eight. A sense of group cohesiveness and trust among members should occur during the first three sessions. A deeper level of sharing and work takes place in sessions four through eight. Eight sessions would allow groups to begin in October and be completed by the winter break in December. A second set of groups can begin after the winter break in early January and conclude prior to the spring break.

GROUP COUNSELING RULES

In the first session, after explaining the purpose of the group and giving a general overview of the activities that will take place during the group sessions, the group leader should explain to the members that like any club or game it is important to have a few rules. Group members should be encouraged to establish the rules that will govern the group. Not only will this encourage the group to feel a sense of ownership of the rules but it is also a way of letting the members realize they have an investment in the group. The group leader should share with the group some of the rules that other groups have used. Some of these rules might include: Members must take turns speaking so that everyone has a chance to share and use good friendship skills; we should not interrupt someone who is talking; and the importance of confidentiality. The counselor should be certain that all members understand the concept of confidentiality. They should be told that what is said in the group, stays in the group. Confidentiality needs to be discussed and examples given as to why it would be wrong to tell anyone what someone in the group said. This discussion is a *teachable moment* in order to promote empathy within the group. It should be emphasized that a group must be a safe place where everyone can be honest and share feelings. The counselor should also encourage the members to be helpful to the other members in the group. The concept of what a support system is should be explained. The counselor should then allow the group to brainstorm other rules while the counselor records them.

It is recommended that the counselor prepare a double-pocket folder for each group member. Rules for the group along with lesson plans for each session would be placed in the folder. This will enable the leader to maintain a good record-keeping system. A good way to begin each session is to hold up the rules and ask a member to read one of the rules. For example, the person who states that confidentiality is one of the rules would also explain what is meant by confidentiality. One way to stress confidentiality is to encourage all members to repeat "What we say in the group, stays in the group." In the first two or three meetings, the group can be asked to explain why this, and the other rules, are important. This procedure only takes a few minutes and enables the members to teach and reinforce the rules to one another.

NAMING THE GROUP

Group members can also elect to name their group. The counselor would solicit recommendations from members for the group's name. After each student has had an opportunity to suggest a name, the members would be asked to close their eyes and vote for only one name as the leader reads out the names. The group leader then informs the members of the name that received the most votes. From then on, the group would be referred to by this name. It is a boost for the self-esteem of the student who suggested the winning name. The group leader should explain the naming process before the recommendations of names are made. Examples of names students have given their groups are: The Feelings Club, Friendship and Activities Club, Beanie Babies, Little Room Big Table Club, The Barney Club, Being a Good Friend Club, The Mind Club, The Cool Friendship Club, Red Fire Dragons, and Peacemakers.

CHARACTERISTIC PROBLEMS TO ANTICIPATE

First and second graders have difficulty sitting still for long periods of time. They can handle a 30-minute session provided that an arts and crafts project or a media presentation is incorporated into the 30 minutes. Games and other activities that allow for movement are effective strategies for maintaining their interest. Children at this age, having a short attention span, are not capable of having long, in-depth conversations. Most likely, despite the rules, they will need to be reminded to take turns speaking and not interrupt someone who is talking. They should be reminded to be good listeners and to share their experiences related to the topic. With young children, each session should focus on only one concept or skill, allowing for ample hands-on learning experiences.

Occasionally, members may state that they do not want to be in the group because they do not need to work on the topic under discussion. The member should be encouraged to remain for that session and then, in a few days, the counselor should meet with the member individually to discuss the reasons for wanting to leave the group. Should the student be insistent on not participating in the group, the leader needs to respect this decision. A positive interaction with the student could pave the way for participation in future groups or individual counseling.

Very young students, students who need to be in constant motion, or students with attention deficits pose a serious challenge when they are in group counseling. An effective method of working with such children utilizes bingo chips. Explain to the group that every time someone uses a positive friendship skill, such as being a good listener, making eye contact, or showing attentive body language, a bingo chip will be placed on the table in front of that person. The group leader can specify any behavior that members are being encouraged to use, stating that the behavior will be acknowledged nonverbally with a bingo chip. Members should be told that there is only one rule that pertains to the bingo chips: "If you move 'em, you lose 'em!" This ensures that the members will not touch the chips and therefore the chips will not become a distraction. Finally, the group leader explains that members will be asked to count their chips at the end of each session and tell the leader how many chips they have earned. The leader will record the number next to their name on the group attendance list. In the event that the member is unable to count, the leader does the counting while the member watches. The group leader keeps a running tally, and during the seventh session, determines the total number of chips each member has earned. During the first session, the members are told that the group member who earns the most chips after the seventh week will get to choose the refreshments for the group's party that will take place during the last session. (The refreshments would be a beverage and healthy snack item. The group leader would be responsible for bringing the refreshments to the last session.) The party is held during the last 10 minutes of the final session. The purpose of the party is explained to the members as a celebration of their hard work and in recognition of all they have learned.

Prior to determining the total chips earned for each student, the group leader should review the elements of good sportsmanship with the group. The leader can ask questions like, "How many of you think you will have the most chips?" "What would a good sport say to the group member who has the most chips?" "Would a good sport say, 'Oh, I wanted to win,' and then stomp his or her feet or pout?" Having this brief discussion with the members prior to revealing the final counts helps to set the stage for a genuine congratulatory experience for the member with the most chips.

Bingo chips can serve a variety of purposes. They can reinforce positive group counseling behavior, help shape the behavior of off-task members in a positive manner, provide an opportunity for members to practice counting (math skills), and learn about and practice good sportsmanship skills. More often than not, the chip winner seeks input from group members regarding the selection of the refreshments. The counselor can encourage and reinforce this collaboration as yet another example of good sportsmanship and positive friendship skills.

CONDUCTING GROUP SESSIONS

The First Session

A number of issues need to be addressed in the first session. They would include

1. Reminding the group of the group's purpose.
2. Telling the group the day, time of day, and number of times they will meet.
3. Describing some of the activities they will do during the sessions (e.g., "We will talk, read stories, use arts and crafts, and even play some games. We will also have a party at the end of our last group meeting to celebrate our hard work and all that we've learned").
4. Asking the members to introduce themselves to the other group members.
5. Establishing and recording the rules that will govern the group.
6. Selecting a group name.
7. Engaging in an "icebreaking" activity.
8. A round of sharing on a preselected subject relative to the group's topic.
9. Distributing permission slips that will be needed for participation in the group.
10. A closing activity in which each member states one thing learned in the group today. This can be something learned about another group member or something learned from the icebreaker activity. A popular practice with young children at the end of each session is to have stickers, a bookmark, or a piece of hard candy that members can select as they line up to leave the counselor's office.

Routines for Subsequent Sessions

It is advisable to develop a routine that is used regularly in all of the group sessions. This helps to organize the group, and members will quickly adapt to the routine. A routine that the writer has found to be effective is as follows:

1. Always welcome the group members individually.
2. Collect the permission slips.
3. Review the group rules by having each member read and explain one of the rules.

4. Briefly summarize what occurred in the preceding session and emphasize any concepts the group learned.
5. Begin the group discussion relevant to the topic. This can be initiated spontaneously by a group member or by a stimulus question from the group leader.
6. For young children, plan some activity related to the group topic.
7. Start a round of sharing on a topic related to the goals of the group.
8. Engage in a closing activity that involves a statement by each student regarding something new learned in the group that day.

It is strongly recommended that the counselor take 10 to 20 minutes after each group session to write a summary of the session and notes about each child's participation. In this way, the group leader can determine the progress shown by each member and note any significant behavior that the group leader may want to share with the teacher or parent. In the event a parent inquires about a child's performance in the group, the counselor can easily refer back to the notes that were taken. Needless to say, when a counselor has several groups running simultaneously, it is impossible to rely on memory to recall individual performances. These notes can also be used when the counselor is involved in team meetings, parent conferences, and consultation with outside therapists who may be seeing group members.

The counselor will want to keep all of the items that members create during the sessions. These can be kept in the member's folder. If students are allowed to take their items home after each session, there is a strong likelihood that the items will be lost or misplaced and never reach the child's home. Using the double-pocket folder, all of the student's work could be placed in one pocket of the folder and a summary sheet explaining each week's topic could be placed in the other pocket. The summary sheet will give parents an overview of what happened each week their child was in the group. At the group's conclusion, the folders would be given to each member to take home. Parents are especially appreciative of the summary sheet because it often answers their questions about the group; it also substantially reduces the number of parent phone calls made to the counselor.

The Last Session

At the sixth session, the members should be reminded that only two sessions remain. At some time during the seventh session they should be told that the final group meeting will be held next week. It is important to prepare the members for the termination of the group. The format for the last session could be

1. Welcome students individually.
2. Briefly summarize what occurred the previous week.
3. Engage in a brief activity related to the topic.
4. Start a round of sharing in which members have an opportunity to share something related to the activity or group topic.
5. Distribute an evaluation form for the members to complete. If a member is unable to read, the evaluation can be read to each child by the group leader.

6. Distribute folders containing the students' work and read the summary sheet.
7. Engage in a closing activity in which members indicate what they liked about the group or a way in which the group has helped them.
8. Have a celebration party.

"Icebreakers"

Icebreakers are used for several reasons. They put group members at ease, promote group cohesiveness, and start the group experience with an activity that children consider to be fun. Elementary school counselors need to be creative and innovative in their work with young children. Developing effective icebreakers is both a challenge and opportunity to show creative talent. Here are samples of icebreakers that children have enjoyed.

1. Draw a shield that fills an entire sheet of white paper. Inside the shield are vertical lines that divide the shield into four equal sections. Make enough copies for every member of the group. Say to the members, "A long time ago, people had shields that were called a coat of arms. These shields told different things about a person. Each of you are being asked to create a shield that shows things you would like others to know about you. In the first section, draw or write something about your family. It could be something that your family helps you with, something you like about your family, or even people who are in your family. In the second section, draw or write something that you are really good at. It might be basketball, soccer, karate, gymnastics, or making cookies. In the third section, draw or write about a good book or something that you have recently read. If you haven't read a book at home, maybe your teacher read a book to you in school. In the fourth section, draw or write what you have a lot of fun doing." When the members finish, conduct a round of sharing in which members take turns sharing what is on their shield with the group. Because groups are small, a round of sharing does not consume a lot of time.

2. Fold a sheet of paper into thirds. Label the top of each third with one of the following: Student . . . Teacher . . . Parent. Distribute one sheet of paper to each member. Ask the members to think of what students, teachers, and parents are responsible for doing. Ask the members to write two things that students, teachers, and parents are responsible for. After they have completed this, ask each member to meet with two other group members and have each of the two group members add two responsibilities to their lists. Now each member will have six responsibilities listed on their papers. Conclude with a round of sharing. This activity lends itself to a discussion about how everyone has responsibilities. This would be appropriate for a study and organization skills group.

3. Draw or find pictures to put on a poster showing faces with various feelings. Feelings could include happiness, sadness, anger, fear, worry, curiosity, etc. Place the poster in the middle of a table. Hand a bingo chip to one member and ask that member to toss the bingo chip onto one of the faces on the poster. The member is then asked to share an event associated with that feeling or something that causes that feeling. Every member would have a turn to toss a bingo chip. The counselor could begin by being the first to toss the bingo chip and share a time that the counselor had the feeling that the bingo chip landed on.

4. Draw the outline of a person. Give copies to each group member and say, "First, on your person's stomach, write or draw something that you worry about. Next, on your person's right leg, write the names of your friends. On your person's left leg, write things that make you mad. On the person's head, write what you think about a lot. On the persons's left arm, write what someone did to you that made you mad. And on the right arm, write what you can do to show your anger without hitting or physically hurting the person." This activity is particularly good for an anger management group. The items that are put on the body parts could vary according to the group topic.

It is safe to say that every elementary school counselor who does group counseling will run groups for children who are experiencing problems due to parental separation or divorce. An example of a divorce/separation group plan follows.

GAME PLAN FOR COPING WITH DIVORCE/SEPARATION

> Group level: 3rd–5th grade
> Number of sessions planned: 8
> Number of members: 5–6
> Time for each session: 45 minutes
> Location of sessions: Counselor's office

(It is presumed that this group will begin in early fall so that it could end prior to the holiday break.)

SESSION 1
Objectives
1. To review the purpose of the group.
2. To introduce group members to one another.
3. To establish group rules.
4. To explore feelings associated with divorce/separation.

Materials Needed
A poster showing pictures that depict a variety of emotional feelings.

Specific Strategies
1. Explain why the group was formed and what the members have in common, that is, each child lives in a home where their parents are either divorced or separated. Explain that living without one parent can be difficult at times, and that it can cause a person's moods to go up and down. Every child who is involved in a divorce or separation experiences different feelings in reaction to the divorce or separation.

2. Have students introduce themselves. Refer to a feelings poster and ask students to identify a feeling they have had about separation or divorce. It is not uncommon for this activity to consume the majority of the first session. This may be the first time students have had the opportunity to talk about or share their feelings, and they may use this session to release pent-up emotions. Students generally find this session and activity to be very cathartic.

3. Explain the importance of having group rules, emphasizing that the rules should allow everyone who wants to talk or share the opportunity to do so. Give examples of rules that students in previous groups have formulated, for example, speak one at a time, no interrupting, say "pass" if you do not want to share, and stick to the topic. After students have brainstormed three to four rules, explain the concept of confidentiality ("What we say in the group, stays in the group") and ask students why this is such an important rule. Stress that they should not share what others have said in the group.

4. Time permitting, and if the group members can read and write, pair up students and pass out an interview questionnaire. Ask students to take turns interviewing one another. When everyone is finished, students introduce their partners to the group. The questionnaire can include items such as name, grade, teacher, who lives in your house, favorite subject, something fun you like to do, something that makes you special, a person whom you respect, anything you want to share. As members introduce themselves, the leader should call attention to similarities among members.

5. Conclude the group session by asking each member to complete this sentence: "One thing I learned in group today was _____ ." If the group members are unable to read or write, the group leader can read this statement and write their responses. Their responses would be placed in the double file folder.

SESSION 2
Objective
1. To examine false beliefs and true statements about divorce and separation.

Materials Needed
Book: *Divorce Happens to the Nicest Kids,* by Michael Prokop.

Specific Strategies
1. Review the previous session and the group rules.
2. Review confidentiality.
3. Review the purpose of the group.
4. Read and discuss the first ten pages of false beliefs and true statements from *Divorce Happens to the Nicest Kids.*
5. Conclude the group by asking each member who can write to complete this sentence: "One thing I know to be true about divorce is _____ ."

SESSION 3
Objectives
1. To allow students to explore and share their feelings about divorce and separation.
2. To allow students to experience the concept of universality, that is, to learn that they are not alone in their feelings and experiences involving divorce and that many of their peers have similar feelings and experiences.

Materials Needed
Copies of a sheet on which there are faces that depict feelings and emotions. They can be drawn or collected from magazines.

(continued)

GAME PLAN FOR COPING WITH DIVORCE/SEPARATION   Continued

Specific Strategies

1. Review the previous session and the group rules.
2. Introduce today's activity: Divorce and separation are a bag full of feelings. Ask each child to think of a question or say something about separation or divorce to the group. Provide an example, such as "How did you feel when you first found out your parents were splitting up?" Prepare a large selection of faces showing different feelings with the feeling written below the face. Have at least fifteen copies of each feelings face available to the students. Tell the students that after a member asks a question or makes a statement, each member should select a feelings face that represents the response to the question. The counselor begins by asking a question. Members choose a feelings face representing their answer, holding it up to the group. Members can have as many turns as time permits.
3. Ask members to share their feelings about experiencing divorce/separation. Point out common feelings shared by group members.
4. Conclude the group session by asking each student who can write to complete the following sentence: "The person I can share my feelings with is _____ ."

SESSION 4
Objectives

1. To explore the issues and experiences that can occur when there is a divorce or separation.
2. To help students become aware of the large number of children who experience divorce each year and the number of books that have been written about divorce as a self-help tool for children.

Materials Needed

A children's storybook dealing with divorce (e.g., *Dinosaur's Divorce,* by Laurie and Marc Brown.)

Twenty-four Popsicle sticks

The children's storybook *Divorce Happens to the Nicest Kids,* by Michael Prokop.

Specific Strategies

1. Review the previous session and the group rules.
2. Open up a discussion about the implications of divorce/separation.
3. Read a story about a child who went through a divorce and had many of the feelings that were discussed last week.
4. Ask the group to guess how many children experience divorce each year. The answer is over one million, and because so many children are involved in divorce, many books have been written to help children who are dealing with parents who are separated or divorced. Have a sufficient number of these books made available to the group.
5. Place twenty-four Popsicle sticks on a table. Each stick should be numbered from 1 to 24. Ask each member to choose four sticks and say, "You are going to help me read a story. Look at the numbers on your sticks. When we get to the page that has your number on it, you will read that page out loud. Then you will share your thoughts about what you read." Begin to read *Divorce Happens to the Nicest Kids.* Open up a discussion on the issues that arise from the readings.
6. Introduce the three Cs. Kids don't *cause* their parents' divorce, kids can't *change* their parents' divorce, and kids can't *cure* their parents' divorce. The three Cs should be written

on a blackboard or paper. Discuss each of the *C*s and explain why it is true. Make a copy of the three *C*s and place it in the child's folder that is sent home at the last session.

7. Conclude by asking each child to complete the following sentence: "One thing I learned today about divorce is _____ ."

SESSION 5
Objectives
1. To continue exploring the various issues and experiences that arise from separation or divorce.
2. To understand the three *C*s and incorporate them into each child's belief system.

Materials Needed
The children's storybook *Divorce Happens to the Nicest Kids,* by Michael Prokof.

Specific Strategies
1. Review the previous session and the group rules.
2. Review the three *C*s.
3. Be certain that each member understands that the three *C*s are true.
4. Continue reading *Divorce Happens to the Nicest Kids*. Continue using the Popsicle sticks to engage students in the reading and discussion of issues addressed by the book.
5. Conclude the group meeting by asking each member who can write to complete the following sentence: "At holiday time, one thing I can do to make myself feel better is _____ ."

SESSION 6
Objectives
1. Continue exploration and sharing of experiences and feelings related to issues concerning the parental divorce or separation.
2. Introduce the board game *My Two Homes.*

Materials Needed
The board game, *My Two Homes,* from Child's Work Child's Play.

Specific Strategies
1. Review the last session and group rules if deemed necessary.
2. Play the board game *My Two Homes,* from Child's Work Child's Play. This game opens up good discussions about parental divorce and separation. Through it, the counselor can explain legal issues concerning divorce and correct many misconceptions a child may have concerning divorce.
3. Inform the group that there will be only two more group sessions.
4. Conclude the group session by asking each student to respond to the sentence: "The hardest thing for me about my parents' divorce or separation is _____ ."

SESSION 7
Objectives
1. To enable the members to share the impact that the divorce or separation has had on their home life.
2. To identify common concerns among group members.
3. To encourage members to identify and focus on positive aspects of their family life.

(continued)

GAME PLAN FOR COPING WITH DIVORCE/SEPARATION   Continued

Specific Strategies
1. Review the last session.
2. Ask each member to tell how things are different for them at home because of the divorce/separation. Note similarities in what the members say.
3. Ask each member to tell the most difficult thing about the divorce or separation.
4. Discuss positive versus negative thinking and stress the importance of being a positive thinker. Encourage the group to think positively about their home life. Ask members to complete the following to make a sentence:
   - What I like most about my home is _____ .
   - I am lucky that _____ .
   - I am looking forward to _____ .
   - I really enjoy _____ .
   - My favorite food is _____ .
5. Open a discussion on the ways members can cope with difficult situations. (Be prepared to offer suggestions.)
6. Conclude the group session by asking students to complete the following sentence: "One way I can cope with difficult times at home is to _____ ."

At the end of this session, the counselor should write a summary sheet that tells what the group accomplished. It could include the topics that were discussed, information the counselor imparted to the group, suggestions that were offered, the activities the group engaged in, and any pertinent facts that would be helpful to the group. This summary would be read at the final group session.

SESSION 8
Objectives
1. To provide an opportunity for the members to take a personal inventory of all that they have learned about divorce and to pass along some of the insights they have acquired to the other members.
2. To terminate the group.
3. To evaluate the group experience.
4. To have a farewell party.

Materials Needed
The summary sheets that were developed in the previous session

Healthy refreshments

Evaluation sheets

Specific Strategies
1. Remind the group that this is the last meeting. Indicate that you hope the group has been helpful to them and that they will be able to use what they have learned to understand and feel better about their parents' divorce or separation.
2. Explain that helping others is often a good way to help yourself. Distribute paper and pencils and ask each member what advice they would give to someone who is experiencing divorce or separation.

3. Review the summary prepared at the end of the seventh session.
4. Ask members to complete an evaluation form.
5. Serve refreshments.

EVALUATING THE GROUP

Evaluating group counseling is important and does not have to be very time-consuming. For the purposes of an elementary school counselor, what is needed after the last group session is data that tell the counselor whether the sessions were useful for the members and whether changes are needed for future groups on a particular topic. The evaluation form should be easy to complete and should not require a lot of writing. For groups that are too young to read or write, the group leader can ask questions of individual children and record their responses. A sample of the member evaluation follows.

Group Name _____

Group Topic _____

We talked about things that interested me: a lot _____ some _____ not much _____ .

I participated in the group: a lot _____ some _____ not much _____ .

The group was: very helpful to me _____ somewhat helpful to me _____ only a little helpful to me _____ not very helpful to me _____ .

The thing I liked best about this group was _____ .

The thing I did not like about this group was _____

_____ .

The counselor may also want to get feedback from teachers. By sharing with the teachers the summary sheet that outlines the topics that were covered in each session, teachers learn about the information and skills students were exposed to in the course of the group experience. The teacher can also be asked to respond to whether there was a noticeable difference in the student's classroom behavior.

GENERAL TIPS FOR GROUP COUNSELING

1. Don't be afraid of making a mistake. When a group leader communicates acceptance and genuine caring for children, members will respond by "forgiving" mistakes the counselor may make. Children at this age are usually nonjudgmental and rather tolerant. By displaying the qualities of genuine caring and concern, the counselor is laying a strong foundation for a positive relationship with students. Students readily detect genuineness and will reciprocate with trust and openness, which are necessary ingredients for an effective group.

2. Be prepared. The lesson plan for each of the eight sessions should be completed prior to beginning the group. The plan should be reviewed 5 to 10 minutes prior to each session.

3. Have all of the materials that will be needed assembled and within easy reach. Because children enjoy touching things and are curious, they will ask questions about things they see.

■ ■ ■ ■ ■

SAMPLE TEACHER EVALUATION

To: _____Teacher_____   Date _____

From: ___Name of Counselor___

Subject: _Group Counseling_____

Topic: _____

The following student(s) have participated in an eight-week counseling group on state the group topic: (Write in the name(s) of the student(s).) The group has ended and attached is a copy of the summary sheet that indicates the topics covered in each of the sessions. I am interested in what you would say regarding an evaluation of the group experience and if you have noted any changes in the attitude or behavior of the student(s). Please respond to the following questions:

1. I have observed significant improvement/change in (write name(s) of each child here).
2. I have observed slight improvement/change in (write name(s) of each child here).
3. I have not observed improvement/change in (write name(s) of each child).

Any comments would be appreciated. _____

_____

You may keep the summary sheets. Please return this evaluation to me or put it in my mailbox. Thank you for your cooperation and for allowing your student(s) to participate in this group.

Materials that will be used in the group should not be seen by the members until they are actually used.

4. Be aware of group dynamics and individual differences. Some members will have difficulty focusing and are easily distracted. These members may get more out of a group if they are seated next to the counselor. The counselor may want to place "role model" members on either side of a member who is working on behaviors that the role models have already mastered. Also, a shy child may feel more comfortable if seated next to the counselor.

5. In the group counseling setting, the counselor acts as a facilitator in the exchange of information among group members. Learning from peers is more effective and lasts longer than adult-directed learning.

6. Every member has strengths and can share a variety of information with the group. The effective leader plans activities and steers discussions in a way that encourages maximum sharing among members.

7. The group leader should make a point to restate important things that are said, compliment member responses, summarize discussions, and encourage members to find solutions to their concerns.

8. Children learn by modeling and the group leader is a significant role model. The group leader should model active listening skills, treat members with respect, be noncritical, and create the situation whereby members can speak without being interrupted. By being a role model, the leader encourages members to incorporate specific behaviors into their repertoire of interpersonal skills.

9. The group leader should be aware that, for some children, the group situation will be the first time these students have been able to express their thoughts, feelings, or ideas to someone who is genuinely interested and who will not be judgmental. The counselor should be aware that group members may be exposed to a set of interpersonal skills that are significantly different from those of the adults who regularly interact with the child on a daily basis. This exposure provides an opportunity for the group member to compare and contrast the effects of different communication styles.

BIBLIOGRAPHY FOR SPECIFIC GROUPS

Divorce/Separation Groups

Group members will begin to identify and express the feelings they associate with their parents' divorce or separation. As members become aware that others in the group have similar feelings, they tend to become more accepting of their own circumstances. Group members are given the opportunity to verbalize their frustrations, anger, and sense of loss. The book *Dinosaur's Divorce,* by Laurie and Marc Brown, is an excellent resource to use in divorce groups. The section that deals with why parents separate or get divorced can serve as a nonthreatening springboard to exploring this topic with the group.

Members are encouraged to communicate their feelings to their parents. They can practice what they want to say by writing a letter to their mother and father in which they mention the things that are bothering them. The counselor should help the members explore what is within the control of the child as it relates to the divorce or separation and what is not within their control. They will also learn and practice effective problem-solving strategies for dealing with their frustrations. Certain anger and stress management techniques can be practiced. The group will see the difference between helpful and hurtful ways of expressing anger. Adolph Moser's book *Don't Rant and Rave on Wednesdays* illustrates a variety of techniques that the members can practice. The group will learn about healthy coping strategies. Helpful information could include the number of divorces that take place every year, the percentage of marriages that end in divorce, the number of children who are involved in divorce, the likelihood of remarriage, and other data pertinent to divorce and/or separation. This information adds to the universality concept that enables group members to feel that they are not alone in this problem. The game *My Two Homes,* from Child's Work Child's Play, is a useful tool to help group members learn facts and to reinforce some of the concepts that are explored in the group.

Other books that are useful with divorce and separation groups would include: *What Am I Doing in a Step Family?* by Claire Berman; *Feeling Angry,* by Joy Berry; *My Mother's House,* by C. B.Christiansen; *Something is Wrong at My House,* by Diane Davis; *At Daddy's on Saturday,* by Linda Girard; *When Mom and Dad Separate: Children Can Learn to Cope with Grief from Divorce* and *When a Parent Marries Again: Children Can Learn to Cope with Family Change,* by Marge Heegaard; *The Divorce Workbook: A Guide for Families,* by Sally Ives, David Fassler, and Michele Lash; *Our Family is Divorcing,* by Patricia Johnson; *How It Feels When Parents Divorce,* by Jill Krementz; *My Kind of Family: A Book for Kids in Single Parent Homes,* by Michele Lash, Sally Ives Loughridge, and David Fassler; *I Think Divorce Stinks,* by Marcia Lebowitz; *Mommy and Daddy are Fighting,* by Susan Paris; *Divorce Happens to the Nicest Kids,* by Michael Prokop; *Let's Talk About It—Divorce,* by Fred Rogers; *Please Come Home: A Child's Book About Divorce,* by Doris Sanford; *I Wish I Had My Father,* by Norma Simon; *Sometimes a Family Has to Split Up,* by James Watson and Robert Switzer; *Complete Group Counseling Program for Children of Divorce,* from The Center for Applied Research; and *The Family Happenings Game,* from Educational Media Corporation.

Friendship and Social Skills Groups

This group will discuss the concept of friendship, how to make and keep friends, reasons why it can be hard to make friends, and self-esteem issues. The group will brainstorm various friendship skills and, when possible, role-play them. Helpful and hurtful ways of expressing angry feelings will be explored, and helpful strategies will be cited and practiced.

Members both learn about and practice the art of giving and receiving compliments and the concept of what it means to have a positive sense of self. Members are asked to identify their strengths and what they observe as strengths in other group members. The group will discuss empathy and sensitivity as important concepts for making and keeping friendships. Group members will learn that change *is* possible and anyone who wants to change *can* change. The group will discuss why certain changes are necessary and why change is difficult to accomplish.

Some books to use for groups dealing with friendship and social skills groups include: *Being Bullied,* by Joy Berry; *Bully on the Bus,* by Carl Bosch; *Double Dip Feelings,* by Barbara Cain; *The Meanest Things to Say,* by Bill Cosby; *Today I Feel Silly and Other Moods That Make My Day,* by Jamie Lee Curtis; *Cap It Off With A Smile,* by Robin Inwald; *Feeling Left Out,* by Kate Petty and Charlotte Firmin; *Making Friends,* by Kate Petty; *My Many Colored Days,* by Dr. Seuss; *Joshua T. Bates Takes Charge,* by Susan Shreve; *I Want Your Moo,* by Marcella Weiner; *A Cool Kid Like Me,* by Hans Wilheim; *Sometimes I Feel Like I don't Have Any Friends,* by Tracy Zimmerman; and *Making Friends With Feelings Kit: Bag Your Feelings, Dealing With Feelings Kit, Worry Kit,* and *The Kelly Bear Behavior Kit,* all from Therapeutic Games from Marco Products, Inc.

Anger Management Groups

The concept of anger will be discussed. What makes a person get angry? What triggers your anger? How is anger expressed? What are good ways to express anger? What are bad ways to express anger? Group members will learn and practice "I" messages. They will be encouraged to use constructive "I" messages both within and outside of the group. For example, instead of saying, "Tommy, when you look at me like that, I feel like hitting you," the member would say something like, "Tommy, when you look at me like that, I feel scared and mad. I would like you to tell me what you are thinking instead of just looking at me."

Members will practice safe ways of expressing their anger. For example, they can run around outside, yell outside, crumple or rip up old papers and throw them into a trash can, write their feelings in a journal, or draw. Members can also be asked to identify and share with the group one or two new strategies that could be used to control their anger. During subsequent sessions, members would report on their successes with these strategies.

The concept of self-control should be discussed. What is self-control? Does everyone exercise different degrees of self-control? How can we increase our level of self-control? Members will learn about the relationship between self-control and the ways we choose to express our anger.

There would be a discussion on consequences and how a person can anticipate consequences. The group will be encouraged to "think ahead" and become aware of how easy it is to predict the outcomes of our behavior. Realistic situations would be posed to the group for their responses. For example, "What would you expect to happen if you got angry at your teacher and called her a name?" or, "What would you expect to happen if your teacher gave you a homework assignment and you didn't do it?"

Group members will learn relaxation techniques (e.g., count to 10, do deep breathing, tense and loosen muscle groups, and talk your whole body into a relaxed state). Problem solving will be discussed and a model for problem solving will be offered. Older students can compile a list of their rights as students followed by a discussion on their responsibilities that accompany these rights. Members can brainstorm examples of when someone's rights are being violated.

Group members will discuss why what they *think* leads to what they *do*, and why we are responsible for our actions. The counselor would also try to get the group to understand that "they own the problem" and not blame others for their behavior.

Books that can be helpful for anger management groups include: *Feeling Angry,* by Joy Berry; *Don't Pop Your Cork on Mondays,* by Adolph Moser; *The Mad Family Gets Their Mads Out,* by Lynne Namki; *Relax,* by Catherine O'Neill; *Feeling Left Out,* by Kate Petty; *Too Smart for Trouble,* by Sharon Scott; *The Very Angry Day That Amy Didn't Have,* by Lawrence Shapiro; *I Was So Mad,* by Norma Simon; *Alexander and the Terrible, Horrible, No Good, Very Bad Day,* by Judith Viorst; *Volcano in My Tummy,* by Pudney Warwick; *Hot Stuff to Help Kids Chill Out,* by Jerry Wilde; *Monster Boy,* by Christine Winn; and *Warrior and the Wise Man,* by David Wisniewski. The following therapeutic games from Marco Products, Inc. can also be used: *Anger Control Bingo, Keep Your Cool Game, The Grouchy Ladybug,* and *Ladybug Puppet.* There are also therapeutic games from Child's Work Child's Play, (e.g., *The Angry Monster Machine and Workbook, The Coping With Anger Target Game,* and *Stop, Think and Relax Game*).

Grief and Loss Groups

The counselor should first make an assessment of how difficult it is for each member to talk about the death of a loved one. Children who are not ready to talk about their loss may need individual counseling prior to participating in a group. An initial activity can be to ask the members to draw a picture of the person they loved who has died. They should be encouraged to talk about the person and can be asked to share: "What will you remember about _____ ?"

With older children, the members could be asked if they know how the person died. Group members can be asked, "If you have questions about what happened to _____ , who can you ask?" The counselor should encourage group members to ask their parents any questions they have about the deceased person. They should also be encouraged to express their feelings instead of holding their feelings back.

There are a number of excellent selections in the book *When Dinosaurs Die—A Guide to Understanding Death,* by Laurie and Marc Brown. The counselor can read a page or two at various times throughout the group to serve as a springboard for discussion and education about death. This book can also be used to explore the different customs associated with death and the grieving process. Members may be willing to share their family's customs.

Perhaps the most effective strategy to use with grief and loss groups is to encourage catharsis. The members should know that the group is a safe place to talk about feelings, to cry, to express anger, and to ask questions. The school counselor is advised not to attempt to respond to questions that have religious or cultural implications. Instead, the counselor should refer the child to a responsible adult in the home. The counselor can even speak with the adult in the home and share concerns as to how the child is reacting to the loss. It can be important for the counselor to learn what the child is experiencing at home. Talking with a responsible adult from the child's home will be helpful to the counselor in understanding the child's loss.

The school counselor should also understand that the counselor cannot give members what they want, namely, a return of their loved one. The counselor can point out to the group that we never lose our memories and love for people who are, or have been, special in our lives.

Good books to use for grief and loss groups include: *Grief Comes to Class: A Teacher's Guide,* by Majel Gliko-Braden; *Life and Loss: A Guide to Help Grieving Children,* by Linda Goldman; *When Someone Very Special Dies: Children Can Learn to Cope With Grief,* by Marge Heegaard; *On Children and Death,* by Elizabeth Kubler-Ross; *Gentle Willow,* by Joyce Mills; *The Saddest Time,* by Norma Simon; *The Tenth Good Thing About Barney,* by Judith Viorst; *After the Funeral,* by Jane L. Winsch; *Children and Grief: When a Parent Dies,* by J. William Worden; and a therapeutic game from Child's Work Child's Play, *The Goodbye Game.*

Study and Organization Skills

The counselor can begin with a discussion of why getting a good education is important and what could happen to the students' lives if they don't study. Effective study skills and teacher expectations are good topics for discussion with the group. Suggestions for good study habits would include

1. A discussion of work: Who works? Why do we work? Think about where your parent or parents work and what kind of work they do. View the work you are expected to do in school, including homework and studying, as your work, your job, your responsi-

bility. Just as your parent or parents go to work, so must you go to work. Your work, however, is going to school to learn and to get the best grades you can.

2. Set aside the same time every day for doing schoolwork. Give yourself enough time and don't plan on doing anything until you finish your homework and studying. Make your schoolwork a high priority.

3. Get rid of distractions such as television, computer games, tape players, radio, telephone, etc. Don't try to study and watch television, listen to music, or anything that could distract you.

4. If at all possible, do all homework at one sitting, but take a 5-minute break if you feel tired.

5. Be sure you have a comfortable and quiet place to work.

6. If you are reading, have good lighting.

7. If you are reading, have a pad of paper available in order to takes notes, in your own words, as you read.

8. Be sure you understand what you read. If you don't, read it again. Concentrate on what you are reading.

9. Check all of your homework. Ask a parent or responsible person to check your work.

10. Be sure that you know all of your homework assignments before you leave school. It is a good idea to keep your homework assignments in a spiral notebook. Write the date of each assignment.

Discuss things such as reasons it is important to organize our work, the consequences of not being organized, why is it difficult for some people to be organized, and how we can learn to be more organized. Ask, "Does any member of the group know someone who is organized? What does this person do that makes him or her organized?" "How motivated are each of you to become more organized?" Ask members of the group to talk about their study habits and how organized they feel they are and what they can begin to do to become more organized.

A project can be to ask members to organize their desks. First, they should be asked how they would go about organizing their desks. They need a plan to work from so that they know what they will be doing. Teachers need to be informed about this project and can be asked to check the students' work and give feedback after completion.

Acquiring good study skills and learning how to be organized is an excellent topic for a classroom guidance presentation. Often, teachers assume that students know how to study and organize themselves when, in fact, they do not. The acquisition of good study habits is frequently overlooked or underemphasized in schools. Schoolwide classroom guidance instruction on this topic is something that should be instituted by the counselor as part of a classroom guidance program.

THE CHALLENGE

Elementary school counselors play a significant role for students, teachers, and administrators. They are busy and involved professionals whose work touches the lives of the children they see and impacts on the families of these children. They function as a liaison between the school and home. Their philosophy is grounded in the belief that all children can benefit, in some way, from contact with the school counselor. Elementary school counseling is not just a downward revision of the type of counseling that takes place in middle, junior, or high schools. There are significant differences between counseling with an elementary-school-aged population and counseling with older children. Elementary school counseling is unique and specialized. The challenge for elementary school counselors is to identify and prevent problems that would otherwise become exacerbated in middle, junior, or high school. Group counseling is an important part of a comprehensive guidance and counseling program. Elementary school counselors are vital to the mission of schools.

CHAPTER FOUR

GROUP COUNSELING IN THE MIDDLE AND JUNIOR HIGH SCHOOL

CYNTHIA DRUCKER

North Bethesda Middle School, Bethesda, Maryland

The middle school years, involving grades 6, 7, and 8, or the junior high school years of grades 7, 8, and 9, are challenging for young preadolescents, their teachers, and school counselors. They are also lonely years for many children who feel isolated in their thoughts, feelings, and personal struggles. Middle or junior high school students feel very unsettled in many areas of their lives. They seek autonomy, yet show considerable dependency. They want to be thought of as being mature, yet they easily regress to immature thinking and behaviors. Because they are experiencing both physical and physiological changes, they are self-conscious, very concerned about the way they look, and are inclined to have low self-esteem. They are also moody and fickle and have difficulty placing blame on themselves. Nevertheless, both individual and group counseling can be very effective with this age group because the intellectual development of middle school students enables them to comprehend the objectives of counseling and they are able to communicate well.

Group counseling in the middle or junior high school can be an effective vehicle to support students through these turbulent times. The structure afforded by counseling in a group setting tends to enhance the comfort level of participating group members. Students in middle or junior high schools are willing to share and learn from each other, which enables them to feel valued and important when they can be helpful to their peers.

RATIONALE FOR GROUP COUNSELING IN MIDDLE OR JUNIOR HIGH SCHOOL

One of the major behavioral objectives in the middle or junior high school curriculum is to provide opportunities for students to work in cooperative learning groups. Group counseling parallels this goal. Group counseling can help students become better problem solvers, enhance their decision-making skills, improve their ability to communicate, and elevate their feelings about themselves. These things occur when the group is focused on examining and implementing problem-solving strategies. Success in reaching group counseling objectives has a direct impact on the student's feeling of success both inside and outside of school.

Groups offer students an opportunity to test self-perceptions against reality and can give students a chance to explore new behaviors by approximating real-life situations. Middle and junior high school students are vitally concerned with peer acceptance and peer relationships. Groups afford them an opportunity to relate with and be identified with their peers.

THE MIDDLE OR JUNIOR HIGH SCHOOL COUNSELOR

School counselors in a middle or junior high school setting enjoy the challenge of working with youngsters at this age level and acknowledge that their counselees are always testing the adults in their lives. The middle or junior high school counselor must be knowledgeable about the attitudes, behaviors, and expectancies of preadolescence. Some desirable characteristics of the effective middle or junior high school counselor would include someone who

- Is a person that student's can trust.
- Possesses and maintains a good sense of humor.
- Practices and stresses confidentiality.
- Demonstrates patience, support, and understanding.
- Has realistic expectations.
- Avoids being overly critical.
- Is empathic.
- Shows interest and a caring attitude.
- Is nonjudgmental.
- Is a good listener.
- Does not expect perfection.

- Treats students with fairness.
- Shows respect for diversity.
- Is a good role model.
- Enjoys interacting with young adolescents.
- Understands how middle schools function.
- Works well with teachers and parents.
- Can handle many tasks at any given time.
- Recognizes their own limitations.
- Demonstrates flexibility and adaptability.

CO-LEADING GROUPS

It is desirable to utilize co-leaders in running groups in middle or junior high schools. The daily schedule of the counselor in a middle or junior high school is filled with unexpected events and emergencies. Because there is no way to plan for such occasions, there could be times when it may not be possible for a single group leader to attend the group session. A co-leader, having attended all of the group sessions, could easily assume responsibility for leading the group in the absence of the other co-leader. Although both co-leaders should make every effort to attend all group sessions, a backup system should always be in place in the event a need arises. It is also advisable for the co-leaders to collectively plan each session and jointly review what happened in the group after the session. In the event there are boys and girls in the group, it would be preferable to have both a male and a female co-leader. Because a group leader is also a role model for the group, having co-leaders provides the members with the opportunity to observe more than one leader. The co-leaders often model the behaviors that the group is focusing on as a way of helping the members develop specific skills.

After each session the co-leaders should meet and process what occurred in the session. Some of the issues to be discussed would be: (1) What was the most successful activity that encouraged group interaction and participation? (2) What was the least successful activity that encouraged group interaction and participation? (3) Which group members participated the most? (4) Which group members participated the least? (5) What can be done to improve the next session? (6) Should we stay with our planned goal for the next session? (7) What would be an effective way of beginning the next session?

Although it is important to have developed a game plan that outlines objectives for each session, the group leaders must be flexible and their expectations need to be realistic. The dynamics within the group will often suggest the steps and planning that are needed for the next session. Subsequent sessions are frequently determined, in part, by what happened in the previous session.

Co-leaders must be able to work well together. Any differences between the group leaders' styles or approaches to the group need to be worked out prior to starting the group. Group members should not see inconsistencies or hear arguments between the co-leaders, nor should they witness power struggles between the co-leaders for control over the group. Co-leading is a collaborative effort.

THE FIRST STEPS

At the beginning of each school year the counselor should conduct a needs assessment survey of teachers and students. By completing a student needs assessment survey, students indicate what groups they are interested in joining during the school year. A sample of such a survey follows on page 84.

It would be desirable for the counselors to visit every classroom in order to administer the student needs assessment survey. Counselors can actually reach the entire student body by visiting all of the classrooms in one of the academic disciplines that are required of all students, such as English classes. Not only can the survey be introduced but a brief overview of the counseling program, including groups that will be forming, can be presented. Counselors should stress their experience with groups and how positive and rewarding the results can be for the participating students. With the information gathered from the survey, counselors will be more prepared to tailor a counseling and guidance program directly to the needs of the students and determine the topics for group counseling.

Counselors should also attend grade-level team meetings to learn about the strengths and weaknesses of specific students from the teachers. Referrals to the counselor can come

STUDENT NEEDS ASSESSMENT SURVEY

This survey is attempting to find out if you are interested in talking with your counselor and what your counseling needs might be. You may want to speak with your counselor privately, or you may wish to become a member of a counseling group. Groups will soon be formed on a variety of topics and you may want to be included in one.

Name _____ Grade _____ Team _____ Date _____

Name of Counselor _____

    Directions: Place an X in the first column if you would be interested in becoming a member of a group dealing with the topic mentioned. Place an X in the second column if you would like to speak with your counselor privately about this topic. You may put an X on as many topics as you want.

	Interest in Joining a Group about This Topic	Interest in Talking Privately about This Topic
1. Making friends	_____	_____
2. Helping myself (gaining more self-confidence, feeling better about myself)	_____	_____
3. Handling teasing or being bullied	_____	_____
4. Death of a friend or loved one	_____	_____
5. Getting along better with my family (parents, brothers, sisters, stepparent)	_____	_____
6. Being more organized	_____	_____
7. Improving my study skills	_____	_____
8. Reducing test-taking fears	_____	_____
9. Parental divorce or separation	_____	_____
10. Being more assertive	_____	_____
11. Dealing with stress and pressure	_____	_____
12. Concerns about drugs/alcohol	_____	_____
13. Dealing with angry feelings	_____	_____
14. Feeling depressed/suicidal	_____	_____
15. Other _____	_____	_____

I am also interested in participating in (check all that apply):

    _____ Mentoring or helping younger students
    _____ The peer mediation program
    _____ Helping in the guidance office
    _____ Being a translator for new students who speak _____
    _____ Performing service in the community
    _____ Other: _____

A question I have for my counselor is: _____

_____

from administrators, teachers, parents, and the school nurse. Counselors can identify students who would benefit from group counseling by observing students in classes, in the halls, during lunch, and before and after school. Selecting group members can be a team effort because there are several counselors in middle or junior high schools. Functioning as a planning team also facilitates co-leading groups.

Prior to beginning a group, the group leader, or co-leaders, should interview the potential group members. If it is felt that a student would fit into the group, information about the group and a permission slip should be sent home for a parental signature. Permission slips need to be collected from each member prior to the first group session. The counselor should be prepared to phone the student's home if the permission slip has not been turned in.

Counselors should follow the school's guidelines for obtaining a pass for students to attend group meetings. On either the day before or the morning of the first session, the counselor should take the pass to each member and remind them of the day, time, and place for the group session.

INVOLUNTARY GROUPS

There are both voluntary and involuntary counseling groups in middle and junior high schools. Involuntary groups develop when teachers, administrators, and parents request the counselor to include certain students in a group. Becoming group members would not necessarily be against their will, but their membership in a group is not voluntary. Needless to say, a group consisting of all involuntary members will be different from groups whose members have elected to become part of a group. Both groups can conceivably attain the group objectives, but the group leader should not expect the involuntary group to be as motivated to achieve the group's goals as would the voluntary members. Involuntary groups do not usually become as cohesive as voluntary groups. It is not uncommon for a group to consist of both self-referred and other-referred students. An involuntary group member could conceivably be invited to join a group of students who are self-referred provided the involuntary member agrees to the rules of the group. From the group leader's perspective, an involuntary group member might be placed in a group on a trial basis. Individual sessions might be necessary to encourage involuntary group members to become compatible with the group.

When counseling involuntary students who have been assigned to a group, it is important to inform the members that participation in the group is not a punishment and need not be an unpleasant experience. Instructional groups, as they can be called, provide the group member with both a learning experience and an opportunity to identify and alter the issues that have contributed to a problem.

Middle and junior high school students frequently struggle with angry feelings and are not always able to control their tempers. Students who have been identified as having an anger problem are usually asked or assigned to become part of an anger management group because they are continually getting into trouble and seem unable to change their behaviors without some intervention. Chronic academic underachievers can also be asked or assigned to be included in a group in which they can acquire effective study skills and gain insights into the reasons for their lack of academic accomplishment. Groups for the academic underachiever should be formed early in the school year.

When dealing with groups comprised exclusively of involuntary members, eight sessions may not be sufficient. These groups can even be open groups and run for the entire semester or all year. In an open group, new members can be added at the discretion of the counselor. New members can be oriented by the group leader as well as older members in terms to what the group is working on, what they have discovered, and what changes in attitudes and behaviors are needed to overcome their problem.

The involuntary group is a greater challenge for the group leader, but not one that should be avoided. The counselor should be aware that involuntary group members can be feeling as upset or troubled as self-referred members, but they may not show it. They often deny their problems and mask their feelings with an attitude of apathy and indifference.

GROUP TOPICS FOR MIDDLE AND JUNIOR HIGH SCHOOL STUDENTS

Although topics can be generated on the basis of school crises and the needs of the school community, several groups should be considered fundamental. They would include groups involving

- Making friends.
- Getting along with family.
- Loss through the death of a relative or friend.
- Divorce and separation.
- Dealing with peer pressure.
- Stress management.
- Anger management.
- Self-esteem issues.

- Students with ADD and ADHD.
- Students who are new to the school.
- ESOL students/acculturation issues.
- Students with learning disabilities.
- Social skills issues.
- Organizational/study skills.
- Multicultural issues/sensitivity training.
- Assertiveness issues.

COUNSELING ISSUES IN THE MIDDLE AND JUNIOR HIGH SCHOOLS

In most middle and junior high schools there are three or more counselors and the caseload can exceed a ratio of 350 students to 1 counselor. A middle or junior high school counseling group can consist of six to eight members; the smallest number for a group should be four. Whereas at the elementary school level it is possible to have a mix of one grade level within a group, groups in middle and junior high schools are best handled when the group is limited to one specific grade level (e.g., all sixth graders, all seventh graders, all eighth graders, all ninth graders). There may also be times when it is desirable to have all-male or all-female groups or groups specific to a single racial or ethnic population. For example, if the group is dealing with eating disorders and the focus is on the female body image in our society, an all-female group would be appropriate. Conversely, if the topic relates to issues that males face in society today, an all-male group would be appropriate. Whenever possible, a female counselor should lead the all-female group and a male counselor should lead the all-male group. However, with most topics it is advantageous to have both boys and girls and diversity within the group in order to facilitate real-life experiences. Groups should meet for 40 minutes and allow for an additional 5 minutes to enable the students to pass to their next class.

Middle school students do not have the pressures that high school students have to earn credits toward graduation, which allows for more flexibility in a student's schedule. Most classroom teachers are supportive of the group counseling program and see it as an integral part of a student's school experience. The classroom teachers should be involved in determining the times the groups will meet. It is advantageous to both the teacher and the student to rotate the meeting times of groups so that the students will not miss the same class repeatedly. Some middle schools have rotating schedules that naturally allow for flexibility in meeting times. Schools that have block scheduling allow the counselor to meet with the students for one-half of the block period, which avoids having students miss an entire class.

Parental cooperation is necessary when doing group counseling with middle and junior high school students. The parents of students who have been invited to become part of a group should be informed of the topic; when, how long, and how often the group will meet; and who will facilitate the group. They should know that the counselor is available to respond to any questions related to the group experience. As previously mentioned, parental permission is needed before a student can be admitted to a group. In anticipation of parental concerns, the counselor should tell parents that their child is expected to be responsible for making up any schoolwork that is missed as a result of participation in the group and that teachers are prepared to help the child with makeup work. Parents should also be told that being affiliated with a group will not interfere with any tests given by teachers or schoolwide testing programs. Finally, it should be emphasized to parents that *groups are educational and not therapeutic in nature.* The general goals of a group are for students to learn more about themselves and to develop strategies and coping skills that can enable them to become more successful both inside and outside of school.

One of the keys for a successful group counseling program in middle and junior high schools is for the counselors to develop a well-structured and organized system in which the students, teachers, and parents are well informed about the group. The principal and teachers of the group members should be provided a list of the group members prior to the first group meeting along with a schedule showing where and when the group will meet. This list should be designated confidential and for the eyes only of the teachers involved and the principal. Teachers, of course, will know which children are being excused for group counseling, and the principal needs to have this information in the event a parent contacts the principal and refers to their child's counseling experience. Every effort should be made not to cancel a group session or to change a meeting time or meeting date. From the beginning, group members need to be told that they are responsible for making up all missed classwork, homework assignments, and quizzes. They should know that one of the group leaders will make a point to periodically check with the classroom teachers to ensure that the group members are following through with their promise to complete their assignments. In most instances teachers are willing to work with their students to help them make up their work. Members can meet with their teachers before school, after school, or at lunchtime. In many schools there are late busses for students who attend meetings, practices, and extracurricular activities. Group members should be encouraged to use these services. When several members are from the same class, they can meet as a group with their teachers to make up missed work.

At times a school counselor may be forced to intervene and help a member make up missed work. Counselors could run a homework club that meets once a week after school. Teachers are inclined to cooperate when they see students making a sincere effort to make up missed work. However, students in middle or junior high schools tend to have a problem keeping track of their assignments, and students who are in groups are often in a group because of their negligence in dealing with academic concerns. A system can be established whereby each group member is asked to keep a record of daily assignments from classes that have been missed and have the teacher initial it. The group leaders could ask each member of the group to contact them every morning before classes to be sure that what has been assigned has been completed. If, for some reason, one of the group leaders is not available in the morning, the guidance secretary can check the students' sheet and report later to the counselor if homework was not completed. No system will work without problems, so the counselor may have to use part of the meeting time to remind the group of their academic responsibilities.

When it comes to the attention of a counselor that a student has repeatedly neglected to make up work or turn in assignments, an option is for the counselor to set up a conference with the student and the teacher. The counselor, acting as a facilitator, would receive input from the teacher on what the group member is not doing and needs to do. Then, functioning as a mentor, the counselor would encourage the member to complete the work.

THE FIRST SESSION

At the first group session the leader or co-leaders should review what is expected of the members and what the members can expect to see happen in the sessions. Rules for the group should be established, with an emphasis on the rule dealing with confidentiality. Depending on the group, the group leader(s) can either allow the group to develop the rules or suggest the rules and ask for additional recommendations from the group. It is recommended that group rules be listed in a document that all members must sign. They should understand that their signature indicates that they accept and will abide by the rules. An example of group rules follows on page 89.

SPACE CONCERNS

Finding a suitable place to meet can be a problem. Most middle and high school counselors do not have an office that is large enough to comfortably seat six or more people. Some group activities call for moving around the room, so having adequate space is important. Once a room has been located, the counselor should inform the faculty of the times that a specific

RULES FOR THE GROUP

1. I understand that everything that is said in a group session will be kept confidential. This means that nothing that I hear will be discussed with people who are not in this group.
2. I will respect what other people say. There will be no put-downs or name-calling.
3. I believe that everyone is entitled to their feelings and opinions.
4. I will be supportive of every member of the group.
5. I will not interrupt a member who is speaking. I will take my turn and let everyone have a chance to talk.
6. I have the right to pass, or not comment, on things that are discussed.
7. I agree to be on time and attend every session of the group.
8. I will not talk about members who are absent or students who are not members of this group.

As a member of this group, I agree to follow all of these rules.

Signature _____ Date _____

room will be used. Placing a sign on the door that says, "Group in Session: Please Do Not Enter," will help to ensure privacy. In order to prevent distractions, group members should place any books or personal objects away from where they are seated.

Places that can be used for the group would include the guidance conference room, empty classrooms, the stage of the auditorium, team meeting rooms, the faculty lounge when the staff permits this, the lunchroom when it is not in use, the principal's conference room, or, when the weather permits, outside on the school grounds.

GAME PLAN FOR A STRESS GROUP

What follows is a plan for eight group sessions dealing with stress management. Although each session has been carefully planned, circumstances from the previous session or issues that could arise might suggest to the leaders that the plan should be altered. Group leaders and coleaders must be flexible.

DEMOGRAPHICS

Group topic:	Stress management
Grade level:	Seventh grade
Number of members:	Six
Gender:	Coed
Planned sessions:	Eight
Location of sessions:	Counselor's conference room
Times of sessions:	Odd weeks: Third period (Sessions 1–3–5–7)
	Even weeks: Fifth period (Sessions 2–4–6–8)

(continued)

GAME PLAN FOR A STRESS GROUP   Continued

SESSION 1
Objectives
1. To welcome and begin to get to know the group.
2. To enable the group to get to know each other.
3. To reiterate the purpose of the group.
4. To set goals for the group.
5. To agree upon the group rules and sign a rules contract.
6. To plan an icebreaker to encourage members to feel comfortable with each other.
7. To define/explain the concept of stress.
8. To show the relevance and consequences of stress in the lives of adolescents.
9. To announce the time/day schedule for the remaining seven sessions.
10. To motivate the group to want to return for the next session.

Specific Strategies
1. Members are asked to
    1. Introduce themselves to the group.
    2. State one reason they are in the group.
    3. State one thing they would like to gain from being in the group.
2. Reiterate the purpose of the group and set some goals.
3. Conduct an icebreaker.
4. Explain the importance of having group rules, emphasizing that the rules should allow everyone who wants to talk or share an opinion the opportunity to do so freely. Give examples of rules that students in previous groups have formulated, for example, speak one at a time, no interrupting, say "pass" if you do not want to share, and stick to the topic at hand. After students have brainstormed the rules they feel are important, be sure the concept of confidentiality has been cited as a rule and ask the group why "what we say in the group, stays in the group" is such an important rule. Be prepared to explain why and stress the importance of not sharing what others in the group have said. Rules should be written up and members should be asked to sign a copy to show they have understood and accepted them.
5. Define stress and open up a discussion on stress. Questions directed to the group would include
    - What is stress?
    - When do we experience stress?
    - Why do we need to talk about stress in the middle or junior high school?
    - Is stress always a sign that something is wrong or bad?
    - How can stress affect us? How does it affect each of you?
    In subsequent sessions, aspects of the concept of stress would be discussed in greater detail. The goals of the group leader or co-leader would be to
    - Define the concept of stress and ask for examples of stressors.
    - Raise awareness of how stress can affect us.
    - Identify stressors in general, as well as the personal stressors for each member of the group.
    - Discover coping skills that could reduce stress and enable members to feel more successful in and out of school.

- Introduce deep-breathing techniques to encourage relaxation. Each session will start with a brief breathing exercise. Some school counselors use guided imagery techniques.
- Encourage each member to feel that stress can be controlled and identify specific ways of coping with stress.

6. Announce the time/day schedule for the remaining sessions.
7. Get feedback from members and encourage them to return next week.
8. Summarize the session.

SESSION 2
Objectives
1. To continue to introduce members to each other.
2. To help the group understand more about stress.
3. To explore methods for relaxing.
4. To administer a stress checklist to the group.

Materials Needed
Copies of a stress checklist

Specific Strategies
1. Review the discussion of the first session.
2. Briefly restate the purpose of the group.
3. Review the group rules.
4. Introduce deep breathing as a method of relaxing.
5. Divide the group into pairs. Members of each pair will interview their partners. They should know the name of their partner, likes and dislikes of their partner, two words that describe their partner, and one thing they have in common with their partner (e.g., a favorite food, sport, musical group). After 10 minutes, partners introduce their partners to the whole group.
6. Complete the stress checklist.
7. Share common stressors as time permits.
8. Summarize the session to the group.

STRESS CHECKLIST
Directions: On the checklist below, put an "X" next to those things that cause stress for you. You may make as many "X" marks as you need.

_____ My parents have separated or divorced.
_____ A member of my family or a close friend has died.
_____ I have too many chores or responsibilities at home.
_____ I get into arguments with my parents, brothers, or sisters.
_____ I am not getting along with certain students.
_____ I am not getting along with certain teachers.
_____ Schoolwork is too hard for me.
_____ I have too much homework to do.
_____ I don't like the way I look.
_____ I don't seem to fit in.
_____ I feel too much pressure.

(continued)

GAME PLAN FOR A STRESS GROUP   Continued

_____ I don't have many friends.

_____ This is a new school and I don't feel comfortable here.

_____ I am using or I am tempted to use illegal drugs or alcohol.

_____ Home is too crowded or noisy.

_____ My parents are too strict.

_____ I don't have enough freedom.

_____ I have money problems.

_____ I am teased or bullied in school.

_____ I often feel nervous.

_____ Some people would like to hurt me.

_____ Some students make fun of me.

_____ I am in danger of failing.

_____ I can't keep up with my classes.

_____ Too much is expected of me.

_____ I don't like school.

_____ Sometimes I am hungry.

_____ I don't get enough sleep.

_____ I don't know what to say to people when they talk to me.

_____ I think other people are smarter than I am.

_____ I am jealous of someone.

_____ I would like to have a boyfriend/girlfriend.

_____ I would like to learn how to study.

_____ I have a problem organizing things.

_____ I would like to talk with my counselor privately about a problem.

_____ I get a lot of headaches.

_____ Other _____

SESSION 3

Objectives

1. To define and continue to discuss the concept of stress.
2. To obtain group reactions to the following definition of stress: "A nonspecific response of the body or person to some demand."
3. To differentiate physical from psychological stress.

Specific Strategies

1. Review the second session.
2. Quickly review the group rules.
3. Utilize a breathing exercise for teaching relaxation.
4. Develop a "circle whip" on the question: "What made this week stressful for you?" Use a seven-point scale in which 7 is the most and 1 is the least stressful.
5. Ask members to define stress as they understand the concept.
6. Explain how stress is "a nonspecific response of the body or person to some demand." Allow the group to react to this statement.
7. Homework assignment for the next session: Share with the group a situation that made you feel stressed sometime during the upcoming week.
8. Summarize the session.

SESSION 4
Objectives
  1. To have group members share the stress they felt during the week. (Followup of the homework assignment.)
  2. To identify the causes of stress.
  3. To discuss a specific aspect of stress (see concepts of stress from Session 1).

Materials Needed
Large, blank poster board

Specific Strategies
  1. Review the discussion from the third session.
  2. Quickly review the rules, if needed.
  3. Conduct a breathing exercise to help the group relax.
  4. Introduce the circle whip. Going around the group and following up on the homework assignment, ask each member to identify a stressful experience during the past week.
  5. On a big piece of poster board, make a "Causes of Our Stress" chart with the following columns: School/Family/Peers/Parent Expectations. The group is asked to fill in the chart based on what causes their stress. Upon completion, the chart can be discussed by the group.
  6. Ask the group to respond to the question: "Is stress good or bad for us?"
  7. Summarize the session.

SESSION 5
Objectives
  1. To differentiate physical from psychological stress.
  2. To explain to the group how frustration, conflict, pressure, and adjustment to change are sources of stress.
  3. To continue to collect the stressful experiences of the group members.
  4. To discuss methods of coping with stress.

Specific Strategies
  1. Summarize previous session.
  2. Briefly review group rules, if needed.
  3. Conduct a breathing exercise to help the group relax.
  4. Ask the group for examples of physical stress (e.g., heat, cold, exhaustion, illness). Ask the group for examples of psychological stress (e.g., frustration, conflict, threats, losses, failure, change).
  5. Explain the fight-or-flight response to stress to the group.
  6. Begin to discuss coping with stress (e.g., assuming responsibility for a problem, problem-solving methods, anticipating consequences).
  7. Remind the group that there are only three more sessions.
  8. Summarize the session.

SESSION 6
Objectives
  1. To discuss positive and negative coping strategies.
  2. To evaluate how the group members are dealing with their stressors.

(continued)

GAME PLAN FOR A STRESS GROUP   Continued

Materials Needed
Copies of Personal Stress Management Action Plan

Specific Strategies
1. Review previous session.
2. Quickly review group rules, if needed.
3. Conduct a breathing exercise to help the group relax.
4. Ask the group to name some positive coping mechanisms (e.g., physical exercise, relaxation, sharing stress with others, developing a support system, getting enough sleep, eating a balanced diet, managing time wisely, setting realistic goals, recognizing stressful situations, avoiding stress whenever possible, balancing work and play, being prepared, solving problems, clarifying problems, showing flexibility, and using time more effectively).
5. Ask the group to name some negative coping mechanisms (e.g., avoiding responsibility, giving up easily, blaming others, refusing to discuss issues, using illegal drugs, drinking alcohol, smoking, skipping school, refusing to do homework, denial of problems, overeating, oversleeping, doing things that abuse your body, watching too much television, playing too much, being irresponsible, showing indifference, or inappropriate use of leisure time).
6. Circle whip: How are group members coping with their stressors?
7. Homework assignment: Complete the Personal Stress Management Action Plan.
8. Review the session.
9. Remind the group there are only two more sessions.

PERSONAL STRESS MANAGEMENT ACTION PLAN
Behaviors and techniques I will start to do to reduce stress:

1. _____   2. _____
3. _____   4. _____
5. _____   6. _____

Behaviors and techniques I have used that I will discontinue using to reduce stress:

1. _____   2. _____
3. _____   4. _____
5. _____   6. _____

Name _____ Date _____

SESSION 7
Objectives
1. To follow up on the homework assignment.
2. To define and explain self-esteem.
3. To evaluate how group members are dealing with their stressors.

Materials Needed
Writing paper and pencils for each group member

Specific Strategies
1. Review previous session.
2. Quickly review group rules, if needed.
3. Conduct a breathing exercise to help the group relax.
4. Follow up on the homework assignment. Ask the group to share their Personal Stress Management Action Plan.
5. Circle whip: Share a recent success with the group.
6. Explain the concept of self. Self-esteem is our feeling about our overall assessment of our worth as an individual. It is how much we like ourselves. Ask group members to list three things they like about themselves and share this with the group. Ask them to list three things they would like to change about themselves. Doing this asks the group members to identify their goals. This second list should not be shown to the group.
7. Ask how can we improve our self-esteem (e.g. by becoming successful, doing those things that make us feel better about ourselves, overcoming bad habits, making positive changes, avoiding negative thinking and negative behavior, setting realistic goals).
8. Homework assignment: Referring to the three things the group members indicated they liked about themselves and the three things they would like to change about themselves, ask the members to write what they would do if they really wanted to change themselves. At the discretion of the group leader(s), and with the permission of the group members, this information could be shared with the group.
9. Summarize the session.
10. Remind the group that next week will be the last session.

SESSION 8
Objectives
1. To review the critical learnings from all previous sessions.
2. To cite the goals and extent to which they have been achieved.
3. To recommend to the group what still needs to be done and make suggestions about how these things can be accomplished.
4. To compliment the group for their accomplishments and hard work.
5. To have a group celebration.

Materials Needed
Copies of an evaluation survey

Specific Strategies
1. Review significant accomplishments of the group.
2. Review the goals of the group and the degree to which the goals have been accomplished.
3. Follow up on the homework assignment. If the group voted to share information, then members would tell what they like and do not like about themselves and what they could do to change the things they do not like. If members did not want this shared, the information would be collected by the group leader. Whether shared or not, the information could be used by the counselor for individual counseling follow-ups with group members.
4. Circle whip: How does each member of the group feel about the ending of the group? (It should be noted that the ending of a group can result in a stressful moment for some members of a group.)

(continued)

GAME PLAN FOR A STRESS GROUP   Continued

5. Circle whip: What did each member of the group learn from the experience and what are the members doing differently now as a result of what they learned?
6. Thank the group for the hard work it did and its cooperation.
7. Ask the group to complete a group evaluation sheet.
8. Remind the group that even though the group experience has ended, confidentiality is still expected and is still important.
9. Let the group know that as a counselor in the school you, or their assigned counselor, are always available to talk with them.
10. A light, healthy refreshment can be offered to end the group session.

GROUP EVALUATION
Please respond to these questions.
1. I found this group experience to be worthwhile.   Yes ___   No ___
2. I would recommend being in a group to my friends.   Yes ___   No ___
3. The group made progress in accomplishing its goal.   Yes ___   No ___
4. What I liked most about this group was _____ .
5. What I liked least about this group was _____ .
6. To improve the group I would suggest _____ .

Your Name _____ Date _____

THE CHALLENGE

Group counseling in the middle or junior high school can be a very rewarding experience for both the group members and counselors. A lot of planning and cooperation is required in the setting up of groups. Logistical problems require patience, understanding, occasional arbitration, and common sense solutions. Middle and junior high school counselors are dealing with a population that can be difficult to work with at times, but also one that shows an excited level of interest and appreciation at other times.

There are significant differences in the maturity of sixth- and ninth-grade students. Both grade levels respond well to group counseling and both pose a challenge to the counselor. The challenge of a middle and junior high school counselor is to find ways of effectively working with students who, because they are experiencing physiological changes in their bodies and psychological mood fluctuations, do not always express emotional feelings honestly. They appear to be more aware of themselves than they actually are. Adolescents at these ages are in a transitional period in which they talk as if they are looking forward to the future and are quick to deny their anxieties about the present. Counselors who work with students in grades 6, 7, 8, and 9 are in a position to observe changes in attitudes and behaviors over a critical period in the life of an adolescent.

CHAPTER FIVE

GROUP COUNSELING IN THE HIGH SCHOOL

CATHERINE WILSON

Quince Orchard High School, Montgomery County, Maryland

Present-day school counselor caseloads are making group counseling a necessity at the high school level. If counselors have a caseload of 300 students and if they do nothing but see students all day, every day, they can give each student approximately 3 hours of their time each school year. As other responsibilities, such as team meetings, committee meetings, parent conferences, and teacher consultations are added, those 3 hours begin to dwindle. For any student who receives more of a counselor's time, there is a student receiving less. In order to ensure that each student gets the services to which they are entitled, counseling with groups becomes critical.

Many of the issues that concern high school students center on their social interactions with parents, peers, and teachers. Students at this age are testing their independence. They are learning to accept responsibilities. They are also testing their decision-making and problem-solving abilities. Counseling groups are a microcosm of the larger school and community environments in which the students are developing these new skills. Counseling groups afford students opportunities to try new behaviors in smaller, less-threatening settings and to receive feedback from other group members that will help them move through adolescence.

WORTHWHILE TOPICS FOR USE IN THE HIGH SCHOOL

The topics frequently addressed in high school counseling groups mirror the current issues of families and the larger society and would include divorce, new family configurations, and mobility. Groups that address these issues are formed around support groups for new students, single-parent families, living with stepparents, blended families, family relations, grief, and loss.

There is an increase of violence in society and in schools. More students are also witnessing violence in their neighborhoods, their homes, and in their personal relationships. Students can be helped by membership in groups that address topics such as relationship violence, sexual abuse, sexual assaults, harassment, temper control, anger management, tolerance, or dealing with discrimination and bias. Students often need help to be academically successful in school and to make choices about their futures. Group counseling on topics such as stress, transition to college or work, ADD/ADHD, and school attendance are helpful.

In high schools students are entering into relationships, establishing their own identities, and making choices about drinking, drugs, and sexuality. Group counseling topics to help with these issues might include gay/straight alliances, drug/alcohol support, eating disorders, weight control/body image, women's issues, minority issues, and teen parenting.

DETERMINING THE TOPICS FOR GROUP COUNSELING

In a high school it is considered a best practice for counselors to assess student needs at least every other year. This should be done at the beginning of the school year. The assessment provides high school counselors with information on the current needs of the students, trends in needs for counseling, and changes occurring in the school community. Needs assessments of students, staff, and parents will provide a complete picture of what groups should be formed.

Students often request that a group be formed. This occurs as students become aware that other teens are facing similar issues and when they recognize there is value in sharing feelings and strategies with others who are in a similar situation. As counselors become familiar with a school community and with individual students and families, they often recognize emerging needs of students that could be addressed in counseling groups.

Finally, the goals of the guidance department, the school community, or the school district may dictate topics for counseling groups. Examples would include working with at-risk students to improve test-taking abilities, improving school attendance, or increasing parent participation in-school related activities.

FACULTY AND ADMINISTRATIVE SUPPORT

A key component in running counseling groups at the high school level is obtaining the cooperation of the administration, faculty, and support staff. Obtaining the support of the administration is critical. Development of this support begins by educating administrators about the total school counseling program. This would include the results of current needs assessments as well as the goals and objectives that are student, department, and school focused. Developing support requires that administrators be kept abreast of plans for group counseling, classroom guidance, and parental involvement. It is important that the principal understand the benefits of group counseling, both to the student and to the school. When counseling groups are a priority of the principal, they are much more likely to be supported by teachers.

Obtaining teacher support is very important. The counseling department should keep teachers informed about the counseling program, including the procedures used for including a student in a group. It is also important for teachers to know the procedures for referring a student for group counseling and to know what characteristics make a student a good candidate for inclusion in a group. Through direct contact and in-service training, counselors should educate teachers on the many aspects of the counseling program. Open communication with staff facilitates support of the counseling program. Counselors should be visible in the school and should use avenues such as newsletters and faculty meetings to inform and discuss the counseling program.

PARENTAL SUPPORT

Equally important as the administration and staff support is parental support. Parents need to be apprised of the functions of the counseling program and the topics that will be used for counseling groups. Methods of delivering this information to parents may include newsletters, columns in the PTA bulletins, or conferences with specific parents. It is prudent to have parental permission for students who will participate in counseling groups. This can be done through an opt-out method, that is, by sending home a description of groups projected for the school year and asking parents to notify the guidance office if they do *not* want their child to participate in any groups. Or it can be done by obtaining permission for each specific group. The difficulty with this latter method is that there can be some topics that students are interested in but do not wish to discuss with their parents. High school students often seek the help of a group in order to talk about things they would not discuss with their parents, for example, issues of sexuality or homosexuality. The method used to obtain permission for participation should be arrived at through discussion with the principal.

CO-LEADING GROUPS

The issue of who should lead the group is very important. Although the group can always be run with a single leader, it is recommended that coleaders run a high school group. Co-leaders have the potential to provide a balance in gender, race, culture, age, perspective, and style. Because it is not uncommon for a school counselor to be called upon to assist a student who is experiencing a crisis situation, having coleaders would enable the group to continue to meet when one leader is called away. If counseling sessions are to be viewed as important to students and staff, they should not, if at all possible, be canceled due to the absence of a leader. The co-leader could be another counselor; another staff person such as a nurse, school psychologist, or qualified teacher; or a counselor/therapist from a community agency or one who is in private practice. When the coleader is not a member of the school staff, the counselor should make every effort to be present at all group sessions. It is important for the counselor to know what was said, who said it, and what techniques were employed by the group leader.

SELECTION OF GROUP MEMBERS

Once it is determined that a group will be formed, appropriate students should be selected. Which students are included depends on the nature of the group, the needs of prospective group members, and the characteristics of the group, such as age or gender. Each student who is under consideration for inclusion in the group should be seen individually by the counselor prior to the first session. This meeting would be used to describe the purpose of the group to the student, to explain how counseling groups are conducted, to discuss how often and when the group will meet, to explain the role of the members and the group leaders, and to inform the prospective group member what is expected of members and what they can expect from the group. This is also the time to indicate that there will be certain ground rules, specifically relating to confidentiality.

Factors to consider in selecting students for membership in a group include topic, age, gender, and the overall composition of the group. For some topics, it may be appropriate to mix students from the ninth to the twelfth grades. For example, in an anger management group, younger students can benefit from some of the experiences and problem-solving abilities of older, more mature students. This would also be true for groups dealing with academic pressures, stress, or peer relationships. These are topics where experience and maturity add to coping skills. It may also be appropriate to mix male and female students.

Groups that focus on family issues such as divorce, grief, or blended families may be beneficial to siblings, but the inclusion of siblings in the same group should be avoided. Placing siblings in different groups would allow each sibling the greatest opportunity to share feelings without concern, embarrassment, fear of retaliation, or loss of confidentiality with respect to the other sibling. To illustrate this, if the group were dealing with stepparents, two children from the same family may have different views and feelings about each parent or the family constellation. The siblings may be reluctant to express their true feelings in front of each other.

When forming a group it is also worth considering if all of the members should be currently facing the same issue or whether to include students who have successfully dealt with the issue. This raises the question of whether there should be role models in the group. The technique of using role models within a group is especially effective if the group is seeking to change some inappropriate behavior.

EXCUSING MEMBERS FROM CLASS

Asking teachers to excuse students from class is one of the more difficult aspects of forming counseling groups at the high school level. In high school, teachers are faced with the demands of covering a curriculum that is very full and requires virtually every class period to address the content. Additionally, the school or school system may offer standardized exams or assessments that students must pass to earn credit or to earn a diploma. Students are held accountable for material even if they have not been in class.

Adding to this difficulty is the fact that students who are being considered for counseling groups are often those students who are having academic problems for a variety of reasons. It is not easy to decide if students who are failing would benefit more from remaining in class to receive needed instruction or from joining a group that will, potentially, help them deal with issues that are impacting on school achievement. There is reason to feel that when underachievement or failure has been chronic, it would make sense to look at the causes of the problem and place the student in an appropriate group. For example, a study skills group could be more beneficial to students who have poor study skills and are considered to be at-risk students than leaving them in class and expecting them to change behavior without help.

The best way to have students available to participate in groups is to have the support of the principal and faculty. When the principal sees what groups can do for students, how participation in a group can improve a student's overall performance in school, and that forming groups makes effective use of the counselor's time, it is likely that the principal will support the use of groups. When the principal supports groups, the staff will be inclined to do likewise.

Whenever possible, counselors should collect data that would validate the importance and value of groups. If, for example, the focus of a group was on having better attendance, it would be wise to keep track of attendance before and after the group sessions; if a group dealt with anger management, keeping track of disciplinary referrals before and after the group sessions would be important. Not all group topics can yield measurable data, but when it is possible, it is a good idea to document before-and-after behaviors.

Although the sanctioning of groups by the principal is very important, the counselor should not rely just on the principal for faculty support. As previously mentioned, it is essential that a good rapport between the staff and the guidance and counseling program be developed for the overall program to be effective, respected, and well received. Counselors need to be visible. They should collaborate with teachers whenever possible. They should be viewed as colleagues, not as a different category of staff, and definitely not on a par with administrators. This means that if all teachers have two nights of chaperone duty during the school year, counselors should also have two nights of chaperone duty. If teachers are required to serve on school committees, counselors should also serve on committees. Teachers need to see that counselors are members of the faculty who are attempting to help students. It also helps to set up groups so that they cause as little disruption to classes as possible. This can be done by rotating the group meeting times, by developing an efficient method for getting passes to students, and by informing teachers of student attendance at group meetings for their class attendance records.

A variety of methods are available for excusing a student from class. Passes can be sent to the student's homeroom or first period, passes can be sent to the classroom that the student will be leaving, or passes can be picked up by the students at the guidance office prior to the group meeting. There are advantages and disadvantages to each of these methods. Allowing students to come for their own pass affords greater confidentiality but relies on students to remember and take responsibility for getting the pass. Sending passes to students will act as a reminder of the session but may draw attention to them. The nature of the group and the needs and input of the students will guide the counselor in making this determination.

It is usually easier to ask teachers to excuse students from class if the counseling group does not meet during the same class time for each session. This can be avoided by rotating either the class period or the day of the meeting. For example, the group may meet during first period for the first week of the group, second period during the second week, and so on. Unfortunately, this system makes it difficult for students to keep track of the meeting schedule. For this reason it is often best to send passes to students.

SPACE CONCERNS

In most school jurisdictions throughout the country, the number of high school students is increasing, resulting in schools that are full or overcrowded. This makes finding a space to hold a counseling group very difficult. Few counselors have the luxury of offices that are large enough to hold a group session. There are very few rooms in a school that are not being used for classes that would be conducive to a group meeting and afford privacy. Often counselors are forced to change locations weekly depending on which conference rooms are available. This contributes to confusion in scheduling and the need to remind students of the time, date, and location of each group session. Conference rooms are the most convenient to use when they are accessible. Small groups can meet in the counselor's office, and it is a good idea to survey the faculty as to what classrooms may be vacant at times during the day. In an emergency, and with prior permission, counselors could use the staff dining room or the teachers' lounge, although the use of these places might not be well received by the faculty. Ideally, the location of all meetings should be determined prior to beginning the first session.

GROUP SIZE

The size of a high school counseling group varies, and a number of variables need to be examined prior to determining the group size. The topic of the group and the number of students who are facing that particular issue is a major consideration. The size of available rooms can also determine the number of members. Optimally, a group would range in size from four to ten. Because of the concerns previously described about excusing students from class, it is unlikely that all students will be in attendance for any given session. For this reason, it is practical to begin the group with a few more students than desired. Although the group leaders do not want to encourage any member to drop out of the group, inevitably there will be dropouts. The group, however, should be a closed group. Members may leave, but new members should not be added once the group begins.

FREQUENCY OF SESSIONS

The frequency of meetings and the duration of the group are determined by the goals of the group. If the group is a growth group, such as a group that is looking at self-esteem or one that deals with reducing stress, it is likely that a specific number of sessions will be planned with a specific agenda or topic for each session. Groups such as these often meet once a week for 8 to 12 weeks. If the group is a support group, such as a grief and loss group might be, it is likely that it will meet weekly throughout the school year. Typically, the length of each session is one class period, or about 45 minutes if the school uses block times. Support groups that meet over a period of many months can be open groups.

THE FIRST SESSION

The first session is a get-to-know-each-other meeting. Members should say something about themselves that they want their group classmates to know. They can also include why they are in the group and what they would like to get from being in the group. During the first session, the ground rules that were described in the individual screening meeting should be repeated. Confidentiality should be discussed and possibly repeated each session because of the difficulty and importance of maintaining confidentiality in a group. Other ground rules typically include: only one person speaks at a time, no put-downs, and the option to pass and say nothing to a comment made by a member. The first meeting should also cover the schedule of meetings and whether session times will be rotated. This information can be put in the form of a memo and distributed to the members.

CHARACTERISTIC PROBLEMS TO ANTICIPATE WITH THIS AGE GROUP

Attendance at group sessions is probably the greatest problem encountered in high school groups. As mentioned previously, high school is a time when academic credits count toward graduation. It is a time when students face standardized exams or other assessments that measure mastery of the material covered in class and when troubled students, who are in need of counseling, may have already missed a significant amount of class time. Teachers are often reluctant to release students who have already missed a lot of classes, yet some classes will be easier for a student to miss than others. Poor school attendance is one of the main reasons that students are not successful in school. Including a student who has shown poor school attendance in a group is risky. Attendance at group sessions is important and there is a likelihood that a student's absence could jeopardize the cohesiveness of the group. On the other hand, an effective group could conceivably motivate a student who has been frequently absent to make changes in both attitude and behaviors. Membership in a group can be the best thing that could happen for some students.

IMPORTANT TASKS FOR GROUP LEADERS

It is important for the counselor to give consideration to all of the logistical issues cited and to the selection and screening of students in order for the group to be successful. Additionally, there are elements that should not be overlooked during the course of the group:

1. Structure each session. Plan each session and do not rely on the students to be able to talk spontaneously. Plan a brief activity that focuses the discussion or illustrates a point that the students would be expected to learn.

2. Plan an activity to stimulate discussion if the progress of the group stalls. Use activities in a purposeful way. For most topics, a series of prepared open-ended or incomplete sentences can be used. Members can fill in the blanks and share their responses with another member first, then with the larger group. For example, if the group is dealing with anger management, the activity could start with sentence stems such as

Recently, I got really angry when . . .

One person I always seem to lose my temper with is . . .

When I feel myself starting to get angry, I . . .

I've been able to stop myself from getting angry by . . .

In a group discussing family relationships, members can be asked to draw a picture of their family having a meal together. The group leader might ask, "Who is sitting there? Where does everyone sit? What do they talk about?" In a grief group, the group leader could begin by asking members to write a letter to the person they miss. Some members may be willing to share their letters with the group. Avoid a series of activities that do not facilitate moving the discussion to a deeper level. Announce the plan for each session and allow ample time for summary and closure.

3. Determine if the group will be open or closed. Prior to beginning the group, the counselor should determine if it will be open to new members during the sessions or if it will be closed. Some groups, such as support groups, may be able to absorb new members as the group proceeds. Generally, it is not wise to add new members to groups that are time-limited.

4. Recognize that involuntary membership in a group can result in a difficult group. It will be necessary to plan differently when the members have been involuntarily assigned to the group. It is not uncommon for an administrator to assign a student to a group as a part of a disciplinary consequence. Teachers can also recommend a student for participation in a group. In such cases it is often necessary to help the student see that participating in the group can benefit the student in ways beyond fulfilling punishment.

5. Set goals for the group and have objectives for each session. These goals should be previously determined by the group leader and co-leader and discussed with the students during the screening session. They should also be reviewed at the first meeting.

6. Formulate a plan for handling difficult members of a group. Deal with difficult members individually and privately outside of the group. Difficult group members would be those who do not respect the rules of the group, or members who interrupt, put down other members, monopolize the discussion, or consistently move the group off the task. A difficult member could also be one who refuses to participate or expresses hostility to either the group leader or members of the group. Members who have breached confidentiality should be dealt with privately. It is also a good idea to review the group goals and the expectations of group members with the member who is having problems with rules. If it appears that the needs of the student are greater than can be met in the group, it may be necessary to see the student individually or make a referral to an outside source.

7. Plan to do an evaluation of your group. The co-leaders should evaluate both the individual sessions and the total group experience. Evaluations should assess such things as group member satisfaction, the degree to which group goals were met, and if changes in the members' behavior or attitude seem to have occurred. Evaluating the group sessions can be done by either the counselor or members of the group. The impressions of group members would enable the counselor to know how effective the group has been. Evaluating can be done after each session or after the last group meeting. Session-by-session evaluating would give immediate feedback to the group leader and would inform the leader if changes in future sessions are needed. The evaluation process should be simple, not complicated. Much can be learned by the group leaders from the answers to a few questions. If session-by-session evaluation is being done, questions should be developed for each session. Responses could be either by thumbs up/thumbs down or by asking the members to write their answers. Session-by-session questions could be: "Did the session meet the objectives of the day? Did you learn something new in group today?" If responses are written, the questions could be: "Write down one thing that you learned today, or what new strategy you have learned for dealing with your problem." Another way of evaluating group sessions would be to ask one or two group members to summarize the session for the group. A more detailed evaluation should be conducted at the conclusion of the group.

8. Consider a follow-up, or maintenance session. Depending on how the members functioned as a group, the topic that was discussed, and the degree to which the goals were met, it may be helpful to schedule another session in 4 to 6 weeks as a follow-up. This would help to provide both closure and ongoing support. The decision to have a follow-up session should be made by the group at the last group session. All members need not concur that another session would be helpful, but approximately two-thirds of the group should be willing to reconvene.

SAMPLE GROUP PLANS

Included in this section are plans for two methods of conducting a high school counseling group for transfer students who are making an adjustment to the school. One plan is presented as an ongoing support group; the other is a structured eight-session group. Running a support group for new students would be a good choice for a school in which there is a constant transition throughout the school year and new students are being enrolled each week. A structured eight-session group would be a good choice for a school where the bulk of new students enroll at the beginning of the school year, at a semester change, or in which there is only a small number of new students during the year. In either case, including students who are currently in the school and who are active members of school helping groups, such as peer counselors or mentors, can provide the new students with a familiar face in the cafeteria or in the halls and a classmate whom they could contact should questions arise that they would rather not raise in the group.

There is data to indicate that students whose families move frequently do not achieve academically as well as those students who attend the same high school for three or four years. The goal of a new student group is to help students make a more successful transition to a new school. This group would

- Provide new students with information about the school.
- Provide new students with information about the community.

- Provide new students with an opportunity to discuss issues and feelings related to moving to a new school (e.g., feeling like a stranger, making new friends, getting involved in extracurricular activities, or the things the new student had to leave behind as a result of the move).
- Provide new students with opportunities to meet other new students.

Icebreakers

In the early stages of a group an icebreaker might be needed. Once the group has focused on the topic, the icebreaker will not be necessary. Some examples of icebreakers are

1. Asking the members to introduce themselves by giving their name and grade and asking their opinion on some current topic (e.g., What did they think of the principal's decision about not wearing hats in school? At what age should kids drive a car? Vote? Drink alcohol? Stay home alone?). Or asking members to tell one thing about themselves, their favorite song, a favorite singing group, the last movie they liked, and so on.

2. Forming the members into groups of three and asking them to spend 10 minutes finding out what they have in common. Maybe they are in the same class, wear glasses, have two siblings, or went to the same elementary school.

3. Asking the members to discuss some relevant topic as a pair or in a triad and then having them share the opinions from their small groups with the large group.

4. Asking the members to stand up if the counselor names a trait or activity that applies to them. The group leader might ask, "Who can use a skateboard? Play a musical instrument? Speak another language? Has a pet?" and so on. Each time a member stands up represents an opportunity to learn more about the member by asking for an elaboration on the response.

An Ongoing Support Group for High School Transfer Students

This support group would meet weekly throughout the academic year and may have to meet at a different time each week. Each session would be approximately 45 minutes. Students who enrolled in the school during that week would be invited to join the group. In this way the composition of the group could change each week, necessitating introductions each week and creating discussion topics that do not necessarily build on the session from the previous week. Students could elect to attend the group for as long as they felt it was necessary. For these reasons, the size of the group would vary each week and finding an appropriate place to meet could be a problem for the group leaders. The group leaders would also need to determine if a student is continuing with the group in order to avoid attending classes. In the event the group leaders feel a student is no longer profiting from membership in the group, the student could be asked to stop attending.

Activities would focus on getting to know the school, the community, and each other. One problem with open groups and groups that meet throughout the academic year is that new members may lack the trust needed to feel comfortable in sharing their feelings with the group. Each week should begin with an introduction of the members and an icebreaker activity that allow students to meet one another.

Examples of information that new students need to know would include

- The name of the principal and assistant principals.
- The names of key staff and their roles.
- The names of the counseling team and the counselor to whom they are assigned.
- A description of the comprehensive counseling and guidance program.
- The name and functions of the school nurse.
- The names of the librarians and how the library can be used.
- The persons who are responsible for locker assignments, books, fees, maps and directions for getting around the school.
- Cafeteria hours, regulations, and cost of meals.
- The school store, including hours of operation and what can be purchased at the store.
- The business office and reasons that students go to that office.
- The physical education program and use of the gym.
- The auditorium and when it is utilized.
- Maps of the local community.
- School bus or subway routes and specific information for using mass transit.
- Movie theaters, malls, and other locations frequented by students.
- The school calendar, including school holidays.
- Dates of schoolwide and college-level tests.
- Grading policies and exam periods.
- Special school events such as homecoming or proms and who is eligible to attend.
- Athletic and social events and how tickets are purchased.
- Snow day policies.
- General school procedures (e.g., homework, being absent from school, student rights, etc.).
- School rules, policies, regulations, and their consequences (e.g., dress codes, wearing hats in class, carrying radios in the hall, etc.).
- School traditions (e.g., back-to-school night, career days, field trips).
- Information about the PTA/PTSA.
- Extracurricular activities, meeting times, and how to join clubs.
- The overall sports program and names of coaches.
- School activities, including theatrical productions and service groups.

A STRUCTURED PLAN FOR HIGH SCHOOL TRANSFER STUDENTS

Grade level: Any grade in the high school

Number of sessions: Eight weekly sessions

Time: The time, or class period, would change each week. Each session would be approximately 45 minutes.

- Prospective members would be screened individually prior to the first session. They would have to be willing to be included in the group.
- Parental permission slips would be sent home and returned prior to the first session.
- Procedures and ground rules would be explained at the first session.
- The group would be closed and no new members could join after the first week.
- The size of the group could be from eight to ten students.
- The group would use co-leaders.

SESSION 1
Objective
For group members to become acquainted with each other and review group rules.

Specific Strategies
1. Welcome the group.
2. Allow members to introduce themselves and name the school they last attended.
3. Clarify the goals of the group.
4. Clarify the group rules (these may be posted or the group can develop their own rules).
5. Do an icebreaker activity.
6. Process/summarize the session (processing should be included as a part of the wrap-up for each session). In addition to summarizing the discussion, ask students to comment on the process of each session (e.g., "What did you notice when the group discussed this topic? When John and Billy disagreed about their parents dating, how did they resolve that? We got off the topic for a while. How did that happen? When we got off the topic, did it help or hurt the group? How did the group react when Mary talked about her mother's illness?").

SESSION 2
Objective
For group members to learn about the school and community.

Materials Needed
A list of items the group will be asked to produce for their scavenger hunt

Specific Strategies
1. Open with a quick icebreaker and review the names of the members.
2. Review the group rules.
3. Hold a scavenger hunt. Group members will work with a partner to find locations and specific information about the school. For example, they might be asked to get a Band-Aid from the nurse's office, go to the cafeteria and find out what the lunch will be today, learn the school's fight song, find out the name of the school's mascot, learn the name of the

principal, assistant principals, and librarians. Reconvene as a group and share the information that was obtained.

4. Process/summarize the session.

SESSION 3
Objectives
1. To allow students to share information and traditions about their previous school.
2. To find commonalities between members (e.g., have members lived in the same cities, visited the same countries, play the same sports, etc.?).

Materials Needed
A United States and a world map

Specific Strategies
1. Members are given world or United States maps and asked to identify places they have lived, a place where a special friend lives, a place where they have had an important learning experience.
2. Allow students to share information and traditions about their previous school.
3. Process/summarize the session.
4. Ask students to bring their backpacks to the next session.

SESSION 4
Objective
To encourage members to talk about things that are important to them and things they miss from their former home.

Materials Needed
Group members' backpacks

Specific Strategies
1. Ask "What's in your backpack?" Ask members to take three things out of their backpacks, wallets, or purses that have a special meaning for them. Members first share these in diads, then with the entire group. Discuss whether these things have changed in meaning as a result of their move to a new school.
2. Ask the members to indicate what they miss from their former school.
3. Process/summarize the session.

SESSION 5
Objective
To help members recognize and understand changes in their lives.

Materials Needed
Copies of worksheets that will be used in this session

Specific Strategies
1. Then and now. Give members a few minutes to work independently on a worksheet responding to a list of open-ended statements, such as:

(continued)

A STRUCTURED PLAN FOR HIGH SCHOOL TRANSFER STUDENTS   Continued

Last year my favorite subject was _____ ; this year it is _____ .
Last year on TV I watched _____ ; this year it is _____ .
The biggest problem I had last year was _____ ; this year it is _____ .
I used to wonder _____ , but now I know _____ .
I used to worry about _____ , but now I know _____ .
Last year my friends _____ , but this year they _____ .

2. After sharing responses, discuss ways their lives have changed. Emphasize positive changes.
3. Discuss ways to meet new people and make new friends.
4. Process/summarize the session.

SESSION 6
Objective
To encourage the members to share their feelings about moving to a new school.

Specific Strategies
1. Role-playing. Assign members various family roles and ask them to role-play situations, such as family reactions when the family learned it would be moving, saying goodbye to friends, packing furniture and clothing, or the first day in the new home. Roles are assigned on slips of paper so that the other members do not know how a character is expected to act. Members can role-play the situations either as they experienced them, or they can be given specific roles and traits to act out such as, "Play a 15-year-old girl who is afraid that she won't find any new friends," or "Play a father whose teenaged son just told him that he didn't want to move." Afterwards, identify and discuss the feelings displayed in the role-playing.
2. Identify and discuss how the members reacted to these feelings.
3. Process/summarize the session.

SESSION 7
Objectives
1. To encourage the members to think about the supports they might have for helping them to feel good about moving and about their new school.
2. To encourage the members to know each other better.

Materials Needed
Copies of a list of fifteen factors that facilitate a positive move

Specific Strategies
1. Give students a list of fifteen factors that facilitate a positive move to a new school. Members can be asked to rank the factors in order of importance. There are no right or wrong answers. Members can be asked to explain their choices. Have students work in small groups first and then larger groups. Ask the group to arrive at a consensus, or at least agree on what it considers to be the most important factor. Examples of factors that would facilitate a positive move to a new school would be
   - The counselors in the new school.
   - Number of previous moves.
   - The teachers in the new school.

- Sibling reactions toward the move.
- Academic ability.
- A good family moving plan.
- Grades from previous school.
- Size of the new school.
- Neighbors of the new home.

- A positive outlook toward the move.
- Athletics (participation in or school's performance).
- Making friends in the new school.
- Opportunity for extracurricular activities.
- Luck.
- What is available in the new community.

2. Process/summarize the session.

SESSION 8
Objective
To bring closure to the group.

Materials Needed
Copies of the evaluation form that will be used by the group

Specific Strategies
1. Review the progress toward the originally stated goals for the group.
2. Make plans for any future meetings. (The group may want to meet every few months for maintenance purposes.)
3. Process/summarize this session. The group leader should summarize the eight-week session. Ask the members to name one positive thing they learned about themselves and one positive thing they learned about the group.
4. Evaluation by students. Students would be asked to respond to three questions and one essay item:
   Answer Yes or No to these questions:
   1. _____ Did this group help you adjust to your new school?
   2. _____ Did you learn a lot about the school from this group?
   3. _____ Was this group worthwhile for you?

Please indicate what could improve this orientation program: _____

_____.

THE CHALLENGE

Counseling groups in a high school can be a rewarding experience for both the group members and the counselor. High school students are mature enough to acquire insights into themselves and be responsive to counselors. They realize that they are going through a period of their lives in which they are required to make decisions that can affect their future. During the high school years, students mature physically, socially, and emotionally. Preparing to graduate from high school involves a number of emotions, ranging from excitement and happiness that their twelve years of school will be over to doubts and anxieties about what they will be doing in the future. One of the roles of the high school counselor is to help students prepare to move on to the next phase of their lives. Group counseling can be one method of accomplishing this objective.

CHAPTER SIX

GROUP LEADERSHIP

The effectiveness of group counseling in a school setting is largely dependent on the skill and expertise of the group leader. In some ways, group leadership is analogous to a chef's seasoning a gourmet meal. Some seasoning is necessary for creating a savory taste. Too little will not create the desired results, and too much will spoil the taste. Group leadership in a K–12 setting requires just the proper amount of leadership. Insufficient or inappropriate leadership will result in a group that can go out of control and fail to focus on the group's objectives. Poor leadership can also result in a group that lacks cohesiveness and wastes everyone's time. Too much leadership can translate into overcontrolling that discourages group interaction and a free exchange of ideas. Effective group leadership requires a delicate balancing of control.

Leadership can be defined as *what* the counselor does during the group session to facilitate moving the group toward its objectives. Leadership also addresses *how* this takes place. The *what* of leadership looks at the actions the group leader takes to stimulate discussion and encourage the group to acquire insights into at least partial solutions and remedies. The *how* of leadership is concerned with developing an atmosphere within the group that is conducive to bringing about change as well as maintaining the rules that are needed to make group meetings a safe and comfortable place for the members.

GROUP RESPONSES TO LEADERSHIP

The primary function of the group leader is to do what is necessary to ensure positive group interactions that move the group toward the intended goal. There is no single formula to bring this about because all groups are different and respond in different ways to group leadership. The distinct personalities and behaviors of group members make every group unique. Some of the variables that account for differences in how groups respond to leadership include (1) the age/grade and maturity level of the group, (2) the group topic, (3) the size of the group, and (4) the experience of the leader or coleaders.

In general, younger groups require more leader control to keep the group on task and to encourage participation but less leader control to deal with group discipline, violation of group rules, or the need to protect members. Younger groups are less goal directed and require more structure and direction. Whereas elementary-aged children usually view the counselor as an authority figure, middle school, junior high, and high school students often challenge the group leader. Young children are not always able to differentiate a counselor from a teacher. They see the counselor as a different type of teacher. In middle, junior, and high schools, students see the counselor as an adult friend and as someone who does not try to be bossy. In comparing teachers with counselors, they view the counselor as being less judgmental and more inclined to be their advocate. Leader control at middle, junior high, and high school levels requires that more attention be addressed to the discipline within the group, the enforcement of group rules, and the protection of group members. At middle, junior high, and high school levels, the form of leader control is often contingent on the group topic and composition of the group.

The topic of the group can be a valid predictor of the amount of leader control that is needed. Whereas friendship or grief groups usually require minimal leader control, an anger-management group or an ADHD group would require much more leader control. The group leader will not know how much control is needed until the group meets and begins to interact. Group leaders need to be flexible when it comes to how much control is necessary. Effective leaders exert control when it is needed and know when less control is warranted.

Smaller groups are obviously easier to control. When the group leader anticipates that the topic might result in a group that is difficult to control, reducing the group size by one member can make a big difference in the amount of leader control that will be needed. Anger-management groups can have as few as four members, and an ADHD group might be more effective if only three members were selected. The group leader's goal should be to put together a workable group, rather than a group with impressive size.

Groups are able to sense the experience level of the group leader. The organization and planning that has gone into the group, the leader's body language, ease of communicating, perceived comfort level, and the confidence that is emanated by the group leader communicate to the group whether leading a group is a familiar or a relatively new experience for the group leader. When the counselor trainee has had a good internship or field experience that included practice in running groups under supervision, the key to reducing anxiety concerning competency to run a group is contingent on how new counselors feel about their group skills. Cognitive restructuring, or what we say to ourselves, can be an effective method of reducing anxiety by replacing negative thoughts and fears with positive and constructive perceptions. New school counselors who are able to say to themselves "I can do it" will probably succeed. Conversely, the new school counselor who lacks confidence and has self-doubts, or the counselor who agonizes over the responsibility of being a school counselor, will probably have trouble. Success, or the lack of success, can be a self-fulfilling prophecy. New counselors need to develop a positive mind-set about their skills. One of the functions of counselor educators is to determine the readiness of counselor trainees to be effective as group leaders while they are still students in their graduate programs and under supervision.

There is no such thing as a perfect school counselor or a perfect group leader. There are effective and ineffective counselors and group leaders. There will be times when an experienced group leader will acknowledge being less effective than usual with a particular group. School counselors should govern themselves by the philosophy that the only mistakes we make are those that are repeated. When a mistake becomes a learning experience, mistakes need not be feared.

LEADERSHIP STYLES

The literature on group leadership makes reference to several styles of leadership. The choices that are most frequently employed are *autocratic, laissez-faire,* or *democratic.* Autocratic groups are leader controlled. Member governance and input is minimal. Autocratic leadership is usually seen when groups are very large. Group leaders who utilize a laissez-faire style are essentially allowing the group to control itself. The role of the group leader is relegated to assembling the group. Once assembled, there is really no group leader. Laissez-faire groups do not always have a specific direction; they go wherever the group takes them. The autocratic and laissez-faire styles are inappropriate in a K–12 setting, and a true democratic style can lead to problems because K–12 groups are not mature enough to be self-directing or self-governing. The style that is being proposed in this textbook could be called a *modified democratic style,* that is, goal directed with strong active leadership and, to a large extent, considerable group governance.

LEADERSHIP TASKS

Group leaders are expected to utilize many of the skills that an active counselor practices when doing individual counseling. These skills would include being an active listener, showing respect and empathy toward each member, and saying things in the group that will be helpful to the group members. As it is being used in this textbook, *leadership* refers to the role of the group leader with respect to (1) establishing and maintaining the necessary discipline within the group, (2) keeping the group on task, (3) enforcing group rules, (4) protecting group members, (5) encouraging full group participation, and (6) moving the group in the direction of the stated objectives.

Maintaining Discipline

Many of the expected behaviors included in maintaining group discipline are covered in the rules that govern the group. It is the group leader who must enforce these rules and see that the group does not get out of control. Despite the warmth and the caring attitude of the leader, it is important that the leader be viewed by the members as a friendly but no-nonsense group leader. This means that the leader's attitude and behavior should communicate to the group that there is a task to be accomplished and that the group leader's job is to see that the group moves in the direction of that objective. In essence, the leader is saying, "We may be able to have fun and we can enjoy ourselves, but we are here for a purpose."

School counselors are nonauthoritarian and reluctant to become disciplinarians. This should not be interpreted by students to mean that the counselor is a "pushover" or easy to manipulate. When forced, the counselor *can* become a disciplinarian, albeit a friendly one; the counselor *can* be firm but is always fair; the counselor *can* control a group. When counselors do classroom guidance, they are expected to keep the class under control. When they are functioning as group leaders, they are expected to be able to control the group.

Without control, a group could become a small mob. The tone for the leader's control of the group must be established at the first group meeting.

Keeping the Group on Task

Effective group leaders will keep the group on task. The short-term task is to cover what has been planned for each week, while the long-term task is to move the group in the direction of the agreed-upon goal. It is easy for a group to digress from the topic and begin to talk about a semi-related or unrelated subject. The group leader who works on developing active listening skills will be aware when this is occurring and should make a comment to the effect that "we've strayed off the topic." Straying should be discouraged at the first group session. Reminding the group of its goals at the start of each session can reduce digressing. It is recognized there will be times when the group wants to talk about something that happened in the school community or a news event that is unrelated to the group topic. Again, leader flexibility would allow some digression. Frequent or prolonged digressions could indicate the group's lack of interest in what is being discussed, boredom with the topic, or a leadership problem. The group leader should attempt to understand the reasons for frequent digressions and take the necessary steps to discourage it. Keeping a group on task is not difficult unless the group leader has allowed a pattern to develop that does not discourage digression. A friendly reminder from the group leader is usually all that is needed when digression occurs.

Establishing and Enforcing Group Rules

In a K–12 school setting, groups without designated rules are ineffective, dangerous, and potentially chaotic. The rules that govern a group assist the leader to control the flow of discussion, protect each member, and ensure that there will be orderly discussion, rather than arguments that can get out of control. Rules are first discussed in the screening interview and need to be firmly established at the first group meeting. Developing rules solely generated by the group could be very time-consuming and may result in the omission of critical rules. It is recommended that the leader be prepared to suggest certain essential rules and then permit the group to add to the list. A list of group rules could be

1. Start and end each session on time.
2. Keep everything that is said in the group confidential.
3. Do not interrupt a member who is talking.
4. Show courtesy and respect to all members.
5. Do not verbally attack a member.
6. Do not talk about a classmate who is not in the group.
7. Do not say negative things about teachers or the principal.
8. Participate in every group meeting.
9. Remember the goal of the group and stay on the topic.
10. Treat others as you would want to be treated.
11. Do not monopolize the group meetings.

12. Do not do or say anything that would distract the group or offend a member.
13. Understand that group members who violate a rule may be asked to leave the group.
14. Being a member of the group does not excuse you from doing homework or other assignments of your classroom teacher.

It is recommended that the rules be written down and distributed to each member. Copies can also be sent home to allow parents to become aware of the professional nature of the group experience. The group rules can also be reiterated at the beginning of each session until the leader feels the rules are being followed. A technique that stresses the importance of rules is to ask members to sign their names to the list of rules with a statement that says, "I promise to obey these rules that have been agreed to by the group. I understand that if I break a rule, there may be consequences." Rules can also be posted in the room during the meetings (and removed after the group leaves). Essential rules, such as the need for confidentiality, not interrupting someone who is talking, or not putting a member down, can be reinforced at every group session. When the group is too young to read or sign names, the group leader can read the rules to the group several times and use a handshake with each member to take the place of a signature. Fewer rules may be needed with very young groups, but confidentiality would still be regarded as an important rule. Rules for young groups would focus more on attention span and self-control issues.

It is very important for the group leader to occasionally comment *when the rules have been followed.* For example, when it is appropriate, the leader could say, "I want to compliment the group on the courtesy they showed each other today. No one interrupted and everyone participated. I am pleased to see that you are obeying the rules that you've established."

Protecting Group Members

Protecting group members is a group rule intended to prevent verbal attacks by one member on another. When discussion becomes argumentative and emotionally charged, a member who is prone to overreact or become verbally abusive will often break this rule. Insults, put-downs, name-calling, or harsh criticisms are examples of verbal attacks. When a verbal attack occurs, the group leader must quickly intervene to prevent the victim of the attack from embarrassment and loss of self-esteem. Immediate intervention also communicates to the group that verbal abuse will not be tolerated. Even if the leader feels the member who is being attacked does not appear to be upset and can handle the attack, the leader must intervene. The leader is responsible for providing protection to all of the members when it is deemed necessary. "You're getting too upset, let's calm down" is the message the leader wants to convey to the offender.

When a verbal attack has occurred and before that session is over, the offender will be expected to apologize sincerely to the member who was attacked, and the attacked member is expected to accept the apology. An apology does not necessarily mean that the offending member is being asked to change his or her feelings. It does require, however, the offending member to modify the words and tone of voice that were used. Members are allowed to disagree with something that is said, but they must learn to disagree respectfully and not offend others by what they say or how they they say it. "I think you are wrong" is an acceptable way to express disagreement. Saying "If you believe what you just said, you're stupid" is unacceptable. The obligation to apologize for offending a group member can be made one of the group rules. Depending on the severity of the attack, the group leader might want to make arrangements to speak separately with the offending and offended members. If the group members are to feel safe, there must be zero tolerance for verbal attacks.

Encouraging Full Group Participation

If all of the members are to derive the maximum benefit from the group experience, there needs to be full group participation. Participation means both reacting to what the members have heard in the group as well as willingness to share personal feelings on the topic. During the screening interview, the group leader should discuss the importance of group participation. The prospective member needs to understand that sharing feelings and opinions is expected. Unfortunately, group members will not always behave in the group on the basis of what they committed to do during the screening interview. It is easy for students to say they will actively participate when they are sitting in the counselor's office. When, however, members have heard critical comments made to other members during a group session, a reticent group member might not be able to keep the promise that was made at the time of the initial interview.

The refusal to share experiences, feelings, and opinions can be linked to concerns over confidentiality and how safe it is to speak in the group. It can also be attributed to how the group reacts when members say something, or it can indicate a member's passive resistance to being in the group. Perhaps the most frequent explanation for why a group member does not participate relates to the member's fear of speaking in the group because of low self-esteem. The child or adolescent with low self-esteem will be reluctant to say anything, fearing embarrassment that would lower an already low self-image. Low self-esteem is one of the most common problems seen by school counselors at all grade levels. It is a precursor to the development of social problems, it can explain a lack of assertiveness, and it can even impact on academic performance when it renders a child unable to ask a teacher for help. Low self-esteem can underlie aggression and conduct problems and is often the explanation why children and adolescents describe themselves as being sad or unhappy.

Self-esteem is how we feel about ourselves. It describes both the degree of confidence we have in our abilities and our impression of the way we are perceived by others. Low self-esteem, or a weak self-concept, addresses what this writer terms our CQ, or *clout quotient*. Our clout quotient refers to how much influence we feel we exert in a given situation based on how we feel we are perceived by others. It is a measure of our self-confidence and is directly related to our self-esteem. Individuals who have a high CQ believe that their opinions are important to others, that what they say is valued, and that they are respected. People with a high CQ are usually in control of themselves and often find themselves in control of situations. The more clout we feel we exert in a given situation, the more self-assured, confident, and comfortable we are in that situation. Conversely, if we feel that we have very little clout, we lack confidence and are reluctant to express ourselves for fear we will be criticized, ridiculed, embarrassed, or ignored.

Our CQ varies according to the situation and is, therefore, situation specific. A woman who is the manager of a large department store would probably have a high CQ with her employees, but she could have a low CQ with a teenaged daughter who is rebelling against her authority. Students sometimes feel they have a high CQ with their peers but a low CQ with their parents. Group members who feel they have a high CQ with their fellow group members would not be reluctant to speak in a group.

A way to quantify our CQ is to evaluate it using a seven-point scale, with 7 being the highest and 1 being the lowest rating. The interpretation of our CQ score would be as follows:

7 = We feel we exert a very powerful influence on people or a situation.

6 = We feel we exert a strong influence on people or a situation.

5 = We feel the influence we exert on people and situations is often strong.

4 = We feel our influence on people or a situation is neither weak nor strong.

3 = We feel we do not exert a strong influence on people or a situation.

2 = We feel our influence on people or a situation is weak.

1 = We do not feel we can influence people or a situation.

CQ changes with age, maturity, and experience. People who rate their overall CQ below level 4 have low self-esteem and would tend to be reluctant to speak in a group. Our CQ can be elevated when we reach personal goals, when we feel successful, and when we receive recognition from significant others. Failures and disappointments lower our CQ. Counseling directed at improving self-esteem is one way of effecting change in the CQ.

When one member of a group is not participating, the group leader should arrange for a private meeting to determine the cause and then seek solutions. When several members of the group are not participating, the leader might want to detour from the group's goal and spend a session on how the group can facilitate full group participation. Failure of several members to participate in the group could also signal a problem with the group's leadership. Members who participate will get more from a group than those who do not, and total group participation makes the group more meaningful and interesting for all members.

Moving the Group in the Direction of the Stated Objectives

It would be naive to suggest that any group will completely achieve its goal or stated objective. At the conclusion of the last group session, a successful group should be moving in the direction of attaining the goals of the group. After only eight sessions, friendship problems are not expected to be resolved; a successful friendship group should equip the members with the knowledge and skills needed to pursue relationships. In a successful study skills group, all members will not become good students; the members should have identified good study skills and learned what study skills they need to work on, what they must start to do, and what they must stop doing and should understand that if they utilize what they learned in the group, their grades should improve. A grief group will still mourn the loss of their loved ones after the group terminates, but the hope is that the members will be able to put their feelings into perspective and be more capable of coping with their loss.

Realistically, all members of a group should not be expected to have benefited from the group experience to the same degree. At the conclusion of an anger-management group, some members might try to control their tempers and find acceptable ways to release their frustrations. Other members will respond in their usual manner and show no benefit from having been part of a group. For this reason, it must be stressed that a *group* does not usually attain goals, but *individuals within the group* can change as a result of the group experience. A successful group is one in which the group leader feels that most of the members were able to move in the direction of attaining the goals that were established by the group. A successful group has direction and a better understanding of the problem. The members may even have acquired some insights that would help them to reduce or resolve their problems. Just as group psychotherapy does not guarantee a solution to a person's problems in life, neither does group counseling make any guarantees other than that members should be more knowledgeable about the topic at termination than when the group began. Change is not expected to happen overnight or in eight weeks. With knowledge and a new direction afforded by group counseling, change can occur with time. Neither counseling nor psycho-therapy are cures; they only offer direction.

Moving the group in an appropriate direction is a major task of the group leader or co-leaders. It begins when a group plan, or game plan, is developed that outlines the objectives of each of the eight sessions. The group plan should also indicate the strategies and topics that could meet the objectives of each session and the materials that will be used to implement the topics. A written game plan provides the group leader with both structure and organization. It avoids a hit-or-miss approach that may not end successfully. A game plan can be likened to a road map that shows where you are, enables you to see where you want to go, and provides you with the details of how to get there. In a goal-directed group counseling game plan, the group leader attempts to chart a course that will predictably move the group toward the objectives. This is accomplished by determining what topics will be discussed in each of the sessions and what learning should take place in order for behaviors or attitudes to change. Group counseling is really a learning experience.

The game plan is developed for the benefit of the leader or co-leaders, but game plans are not set in stone. When the group seems to be moving on its own and the group leader feels that the group is going in the direction of the goal, the structured game plan can be put aside. Likewise, depending on what occurs in a session, the leader may wish to alter the planned content of the next session. Flexibility being one of the characteristics of a good group leader, the leader must be prepared to make changes in the game plan when they are deemed necessary.

It may be difficult for the group leader to step back and objectively look at where the group seems to be going. Weekly assessments are important, another reason why it is advantageous to have co-leaders. The co-leader offers another perspective that can help to determine whether each session is moving in an appropriate direction.

OTHER LEADERSHIP RESPONSIBILITIES

There are a number of leadership tasks that do not involve leader control but are part of the leader's responsibility. They involve group communication, active listening, questioning, interpreting, modeling appropriate behavior, problem solving, linking, assigning homework, and reviewing and summarizing.

Task: Communicating

The group leader should encourage group members to direct comments to other members rather than exclusively to the group leader. Members should interact with other members as well as the group leader. If members tend to look at the group leader when they speak and not at each other, the group may not be as cohesive as it should be or the leader may have, inadvertently, created a group that is too leader controlled.

If the members are inclined to look at the leader when they make comments, the group leader should encourage more group interaction. At the first group meeting it is a good idea for the group leader to use and define the word *interaction*. The group leader could say,

> One of the things we are here to do is to interact with each other. We interact when we listen and respond to what someone has said. We interact when we respect the right of someone to speak and when the other person respects our right to speak. When we interact we can agree or disagree with what we heard. We can react by stating our opinion about something or by sharing an experience that we've had. When we are interacting we can ask or answer a question, but it is important to understand that everyone will not agree with everything that someone says. It is also important to know the difference between criticism that is meant to be helpful and criticism that is intended to be hurtful.

The group leader's message is, in essence, that we are not here to hurt others or argue. We are here to discuss things, find solutions to a common problem, and be helpful to one another.

Equally important as group interaction is learning how to communicate. A lack of communication is often viewed as the underlying reason why people have problems interacting. Parents complain that their children do not communicate with them. A disenchanted wife complains that her husband does not communicate with her. Poor communication is blamed for many social and interpersonal problems. In a communication system, there is both a sender and a receiver. In the case of verbal communication, someone talks and someone is there to listen. The sender speaks and the receiver must hear and also comprehend what was heard. Unless there is understanding of what was said, there is no communication. When someone is speaking to you in a language you do not understand, there is no communication. When a parent speaks to a child and the child does not respond, there is no communication. Good communication implies that the listener is also responsive to what has been said.

It is possible to communicate without using words. Facial expressions, gestures, body language, and silence are nonverbal ways to communicate. The boy who shuffles slowly and late into a classroom, touches and bothers everyone he passes, slouches in his seat, folds his arms, makes grunting sounds, grimaces, and closes his eyes and pretends to be asleep is communicating even though he has not said one word. His expressions, body language, and gestures might be saying, "Leave me alone. I am not interested in being here, and you can't make me pay attention." When a teacher asks a student a question and the child is silent, this student is really communicating. What the student is *not* doing is *relating*. The group leader must relate to the group and group members must relate to each other. We relate through speech by showing interest in what was said and by being responsive, empathic, and respectful of the person who is speaking, even if we disagree with what was said. The difference between communicating and relating could be one of semantics; nevertheless, the group leader should encourage the members to verbally relate to one another.

Task: Active Listening

Active listening could be viewed as the primary task of the group leader during the actual group meeting. Listening, however, only takes on importance when the group leader remembers what was said. Taking notes during and after the session is necessary because the leader cannot be expected to retain everything that is said in the group. During the session, the leader should jot down the topics that are being discussed rather than the details of who said what. These notes are not intended to be the same as counseling notes. It is better to write counseling notes after, rather than during, the session. Even though the group leader may not be saying much in the group, members are aware when the leader writes something during a session. For some members, watching the leader write could be a distraction. Also, writing notes during the session reduces the leader's ability to listen attentively to what is being said.

Listening is hearing what someone says. Active listening is hearing, comprehending, and reacting to what was heard. Active listening puts what is said into our memory and allows us to recall it at a later time. Through active listening the group leader is able to follow and remember the key points of the group's discussion. In the K–12 setting, the group leader often participates in the group and needs to be aware of everyone's comments. This means that it is important for the group leader to know not only what was said but who said it. It is also helpful when the leader is able to recall specific things that members have said in previous sessions. Because the group leader is also a role model, active listening encourages the group members to become active listeners.

Task: Questioning

Another reason for practicing active listening is to be able to formulate questions both to individual members and to the group. Questions can be used to accomplish a number of things. They can be used to clarify a member's comment (e.g., "What did you mean when you said some things at home are better now that your father doesn't live with you?"). They can be used to probe for more information (e.g., "What did you do when Billy wouldn't play with you?"). They can encourage the group to do problem solving (e.g., "Does anyone have a suggestion that would help Joanne find time to do her homework?"). They can encourage group members to share their feelings (e.g., "Has anyone else ever felt the way Jackie is feeling?"). Questions can elicit group interactions, keep discussion moving, or let the group reflect on something the leader feels is important (e.g., "Why do you suppose parents get upset when their child doesn't listen to them?").

Questions require answers. If the group leader asks a question of the group and, after allowing sufficient time, no one responds, the question should be repeated and members should be encouraged to respond, even if it means calling on a specific member. If there is still no response, the leader should be prepared to make a comment that would either react to or answer the question. The leader needs to be careful that questions or comments do not put a member on the defensive or make a member feel uncomfortable. The statement, "Andy, you agreed to keep things we talk about confidential. Why did you break your promise?"would force Andy to become defensive. Saying to Andy, "We know that you told your friend something that was said in group last week. Do you agree that this shouldn't happen again?" communicates to Andy that what Andy did was wrong and the group leader is disappointed, but it allows Andy an opportunity to redeem himself. "I just can't believe what I just heard you say, Priscilla" would make Priscilla feel uncomfortable. There are better ways to help Priscilla than to show shock or disbelief in her opinion. "What you just said is interesting, Priscilla. I'd like to talk with you about it some time" would not make Priscilla feel guilty about something she said. It is also not a good practice to question a member's thinking. "I'm disappointed that you feel that way, Sandra" leaves Sandra without an acceptable ego-saving response.

Task: Interpretation

Interpretation is one of the most important techniques active counselors utilize when doing either individual or group counseling. It is used to help counselees or group members gain an understanding of the possible reasons or causes of their problem of which, heretofore, they were unaware. Interpretation can form the basis for the acquisition of insights. Insights can lead to solutions because insights help to identify the source of a problem. With insight, we have both an explanation and a direction. Once we have gained insight, we have a choice. We can either do what is needed to change a situation or we can elect to do nothing. When done effectively, interpretation enables the counselee or group member to be able to say, "Now I know why I . . . ."

Interpretation is not a term that school counselors often use when describing what they do in the process of counseling. It is not a term that is often discussed in textbooks used in counselor training programs. Calling what happens in counseling interpretation, however, is a matter of semantics. To illustrate this, a competent school counselor should be able to offer at least five reasons why a student could be underachieving, five reasons why a child is shy, five reasons why a child is showing hostility toward peers, five reasons why a child underachieves, and five reasons to explain why a child has poor social skills. In other words, school counselors speculate. Using logical reasoning, they develop impressions of what might cause a specific problem. This is a part of their training. Using the technique referred to as *linking,* counselors and group leaders can show how a counselee or member's previous comments are related to what was just said. In essence, the counselor is using interpretation in counseling, but it is not being called interpretation. Any time a counselor offers a possible explanation as to *why* a counselee could be showing resistance, *why* a student might be failing English, or *why* a kindergarten child cries when the mother leaves the classroom, the counselor is utilizing interpretation. When what the counselor says enables a counselee or group member to say, "Hmmm, that might explain why I . . . .," that member now has insight made possible through the counselor's interpretation.

Interpretation involves speculation, assumptions, intuition, and educated guesses. It is based on knowledge of such things as demographic information, qualitative data obtained from interviews, observations collected by the group leader, or quantitative data derived from standardized test scores. It also comes about through the knowledge the counselor has acquired through professional training and experiences from practice. Interpretation involves drawing conclusions that are based on everything the counselor knows about the counselee or group member.

To illustrate this, let us assume Laura is a member of a social skills group. In the screening interview, she told the counselor that she is very shy. In each of the first three sessions, Laura stated one fact to the group about herself and her shyness. We will call these *facts* A, B, and C. In the current session, the group leader hears Laura mention fact D. It should be assumed that Laura knows facts A, B, C, and D because she was the person who told the group these facts about herself. These facts could be isolated, related, or semi-related things. Unfortunately, knowing facts A, B, C, and D has not given Laura the insight that would help her understand why she is shy, nor have these facts enabled her to know why her problem has persisted or what she would need to do if she wanted to overcome it. When the group leader can link facts A, B, C, and D and, drawing a conclusion from experience, knowledge, and intelligent speculation, offers Laura *message E,* and if Laura ponders *message E* and says, "Well, that *could* explain why I can't walk up to someone I know and say, 'Hi,' or why I never raise my hand in class," the group leader has probably made an accurate interpretation and Laura is in the process of acquiring insight. Learning and understanding message E could be one of the keys needed to help Laura overcome her problem. It would also offer her some direction as to what she might begin doing to become less shy.

Insights by themselves, however, do not solve problems. Knowing the cause of a problem is not an automatic solution to the problem. This is especially true for children when the source of their problem lies beyond their control. A child who has low self-esteem could develop insight and realize that emotional abuse from parents and siblings is a major explanation for why his or her self-concept is low. Insights will not change this child's self-feelings *unless or until* the environment changes. Unfortunately, the child must continue to live in the environment that is causing the problem. In a situation like this, having identified the source of the problem, insight would enable the counselor to recommend an environmental intervention. Counseling could be directed at helping the child learn coping skills and ways to deal with a situation that is beyond his or her control. Counseling could also help remove the child's feeling of guilt or responsibility for the problem.

In order to make interpretative statements, school counselors need to have a working knowledge of normal child and adolescent development, an understanding of the basis for deviant behaviors in children and adolescents, the ability to reason logically and engage in rational thinking acquired through life experiences, the ability to be incisive, and respect for their own ability to think. Although the process of interpretation can be explained and demonstrated to counselors and counselor trainees, the ability to make good interpretations relies on intangible skills acquired by thinking through the presenting problem in order to speculate on what might explain the behavior. Counselors who lack curiosity about reasons for behavior and focus mainly on *what* a person is doing will not get practice in understanding the dynamics of a person's behavior. Interpretation is also aided by feeling grounded in theories of personality and theories of counseling. If, for example, a group member is viewed as being highly competitive, rebellious, and envious, and if the group leader learns that this group member has both an older and younger sibling, it would be helpful to remember what Alfred Adler had to say about birth order and the middle child. If a member of an anger-management group is frequently and harshly punished by a father or is tormented by a sibling, it would be helpful to remember what Sigmund Freud said about the defense mechanism of displacement and how we shift our aggression from the real source to a safe source.

Because interpretation is expected to result in the acquisition of insights, this technique will not be effective with children who are usually regarded as being too young to acquire insights. A general rule is that children under the age of 8 will have difficulty developing insights. This would suggest that using interpretation that might lead to insight should be restricted to children who are in the third grade or beyond. This does not preclude the group leader from encouraging a younger child to understand a basis for his or her behavior, but the child may not be able to internalize the explanation. In school settings, interpretation is most effective with a middle, junior high, or high school population.

Task: Modeling Appropriate Behavior

One explanation for a child's behavior can be expressed as "monkey see . . . monkey do." If the group leader expects the group to show respect, courtesy, and the other behaviors stated in the group rules, it is important that these behaviors be demonstrated by the leader and/or co-leader. Group members will not respect the leader whose actions say, "Don't do as I do; do as I say." Modeling teaches through being observed. The group leader should consistently demonstrate the behaviors that reinforce the group rules. School-aged children are impressionable. The skills and behaviors that are modeled by the group leader can be consciously or unconsciously incorporated into the personality of group members. It should be noted, however, that some members will model after the leader and also their peers and fellow group members. Within a group there will often be a member who is charismatic and admired by the group. The behavior of such a member can have either a positive or a negative influence on the members. It is fortunate when the group model is demonstrating desirable qualities. It is unfortunate when the charismatic model is not a good role model.

Modeling can also be used as a deliberate strategy when the leader feels there is a need to improve a behavior through negative modeling. Negative modeling is consciously modeling inappropriate or unacceptable behavior in order to make a point. For example, if there is too much interrupting going on in the group, the leader could model excessive interrupting to show the group how difficult it is for a member to say something. Once the point has been made, the leader should explain to the group the purpose of the negative modeling and the appropriate behaviors that will be expected in the future.

Group members in middle, junior high, or high school are keen observers. They are very aware when the group leader is confused, having doubts about how to proceed, is disorganized, or seems to be experiencing anxiety. Unintentional negative role modeling on the part of the group leader frequently results in a group that becomes disorderly and will not move toward its objectives. Beginning counselors in secondary schools who doubt their group leadership skills should pair up with an experienced co-leader until they feel confident about their ability to run a group effectively. In an elementary school setting, where there is usually only one counselor, co-leading with a counselor from another elementary school might be difficult to arrange because this would leave the visiting counselor's school without a counselor during that time period. Turning to a middle school counselor or a qualified person from a mental health agency for help might be a viable option.

Task: Problem Solving

Attitude or behavior changes, in some way and to some degree, are the ultimate goals of counseling. Change does not occur without problem solving. In group counseling, problem solving is accomplished by the group with the assistance of the group leader. There are a number of models that can be used for problem solving. It is unlikely that a K–12 group would be knowledgeable about such models or the techniques that can be used for problem solving. It falls on the group leader to propose a problem-solving model because it would not be time-effective for the group to develop its own model.

A simple and uncomplicated problem-solving model that could be presented to a K–12 group would be as follows:

1. Develop a clear statement of the issue or problem that needs to be reduced or resolved.
2. Having determined the issue or problem that needs to be resolved, identify what would be considered an ideal outcome.
3. Without spending too much time on the ideal outcome, define what would be a practical or realistic outcome. This is the outcome the group would eventually be addressing.
4. Brainstorm all possible solutions, even those that are unrealistic, impractical, or seemingly impossible to accomplish.
5. Eliminate the solutions that are unrealistic, impractical, or impossible to accomplish.
6. Arrive at one or two workable solutions and eventually decide on a single solution.
7. Determine all of the things that must be done in order to accomplish this solution.
8. Begin to do those things. The things that need to be done should be written down and frequently reviewed. Essentially, a checklist will be developed that provides direction and the structure needed for solving a problem.

In order to focus the group on problem solving, the group leader should make a point of frequently asking how the group would solve specific problems that come up in the course of discussion. For example, Greg, who is in a divorce group, tells the group that in addition to having to learn to live without both parents, he is failing math and English and he will not be eligible to play basketball for the school unless he can pass both of these subjects. The group could be asked to help Greg develop a plan that might help him pass his subjects. Using the model just cited, Greg would end up with a game plan that should suggest specific things he would need to do if he wants to improve his grades in order to play basketball. Effective problem solving involves the creation of a game plan. The extent to which the plan can be implemented determines the extent to which the problem can be successfully resolved.

It should be realized that all problems cannot be solved using this or any model. Some problems require time, acceptance of circumstances, and adjustment to a situation. There are also problems that are beyond the control of the member. Grief over the loss of a loved one is an example of a condition that needs time, acceptance of circumstances, and adjustment. Parental or environmental problems are examples of problems that are beyond the control of the member.

Faced with a problem, many school-aged children never think about what *they* can do to solve their problem. They do not assume responsibility for finding a solution. Overly dependent children look to others to solve their problems. Angry children show indifference to problem solving, and children who have low self-esteem doubt their ability to solve problems. When the group leader feels that the group is lacking in problem-solving experience, it would be necessary to digress from the group plan and discuss a model for doing problem solving. A number of life experiences could be posed to the group as examples of problems that need solutions. With an introductory level group, the group leader might pose these kinds of questions to practice problem solving:

- What would you do if you came into your home and you smelled smoke?
- What would you do if you forgot your lunch money?
- What would you do if someone from your school called you a bad name?
- If a new student came into your class and you wanted to meet him or her, how would you go about doing it?
- If your teacher often scolded you and you didn't like to be scolded, what would you do?

Questions such as these would be adaptable for use with the problem-solving model described. After the group shows it can solve practice problems, it can be asked to work on the topic that was the reason they became members of the group. In an assertiveness training group, the group leader might say, "Now that we have done so well solving the practice problems, let's look at the problem you are all facing, namely, how to be more assertive. Let's first develop a clear statement of the specific assertive issue. Then let's identify what the ideal outcome would be. Next we'll define what a practical or realistic outcome would be. Then we'll brainstorm for all possible solutions," and so on.

Task: Linking

Linking occurs when the group leader relates what is said by one member to what another member has said. In so doing, the leader ties both comments together, showing how they are either similar or different. Linking serves to make the group aware that group members will sometimes think alike and also that it is all right to have different feelings and opinions about something. Linking requires the group leader to be attentive to what has been said and who has said it. The leader can also encourage the group to do linking in order to increase the active listening skills of the group. "Does anyone recall what person in this group said something similar to what Amanda just said?" puts the group on notice that the leader expects them to both listen to what is said and also try to remember the member who said it. Linking can be used when the leader wants to identify the issues on which group members either agree or disagree and to point up contradictory statements made by a group member. As previously mentioned, linking comments from the past with what has just been said is a technique used in making interpretations.

Task: Assigning Homework

From time to time, and depending on the topic of the group, the leader may assign homework. Homework should always be something the members *can* accomplish and something that will move the group in the direction of its objective. Homework, when it has been successful, can also encourage the members to feel a sense of accomplishment and success. For example, in a friendship group that has met three times, the group leader might assign each member to say hello to a boy or girl to whom they had never spoken. The group would have to agree that this is a worthwhile assignment, and each member would be expected to commit to doing it. At the next meeting, the members would discuss their experience and how they felt when they succeeded or, if they were unable to carry out the assignment, why it was difficult for them to do the homework. In an anger-management group of youngsters who tend to be physically aggressive, after discussing alternative ways to deal with anger, a homework assignment could be to ask the members to use a nonphysical method of controlling their frustration *one* time in the upcoming week and report to the group what nonphysical method they used and how they felt afterwards.

Although the group leader expects all members of the group to complete assignments, in reality all members will not do their homework. Members who have a history of not doing classroom homework, or members who do not take the group seriously, will probably have some excuse for not doing the assignment. Members who have not succeeded in doing the assignment should not be penalized or made to feel as if they had failed. Not doing homework should be viewed as a lack of readiness to do the task, a lack of motivation to take a risk, fear of failure, fear of embarrassment, or a negative attitude toward the group's goal. It is important for the group leader to understand the reasons and take steps to help the member be successful the next time. It is often necessary to talk with the member privately.

Homework assignments have a purpose. When assignments have been successfully carried out, members gain confidence and feel better about themselves. Success in assignments also encourages group cohesiveness because the members have an experience to share. A successful homework assignment can be viewed as a step toward the group member's goal.

Task: Encouraging Members to Help Others

During the screening process and when the counselor is discussing the expectations for a group member, one of the things that should be mentioned is the importance of being helpful to other group members. Even though students become members of a group to overcome a personal problem, they should understand that they might be helpful to classmates experiencing the same problem. This writer feels that the responsibility to help other members is not stressed enough in group counseling and is often nonexistent in some K–12 groups. Group members can be helpful to their fellow members in both direct and indirect ways. Members offer direct help by what they say to the group and what they say to a group member. If Betty, who is in a grief group, says, "We shouldn't forget that we will always have the memories of the people we've loved," Betty is saying something that could be helpful to the group. When she says, "I understand what you're saying, Peggy. I feel my mother is with me all of the time, too," she is helping Peggy. When members offer comfort to their fellow members by showing empathy and understanding, their support is felt.

Members offer indirect help when they share how they have handled a situation. In a group working on being more assertive, Ellen, a high school senior, might say, "I'm tired of being pushed around by Elizabeth, my so-called friend. So yesterday I said to myself, 'No more!' So when Elizabeth asked me to drive her home after school, I said, 'I can't. It's not convenient for me.' I've never stood up to her and said no before and, I've got to tell you, it felt real good!" The way Ellen handled this situation could have a positive impact on the other members, who might then say to themselves, "No more!" when they are faced with an intimidating situation. Whenever members share a way they have handled a situation effectively, the other members are hearing something they could potentially use.

Another way a group leader can encourage members to help their fellow members is by frequently asking if anyone has a suggestion that would help a particular member. By positively reinforcing helpful comments, the leader encourages helpful behavior. "Heather, that was a very good suggestion you offered Cheryl. How does the group feel about it? How do you feel about her idea, Cheryl?"

The group leader can also create stimulus situations by asking members to role-play. To illustrate this using an anger-management group, the leader could ask George and Daryl to play a role that the leader would create. The group leader says to George, "Pretend that you are working on controlling your temper. This isn't easy for you since you think you're tough and you often get into fights. Let's suppose that after school, Daryl, a boy you're not supposed to like, says to you, 'You're a yellow-bellied, fat sissy.' Show us how you would handle this situation. Remember, you're trying to control your temper." After listening to the interaction between George and Daryl, the leader would turn to the group and say, "How does the group feel about the way George handled this situation?" Using a variation of psychodrama, the group leader could set up scenes between several members of the group using scenarios related to the group's topic and then discuss what took place. Role-playing is fun for the group and can help members rehearse thoughts and actions.

In addition, groups often produce friendships that did not exist prior to the group's existence. Being in a friendship group subtly encourages members who are seeking friendships to turn to each other as new friends.

DEVELOPING STIMULUS QUESTIONS

It has previously been suggested that the leader should have prepared questions to begin a session or to use when the discussion seems to be lagging. These should be open-ended questions that have been developed to elicit a response from the group or group member. Similar to good leads, they should begin with the words *how, when, what, tell us,* or, on occasion, *why.* In a friendship group, a question could be, "What are some of the things that prevent you from going up to someone at recess and saying, 'Hi. Can I play with you?'" or, "How would you know if someone wanted to be your friend?" In a divorce group, the leader might ask, "What has been the biggest difference in your house since your parent left?" or, "What problems have you had at home since your parents separated (or were divorced)?" In an ADHD group, the group leader could ask, "Tell me what you think it means to have ADHD," or, "What kinds of things have you learned to do to control your ADHD?"

Stimulus questions are designed to encourage group discussion. With upper primary groups and beyond, the group leader could assign homework asking the members to suggest one question that would be good for group discussion. In order to prevent inappropriate stimulus questions, these suggested questions should be screened by the group leader.

REVIEW AND SUMMARY

It has been mentioned that each group session should begin with a brief review of what the group discussed at the previous meeting and where it left off. If the group leader has taken good notes, specific members could be mentioned as having made certain comments. This encourages members to participate because children of all ages like the recognition of having made a statement that the leader wrote down and repeated to the group.

During the last two or three minutes of each session, the group leader should summarize what was said in the session. This summary forms the basis for what the group leader would use to begin the next session. In all probability, the summary is what the members will carry out of the meeting. At the final session, it is helpful if the members receive summaries from the seven previous sessions. As a last activity at the final meeting, they could be asked to write what they remember about the current meeting in order to have something written that summarizes the final meeting. This provides documentation on what took place in their group experience; it is also a document that parents, teachers, and administrators might like to see.

A HANDFUL OF BE'S   *To summarize the tasks of the group leader, let us review what is expected of a leader. In order to run a successful group, leaders should*

- Be well prepared.
- Be sincere.
- Be empathic.
- Be relaxed.
- Be sensitive to the feelings and needs of the group.
- Be aware of what is happening at all times.
- Be helpful whenever possible.
- Be careful not to allow anyone to say something that might be harmful to a member.
- Be knowledgeable about the group topic.
- Be goal directed.
- Be a good listener.
- Be flexible.
- Be a facilitator of discussion.
- Be an active leader.
- Be in control of discipline within the group.
- Be in contact with parents in order to get their permission.
- Be prepared to enforce the group rules.
- Be realistic in goal setting.
- Be themselves.

It is really not difficult to be a group leader and run an effective group. Group leaders must approach the task of leading a group with the confidence that enables them to feel that they will be able to deal with whatever happens. (The problems that typically develop with groups will be discussed in the next chapter.) The group's goal should be thought of only as a direction that will never be fully reached. In a successful group, the group and the group leader(s) will have been successful if they have effected a degree of change in each member.

CHAPTER SEVEN

PROBLEMS AND SOLUTIONS

Things do not always go the way they are planned. Despite the best preparation, a well-developed game plan, proper screening, meticulous concern with the details of starting a group, and having the know-how to run a group, group counseling does not always succeed. The wise group leader will anticipate that problems will arise from time to time and not panic or become discouraged when they occur. The critical issue is not whether problems can arise, but whether a group leader feels confident to deal with whatever happens. Problems require solutions.

Some things can be done that might prevent problems with a group. They fall into the categories of what the leader *should do* and what the leader *should avoid doing* in order to prevent problems. Primary prevention addresses the problems that can be averted through careful preparation prior to the first group meeting. Reviewing what has been previously mentioned, this would include the selection and screening of prospective group members, determining the proper number of group members, obtaining signed parental permission slips, coordinating meeting times with the teachers involved, preparing group plans for each session, and finding an appropriate room for meeting. Secondary prevention refers to how group leaders handle individual and group problems that occur during the group sessions. These problems would include a failure of a member to respect the group rules, distracting behaviors, a lack of group cohesiveness, and those things that prevent movement toward the group goals.

If you were to ask a counselor how a group seems to be going, a response you might get would be "this is a good group" or, "this is a difficult group." Despite using similar procedures for selecting members and preparing group plans for each session, some groups run smoothly while other groups have problems. Problems that involve the total group are different from problems that result from the actions of individual members. Although the group topic and composition of the group can sometimes explain the reason a group is having problems, even groups that predictably would not be difficult to run could have problems.

When a problem can be viewed as a learning experience that needs a solution, it will be less threatening or intimidating. What follows are some of the more common problems that a group leader will encounter and ways to resolve or reduce them.

PROBLEMS INVOLVING THE ENTIRE GROUP

Groups, being comprised of individual members, are often a reflection of the problems members carry into the group. If anger management is the group topic, the group leader should expect to see members who are probably lacking self-control and inclined to act out their angry feelings. If a divorce group is being run, the group leader could expect to see members whose lives have been temporarily upset and who may still be reacting to the disruption of the family. Most group members are faced with problems that result in frustration, anger, or disappointment. These feelings can be transferred to and reinforced by the group. It should be assumed that other members of the group share similar feelings. For this reason, negative feelings of individual members are often intensified by the group. In order to develop a proper mental set, the group leader should speculate about the inherent nature of each group and not make unrealistic assumptions. It would be unrealistic to assume that the composition of a group dealing with anger management will be similar to that of a group who has experienced the loss of a loved one. Every group is unique. The counselor, having done a pregroup screening interview with each member, should be able to feel that the composition of a particular group is somewhat predictable.

A group problem exists when one or more of the members have an attitude that results in counterproductive behaviors. An example of this would be a group that is out of control. An example of this would be a group that is out of control. This could be seen when the conduct during a session consists largely of inappropriate and frequent laughter, silliness, inattentiveness, and rejection of the leader's attempts to move the group toward the agreed upon objectives. Group problems can occur when a charismatic, or popular, group member does not take the group seriously and others follow the example, when members will not focus on the topic, or when they view group sessions as a play period. Group problems can develop when members have not been carefully screened and are not ready to be in a group. Group problems can also result from the ineffectiveness of the group leader.

When working with introductory and primary level groups, problems often arise from the immaturity of the members. Group counseling with young children at the introductory level usually will involve the use of play media, such as hand puppets, toys, crayons, clay, and doll figures. Children at this level are often unable to verbalize their conflicts and frustrations. Very young children can be unaware that they even have a problem. Because they may not be aware of what *normal* feelings are, they accept their troubled feelings as if they were common to all children their age. A teacher or counselor can identify the young child who appears to be sad or is showing signs of being unhappy. Their faces and body language deliver the message that they are troubled. Young children tend to be dependent on others to do their problem solving and need to learn that they must assist in problem solving. Until they are 8 or 9 years of age, it is difficult for most children to comprehend a cause–effect relationship that might be underlying their problems. They are inclined to focus on the present, and it is difficult for them to develop plans that lead to solutions. Young children often show an inability to comprehend the purpose of a group. They see group counseling more as a social opportunity than one that is directed at change through interaction. When they are old enough to perceive they have an academic or learning problem, the awareness is usually the result of external pressure they feel from parents or teachers. Leader problems with introductory and primary level groups are often due to unrealistic goals and expectations.

Problems with middle, junior high, and high school groups are largely attitude and control problems. In many cases, the potential for these problems can be identified at the screening interview. Problems seen with groups at this age level frequently occur as a result of disruptions, absences, a refusal to abide by the rules of the group, or the inability to take the work of the group seriously. The resistant, indifferent member can have as much negative influence on a group as does the member who dominates the group or tries to control the group leader.

Lack of Group Cohesiveness

Groups that have problems do not become cohesive. Cohesiveness refers to the bonding that occurs within a group and relates to how unified the group is with respect to purpose and the respect shown between members. In a cohesive group, there is mutual respect and members feel that it is safe to interact. The group leader is largely responsible for creating the bond between members. Cohesiveness is encouraged when the leader frequently and judiciously points out the common problems shared by the group and when the group begins to feel members are working toward a common goal. Cohesiveness is also encouraged when the group leader links comments that have been made by members to what is being said and when there is positive interaction between members. It develops when the group leader expresses enthusiasm and a positive attitude. Finally, cohesiveness is strengthened when the group leader uses the pronoun *we* in making reference to the group. For example, "*We* had a good session today. I was very pleased to see that everyone participated and *we* said important things. We're moving closer to *our* goal. Let's be sure that *we* keep it up." The pronoun *you* removes the leader from the group (e.g., "You had a good session today").

The ideal group would have full cohesiveness among all members. When this occurs, all group members show they care about each other and they function as a support group. Groups at the introductory and young primary levels do not tend to become cohesive, although some older primary groups might show signs of moving towards cohesiveness. Intermediate and secondary groups have the potential to become fully cohesive. Partial cohesiveness can be seen when cliques form within the group, a common occurrence in which some of the members bond with each other but one or two members are excluded from the bonding and feel isolated from the majority of the group. The leader should be aware of cliques as they form and should discourage them. Changing the seating arrangement is one way to discourage cliques, although members are free to make comments from any seat in the room. Deliberately inserting members who are not part of the clique into the discussion is another way to break up a clique. It is not unusual for members of the clique to maintain contact with each other outside the group situation. When the group leader feels a clique is having a negative impact on the group, it might be necessary to discuss with the clique members, as a group, the importance of cohesiveness and how their subgroup is a threat to the cohesiveness and productivity of the whole group.

Negative Thinking

At the initial group meeting, it is important that the group leader encourage the members to believe that to some extent the group has the potential of moving toward the group's goal. The group needs to believe that change is possible and that the group sessions will be beneficial if members work together. This is positive thinking. If the group doubts that this will happen, or if it believes that nothing will change as a result of the eight sessions, the pessimism results in negative thinking. Problems that involve the entire group often occur as a consequence of negative thinking. Negative thinking usually results in negative member behaviors, which tend to be oppositional and resistant to change. The signs of negative behavior in a group are showing indifference or apathy and not doing what is asked. Negative thinkers are inclined to be stubborn, argumentative, and quick to complain.

Negative thinking, as a personality trait, can be formed from experiencing frustrations and disappointments. It reflects dissatisfaction and bitterness toward important life situations. In school-aged children, these situations could be home based, due to problems in school, or the result of unpleasant life experiences, including inadequate social relationships. Frustration will intensify when children feel helpless to change either the situation or the person who frustrates them. As a result, negative attitudes develop. To illustrate this, children become frustrated when they are constantly being chastised by their parents for not getting good grades. When they are either unwilling or incapable of doing what is needed to raise their grades, it is easy for them to develop a negative attitude toward school because school is the underlying cause of parental criticism. Their negative attitude expresses frustration, anger, helplessness, and resentment both to parents and teachers. In an attempt to maintain their self-esteem, they often blame someone other than themselves. They might try to convince their parents that their teacher is a "bad" or unfair teacher and blame the teacher. Or they might say that their parents expect too much from them. They often rationalize by saying that school is boring, that going to school is a waste of time, that school doesn't teach relevant things, or that school cannot teach them to do what they want to do the rest of their lives. Many students who have negative attitudes toward school do not really believe the negative things they say about school. They say what they feel will justify their attitude and behavior.

Negative thinking can be seen with introductory- or primary-level age groups. The child who has been spoiled and demands his or her own way, or the child who is expressing an excessive need for autonomy and rejects controls, is often oppositional and uncooperative. Their response to hearing the word *no* can sometimes be catastrophic. Although their reaction is usually more volatile at home than it is in school, teachers and school counselors can identify the children who show negative behavior when things do not go their way. Middle, junior high, and high school students often display high degrees of negativity. Emanating largely from disappointments and events that have had a negative impact on their self-esteem, preadolescents and adolescents use negativism as a defense against further disappointment. They will be less disappointed if they never expect life to go the way they would like it to go. This cause of negative thinking relates to the unconscious use of the ego-defense mechanism known as *emotional insulation.*

People who utilize emotional insulation do not allow themselves to believe they will get what they want. In order to avoid being disappointed, they seldom expect things to happen the way they want them to happen. Emotional insulation occurs when we protect our emotions by acquiring a somewhat cynical attitude. It is a mind-set that teaches us we will not be disappointed, hurt, or upset if we never expect to get what we really wanted. When our emotions are insulated we are prepared to adjust to not having what we want. As an example, a 12-year-old girl whose parents are divorced and whose father has not had any contact with her for five years, could tell herself not to expect a birthday or Christmas present from her father this year. She rationalizes that since she has not had a gift from her father for five years, there is no reason to expect one this year. This child has insulated her emotions to protect herself from being disappointed and hurt if she does not get a birthday or Christmas present. This does not mean she will not care if she does not get presents from her father, but it will hurt less if she is prepared not to receive them. Not expecting gifts from her father is a negative attitude caused by emotional insulation.

If you have ever purchased a lottery ticket worth millions of dollars if you have the winning numbers, it is doubtful that, having paid a dollar for the lottery ticket, you then make plans to spend all of the money you might win. When the numbers on your ticket do not match the winning numbers, you might feel some degree of disappointment, but it is unlikely that it would send you into a major depression or that you would go into a rage. When you purchased that ticket, you unconsciously insulated your emotions by saying to yourself, "The odds of my winning are one hundred million to one. I doubt that I will win." As a result, you can take the failure to win the millions in stride. Some degree of emotional insulation is a necessary adjustment mechanism. Children and adolescents are vulnerable to overreacting to disappointments until they learn that they should not expect to get everything they want. Children or adolescents who have not learned to insulate their emotions somewhat can become devastated when they do not get what they want. Their rage and explosive reactions send the message that it is difficult for them to tolerate frustration and that their expectations for themselves and others are not realistic. Inadvertently, their parents may have programmed them to believe that they can expect others will satisfy their wants and needs just as the parents have. Whereas some emotional insulation is desirable, overinsulating our emotions can be harmful. Overinsulation, or insulating our emotions to excess, can produce indifference and apathy, which are variations of negative thinking. Overinsulation can prevent us from trying to solve our problems. The highly cynical person has a what's-the-use? attitude.

Negative thinkers are not always aware of their negative thinking because they are able to justify their attitudes and behaviors. They fail to realize that they are describing that proverbial glass of water as being half-empty, rather than half-full. Negative thinkers see the hole of the doughnut, not the doughnut. They are not even looking for the positives in a situation. The group leader needs to call negative thinking to the attention of the group when it becomes habitual. If negative thinking by the group is viewed as a problem that could prevent movement toward the group's goal, overcoming negative thinking should become a subgoal that requires immediate attention.

One way to call attention to negative thinking would be to encourage the group to say things that are positive. A group homework assignment could address this objective. The group could be asked to practice positive thinking by adding a positive statement to every negative comment they make during the week. This would require the members to become aware of their negative thinking and begin to look at the positive things about people or situations. For example, if Larry says, "Tomorrow is our picnic. I'll bet it will rain tomorrow," Larry would then be expected to say something positive like, "Even if it does rain, we can still have fun." Negative thinkers are inclined to overuse the words *always* and *never.* For example, "We never have fun in school," or "My teacher is always scolding someone." Negative thinking can also underlie passive resistance. Refusing to participate in the group discussions, coming late or missing a group meeting, not doing a homework assignment, or showing indifference in discussions are examples of passive resistance and signs of negative thinking.

Lack of Motivation

In athletic competition, a coach gives the team a motivational pep talk before the game. The coach needs to exude enthusiasm and convince the team that it can win the game. It was mentioned earlier that the group leader needs to express enthusiasm. The reason is similar to why the coach gives the pep talk, but the goal is slightly different. For the coach, winning the game is comparable to the feeling the group leader gets when the group shows movement toward the goal. The purpose of the leader's enthusiasm is to motivate the group. Motivation is the key to success in most things we do. Assuming a student has the ability to achieve academically, a lack of motivation is often the underlying explanation as to why the student underachieves. Students who underachieve are often accused of being lazy, but more accurately they could be accused of *situational laziness,* for many so-called lazy students could play a sport or video game ten hours a day. Lazy is not the correct label for these students. They are just not motivated to do what needs to be done in order to succeed in school. A lack of motivation, to some degree, can also explain why a group does not show movement toward the group's goal. This writer regards how to motivate students to achieve their academic potential as the number-one problem in educating children of all ages. The secret of how to motivate students has eluded educators. Teachers have used countless strategies to try to motivate students—verbal praise, star charts, pep talks, candy, privileges, or behavioral contracts. Rewards of all kinds seem to work for a while, but in time they become ineffective. There is no universal motivator—what motivates one child may not motivate another child.

The secret of motivation may lie in revising the old proverb "You can lead a horse to water, but you can't make it drink." But add the words, ". . . unless you give the horse salt." Now the horse *will* drink! The solution to the motivation problem could lie in determining what each child's *salt* would be, what would motivate a particular child. Our salt, however, changes throughout our lives. What motivates an 8-year-old child is not what motivates a 16-year-old adolescent. Motivators are based on what we want or need at any given time. A child may need parental praise at 10 but would probably prefer peer recognition at 15. An important question counselors might ask themselves is "What is my salt?"

Motivation to do something will be increased when the person is directly involved in the task. Telling a group how to go about making friendships is not as effective as developing a series of demonstrations in which the members role-play meeting someone for the first time. A math teacher might motivate students to do their homework when students are selected to show the class how they solved a homework problem. Motivation also increases as a result of success. Getting an A on a spelling test might result in high motivation to get an A on the next test. Utilizing both the principles of involvement and success, the group leader should make certain that all members are active participants in the group and should make the group aware of any degree of change, improvement, or success in the group. Rewards and positive reinforcement also help to motivate groups. Positive reinforcement can occur when the group leader acknowledges an insightful statement made by a group member or explains why today's session was a very good one. When the leader makes a point of praising a group member who has said something helpful to another member, others are encouraged to help their fellow members. A reward can be a party at the last group meeting if the group has shown movement toward the goal. With introductory and primary groups, rewards can be icebreaker activities at the end of a session.

Enthusiasm is expressed by facial expressions, words, and vocal inflections. The group leader's eye contact with the group, occasional smile, use of encouraging, positive words, and appropriate excitement in vocal inflections can indicate the leader's apparent enthusiasm. The group leader's reaction to the group can also be a barometer measuring how motivated the group seems to be. Why a group seems to be highly motivated or why one is flat can be a reflection of the way the leader speaks to the group.

The Silent Group

A problem has occurred when the entire group goes silent. Unless the group leader is prepared to begin each session with a summary review of the previous session and has developed stimulus questions, group silence could start each session. Group silence often means that no one has anything to say, no one knows what to say, or no one wants to be the first to say something. It could also signal that the group is showing resistance or is bored. Group silence can occur when the group feels that talk on a topic has been exhausted and that the group is ready to move on. When silence occurs during the last 5 or 10 minutes of a session in introductory or primary groups, it could be the group's way of asking the group leader to begin a group-oriented activity. Silence in older groups can send a message that the group is too dependent on the group leader to initiate the discussion and is content to wait for the group leader to speak.

What often occurs when the group goes silent is a "waiting-out" game in which the leader waits for someone in the group to say something, and the group waits for the leader to say something. It becomes a variation of what could be called a game of "verbal chicken." When silence occurs in the midst of a group session, it is recommended that the leader allow about 30 seconds of silence before saying something. Waiting longer could be awkward and might lower the morale of the group. However, 30 seconds can seem like a long time. What the leader does in those 30 seconds is important. It would not be appropriate for the leader to show nervousness or irritation, neither would it be proper for the leader to engage in some distracting behavior, such as writing notes, looking around the room, or checking the time. During what seems to be 30 seconds, the leader should casually and slowly look at each member as if to say, "Why don't you say something?" When all of the members have been looked at and no one has volunteered to say something, the leader should be prepared to pose a stimulus question or move to a new topic. If the time for ending the session is near, opening up a new topic is not advisable; reviewing things that had been said would be more appropriate. Letting the group leave early is not recommended because students would then be walking around the building during class time and it would be embarrassing to have to explain to the administrator why the group did not remain until the scheduled time for departure. Early release could also set a precedent that would encourage silence in the future in order to bring the session to an end. There is always a reason for a silent or nontalkative group. The group leader needs to discover the reason.

MEMBER PROBLEMS

Hostile or Verbally Aggressive Behavior

Everyone is capable of getting angry once in a while. Here, however, the discussion focuses on individuals for whom anger and hostility are frequent characteristics of their personality and behavior. Groups do not bring out verbal hostility in a student unless that student has a history of being verbally hostile. Likewise, membership in a group will not prevent a student who is hostile from displaying anger. The best defense against verbal hostility is prevention. Prior to meeting with an anger-management group, the group leader needs to do at least two things. First, at the initial interview, and in a friendly, nonauthoritarian way, the group leader should make the prospective member aware that proper behavioral control will be expected. The member would need to promise the leader to make an effort to exert self-control. The prospective group member needs to have a clear understanding of the expectations for group members as well as the goals of the group. It is what this writer calls a "welcome . . . but" invitation to the group. In essence, the message is "I want to encourage you to become a part of this group and I think you will find it worthwhile. If the group is successful, and I have reason to feel it will be, you should be able to enjoy school more and stay out of trouble. But, the group will have rules and one of them is that no one in the group is allowed to say or do anything to hurt a member of the group. If you are willing to make a promise to me that you will try hard to control your temper, I would be very pleased to invite you to join our group." If unable or unwilling to make this promise, the student should be asked to begin individual counseling with the counselor.

The second thing the group leader should do is to give the member a nonverbal sign that the group leader will use when it is felt that the member may be about to lose control or become offensive. The sign would be a way of saying, "Time out. You're getting too upset." The time-out sign used in athletic competition by making the letter T with both hands is effective. It is important that the sign be used *before* the anger becomes intense, much like stopping a rolling snowball at the top of a hill before it has been allowed to become larger and gather momentum. The prospective group member would have to agree to accept the time-out sign as a signal for calming down. Prevention requires the group leader to be an active listener and respond quickly when a member seems to be losing his or her temper or when the group seems to be getting out of control.

In an anger-management group, the counselor will have assembled students who have been identified as verbally hostile and/or physically aggressive. The group leader needs to remember that aggressiveness and verbal hostility are just symptoms of a problem. Individual counseling in addition to group counseling should be considered for members in anger-management groups in order to help each member gain some insights into his or her behavior. Although this would mean that the student would have to be excused from class more than once a week, it is justifiable when there is hope that the combination of both individual and group counseling might reduce the problem. Students who are verbally hostile and/or physically aggressive disrupt classes and pose a danger to the school community. Whatever is needed that might alleviate or ideally, eliminate, the problem is worth whatever it takes to effect this change. The individual counseling can be done every other week, which would mean that the student would meet one-on-one with the counselor four times in the eight weeks. A goal of the counselor could be to determine the problem that is responsible for and contributes to the aggressive behavior. Individual counseling sessions would be supportive and could reinforce any positive behaviors that are seen in the group. Individual counseling can be less threatening for the student who is also meeting with the counselor in a group. Rapport transfers from one situation to the other. Should the counselor feel that the student's problem is too severe and goes beyond what can be handled by a school counselor, a referral to an out-of-school source should be made.

The Silent Member

Ed was a fifth-grade group member who was reluctant to talk during the first two group meetings and gave one-word responses to the group leader's questions. He appeared to pay attention to everything that was said but did not interact with the group. Ed would be considered a silent member. He could be expressing fear and feelings of low self-esteem, he could be communicating either passivity or passive-aggressive behavior, or he could also have been reacting to the composition of the group, which would be the case if he felt intimidated by someone in the group. Before taking steps to encourage Ed to participate in the group, the group leader should attempt to understand the reasons for Ed's lack of participation. Although it would be appropriate for the group leader to encourage Ed to speak more in the group, it might be inappropriate to *force* Ed to participate until the counselor learns why he was not participating. This investigation should be handled privately in one or more individual counseling sessions. In all likelihood, the screening interview would have suggested that Ed might have difficulty talking in the group. But because Ed had agreed to be in the group knowing the expectations for a group member, the group leader could assume that Ed knew what was expected and, at the time of the screening interview, was willing and able to participate. Ed may really have wanted to be able to talk in front of the group, but something occurred that made this difficult or impossible.

The group leader must be empathic toward Ed and try to view the problem from his perspective. If it is learned that Ed would like to become more active in group but is having a hard time doing so, the leader should encourage Ed to be spontaneous once or twice during the next group session. More spontaneity should be encouraged in subsequent sessions. Ed should know that the leader will occasionally call on him for input or a reaction during a discussion. The leader needs to reinforce Ed's efforts and willingness to take risks. Verbal reinforcement should be given to Ed after each session and during individual counseling. The group leader should view Ed's silence or reluctance to speak as a symptom of a problem. Helping Ed to acquire some insight into the reasons for his silence and encouraging him to do whatever is necessary to overcome his reluctance to speak would be counseling goals. Ed would have to commit himself to being willing to take calculated risks, one of which would be to consciously make an effort to begin to speak in the group. If Ed's problem is due to poor self-esteem, he should understand that speaking in the group is one way to enhance his self-esteem. If he is intimidated by a member of the group, Ed needs to face up to the problem knowing that the group leader is there to help him. Feeling intimidated by someone usually indicates a tendency to devalue the self. Ed needs to view himself as a person who is valuable both to himself and others.

Silence can be due to other reasons, however. If listening to what others in the group are saying makes a member uncomfortable, or when what others in the group are saying intensifies painful emotions, silence is understandable. This is a common reaction to the emotion of grief due to the loss of a loved one. Grief groups are different from other groups in several ways. In a grief group, the leader's voice should not be one of exuberance, but one of compassion. The group goal does not usually involve behavioral changes but is related more to helping individual group members obtain some emotional comfort, support, and acceptance of a painful reality. Predictably, there will be more silence in a grief group because the members will be reacting to their loss and reflecting on memories. They may have difficulty expressing their feelings. They also realize there is no acceptable solution to their problem. No one can give them what they want; no one can relate to their personal loss. Silence in a grief group could also indicate that members are not ready to talk about their loss, and the leader should not force this readiness. Members of grief groups are often showing signs of varying degrees of depression. This would certainly be true if they have experienced a recent loss. In the event the group leader feels that the member appears to be significantly depressed, or if the grievance time has been excessive, a conference with the parents might suggest that the parents should consult with their pediatrician or an out-of-school referral should be made to a mental health professional.

Violating a Group Rule

As previously stated, although the existence of group rules is mentioned in the screening interview, the actual rules that will govern the group should be established at the first session. Both the consequences and the process for dealing with breaking a rule should also be stated so that the group knows, in advance, what would occur when a rule has been broken. Consequences for breaking a rule can range from being reminded of the rule, to receiving a warning, to being asked to leave the group. Some violations can be handled privately by the group leader, whereas others need to come to the attention of the entire group. The leader could call being impolite or verbally abusive to the attention of the violating member and ask that the offender apologize to the member in front of the group. Breaking the rule about interrupting could be handled by simply reminding the offending member of the rule against interrupting. Missing a session, coming late, monopolizing the group, or being disruptive should be handled privately. Because it is critical that members feel safe to speak in the group, a member who has broken the rule involving confidentiality could either be given a warning or asked to leave the group. The warning could be stated in front of the group. If the member's breach of confidentiality warrants being asked to leave the group, this should be handled privately, outside of the group. Being asked to leave is a severe action that might be taken if the group leader feels the violation was extremely harmful to the member whose privacy was violated. When the group leader feels that the violation of trust was such that the group's ability to feel free to talk has been compromised or destroyed, asking the member to leave would be necessary. The decision to remove a member from a group is made by the group leader and co-leader. The group should be informed that confidentiality has been breached and of the action that was taken.

When a member is asked to leave the group, the member's parents need to be notified, in writing, and given a minimal explanation without revealing the details of what their child said that broke the rule of confidentiality. It is sufficient to say that their son or daughter broke the rule of confidentiality and had known that breaking this important rule could result in being asked to leave the group. Expulsion from a group does not necessarily mean the student could not be in another group at some later time. The student's teacher should also be informed of the decision with the same minimal explanation. The group leader is still ethically bound to maintain confidentiality and is not permitted to discuss the details of what happened. The group leader's ethic of protecting the group member would remain.

The Nonsharing Member

There is a difference between the silent member and the nonsharing member. The silent member does not talk. Nonsharing members talk but avoid talking about themselves. Nonsharing members listen to others and may be quick to respond to the issues and problems that others present. However, when it comes to discussing *their* issues or *their* feelings, they will be evasive and noncommittal. It usually takes the group leader at least two sessions to realize that a member is nonsharing. Because they are active in the discussions and can be very helpful to others, the group leader can be misled into thinking this member is functioning well in the group. On reflection, the group leader should realize that this member has not shared anything personal with the group. Attempts to have the member talk about personal feelings or experiences will have been met with resistance. When asked a direct question, the nonsharer will give one-word responses, deny, or not admit to feeling the way other members do. The impression nonsharing members try to give is that they are handling their situation very well and really do not need the group for support or assistance. Even if this is true, sharing members would be expected to talk about how they are dealing with the issues.

There are at least eight possible explanations of why a member would be nonsharing.

1. The first, and perhaps the most common, explanation is the member's concern over the safety of talking in the group. Although confidentiality is stressed, members cannot be certain that what is said in the group will stay within the group. Logically, if the member says nothing, nothing can be repeated. Nonsharing members could be playing it safe.

2. The need of group members to maintain and protect their image is a second reason why members can be nonsharing. By showing their best side and not allowing others the opportunity to know the person they really are, nonsharers prevent others from knowing their weaknesses or forming negative opinions. Their fear is that exposure could alter the image they are trying to create.

3. Denial, in order to avoid embarrassment, is a third explanation for nonsharing. Some members cannot admit they have problems and would be embarrassed to talk about their environmental situation if they feel it could be viewed by the group in a negative way. For example, it would not be easy for Eleanor to tell the group that her father is in jail or that her mother sleeps all day and is out all night. When the group is talking about parents or home conditions, Eleanor has nothing to say. Denial can also be seen when a member is not able to *own the problem* and blames others for personal shortcomings. Bob is in conflict with his parents and freely talks about how unfair and demanding they are. He vents his anger at how they have punished him for insignificant things and tries to convince the group that his parents are to blame for his unhappiness. He even attributes his poor grades to their actions, which prevent him from studying. Bob is unwilling to talk about his contribution to the problem and how his negative attitude and oppositional behavior triggers their behavior.

4. Some children are naturally secretive. They choose not to share their attitudes and feelings with others and strive to create a mystique they feel differentiates them from their peers in a positive way. Secretive people feel they have something to hide. Whether they do or don't, the perception that they do is enough to maintain their secrecy. The need of some members to keep their lives private is a fourth explanation for nonsharing.

5. A fifth reason for nonsharing can relate to cultural factors. In families where children have been told by parents that family problems should never be discussed outside of the home and that telling others your problems is a sign of weakness, nonsharing members could be complying with parental or environmental influences. Before being critical of a member for nonsharing, the group leader should investigate the possibility that the member has been discouraged from sharing feelings or experiences with people who are outside of the family.

6. A sixth, and related, reason for nonsharing could be the member's lack of familiarity or discomfort with expressing or sharing feelings. There are homes in which personal feelings are rarely discussed and the opinion of the child is not welcomed. The expression "children should be seen and not heard" still applies in some families. For a child living in such an environment, sharing is a new experience.

7. The seventh explanation for nonsharing is that it could be due to passive-aggressive behavior. In this instance, aggression is being expressed passively by what could be called the *sin of omission,* or what we fail to do. Knowing it is expected that members will talk in the group, the passive-aggressive member is oppositional and refuses to interact. Passive-aggressive behavior should not exclude a student from being placed in a group, but the leader should anticipate nonsharing behavior that needs to be addressed in individual counseling.

8. An eighth explanation for why a member is nonsharing relates to how the member handles emotions. If members know that they tend to become overemotional when they talk about certain subjects and fear they might cry, lose control, or embarrass themselves, not sharing would prevent this from happening. Members who feel they are not able to control their emotions will not share their feelings or experiences because they feel it is not safe for them to talk, not because they cannot trust the group, but because they do not trust themselves. From the group leader's perspective, there are valid reasons for recommending one-on-one counseling for nonsharing members; they might not be ready to be in a group.

The Monopolizer

Group leaders will occasionally encounter a member whose need to talk excessively threatens to dominate the group. This member is either consciously or unconsciously attempting to control the group through the amount of the time the group is forced to listen to what the member is saying. Unless the leader takes action to curb what seems to be frequent, nonstop monologues, this member could upset and ruin the group. Eventually, the monopolizer antagonizes the other group members and the group's frustration ultimately turns to anger. Should this occur, the group leader finds that instead of discussing the topic and moving toward the group goal, the energy of the group is spent expressing hostility toward the monopolizer.

There are a number of reasons that might explain why a group member monopolizes the discussion. People who are loquacious often use speech to gain attention and take control of a situation. If this is the usual and customary behavior of a group member, it is possible that by dominating the discussion the member feels the group will be impressed; this enhances the member's self-esteem. People who monopolize a group can be sending a message that says they feel they know more than anyone in the group; speech is the vehicle they use to get respect. They justify their behavior by believing that what they say is more important than what others say. Excessive talking can be a way to expresses their need to feel superior. Figuratively speaking, speech is a lasso—as long as you are talking to someone you are holding that person captive until you stop talking. In normal conversation, listeners do not feel as if they are captives because a speaker does not usually talk very long without letting another person speak. Monopolizers, on the other hand, are out to "take prisoners." Once they have an audience, they enjoy the attention and hold the spotlight. Most monopolizers are not good listeners and really do not care to hear what someone else is saying. In middle, junior high, and high school groups, the group monopolizer may think that the group leader is inadequate and therefore feels it necessary to take charge and become a self-appointed co-leader or leader. The signs of this would be the monopolizer's open defiance or criticism of the leader and belittling of what the leader says in front of the group.

The solution to the problem of the member who seeks to dominate the group is meeting privately with the monopolizer with the purpose not of scolding or punishing, but of conveying the message that monopolizing the group is thwarting the goals of the group because the members are not getting the time they need during a session to express their concerns and feelings on the group topic. The counselor must not discourage the monopolizer from participating in the group, but rather encourage more consideration of all the members. If need be, the counselor may interrupt the monopolizer during group. Although not interrupting is one of the group rules, in cases in which the leader needs to prevent monopolizing by a member, the leader should be prepared to interrupt. The need to monopolize a group is yet another symptom of a problem; the counselor should deal with the symptom and also focus on the problem.

A Missed Session

It is unlikely that every member will attend all of the group sessions. Likewise, there will be times when an emergency will force the cancellation of a group session. A canceled group session can be rescheduled, or it might be possible to extend the group one week to provide for the number of meetings that had been planned. There is no way a member can make up a missed session. In most instances, there is not much the group leader can do to inform the member of what was missed. The exception to this would be a homework assignment. It is recommended that the leader contact the member who missed the session and, at an individual session, allow the member to talk about how the assignment was carried out.

Another problem arising from absence is the absence of several members of the group for valid reasons. As a rule, three members of the group are needed to constitute a quorum. When only two members show up, the group should be canceled, although the group leader could elect to meet with the two members, not as a group session, but to evaluate the progress the two members are making. Under these circumstances, the group should still try to get in the number of sessions that had been planned even if it means extending the group one more week. Inasmuch as a group depends on interaction, when the group is too small, the potential for interaction is reduced. This policy should be announced at the first group session.

Unexcused absences need to be handled in a different way. The "I forgot" excuse can be legitimate, but it can also be a sign of resistance. If a member is not present when the group convenes, some group leaders send a member who is present to the missing member's classroom. This writer does not recommend doing this. The missing member could be absent from school or have decided not to attend group that day, and the member who is sent to find the student will be absent from the group for several minutes. It is not fair to ask the group to wait for members to arrive because one of the group rules is that the group starts and stops on time. Informing members and teachers on the day of the session should be sufficient to remind members of their responsibility. There will be times when a group member informs the counselor, prior to the group meeting, of a valid reason for not attending. Making up a test or doing something for a teacher are valid reasons, as are illness and an excused absence from school on the day the group meets. The group leader should not expect perfect attendance at all group sessions.

When absence can be attributed to resistance, a private talk with the group leader is necessary. Resistance does not always mean the member wants to drop out of the group, but there is a strong possibility that this will happen. The counselor should not force a resistant group member to attend group. A group member always has the option of dropping out. The counselor should be honest with the member, and if the counselor feels that dropping out is a mistake, the reasons should be stated to the member. Just as when a member is asked to leave the group, when a member drops out of a group parents must be notified, in writing, that their child has made the decision to terminate group membership. No reason needs to be given other than it was the member's decision. Parents should be discouraged from trying to pressure their child into changing that decision. The member's teachers should also be notified when a member drops out.

ETHICAL PROBLEM: OPENING PANDORA'S BOX

All school counselors face a potential danger every time they see a counselee for individual counseling or whenever they run a group session. The danger lies in the intense feelings that can be released when something that is said by the counselor or a member of a group sets off a strong emotional reaction by a group member. The reaction can be either explosive or subdued. An explosive reaction is externally directed and is seen when a group member goes into a rage, loses self-control, verbally lashes out at the counselor or group member, or becomes physically aggressive by either hitting or destroying something. A subdued reaction is internally directed and is seen when the group member becomes instantaneously silent, sobs or cries uncontrollably, or walks out of the room.

An experienced counselor can often predict the group member who may be prone to having a strong reaction to a verbal stimulus. A member of a grief group who is having a difficult time dealing with loss might become devastated by something that was said and lose emotional control. A member of an anger-management group might respond to something that was said by becoming verbally hostile or physically abusive. But there are many times when Pandora's box is opened suddenly and without warning. It is not always possible to know what could trigger an emotional outburst. Some children, because of their circumstances and life experiences, walk around with the proverbial chip on their shoulder and welcome an opportunity to displace their anger when they perceive it is safe to do so. The counseling situation is often seen as a safe place to vent feelings. Children and adolescents who are reacting to feelings of inner turmoil, frustrations, unresolved conflicts, unhappiness, or stress over a period of time can build up emotional pressure that needs to be released. The emotional release occurs when they are no longer able to hold back or control their feelings. Many school-aged children have problems whose roots are hidden beneath, yet close to, the surface of their awareness. The events or memories that a child or adolescent does not want to remember because they are too painful, upsetting, embarrassing, or ego threatening could be either suppressed or repressed. When something is said by the counselor or someone in the group that prompts a member to recall an unpleasant event, either directly or by associating the comment with something in the member's past, the recollection becomes upsetting, and Pandora's box has been opened. When this occurs, calming the student can be very difficult.

Active counselors run the risk of releasing strong feelings from group members. In response to a probing question, Glenn, a 12 year old in an assertiveness group, might begin to talk about the way he has been treated by his peers. If the group leader says, "Tell us more," and if Glenn has had a recent bad experience in which he felt intimidated and embarrassed, he may take this opportunity to say things that he has wanted to say but until now could not. What might follow could be a tirade on how angry and hateful he feels. The more Glenn talks, the more he expresses his true feelings in an uncensored way. From the tone of his voice and the words he is using, the group leader can begin to understand the severity of Glenn's emotional pain and the impact certain experiences have had on him. Glenn is experiencing catharsis, and what he is saying needs to come out. His outburst could be frightening, however, for the group members or even the group leader. Even passive counselors or group leaders who ask few questions and reflect what they hear a counselee say could, inadvertently, bring to the surface memories and feelings that can be disturbing for the group member.

Opening Pandora's box occurs more often in individual counseling. It seldom occurs in introductory- and primary-level groups and does not happen frequently with intermediate- and secondary-level groups. Nevertheless, the counselor should be aware of what *could* happen and be prepared to take the necessary action. If, for example, Glenn loses control and goes into a rage, screams, begins to make threats, or starts to cry, the counselor might want to walk him out of the group room and into a private place. Essentially, the group leader now must try to close Pandora's box. Although the initial objective would be to attempt to calm Glenn down, this may not be possible until Glenn has finished reacting. Once Glenn has regained his composure, he could be invited to return to the group. In Glenn's presence, the group should be reminded of the rule of confidentiality and that what was seen or heard must not be shared with anyone. This needs to be said several times.

In response to an outburst, the group leader must not panic. There is no reason to abruptly end the group session. The sky has not fallen down, but red flags are being displayed. If Glenn's emotional reaction is seen as a call for help, the group leader has a decision to make. Should Glenn be asked to see the school counselor on an individual basis for a while and continue in the group, or should the counselor make arrangements to meet with Glenn's parents to discuss an out-of-school referral? If, after talking with Glenn one or two times, the counselor feels that Glenn's problem goes beyond the counselor's skills or availability, the counselor could suggest to Glenn that there seems to be a need to do more exploring in some areas and that involving his parents in the exploration would be advisable. In a very nonthreatening way, Glenn should know that his parents will be asked to meet with the counselor. The other necessary actions for the school counselor would be to inform the principal that Glenn's parents have been asked to meet with the counselor and the plan is to make a referral to an out-of-school professional resource. It is important that the counselor not breach confidentiality with the principal and only indicate impressions and the rationale for the actions. The next thing would be to arrange to meet with the parents. Finally, in accordance with the school's referral policy and the ethical responsibility of the counselor, an appropriate referral should be made. This writer feels that the principal should be informed when out-of-school referrals are recommended, unless the principal indicates that it is not necessary to do so.

It should be reiterated that Pandora's box is not opened very often. Because there is always the possibility that it *could* be opened, the group leader needs to know how to handle the situation should it ever occur. It is also important for the counselor to realize that opening Pandora's box is not a mistake. When it occurs, a problem has been identified and the proper actions can be taken so that a child can receive help. A youngster who is troubled with conflict, whether conscious or unconscious, is a child who hurts.

REVIEW AND SUMMARY

To review those things that group leaders can do to prevent group counseling problems from developing,

1. Early in the school year, inform the administration, faculty and parents that your comprehensive guidance and counseling program includes group counseling.

2. Establish good rapport with the principal and faculty in order to facilitate their cooperation.

3. Distribute needs assessment surveys to teachers, parents, and students for suggestions of group topics. Involving the entire school community will create visibility and interest.

4. Screen your prospective group members through a brief interview.

5. Inform the parents of prospective members that their child has been selected to be in a group and inform them that they must return a signed permission slip.

6. Request the schedules of teachers to determine convenient times for the group to meet.

7. Stagger the meeting times in accordance with the schedules of the faculty.

8. Request teachers to excuse the selected group members from their classes at designated times.

9. Inform the teachers of group members the number of planned sessions, dates, and times for each session. Deliver a note to the teachers on the morning the group is scheduled to meet as a reminder.

10. Plan to use co-leaders when it is convenient.

11. Establish, enforce, and reinforce group rules.

12. Set a realistic goal and subgoals for the group.

13. Teach the group what is expected of group members.

14. Develop a game plan for each session.

15. Prepare open-ended stimulus questions in advance that can elicit responses.

16. Use an icebreaker at the first session and whenever it is deemed necessary.

17. Maintain control of the group.

18. Take notes for the summary of each session and the review that starts a session.

19. Be a good role model for the group.

20. Encourage all members to participate in the group.

21. Reinforce good participation with verbal praise.

22. Start and stop each session on time.

23. Assign constructive and realistic homework when the group is ready to carry out assignments.

24. Include children from a diverse ethnic population in groups.

25. Focus on problem solving.

26. Practice good leadership skills.

27. Remember that you have been trained to be a counselor and use your counseling skills at all times.

28. Be prepared to offer concrete suggestions in order to move the group toward the goal.

29. Discourage members from monopolizing, distracting, digressing, or otherwise impairing the group.

30. Plan for a farewell party the last 10 minutes of the final session.

There are also things that the group leader should avoid doing to prevent group counseling problems:

1. Do not presume that groups are appropriate for every problem or every student.

2. Do not expect that six or eight sessions will resolve the problem being discussed. At the conclusion of a successful group, the group should be moving in a direction that could resolve or reduce the problem.

3. Do not force a student to become a member of a group.

4. Do not include someone in the group who is unable to communicate or would not be able to comprehend what is being discussed.

5. Do not let a member dominate or monopolize the group.

6. Do not try to run groups that are too large. Seven members with older groups should be the maximum. Let grade level, topic, and space determine your group size.

7. Do not have more than a single grade difference in the group.

8. Do not run an open group, unless the group is planned to run throughout the year.

9. Do not allow visitors to observe the group.

10. Do not show anger, frustration, or upset to the group.

11. Do not permit lengthy digression from the group's topic.

12. Do not panic when something goes wrong. Evaluate the situation and determine what needs to be done. When in doubt, consult with a colleague.

13. Do not be discouraged when one session does not go according to plan. Determine the reason and do some problem solving.

14. Do not allow the group to talk about students who are not in the group.

15. Do not allow the group to talk about teachers or the principal.

16. Do not allow members to attack or become verbally abusive to each other.

17. Do not forget to stress confidentiality at every group session.

18. Do not break confidentiality when consulting with teachers or parents.

19. Do not let the group "gang up" on a member.

20. Do not lecture to the group.

21. Do not assign homework until you feel the group is ready to carry it out.

22. Do not forget to mention the terminating date of the group several weeks prior to the last meeting.

23. Do not yield to pressure to do something you feel is professionally inappropriate (e.g., yielding to pressure to add members to the group).

24. Do not engage in unethical conduct.

25. Do not hesitate to ask a group member to have an individual conference when you deem it necessary.

26. Do not discuss what is said in a group outside of the group.

27. Do not allow a group member to remain silent throughout a session.

28. Do not allow members to avoid doing their class homework or class assignments.

29. Do not forget that the group leader is a role model.

30. Do not expect perfection. A counselor-trainee is only expected to have entry-level skills. With experience and confidence leadership skills will improve. Be patient with yourself.

After the last group session the group leader, or co-leaders, should do an evaluation of the group experience. Evaluations should be both informative and diagnostic. The informative component should show the group leader which group members benefited from the group experience and how well the group moved toward the goal. It would address the strengths and weaknesses of individuals and the group. Diagnostically, an evaluation would allow the group leader to understand what contributed to either the group's success or lack of success. The diagnostic components of the evaluation would raise and answer *what* or *why* questions, depending on how successful the group experience has been. What made the group cohesive, or why didn't the group become cohesive? What enabled the group to interact so effectively, or why didn't the group interact effectively? An evaluation would also let the group leader know what was effective and what changes should be considered for future groups.

A member-by-member assessment does not have to be a time-consuming or complicated process. An example of a group member assessment follows. Progress can be measured by using a five-point scale with 5 being the best and 1 being the worst. The numbers would correspond to significant, much, some, very little, or none. The categories evaluated can be attitude, behavior, and overall.

Topic: Divorce/Separation
Grade level: Seventh grade
Dates of sessions: October 2, 9, 16, 23, 30
                   November 6, 13, 20
Co-leaders: Allan Williams and Karen White
Scale: 5 = significant change
        4 = much change
        3 = some change
        2 = very little
        1 = no change

	ATTITUDE	BEHAVIOR	OVERALL
Frank	5	4	4+
Ann	4	4	4
Eddy	2	1	2
Alice	5	5	5
Tom	3	4	4–

Assessing the group requires the use of different criteria. The group leader would be looking at those qualities that make groups effective, including group cohesiveness, direction toward the goal, group interaction, respect for group rules, group behavior, group session plans, and leadership. The numbers, using a five-point scale, would correspond to

5 = very good
4 = good
3 = acceptable
2 = could have been better
1 = not good

For example,

Group cohesiveness	4	Group behavior	4
Goal direction	4	Group session plans	4
Group interaction	4	Leadership	4
Respect for rules	5	Overall evaluation	4

The diagnostic component of evaluating a group does not lend itself to the development of quantitative data. Answers to questions of why something did or did not happen in the group are speculative and based more on logical reasoning and experience than raw data. They can best be discussed with a co-leader. In the absence of a co-leader, the group leader could talk with a colleague or just find a quiet place and reflect.

When the group has shown movement in the direction of the group's goals and the last session is over, the group leader(s) should feel a sense of accomplishment. A successful group leader can feel that the members have profited from the experience. When a group has been successful, everybody learns something.

CHAPTER EIGHT

MULTICULTURAL GROUP COUNSELING IN THE SCHOOL SETTING

CHERYL C. HOLCOMB-McCOY
University of Maryland

Schools today are more multicultural, multiracial, and multilingual than ever before. By the year 2050, it is estimated that public schools in the United States will consist primarily of students of color, and in major cities White students will be a numerical minority. School counselors will undoubtedly be implementing group counseling with students of varying ethnic/racial backgrounds. Unfortunately, school counselors rarely examine the effect of culture on group process. They are also less likely to explore how their own racial/ethnic biases and behaviors can affect the progress of a counseling group.

This chapter will provide guidelines for school counselors who implement groups with children from ethnically dissimilar backgrounds. In addition, an overview of the characteristics necessary to become an effective multicultural group leader will be discussed. A model of implementing an ethnically homogenous group in an elementary school will be outlined. Finally, a checklist for assessing a school counselor's multicultural competence will be provided.

IMPORTANT TERMINOLOGY

Although the terms *multicultural, ethnicity,* and *race* are used interchangeably by most laypersons and counseling professionals, the terms have distinct meanings and implications. For the purpose of this chapter, the term *multicultural* will be used to describe any relationship that includes persons of different ethnic/racial backgrounds. *Ethnicity* refers to persons descending from a particular geographic region (e.g., African American, Italian American, Greek American, Asian American, Native American, Hispanic/Latino American).

Race tends to be more of a political term used to describe groups of individuals along ethnic lines. For example, although African American is an ethnic identification, many persons refer to all persons of African descent as *Black,* which is a racial identification. Likewise, *White* is a racial identification depicting such ethnic groups as Italian Americans, Greek Americans, and so on.

Although the writer is very aware of the countless cultural groups (e.g., age, gender, sexual orientation) that students may identify with, this chapter will focus primarily on group counseling issues surrounding the ethnic/racial differences among group members.

TRADITIONAL GROUP COUNSELING ASSUMPTIONS

Bias in school counseling groups can result from a school counselor's adherence to traditional or Eurocentric group counseling theory and assumptions. An increased awareness of the limitations of traditional counseling assumptions will decrease school counselors' misinterpretation of culturally bound group behavior as deviant and/or inappropriate. This section will include a discussion of cultural contradictions in traditional group counseling theory.

Several traditional group counseling assumptions conflict with the beliefs and behaviors of various cultural groups. One of the most obvious group counseling assumptions is that group members need to self-disclose in order for group cohesion to occur. Talking is perceived to be essential to the development of a group. The implied expectation is that group members speak English in a group. However, self-disclosure and talking in a group setting are not valued by all cultures. For instance, many Asian cultures believe that it is better to be silent than to ramble on and say nothing important or say something that is not carefully thought out.

In addition to being expected to talk, traditional group counseling theory assumes that group members will self-disclose information regarding personal life occurrences, relationships with significant others, and personal thoughts and feelings. Many cultures may view these types of self-disclosures to be appropriate only within the family or with authority figures (e.g., clergy, elders in the community) and not with their peers. A Latino mother of a 12-year-old boy might have reservations about her son participating in a group for children who are experiencing divorce because she believes family problems should never be discussed outside of the family. Likewise, a Jewish student might tell his counselor that he would rather discuss personal issues with his rabbi than disclose to his peers in a group.

In group counseling it is also assumed that group members will respond spontaneously whenever they have a reaction to something that has been said or done in the group. Many group leaders do not require members to raise their hands when they want to speak. A standard rule is to listen to one another without interrupting. Students are expected to talk to one another and not direct every response to the group leader. Some students from cultures where structure and authority are highly regarded might have difficulty with this expectation. For example, Thu, a Vietnamese student, tended to speak only in her group when the leader specifically addressed her. She told the counselor that in her culture persons of authority are highly regarded and a person only talks when they are asked to speak.

GUIDELINES FOR MULTICULTURAL GROUP COUNSELORS

An effective multicultural group leader is the key to a successful multicultural group. The effective group leader must not only be sensitive to the distinct cultural differences between members but must also be aware and knowledgeable of personal cultural biases and prejudices. Furthermore, group leaders must value diversity and be willing to accept the attitudes and beliefs of the group members about other racial/ethnic groups as well as various perceptions about American society.

Group counselors within the school setting must be able to facilitate the multicultural and/or ethnic identity development of group members. This can best be done by understanding and acknowledging the reality that many ethnic minority students are socialized within a society in which minorities have a history of suffering from prejudice and discrimination and by understanding the concepts of powerlessness and *White privilege.* White privilege is the systemic, oftentimes unearned, advantage that White individuals possess because of their skin color. Group counselors also facilitate the counseling process by encouraging group members to explore their ethnic and racial heritages and experiences. The group leader should be able to help group members develop group norms that reflect the various cultural values and perspectives of the group members. For example, students from cultures where persons of authority are considered wise and insightful might develop a group norm of never interrupting the group leader when the leader is talking. Essentially, it is imperative that school counselors encourage group members to explore and examine their own personal or interpersonal issues within the context of a multicultural student population. To illustrate this, in a group designed for enhancing the self-concept of sixth graders, a Korean student might explore the Korean ethnic heritage and discuss it within the context of a predominately White school and community. This exercise would further enhance the identity of this student as a Korean living in the community.

In addition to being able to help students facilitate their own multicultural and ethnic identity development, group leaders must be cognizant of the tendency to stereotype. Stereotyping is the process of using rigid preconceptions to describe and understand all members of a particular group, regardless of the variations that exist within that group. When school counselors act on these preconceptions, they approach culturally different students in groups monolithically, using a dominant, inaccurate point of view. The following example illustrates this point:

Clara, an elementary school counselor, initiated group counseling for fourth-grade students who have a low self-concept. The group consisted of two White girls, one African American girl, two White boys, and one African American boy. Group sessions centered on highlighting the strengths and talents of the group members. One activity required students to draw pictures of themselves performing an activity that they were good at. Maleek, the African American male group member, drew a picture of himself playing soccer. When Maleek showed his picture to the group, the counselor said, "Maleek, I'll bet that's a picture of you playing basketball!" Maleek appeared irritated and remarked, "Why does everyone think I play basketball?"

Some group counselors tend to combat stereotyping by acting as if all of the students in a group are the same, that is, by attempting to be color-blind. This is also inappropriate because it shows a lack of respect by not acknowledging a group member's cultural/ethnic identity. Take, for example, Bill, a high school counselor. Bill initiated a group for eleventh graders to introduce them to several different colleges. Bill decided to select colleges that most White students would want to attend. In one of the groups, a Hispanic student complained to Bill that he did not include any colleges or universities with large numbers of Hispanic students. Bill, noticeably upset, exclaimed, "I wanted to introduce the same schools to everyone. I didn't want to separate the colleges according to their ethnic minority student percentages!" Although Bill's intentions were well-meaning, introducing schools of varying types and student populations would have been more appropriate. Just as students differ with regard to race and ethnicity, so do their choices in colleges. By avoiding issues pertaining to race and ethnicity, Bill failed to respect those students and the colleges that are different from the norm.

In addition to their own stereotyping, group counselors must also be able to recognize and challenge stereotyping by group members when it occurs (e.g., group members assuming that an African American male student enjoys basketball or group members assuming that an Asian student is talented in math). The group leader should immediately acknowledge and correct the stereotype. Students should then be encouraged to discuss the damaging effects of acting on stereotypes: "Was this assumption fair to Maleek? How do you think he felt, especially if he does not like to play basketball?"

SCREENING, SELECTION, AND PREPARATION OF POTENTIAL GROUP MEMBERS

The screening and selection of group members is essential to the success of a counseling group in schools. It is necessary for school counselors to select students who are capable of successfully working in a group and, at the same time, will benefit from group counseling. The cultural beliefs that students have about counseling must be considered because group members must be willing to examine a presenting problem and experiment with new solutions to that problem. A Taiwanese student who has difficulty discussing his problem with other students due to cultural beliefs should either be seen individually or referred to another source of help (e.g., clergy within the student's culture or a counselor with the same ethnic background). In a screening interview, it is important for the school counselor to explain the purpose of the group in a manner the student can understand. This is especially important for students whose first language is not English. If language is seen as a barrier during the screening interview, it will probably be a concern in the group interaction. During the screening interview, the counselor should determine if a student might feel more comfortable in a group that is ethnically and/or linguistically similar.

Factual information about a student's presenting problem and/or current situation within a cultural context is also important to assess during the screening interview. School counselors should ask prospective group members questions not only about their presenting problems but also how their culture affects their concerns. An immigrant from El Salvador being screened for a friendship group might be asked, "How has emigrating to the United States influenced or affected your ability to make friends?" The member's response to this question would allow the school counselor to gain insight into how the culture and past experiences impact on the student's friendship concerns.

It is also important to ask ethnic minority group members to discuss their beliefs about counseling, particularly group counseling. Questions related to their expectations of the group and perceptions of group counseling may provide the group leader with useful information on which to base group activities and group structure. It may also help the counselor screen individuals whose expectations are unrealistic or culturally incongruent with the counselor's approach to group counseling.

In addition to screening potential group members, it is crucial for school counselors to prepare all group members for the group experience. Group preparation can consist of providing information about the goals, techniques, and expectations for group counseling. During the screening interview, a school counselor might examine the goals and expectations with regard to the students' belief systems. For example, a counselor might indicate that support and participation are valued in group counseling and could ask the group, "How would you show support to Min Chu? How do you receive support from your family? Peer group?" A discussion of the responses to these types of questions can give a group member some idea of what the group will be like, and it helps the counselor understand the student's ability to achieve the goals of the group as well as provides information on the student's style of interaction.

GROUP COMPOSITION

Counseling groups in schools may be racially or ethnically homogeneous or heterogeneous. Homogeneous groups consist of members from similar ethnic or racial backgrounds. For instance, a school counselor might initiate a group for African American girls or a group for Latino boys. Heterogeneous groups, on the other hand, consist of members who represent various ethnic/racial groups. It is important to remember that there can be heterogeneity within homogeneous groups. A homogeneous group of Latino girls could be diverse in terms of socioeconomic background and ethnic designation (e.g., Mexican, Puerto Rican, Cuban). School counselors, therefore, must be cognizant of both commonalities and differences among members of a presumably homogeneous group. Every group is heterogeneous in some way. This writer feels that there is an appropriate time for using both types of groups. A rationale is offered for when a racially homogeneous group is most effective and when a racially heterogeneous group is most effective.

Rationale for Homogeneous Groups

Ethnically or racially homogeneous groups typically provide students with an opportunity to explore their racial/ethnic identity. This is usually true because members are more apt to share cultural experiences and express their questions regarding the development of their identities. In addition to providing a place for members to share identity conflicts, ethnically homogeneous counseling groups tend to inspire more immediate trust and group cohesion. These groups may have less conflict, more mutual support, and better attendance.

One possible pitfall of ethnically homogeneous groups is that the leader and members may assume similarities and deemphasize the differences among members. For example, a group leader might focus primarily on the ethnic background of a group of Native American sixth graders and not acknowledge their various family traditions, socioeconomic backgrounds, or gender identity issues. In addition to overlooking differences, stereotyping of ethnic group characteristics might ultimately cause a homogeneous group to be less productive and more superficial. A school counselor might initiate a group for African American fourth-grade girls who are struggling with self-esteem issues. It is important for the school counselor not to assume that these girls possess stereotypical characteristics of African American women, such as living in a single-mother-headed household, having a low socioeconomic status, or having a sassy personality. School counselors must acknowledge differences in group members and the significance of these differences in terms of how the members view themselves, their views of their own and other groups, their views of the dominant group, and how they function in school. Therefore, school counselors who lead homogeneous racial/ethnic groups need to acknowledge similarities and differences, as well as strengths and vulnerabilities, of group members so that they can clarify relevant issues of identity.

Intelligent Black Males (IBM) Mentoring Group: An Example of a Racially Homogeneous Group for Elementary-Aged Black Males

To illustrate the aforementioned elements of a homogeneous group in schools, a group for Black male students in an elementary school will be described in this section. Although this group counseling model targets a specific group, many of its components have relevance to all students.

Data on the status of African American boys is alarming. Black male students, for example, are far more likely than other groups to be placed in general education and vocational high school curricular tracks than in an academic track. They are three times more likely to be placed in special education classes than in gifted and talented classes, and Black male students are suspended from school more frequently and for longer periods of time than other ethnic/gender groups (Lee, 1992). This troubling profile is further compounded by the fact that teachers, counselors, and administrators exhibit lower expectations for Black males. For these reasons, it is critical for counselors to implement programs and provide opportunities for Black male students to maximize their potential.

To address the need to empower young Black males, this writer developed a mentoring program for Black male students (grades 3–5) at a local elementary school where ethnic minority students (i.e., Black and Hispanic) were performing disproportionately lower on achievement tests. The initial efforts were aimed at raising self-respect, promoting racial/ethnic pride, and overcoming the obstacles to their educational needs. The program, based on the work of Lee (1992), included two components: mentoring and group counseling. Mentoring, the first component, consisted of matching the boys with a Black male mentor from the community. The mentors, who were screened for participation in the program, were required to mentor one boy for the entire school year. The mentors met with the boys at least once a week and accompanied the boys on cultural field trips (e.g., Blacks in the Wax

Museum, tour of the home of Frederick Douglass). The overall goal of the mentoring component was to provide the boys with an opportunity to interact with a positive Black male role model on a consistent basis. The group counseling component consisted of a six-week group counseling module implemented by the school counselor and a teacher. An overview of the group format is presented here.

Goals for Group Counseling

1. To improve the academic achievement of African American males (grades 3–5) by instilling in the boys a sense of ethnic pride and self-confidence.
2. To enhance the self-concept of African American males by developing within them a sense of ethnic pride.
3. To assist African American male students in exploring possible career and personal goals.

Participants.   The Black boys in the Intelligent Black Male (IBM) Mentoring Program were required to participate in a six-week group. The sessions were held after school from 3:30 to 4:15 P.M. in the school counselor's office. No more than six boys were in a group at one time and the groups were divided according to grade level. Third-grade boys were in one group, and fourth- and fifth-grade boys were in another group. The co-leaders of this group were the school counselor, who is an African American woman, and an African American male teacher.

Before the first session, the group leaders met with prospective group members and their parents. This program orientation was needed in order to explain the purpose and nature of the group as well as the importance of regular attendance. Confidentiality and the limits to parent feedback were explained and group leaders stressed the importance of building trust. Throughout the orientation, the boys and their parents were encouraged to ask questions. Parent permission slips were signed at the conclusion of the orientation.

Next, an outline of the group sessions for the third-, fourth-, and fifth-grade boys was provided. Session topics could vary according to the needs and grade level of the group members.

SESSION 1: GLAD TO BE ME!
Session Goals

1. To enhance the participants' self-esteem by highlighting their unique personalities.
2. To develop group rules.
3. To begin to develop a sense of cohesiveness between the boys and group leaders.

Materials Needed

Group rules chart, chart paper or chalkboard

Procedure

The group leader began by explaining the purpose and goals of the group. Members were asked what they expected of the group. Next the group members were asked to introduce themselves by stating their names and an animal that best describes their personality and why. For example, "My name is Jared and my personality is like a lion because I am strong and courageous." After the introductions, standard group rules were discussed. The standard rules were

1. Be respectful of others and self.
2. Keep everything in the group confidential.
3. Listen to others.

Group members had the opportunity to add other rules. Examples of additional rules included don't joke around, speak so that others will hear you, and keep focused on the session's topic(s).

SESSION 2: WHEN I GROW UP
Session Goal
1. To explore future goals and expectations and what it will take to realize them.
2. To highlight the relationship between present academic achievement and future goals.

Materials Needed
Chart paper or chalkboard

Procedure
1. Introduce the concept of the twenty-first century. Explain the significance of the start of a new century. Stress the fact that they will be young men in the twenty-first century.
2. Initiate a group discussion that includes the following questions:
   - How old will you be in 2010, 2020, 2030, and so on?
   - Where do you think you will be living in those years?
   - Will you be married? Have children? What kind of job will you have?
   - How can doing well in school now help you when you are grown up in the twenty-first century?
   - What things are you learning in school now that will help you in the twenty-first century?

SESSION 3: DEALING WITH DIFFICULT SITUATIONS
Session Goals
1. To have group members examine the dynamics of the academic and social problems they confront as students.
2. To have group members develop appropriate strategies and techniques for confronting these challenges.

Materials Needed
Chart paper or chalkboard

Procedure
Ask members to list problems they have in school. Record these problems on the chalkboard. Lead a group discussion by asking members the following questions:
   - Do you feel that you are treated differently from the Black girls, Latino students, Asian students, White students in the school?
   - Most of the time when you get into trouble in school, is it your fault or do you think that teachers are just picking on you?
   - What can you learn from having difficult times in school?
   - What can you do to keep from having difficult times in school?

(continued)

Continued

> After discussion, role-play confrontations or problems in school and then discuss how the problems can be solved. Possible problem situations could include coping when being teased, feeling left out, peer pressure, and disagreement with teachers.

SESSION 4: AFRICAN AMERICAN HEROES
Session Goal
To examine the boyhood of famous African American men in order to gain a greater appreciation for and understanding of the foundation for their accomplishments.

Materials Needed
Excerpts from biographical information on famous African American men. The *Encyclopedia of African American Heritage* by Susan Altman (this is an excellent source for this activity).

Procedure
1. Read, or have members read, brief biographical information focusing on the boyhood of famous African American men such as Arthur Ashe, Ralph Bunche, Frederick Douglass, Muhammed Ali, W. E. B. Du Bois, Langston Hughes, Jackie Robinson, Bill Cosby, Malcolm X, Martin Luther King, Jr., or Jesse Jackson.
2. Have participants compare their boyhoods to the famous African American men's boyhoods.
3. Lead a discussion on what we can learn from these famous men.

SESSION 5: OCCUPATIONS OF AFRICAN AMERICAN MALES
Session Goals
1. To examine the occupations of contemporary African American men.
2. To highlight the role education plays in obtaining a place in the world of work.

Materials Needed
Occupation questionnaire, chart paper or chalkboard

Procedure
1. Prepare a questionnaire about African American men in various occupational roles.

Do you know an African American man who is an auto mechanic?	Yes	No
Do you know an African American man who is a dentist?	Yes	No
Do you know an African American man who is a teacher?	Yes	No
Do you know an African American man who is a pilot?	Yes	No
Do you know an African American man who is a doctor?	Yes	No
Do you know an African American man who is a musician?	Yes	No
Do you know an African American who is a custodian?	Yes	No
Do you know an African American man who is a nurse?	Yes	No
Do you know an African American man who is an accountant?	Yes	No
Do you know an African American man who is an engineer?	Yes	No

2. Have members complete the questionnaire. When they are finished, total the number of people who know men in each category. Discuss the following question: "When these men were your age, do you think they were good students in school? Why?"

3. Have group members discuss which subjects one would have to be good at to be a success in each of these categories.
4. Remind members that the next session is the last session.

SESSION 6: I BELIEVE I CAN FLY
Session Goal
To synthesize group members' learning and experiences from the program into a personal plan.

Materials Needed
Chart paper or chalkboard, blank paper for personal action plan

Procedure
1. Discuss with the participants the meaning of school success. What is it that you want to achieve in school? How are you going to achieve that success? Ask the participants to complete the following statements:
   When I am in school I will _____ .
   When I am at home I will _____ .
2. Have each person complete a personal action plan with his ideas for school success.
3. Have both the group member and his mentor sign the sheet. Share copies of the plan with parents and teachers. Ask each member to share with the group why he feels that he will be a success in school.
4. As a final activity, have the group attempt to compose their own rap about academic success.

Although the IBM group is designed for African American male students, it can be modified for students of other ethnic backgrounds. It should be remembered that the goal of this type of homogeneous group is to provide students with an environment where they can build cohesion and universality. The group was successful with co-leaders, but it can be implemented with one leader. It is important, however, that at least one leader of this group be an African American male.

Rationale for Heterogeneous Groups

Racially and ethnically mixed groups in schools reflect not only our society's race relations but also race relations in the school. Heterogeneous groups may reenact racial dynamics among students that ultimately provide the school counselor with valuable information for possible schoolwide programs and classroom guidance. Members of an ethnically/racially heterogeneous group have the opportunity to develop more understanding of themselves and others. Most important, they will develop skills in relating across differences.

Racially/ethnically mixed counseling groups present challenges for group leaders and group members. First, in groups where ethnic minority members are underrepresented, conscious and unconscious group dynamics can create a social microcosm of unproductive racial interactions that taint cross-racial relationships. For instance, being the only ethnic minority member in a group may make it difficult for that member to share experiences with others or cause that member to feel isolated. A student who is the only visible minority student in a group may feel inferior, feel compelled to agree with the majority, or may question his or her own judgment. When leading mixed racial/ethnic groups, it is imperative for school counselors to encourage mutual empathy among members and facilitate trust and safety among minority members so that they will feel safe to share experiences they do not usually discuss in mixed groups. It is equally important for group leaders to encourage White group members to listen and accept the experiences of ethnic minority group members.

Acculturation Issues in Group Counseling.   Acculturation is the process that includes changes an individual undertakes as a result of interaction with a second culture. This process occurs in the following stages: (1) the precontact phase in which each independent cultural group has its own characteristics, (2) the contact phase in which groups interact with each other, (3) the conflict phase when pressure is exerted on the nondominant group to change in order to fit in with the majority group, (4) the crisis phase when the conflict comes to a head, and (5) the adaptation phase during which relations between the two groups are stabilized (Berry and Kim, 1988). The specific stage/phase of acculturation can significantly influence a student's receptiveness to group counseling. For example, an Asian student in the conflict stage might be less apt to participate in group counseling because of his/her culture's values against self-disclosure. In contrast, a Latino student who is clearly in the adaptation phase would likely be more receptive to group counseling with diverse students.

Ethnicity of the Group Leader.   Group leaders of any ethnic background will experience challenges when leading mixed racial groups. Counselors are often confronted with issues related to their philosophical and/or political perceptions that are in conflict with group members' beliefs. A Hispanic group member might disclose to the group that she is distrustful of all White people and that she believes the entire school system consists of racist individuals. The White group leader in this situation must validate, but not necessarily agree with, the member's perceptions and be prepared to process or discuss these perceptions with group members. White group counselors are sometimes challenged because of ethnic minority student perceptions that their knowledge of other cultures is not credible. Essentially, it is necessary for White school counselors to become aware of their vulnerability to imposing their own cultural perspectives and values on ethnic minority students.

Ethnic minority school counselors might experience other challenges. Ethnic minority group leaders might experience aggression from both White and ethnic minority students because of internalized perceptions that ethnic minority individuals lack the skills to be leaders. Inasmuch as ethnic minority persons are often stereotyped as not occupying authority positions, it is difficult for many students to acknowledge and respect their authority. Ethnic minority school counselors might also have difficulty openly discussing the significance of their own racial and ethnic identity. As a result, ethnic minority group leaders will often choose to ignore or avoid racial topics when interacting with students. This is not helpful to students; counselors can model how to discuss topics related to race and ethnicity. This modeling of positive race dialogue in the group setting builds the foundation for positive race relations in the classroom and other school settings (e.g., the playground, the cafeteria).

Group Guidance Related to Race and Ethnicity Issues

Group guidance or classroom guidance is a wonderful avenue for school counselors to address race and ethnicity issues in the schools. Group guidance, unlike group counseling, is used to relay information or to instruct a large group of students. The format for group guidance sessions is very similar to a regular lesson, in which objectives are formulated and activities provided as a means to achieving the objectives. One of the benefits to implementing group guidance is that the counselor is able to interact with large numbers of students. Group guidance is an excellent means for school counselors to address cultural sensitivity and issues pertaining to diversity. The counselor can help students become more culturally sensitive by implementing group guidance sessions that are focused on the following objectives: (1) accepting and appreciating differences in others, (2) learning accurate terminology (e.g., racism, prejudice, ethnicity, oppression) when discussing issues related to cultural sensitivity, (3) exploring one's own biases, and (4) learning about diverse cultures and ethnic groups.

Group guidance units related to race are most successful with students in grades 4 and above. The ability to think analytically and abstractly is necessary in order to understand the construct of racism. Counselors should also take care to develop guidance lessons with small-group activities. Student interaction and discussion is perhaps the best avenue for addressing racism and prejudice. For example, students can meet in small groups to talk about their ethnic and/or racial histories. Having students recognize each other's ethnic heritage can help them recognize the uniqueness of different cultural groups and dispel stereotypical beliefs. Many White students will comment that they have no ethnic heritage! When this remark is made, school counselors should encourage them to research their family histories and to talk to grandparents or older family members to gain historical family information. They can investigate such things as where their ancestors came from and why they came to America. Gathering this information in combination with discussing their race of origin helps students develop a sense of racial identity.

School counselors can also use group guidance to discuss the impact of racism and prejudiced behavior in our society. Lessons regarding such controversial topics as racism and prejudice should be well planned and geared to students in grades 4 and above. Group guidance can include the following activities:

1. Case studies related to students of color and racism. Students are given cases and asked to discuss the feelings of characters and ways to solve the problem of dealing with prejudiced behavior.
2. Define stereotypes and brainstorm stereotypes that students have or have heard about different groups of people. Discuss the danger of stereotypes.
3. Interviews of classmates about their experiences with prejudices and biases. This activity is then followed by a group discussion.
4. Invite people of color from the community to discuss their personal racial/ethnic histories. This activity can be done in a large auditorium with 60 to 65 students. Students should have prepared questions for the panelists about dealing with prejudice, racism, and oppression.

Counselors should never attempt to introduce topics dealing with race unless they are comfortable discussing the topic themselves and comfortable with the possible discomfort that others might feel Many members of a faculty will want the school counselor to water down race discussions and only explore different cultural groups. For example, the school counselor might be asked to implement classroom guidance lessons that feature a particular ethnic group each week. It is assumed that by learning about the foods, clothing, and cultural artifacts of an ethnic group, stereotypes and biased beliefs will somehow be dispelled. Many schools even choose to sponsor such events as Cultural Awareness Days and International Nights. These events are wonderful and enable people to feel good, but they avoid issues related to discrimination, oppression, and racism. Only a few schools choose activities that openly address racism in the school community. Activities such as parent discussion groups about developing a positive racial/ethnic identity and workshops on how to talk to children about racism are excellent avenues for schools to involve parents in the process of combating prejudice and racism.

The first step in the process of combating racism is for coulselors to see themselves as racial beings. Counselors must openly discuss the manifestations of racism, prejudice, and discrimination with colleagues and students. Books that school counselors can read before addressing racism in their guidance activities are *Race Matters* by Cornel West (1993), and *Pedagogy of the Oppressed* by Pablo Freire (1999), and *Why Are All the Black Kids Sitting Together in the Cafeteria? And Other Conversations About Race* by Beverly Tatum (1999).

BECOMING A MULTICULTURALLY COMPETENT GROUP LEADER

Becoming a more culturally sensitive and multiculturally competent group counselor is a developmental and methodical process. In the writer's opinion, there are activities that one must participate in to ensure growing toward becoming culturally sensitive. Those activities include (1) reading literature and attending workshops, seminars, and classes that focus primarily on other cultures and ethnic groups. A school counselor should attend at least two conference sessions per year on multicultural issues. Counselors should also read at least two books a year that are written by and about a cultural group other than their own. By studying and discussing the history of minority groups, a person becomes aware of dangerous stereotypes and the manifestations of being historically oppressed. (2) Identifying one's own racial and ethnic origin(s) and the privileges or liabilities that are associated with having that ethnic origin. Recognizing the privileges of one's race often assists in understanding oppression. (3) Reading the research and literature pertaining to the ethnocentrism in mental health disciplines. (4) Visiting the home or church of someone from a different ethnic, cultural, or religious group.

It is essential for group counselors in schools to challenge not only the content (e.g., biases, prejudicial beliefs) of what they are thinking but also the way and process by which they act on that content. In addition to becoming aware of cultural biases and beliefs, school counselors must have adequate knowledge of other ethnic/racial group norms and perspectives. More specifically, school counselors must be aware of the institutionalized racism and ethnocentrism existing in schools as these are manifested in low achievement levels of ethnic minority students, disproportionate numbers of ethnic minority students placed in special education tracks, and an increasing number of ethnic minority students who choose to drop out. Furthermore, because of the lack of attention to many ethnic minority issues, group leaders need to actively seek out literature, information, experts, workshops, seminars, and courses that address unexplored areas of education (e.g., racism in education, White privilege in education).

In order to continually assess one's multicultural competence, the following checklist can be used by school counselors. Those items in which the counselor rates competence as *somewhat competent* or *not competent* are areas of needed improvement and should be addressed immediately.

SCHOOL COUNSELOR'S MULTICULTURAL COMPETENCE CHECKLIST*
(1) Not competent, (2) Somewhat competent, (3) Competent, (4) Extremely competent

1. I can discuss my own ethnic/cultural heritage　　　　　　　　1　2　3　4
2. I am aware of how my cultural background and experiences have influenced my attitudes about psychological processes.　　1　2　3　4
3. I am able to discuss how my culture has influenced the way I think.　1　2　3　4
4. I can recognize when my attitudes, beliefs and values are interfering with providing the services to my students.　　1　2　3　4
5. I verbally communicate my acceptance of culturally different students.　　1　2　3　4
6. I nonverbally communicate my acceptance of culturally different students.　　1　2　3　4
7. I can discuss models of Racial Identity Development.　　1　2　3　4
8. I can identify the cultural basis of my communication style.　　1　2　3　4
9. I can identify my negative and positive emotional reactions toward persons of other racial and ethnic groups.　　1　2　3　4
10. I can identify my reactions that are based on stereotypical beliefs about different ethnic groups.　　1　2　3　4
11. I can discuss within-group differences among ethnic groups (e.g., Puerto Rican student vs. Cuban student).　　1　2　3　4
12. I can discuss how culture affects a student's career choices.　　1　2　3　4
13. I can discuss how culture affects the manifestations of psychological disorders.　　1　2　3　4
14. I can describe the degree to which a counseling approach is appropriate for a specific group of people.　　1　2　3　4
15. I can explain how factors such as poverty and powerlessness have influenced the current conditions of at least two ethnic groups.　1　2　3　4

*Taken from Holcomb-McCoy, C., & Myers, J. (1999). Multicultural competence and counselor training: A national survey. Journal of Counseling and Development, 77, 294–302.

16. I can discuss how the counseling process may conflict with the
cultural values of at least two ethnic groups.   1   2   3   4

17. I can list at least three barriers that prevent ethnic minority students
from using counseling services.   1   2   3   4

18. I can discuss the potential bias of two assessment instruments
frequently used in schools.   1   2   3   4

19. I can anticipate when my helping style is inappropriate for a
culturally different student.   1   2   3   4

20. I can help students determine whether a problem stems from racism
or biases in others.   1   2   3   4

SUMMARY

Ethnic minority students will, in a short time, become a majority of today's public school population. When leading groups in school settings, effective school counselors must be aware of the diversity of students and actively seek to be more culturally knowledgeable and aware. Counselors must recognize their own stereotypical and prejudiced beliefs about other cultures and ethnic groups; realize that traditional theories and techniques of group counseling reflect the majority culture's history, beliefs, and values; and recognize the relationships/dynamics between culturally and ethnically different persons.

The challenge for group counselors in schools is to accurately clarify their own values, acquire knowledge of other cultural groups, recognize racism in educational institutions, work diligently to dispel racism in schools, and learn group counseling strategies that are appropriate for groups with ethnically and culturally dissimilar members. This process is by no means easy. It should be remembered that it takes courage and the initiative to venture outside of one's habitual ways of interpreting and leading groups.

REFERENCES

Berry, J. W., & Kim, U. (1988). Acculturation and mental health. In P. R. Dasen, J. W. Berry, & N. Sartorius (Eds.), *Health and Cross-Cultural Psychology: Toward Applications.* Newbury Park, CA: Sage, 207–236.

Freire, P., Holcomb-McCoy, C., & Myers, J. E. (1999). Multicultural competence and counselor training: A national survey. *Journal of Counseling and Development, 77,* 294–302.

Lee, C. C. (1992). *Empowering Young Black Males.* Ann Arbor, MI: ERIC/CAPS.

Tatum, B. D. (1999). *Why Are All the Black Kids Sitting Together in the Cafeteria? And Other Conversations About Race.* New York: Basic Books.

CHAPTER NINE

GROUP PLANS

The cornerstone of group counseling is the plan that is developed to outline the contents of each of the proposed group sessions. A group plan, or game plan, is equivalent to a lesson plan used by teachers to indicate their daily curriculum. Without a group plan, the inexperienced group leader has little idea of where the group is really headed and almost no reference point for how the group is expected to achieve its objective. Referring back to the road map analogy, group counseling without a group plan is like driving on an unfamiliar highway with no road signs and relying only on sense of direction to end up at the proper destination. Getting lost on a highway will result in a delay in arriving at a destination; group leaders who *get lost* or do not know where they are going can waste students' time and possibly harm five or six students who expected to receive help.

A group plan is not difficult to develop. It should begin with a clear and realistic understanding of the group's objective. Once the topic has been selected, the general objective is easily defined. A divorce group would be directed at helping the members adjust to their new parental arrangement; a social skills group would need to understand what has prevented them from having friends and how they can begin to make friendships. Looking at the objectives of the group, the counselor, as the group leader or facilitator, should ask the obvious question, "How can we get there?" To find the answer means searching for the topics or subgoals that need to be addressed in order to move in the direction of the final goal. A logical point of departure for developing the game plan is to clarify the problem and define terms. For example, to clarify the problem in a stress-management group, the group leader might decide that the first session should present an overview and preview of the topics that will be raised in each of the eight sessions. That would mean defining stress and looking at the causes of stress. In subsequent sessions, the group would examine what stressors are for each group member, how pressure relates to stress, what situations tend to be stressful, how stress can become habitual, and most important, effective ways to manage personal stress.

It is helpful when group leaders can personalize the problem by putting themselves into the situation. In personalizing the problem with a separation/divorce group, an elementary school counselor might think, "Assume I am 10 years old and my parents are divorcing. How might I be feeling? What would I need to understand that could help me deal with my feelings? What attitude should I develop that would help me to adjust to my new home situation? In short, what is it going to take to enable me to cope with a situation over which I have no control?" If a high school group is dealing with the problem of low self-esteem, the group leader could think about a series of questions: "Assume I am a teenager who has low self-esteem. I should have a clear understanding of what self-esteem means and how I really feel about myself. It would be important for me to know why I feel the way I do and what would have to happen that would make me feel better about myself. Is there anything that I like about myself? What changes would I like to see in myself? Do I have any personal goals? How can I go about becoming the person I want to be? What could prevent me from becoming that person? How can I solve my problem? Can I really change?" Self-questions can provide the stimulus for developing the group plan.

Group plans should be based on logical, realistic, and predictable outcomes. They should consist of attainable subgoals as well as both creative and innovative ways to achieve these subgoals. In recognizing the limitation imposed by time and the school setting, the group leader must be aware of the maturity of the group and be careful not to attempt too much or move too rapidly. The group plan for certain remedial groups could follow a sequential development in which a group session builds on the previous group session. In a study skills group, for example, the session that addresses the physical conditions that are conducive to studying should precede the session that looks at strategies for comprehending what has been read. In a friendship skills group, the session dealing with the kinds of attitudes and behavior that prevent the acquisition of friends should follow the session that identifies behaviors that usually result in making and keeping friends. The sequence of the group plan often proceeds in a progressive way so that sessions build on each other.

Support groups, however, do not always involve progressing from one topic to another. Grief/bereavement groups need not be highly structured, and each session does not necessarily build on the previous session. Nevertheless, it is important that there be some plan for grief/bereavement groups that can cover all feelings related to grief and bereavement. On the other hand, a support group for students who are at risk of dropping out of school could be organized in such a way that topics can build on each other. For example, "Last week we talked about the advantages and disadvantages of dropping out of school. Today let's look at the advantages and disadvantages of staying in school." Preventive groups, as in classroom guidance activities, should be structured and planned in a sequential way to allow the counselor to cover the material that has been planned in the time allotted.

GROUP PLANS FOR GROUP COUNSELING

The group plan provides the group leader with a systematic approach to moving a group in the direction of the group's goal. The extent to which a group leader adheres to the group plan varies according to the maturity of the group, the quality of the group's interactions, the cohesiveness of the group, the motivation the group has to move toward the goal, and the experience of the group leader. The group plan is essentially an agenda. At some time during the six or eight sessions, most of the items that are on the agenda should be covered or discussed. Nevertheless, a group leader must be flexible and know when it is advisable to deviate from the proposed session plan. The group leader must exert good judgment and recognize when a discussion that is underway is more beneficial than what was next on the planned agenda. Time is frequently the enemy of the group leader. Group sessions have a time limitation in terms of both the length of time for a session and the number of planned sessions. For this reason, the group leader should not try to plan for more topics than could be covered in a group session. It is, however, better to plan for more than not plan for enough. The size of the group and the quality of interaction often suggest the number of topics that can be discussed in a given session.

The group plan can be divided into four sections. The first section is a statement of purpose, or objectives. It tells what the session is expected to accomplish. The second section looks at the materials that will be used and what needs to be collected prior to the session. Materials, including blank paper, topic-oriented games, posters, construction paper, a chalkboard and chalk, crayons, scissors, or an overhead projector or a video, might be used with all group levels. The third section of the plan details the specific strategies that will be used in a session. Strategies include what the group leader plans to say to the group, group activities, topics for discussion, and homework assignments. The specific strategies address what was stated as the purpose of the session. A brief summary of what was accomplished would conclude the session. This summary would be restated at the opening of the following session as a reminder of what had occurred in the previous meeting and what was being discussed when the session ended.

At the final group meeting, there should be an evaluation of the group experience both in terms of individual growth and the extent to which the group, as a whole, accomplished its objective. Group members would be asked to complete a short evaluation. Teachers would also be asked to evaluate the progress or changes they saw as a result of the group experience. Both evaluations are important to the group leader.

What follows is an example of a group plan for seventh graders who need to improve their self-esteem. It is developed for a middle school setting.

GROUP PLAN FOR DEVELOPING SELF-ESTEEM

Group level: Seventh grade
Number of sessions planned: 8
Number of members: 5 or 6
Gender: Male or female
Time for each session: 35 to 40 minutes
Location of sessions: Counseling conference room
Group leader: Single leader (co-leading is preferred)

PREGROUP PREPARATION
At a screening interview, each prospective member would be told the purpose of the group, the number of times the group would meet, that there would be rules they will be expected to follow, and that one of the most important rules is confidentiality. During the screening interview, the school counselor would briefly indicate how groups function and what is expected of a group member. Essentially, they would be told that they will be expected to listen to what is being said, share their opinions and feelings with the group, show respect to group members, and try to help their fellow members by being a good listener, offering suggestions, and showing friendship. These points would be repeated at the first group meeting for emphasis. If students show interest in becoming members of the group, the prospective members would be asked to have a parent

continued

Continued

sign a permission slip. They would be told the date of the first meeting and that they could not participate in the group until the signed slip was returned. If the slip is not returned before the first meeting, they would not be permitted to be in the group.

SESSION 1
Goals
1. To review the purpose of the group.
2. To introduce group members to each other.
3. To present an "icebreaker" to relax the group.
4. To establish group rules.
5. To have students sign a contract stating they are willing to abide by the rules.
6. To begin talking about self-esteem.

Materials Needed
Chalk and chalkboard
A Rules Agreement
Blank sheets of paper

Specific Strategies
1. Explain why the group was formed and establish group goals.
2. Ask members to introduce themselves by stating their (1) name, (2) name of teacher, (3) some things they have fun doing, (4) some things they don't like to do.
3. Introduce a 10-minute icebreaker. The group leader says, "You are walking along a beach near the water on a hot summer day. As you walk, you are looking down at the sand. You see a bottle that's almost buried in the wet sand. You stop and pick up the bottle. There is a cork in the top of the bottle and when you look inside you see a little statue. You're curious about that little statue. You take the cork out and all of a sudden, the statue starts to move and a genie begins to come out of the bottle. As the genie comes out, he gets larger and larger. You watch as the genie becomes a giant. You are not afraid because the genie is smiling. Finally, the genie is completely out of the bottle. He is wearing a turban and a flowing robe and has a large sword strapped to his side. The genie bows to you and says, "Don't be afraid of me. I want to thank you for letting me out of this bottle. I've been trapped in it for many years, and you are the first person who took the time to take the cork out of the bottle and let me out. Now I will reward you for your kindness by allowing you to have three wishes. You may wish for any three things you would like and I will grant your three wishes." Then say to the group, "If this had happened to you, what would you tell the genie? What are your three wishes?" The group leader should write down each member's wishes to gain insights into the needs and maturity of the members.
4. Explain to the group the importance of having group rules. Prepare, in advance, a Rules Agreement for the members to sign. Ask the group if it would like to include other rules. Write these rules down and distribute copies to each member at the next session. Explain the consequences of breaking a rule.
5. All group members are asked to sign a Rules Agreement:
    I, _____ , have heard and understand the rules that my group will be using throughout our group sessions. I feel all of the rules are important and I understand that breaking a rule can have serious consequences. I promise not to break any of the rules.
    Signed _____ Date _____
    In the event the members cannot write their names, a handshake would suffice.

6. Begin a discussion about self-esteem.
   - Self-esteem is how we feel about ourselves.
   - Self-esteem is also how we think others feel about us.
   - What are some ways we can feel about ourselves?
   - Why do you think we feel the way we do about ourselves?
   - Do you think our self-esteem can change?
   - What would make our self-esteem change?
   - How much do you like yourself ? (Ask members to rate themselves using a seven-point scale with 1 being lowest.) The leader should make note of the number members assign to themselves. This question will be asked again at the last group meeting.
7. Summarize the session.

SESSION 2
Goals
1. To review the summary of the first session.
2. To present a brief icebreaker to relax the group (optional).
3. To continue to discuss self-esteem.
4. To evaluate each member's feelings about personal successes.
5. To begin discussing ways to become successful.

Materials Needed
Chalk and chalkboard

Specific Strategies
1. Review the summary of the first session.
2. Review the group rules.
3. Icebreaker. Who has
   Been to a theme park (e.g., Disneyworld, Busch Gardens, King's Dominion)?
   Played a musical instrument?
   Caught a fish?
   Made something in the kitchen (e.g., brownies, fudge, sandwich, etc.)?
   A dog, a cat, a fish, a bird at home, etc.?
4. Resume the first session's discussion of self-esteem. (See item 6 from the first session.)
5. Ask all members to mention something that made them feel successful.
6. Ask members to name something they would like to accomplish and what they would have to do in order to successfully accomplish it.
7. Summarize the session.

SESSION 3
Goals
1. To encourage each member to set personal goals.
2. To discuss what it takes to be successful.
3. To continue to discuss self-esteem and ways of gaining success.

Materials Needed
A copy of the group's rules

Specific Strategies
1. Review the summary of the second session.
2. Review the group rules, if necessary.

continued

Continued

3. Present a brief icebreaker. Who has
   Flown in an airplane?
   Made a snowman?
   Had a stomachache?
   Slept outside?
   Been to a zoo?
   Been a patient in a hospital?
4. Open a discussion on the characteristics of successful people.
5. Ask members to identify one or more personal goals.
   - What would you like to be able to do?
   - Why would this make you feel better about yourself?
6. Summarize the session.

SESSION 4
Goals
1. To continue discussing personal goals and examining the obstacles that would need to be overcome in order to attain these goals.
2. To continue discussing self-esteem.

Materials Needed
Chalk and chalkboard
A copy of the group's rules
Blank sheets of paper
Predetermined homework assignments for each member

Specific Strategies
1. Review the summary of the previous session.
2. Review the group rules, if necessary.
3. Ask all members to talk about the personal goals they have set.
4. Determine the obstacles members feel they would have to overcome in order to attain the goals they have set for themselves.
5. Assign buddies to form diads. Each member of the diad is asked to help the buddy develop a plan for attaining a personal goal. Allow time for this diad meeting.
6. Buddies will also assist members in finding solutions for obstacles that need to be overcome in order to reach their goal. Write down all suggestions that are offered.
7. Indicate an appropriate assignment for each group member and request that this "homework" be done by the next meeting. Homework should be directed at helping members do something that would approach the goal that they have set. (For example, Bryan wants to get a better grade in English. His homework could be to ask his teacher what he needs to do to get a better grade and then begin to do it.) The homework assignment could come from things the buddy discussed with the member.
8. Summarize the session.

SESSION 5
Goals
1. To review the personal goals for each member.
2. To check on the group's homework assignments.
3. To talk about motivation in general and motivation to accomplish personal goals in particular.

Materials Needed
Blank sheets of paper

Specific Strategies
1. Summarize the previous session.
2. Quickly review the group rules, if necessary.
3. Check on homework. Praise those who were successful and help those who were not successful in completing their homework assignment.
4. Open a discussion on motivation.
   - What is motivation?
   - Why is motivation important?
   - What are you motivated to do?
5. Discuss the importance of being highly motivated to succeed. One way of presenting motivation is to differentiate the *should* level of motivation from the *will* level of motivation, from the *must* level of motivation. The *should* level only tells us that we know right from wrong. This does not often motivate us to change. Everyone knows that we *should* do what our parents ask us to do and we *should* do our homework, but some students don't listen to their parents or do their homework. Allow the group to mention other things we *should* do. The *will* level is like a promise. When we do what we promise we *will* do, we get respect. You may have said, "I *will* keep my room neat or I *will* go to bed when my parents tell me." Unfortunately we don't always do what we promise we will do. Allow the group to mention other things they have said they *will* do. The *must level* is very different from the *should* and *will* levels. The *must* level has a consequence that we don't want. The must level has an *or else* attached to it. For example, you *must* listen to your parents or else you will be punished. You *must* do your homework *or else* you will not get good grades and you might not be allowed to watch television. You *must* brush your teeth *or else* your teeth will get cavities and you could have a toothache. Or, you could say to someone who smokes cigarettes, "You *must* stop smoking *or else* you will become addicted to nicotine and you could develop lung cancer." In order to be highly motivated, we need to be at the *must* level.
6. Refer to the *must level* of motivation and determine the consequences for members who will not be successful in attaining their personal goals. In other words, what is the *or else* if they do not attain their personal goals?
7. Summarize the session.

SESSION 6
Goals
1. To continue to discuss motivation to succeed.
2. To continue to look at personal goals.
3. To examine a model for problem solving.
4. To discuss risk taking and why it is sometimes hard to take a risk.

Materials Needed
Chalk and chalkboard
Blank sheets of paper

Specific Strategies
1. Review the summary of the previous session.
2. Quickly review group rules, if necessary.

continued

Continued

3. Continue previous session discussion on topics of motivation, goal setting, and overcoming obstacles to attaining the goals.
4. Look at a problem-solving model. For example:
   - Develop a clear statement of the problem/concern.
   - Identify what the ideal outcome would be.
   - Define a realistic outcome.
   - Brainstorm for all possible solutions to the problem/concern.
   - Eliminate the solutions that are unrealistic, impractical, and impossible to achieve.
   - Arrive at one or two workable solutions to the problem/concern and eventually decide on a single solution.
   - Determine all of the things that must be done to accomplish this solution.
5. Talk about risks and why it can be difficult to take a risk.
   - You could fail in doing what you try.
   - You could end up feeing rejected, embarrassed, sorry you tried, or end up feeling worse.
   - You might not know what you should say or what you should do when you take a risk.
   - You don't feel ready to take a risk.
6. Talk about the consequences of not taking risks.
   - Nothing changes.
   - You could become disappointed or angry with yourself for not trying.
   - Things can go from bad to worse.
7. As a homework assignment, ask all members to come up with a solution to one thing that they *must* do in order to feel better about themselves.
8. Remind the group that there are only two more sessions.
9. Summarize the session.

SESSION 7
Goals

1. To check on the progress of each member.
2. To review the concepts of motivation and problem solving.
3. To check on the homework assignment.

Specific Strategies

1. Review the summary of the previous session.
2. Briefly review group rules, if necessary.
3. Check on the homework assignment. Did any member take a risk?
4. Check on the progress each member has made on attaining personal goals.
5. Review information about self-esteem, personal success, motivation, and problem solving.
6. Remind the group that the next session will be the last meeting.
7. Summarize the session.

SESSION 8
Goals

1. To review the group's goals.
2. To indicate progress shown by specific members of the group.
3. To identify what each person needs to continue to work on.
4. To evaluate the eight sessions.

5. To terminate the group and arrange for follow-up.
6. To have a 5-minute party.

Materials Needed
Blank sheets of paper
Member evaluation form
Healthy refreshments
Evaluation forms for group members
Evaluation forms to be given to teachers

Specific Strategies
1. Review the topics covered in the previous sessions.
2. Examine the progress made by individual group members.
3. Knowing that the group will not be meeting again, ask members to suggest a homework assignment for themselves that they can work on after the group ends.
4. Using the question from the first session, ask each member, "How much do you like yourself?" On a seven-point scale with 1 being the lowest, record the number and compare it with the number given at the first session.
5. Ask each member to evaluate personal and group progress. The group leader could say, "Because this will be our last session, it is important that I learn if this group accomplished what we set out to accomplish. Please answer each of these questions by putting a circle around either the word *yes, no,* or *maybe.*" The group leader then distributes a sheet on which the following questions are written. The group leader reads each question to the group.
    1. Do you have a better understanding of what self-esteem means? Yes No Maybe
    2. As a result of having been in this group, are you more aware of what you can do and those things you need to improve in? Yes No Maybe
    3. As a result of having been in this group, have you been able to define your personal goals more clearly? Yes No Maybe
    4. As a result of having been in this group, do you have a better understanding of the things that have prevented you from reaching your personal goals? Yes No Maybe
    5. As a result of having been a member of this group, do you have a better understanding of what is meant by motivation? Yes No Maybe
    6. Do you have a good understanding of what is meant by a *must* level of motivation? Yes No Maybe
    7. As a result of having been in this group, do you feel you can do a better job of problem solving? Yes No Maybe
    8. Do you feel you accomplished something as a result of having been a member of this group? Yes No Maybe
    9. Do you feel more prepared to take good risks? Yes No Maybe
    10. Would you want to be included in another group some day? Yes No Maybe
    If there were things about this group that you did not like, please indicate what they were.

_____ _____ _____

Members are asked to arrange for an individual meeting with the counselor in about two weeks to report on their last homework assignment and overall feelings about attaining their personal goal.

An evaluation form should also be given to the teachers of the group members.

continued

Continued

TEACHER EVALUATION

An eight-session group dealing with self-esteem issues has just concluded. As you know, your students Marsha, Fred, and Eleanor were in this group. I would appreciate your input as to their personal growth and any change you may have noticed in these students as a result of the group experience. Your answers to this evaluation will be treated as confidential. They will be used only to help the guidance and counseling program assess the effectiveness of this group and to make any needed changes for future groups. Any comments will be especially appreciated.

Your name _____ Grade _____ Date _____

Using the following scale from 1 to 5, rate each of your students.

5 = a lot of change/improvement
4 = much change/improvement
3 = some change/improvement
2 = little change/improvement
1 = no change/improvement
0 = cannot say/no opportunity to observe

Re: Marsha

_____ Growth and progress in matters pertaining to self-esteem
Comments:
_____
_____

Re: Fred

_____ Growth and progress in matters pertaining to self-esteem
Comments:
_____
_____

Re: Eleanor

_____ Growth and progress pertaining to self-esteem issues
Comments:
_____
_____

Please indicate any comments that may have been made by these students pertaining to the group or group sessions that you feel free to share.
_____

If you are interested in talking about this group, let me know and I will arrange to meet with you. Your cooperation in making the group counseling program successful is greatly appreciated. Please return this evaluation form to me or put it in my mailbox.

_____ , NCC
Sixth-Grade Counselor

GROUP PLAN FOR ACADEMIC UNDERACHIEVERS

This section discusses an eight-session plan for students who have been identified as not achieving their academic potential. Students can be said to be underachieving when there is a discrepancy between the student's intelligence, as measured by a standardized intelligence test, and academic achievement, as measured by a standardized test of achievement. Even in the absence of the necessary standardized measurements, experienced teachers are often able to identify those students whom they feel should be getting higher grades.

There are several explanations for academic underachievement. One explanation is a policy of social promotions. Social promotion is a common practice in many school systems. To illustrate, a fourth-grade student who is functioning below grade level would be *promoted* or, more accurately, *placed* in the fifth grade because of age, rather than readiness. This results in a student who will not be able to function at a fifth-grade level because the student would be lacking the readiness, or fundamental skills needed, for being successful with the fifth-grade curriculum. Being socially promoted to the fifth grade would, undoubtedly, please the child, and it may please the parents, but being placed in a learning situation that is too advanced would not be in the child's best interest. Social promotion also rewards the student who has not earned promotion and reinforces the behaviors that contributed to the lack of academic achievement. As social promotions continue year after year, the student falls farther behind academic expectations and eventually is so far behind that catching up may not be possible without receiving extensive tutoring. It should not be surprising that these students become dropouts when they reach the legal age of quitting school.

Intervention with students who are underachieving should be initiated as soon as the problem is recognized. Underachievement can usually be identified in the elementary grades. It is not too late to intervene at the junior high or middle school levels, but it can be too late once the child is in high school.

Underachievement is seen in students who have a negative attitude toward school and lack the motivation to succeed academically. What makes underachievement an unfortunate problem is that these are children with ability and the potential to be successful in school. The group plan that follows addresses seven reasons that underlie the causes of the problem. These reasons are

1. Personal problems. Children who underachieve often have personal problems that distract them from attaining their academic potential, which includes having a negative attitude toward school.
2. Values. Education, as offered in schools, is not sufficiently valued.
3. Motivation. The motivation to succeed in school is low or lacking.
4. Home environment. The home environment can produce underachievement when one or more of the following conditions are present:
   a. Education is not sufficiently valued by parents.
   b. Home does not offer the child an adequate support system for being successful in school.
   c. Parents are unaware of their role in helping their child succeed in school.
   d. Parents are unable to help their child succeed in school.

    e. Communication between the school and home is inadequate.

    f. Parental attitudes toward school are negative, which rubs off on the child.

5. Peer pressure. When a student has friends or identifies with a group that rejects school, it is unlikely that the child will acquire different attitudes. Peer pressure can produce underachievement when any of the following conditions are present:

    a. The peer group does not value education, and academic achievement is a low priority.

    b. The child elects to adopt the values of the peer group.

    c. The peer group is involved in behaviors that can affect ability and school performance, such as truancy or the use of illicit drugs.

    d. The peer group discourages academic success through ridicule and other verbal punishing.

6. Priorities. School attendance and school performance are not high priorities for the student. Frequent excuses given by students who are underachieving are that school is boring or what is being taught lacks relevance.

7. Teacher attitudes. The attitude of teachers toward children who underachieve can also become a contributing factor. Teaching a student who has a negative attitude toward school and also shows oppositional behavior becomes a huge challenge for a teacher. Understandably, teachers often lose patience with underachieving students when they also disrupt the class, defy or reject the teacher's authority, or refuse to cooperate with a teacher's expectations. Regardless of the size of the class, there is only so much time a teacher can devote to a single student. Students who show an indifference to learning do not encourage teachers to take time away from those students who show an interest in learning. At some point, many teachers give up trying to change resistant attitudes. This serves to exacerbate the problem of underachievement.

    The group counseling that is planned for these students differs somewhat from the usual eight-session model. It is a more intensive, multifaceted model requiring parental and teacher involvement and if used in a middle, junior high, or high school, should be co-led. It requires each of the members to attend eight 40-minute group sessions and also four 30-minute individual sessions. There would be six members in the group divided into two teams, three members in Team A and three members in Team B. The group members would have the option of naming their teams. One co-leader would be responsible for conducting the two individual counseling sessions with Team A, and the other co-leader would conduct the two individual counseling sessions with Team B. In the fifth week, the leaders would switch teams. In this way, both co-leaders will have had one-on-one contact with all members.

    The purpose of the individual counseling sessions would be to (1) get ongoing member reactions to the group, (2) discuss the progress seen in the classroom from teacher input, (3) examine personal concerns that could be contributing to the academic problem, and (4) reinforce what is being discussed in the group. One of the subgoals of the leaders would be to encourage the group to become cohesive. The group would make plans to have lunch together at least three times a week, and the group leaders should join them for lunch at least once a week. There would be homework assignments that would require some group collaboration, and members would be encouraged to refer to each other by name during the sessions, for example, "Don, I don't agree with you" or "I feel the same way, Joe." Frequent use of group members' names would aid in the bonding of the group. A photograph of the group and leaders would be taken at the first group session and would be posted in the group counseling location during all of the group sessions. Each member would be asked to sign the photograph and copies would be distributed to group members after the last session.

One parent, preferably both parents, would have to agree to actively participate in the program. Parents would be expected to attend two 1-hour parent-only group sessions. The first session would come after the second week of the program, and the second session would come after the seventh week. Parental involvement is a necessary part of the program because parents are assigned a role in helping their child attain grade-level performance.

Teachers have an important role in this program. The group leaders would meet with the teachers whose students are in the program to explain the details of the plan. They would be asked to follow the progress of their students who are in the group by completing a weekly progress report (see page 184) and by indicating what fundamental skills need to be addressed. A tutorial system utilizing classroom and/or resource teachers would be established.

The group members would be identified largely by teacher referral. This is not intended to be a group for students who exhibit severe school conduct problems, but rather for those students whom teachers feel are functioning below grade level and who have the potential for improving their grades. The co-leaders could approach a grade-level team for referrals. The screening interview with prospective group members would focus on the student who is interested in eventually being able to function at or near grade level and is willing to be cooperative. Students would be told that they would meet eight times as a group for 40 minutes and that every member would be seen four times for a 30-minute individual counseling session. They would also be told that their parent or parents would be required to participate in the program. Parent meetings would be early in the evening in order to accommodate parent work schedules.

If the student is interested in joining this group, a parent would be contacted and invited to participate in the program. The group leader would impress on the parent the importance of the group, why their child needs to be in this group, and that such an opportunity may not happen again. The group leader should also inform the parent that their child has more ability than is being shown and that their child's teachers will also be involved in the program. Parents would be told that unless they are willing to participate, their child cannot be in the program. A signed permission statement would have to be returned to the group leaders. This statement would commit the parent to attend both of the parent-only meetings.

Target population: Seventh-grade students
Number in the group: Six
Gender   Mixed or homogeneous
Number of group sessions: Eight
Number of individual sessions: Four
Time for each group session: 40 minutes

continued

Continued

Time for four individual sessions: 30 minutes
Location: Counseling conference room
Leadership: Co-leaders
Time: Two-tier staggered days and times
Planned follow-up: Four weeks after the last meeting

SESSION 1: INTRODUCTION
Goals
1. To welcome the group and introduce members to each other.
2. To introduce the co-leaders and explain the format of the group plan.
3. To identify the purpose of the group.
4. To establish group rules and the consequences of breaking a rule.
5. To review the expectations for membership in this group.
6. To get feedback from the group as to what each would like to accomplish in the group.
7. To present an icebreaker.
8. To announce the meeting schedule and method of informing members of meetings.

Materials Needed
Six copies of the Statement of Commitment (see page 184)

Specific Strategies
1. Explain the objectives of the group plan and all of the details of the program. Be sure the group understands what it will be expected to do. Explain how bonding, cohesiveness, and helping one another is important for the success of each group member.
2. Establish group rules. In addition to the standard rules and an emphasis on confidentiality, the need for perfect attendance should be stressed. Members should feel that it is a privilege to have been selected for this group.
3. Ask all members to indicate specific target goals or what they would like to accomplish through being in the group. Record their comments for future use.
4. Ask members to commit twelve weeks of their lives to working at changing their attitudes toward school by becoming highly motivated to improve their scholastic performance. The group will meet for eight weeks, and a single follow-up session is planned four weeks later. Explain how these twelve weeks could change a group member's future in school and, quite possibly, what the member will do after graduation. Impress upon the group that these twelve weeks could have a positive impact on each member's life. The group leaders would ask each member to sign a statement of commitment.
5. Icebreaker. Ask each member:
    a. What would you say was the greatest invention?
    b. If you were on an island by yourself, and there was no electricity or telephone, what three things would you like to have with you?
    c. What would you do if you found an envelope on the street with nothing written on it and fifty 20-dollar bills were inside?
6. Inform the group of the staggered meeting schedule, describe the process by which they will be reminded of each meeting, set up the schedule for individual counseling sessions, and assign the groups to their first co-leader.
7. Announce that next week the group will begin to talk about motivation. Ask the group to think about the things they are motivated to do and report this to the group the next week.
8. Summarize the session.

SESSION 2: ASSESSMENT OF MOTIVATION I
Goals
1. To understand what each member is motivated to do.
2. To assess the motivation each member has to become successful in school.
3. To discuss each member's current priorities.
4. To begin to discuss motivation.

Materials Needed
A copy of the group rules should be brought to each group session.

Specific Strategies
1. Review the summary from the previous session.
2. Review the group rules.
3. Follow up on the assignment from the previous week to learn what each member is motivated to do (e.g., be a better ball player, become stronger, become rich, get a boy- or girlfriend).
4. Explore the basis for each member's attitude toward school.
5. Determine each group member's priorities and priority for schoolwork.
6. Inquire what it would take for each member to consider changing attitudes toward school to make learning a high priority.
7. Begin a discussion on motivation: what it is, why it is important, how we become motivated, and why becoming motivated can be difficult.
8. Homework assignment: Each member would be asked to set a target goal for improving classroom performance. A goal could be to complete a given number of homework assignments, ask a teacher for help, make a commitment to study for tests, or cooperate better with teachers.
9. Summarize the session.

SESSION 3: MOTIVATION TO SUCCEED
Goals
1. To continue the discussion on motivation from the previous week.
2. To open a discussion of the concept of success.
3. To discuss the concept of commitment.
4. To talk about study skills.

Materials Needed
Guidelines for good study skills for distribution to the group

Specific Strategies
1. Review the summary from the previous session.
2. Review the group rules, if necessary.
3. Follow up on homework. Ask members to indicate their target goal for improving their classroom performance.
4. Discuss the feelings of each member relative to
   a. How their parents view school.
   b. How their peers view school.
   c. How their siblings view school.
5. Explain motivation according to *should* levels, *will* levels, and *must* levels (see Session 5 of the self-esteem group plan, page 171).
6. Ask how each member can become motivated at the *must* level to attain goals.

continued

Continued

7. Open a discussion on the meaning of success. Why is success important? What does it take to be successful? Who are the people they know who are successful?
8. Open a discussion on commitment. What is meant by a commitment? Why is it important to be able to make a commitment? Why can it be difficult to make a commitment? Have any members ever made a commitment? If so, to what? Will each member make a commitment to improve their attitude toward school?
9. Homework assignment: Ask members to pick one subject with which they are having a problem and to ask that teacher what they could start doing that would improve their grade. Report the results to the class next week.
10. Distribute guidelines for good study skills.
11. Summarize the session.

SESSION 4: VALUES
Goals
1. To begin to examine values.
2. To assess the value each member places on education.
3. To discuss how values change throughout life.
4. To have members identify their immediate and future goals.

Specific Strategies
1. Review the summary from the previous session.
2. Review group rules, if necessary.
3. Ask each member to report on the homework assignment. What classroom subject was selected and what was done that could improve the grade in that class?
4. Open a discussion about values. What is a value? How do we acquire our values? Can values be changed? What are some of the values of the group members? Why is education a value?
5. Open a discussion on how our values change throughout life.
6. Ask each member to identify immediate goals and future goals. How realistic are their goals? What would they have to do if they are to meet their goals?
7. Discuss why doing our best in everything we do is both a value and a goal.
8. Homework assignment: Ask several friends what is important to them. Report the findings next week in group.
9. Summarize the session.

SESSION 5: CONSEQUENCES
Goals
1. To examine how all behavior has some consequence.
2. To examine the importance of our actions.
3. To understand the importance of graduating from high school.
4. To discuss the problem of feeling bored in school.

Specific Strategies
1. Review the summary from the previous session.
2. Ask the group to talk about the progress being made in class.
3. Open a discussion on how the past can explain the present and how the present can predict the future.

4. Examine the consequences of certain behaviors, including:
   a. Breaking laws.
   b. Hurting people's feelings.
   c. Physically hurting someone.
   d. Using illegal drugs.
   e. Getting poor grades in school.
   f. Dropping out of school.
5. Discuss role models and ask members to identify their role models.
6. Ask for reports on the homework assignment of finding out what is important to their peers.
7. Open a discussion on why students feel bored in school.
8. Ask the group how we can overcome feeling bored.
9. Summarize the session.

SESSION 6: SCHOOL PROGRESS AND PRIORITIES
Goals
Prior to this session, the co-leaders would have spoken with the teachers of the group members to learn if they have observed any changes in their students' attitudes or performance.

1. To evaluate the progress members have made in their schoolwork (e.g., test scores, turning in homework, classroom participation, attendance, teacher comments, specific problems).
2. To report on teacher comments that would reinforce the progress of specific group members.
3. To determine what help is needed for each member in specific classes.
4. To review the target goals that each member set in the second session.
5. To determine the priority of each group member for scholastic achievement. (A five-point scale could be used to help them evaluate their priority for doing schoolwork.)

Materials Needed
Reports from teachers indicating the progress of members (not to be distributed)

Specific Strategies
1. Review the summary from the previous session.
2. Ask members to report on classroom progress.
3. Share positive teacher comments with the group.
4. Ask members what help they could use in specific subjects that would improve their classroom performance and grades.
5. Check progress made on the target goals each member set (from Session 2).
6. Ask members if they see evidence that their parents' attitudes toward school have changed as a result of the first parent-only session.
7. Open a discussion on priorities.
   a. Define priorities.
   b. Describe how we establish our priorities.
   c. Ask what priorities are set for us by others.
   d. Discuss why school achievement needs to be a high priority.
8. Homework assignment: Assign the group to identify one reason that might explain why students have negative attitudes toward school in preparation for next week's discussion on negative attitudes.
9. Remind the group there will be two more sessions.
10. Summarize the session.

continued

Continued

SESSION 7: NEGATIVE ATTITUDES AND PEER PRESSURE
Goals
1. To define negative thinking.
2. To identify the basis of negative thinking.
3. To open a discussion on negative attitudes toward school.
4. To examine peer pressure.

Specific Strategies
1. Review the summary from the previous session.
2. Ask members to report on academic progress.
3. Open a discussion on negative thinking.
4. Follow up on the homework assignment. Ask each member to cite one reason that might explain why students would have a negative attitude toward school.
5. Discuss the impact of negative thinking on all aspects of life.
6. Talk about an antidote to negative thinking, such as becoming a positive thinker.
7. Define and ask the group for examples of peer pressure.
8. Discuss how peer pressure can be both helpful and harmful to us.
9. Ascertain if group members have felt peer pressure because of changes they may be making in their attitude toward school.
10. Open a discussion on why we get bored with something.
11. Remind the group that next week is the last session.
12. Summarize the session.

SESSION 8: PERSONAL PROBLEMS
Goals
1. To identify personal problems that can have a strong influence on school performance.
2. To show how distractions affect school performance.
3. To review the topics from previous sessions.
4. To evaluate the progress made in the group counseling.
5. To close the group sessions with a light refreshment.

Materials Needed
Evaluation forms for students
Evaluation forms for teachers
Healthy refreshments

Specific Strategies
1. Review the summary from the previous session.
2. Ask members to report on their academic progress.
3. Ask members how personal problems can affect school performance. Cite as examples when we are upset about something that happened at home or with a friend, when we are angry and are thinking about the thing that made us mad, when we are in trouble and worry about what will happen to us, when we are afraid that someone in school will tease or bully us, when we are too shy to ask a teacher for help when we don't understand something.
4. Ask the group to name things that can distract them from doing their best in school. Examples could be worrying, fear, feeling rejected by a boy- or girlfriend, not feeling

well or having pain, thinking about what we are going to do after school, a problem at home, or remembering something that made us mad.

5. Review the key topics from the past seven weeks. This would include reference to motivation in general, motivation to succeed, priorities, education as a value, negative thinking, current and future personal goals, anticipating the consequences of behavior, overcoming peer pressure, reducing boredom, and removing distractions that would affect our school performance.

6. Distribute an evaluation form to the members (see page 185).

7. Have a light refreshment and thank the group for its cooperation. Inform the members that they are encouraged to make an appointment to see one of the group leaders for individual counseling.

FORMAT FOR PARENT-ONLY GROUPS

Parents would meet each meeting for 1 hour at a time convenient for the parents and group leaders. Early evening is recommended. At the first meeting, it is important that the principal, or an assistant principal, welcome the group and introduce the group leaders. The sessions would be discussions more than lectures, but the first meeting would begin with an explanation of what the program seeks to accomplish, a listing of the categories that will be covered in the eight sessions, the role of the teachers in the program, and the role of parents. Specifically, parents will be asked to communicate to their child (1) that they support the goals of the group plan, (2) that school and education are important values, (3) that they want their child to succeed in everything they do, (4) that success in school is very important, (5) that they will be following their child's progress more than they have, (5) that they will expect their child to do all homework assignments, and (6) that they will encourage their child to have perfect attendance and not be late for school. These points would be distributed to the parents in writing.

Discussions would be opened on such topics as

1. Parental views about education.
2. Parental views about the school.
3. Specific ways parents can help their child become more successful in school.
4. Problems parents may be having with the school.
5. Parental aspirations for their child.
6. Concerns parents have about their child.
7. Distractions parents feel could be impacting on their child's classroom performance.

The second meeting would discuss and evaluate changes parents are seeing in their child. The meeting could pursue any topics not covered in the first meeting and would encourage feedback on any subject related to their child's education. It should be geared to motivating parents to stay on course and assume some responsibility for their child's school success. Parents would be encouraged to inquire frequently about their child's progress, check with teachers to ascertain that homework is being completed, and discuss the results of test scores and grades. One objective of meeting with parents is to make the child aware of parental interest in the schoolwork and to encourage parent–child interactions on school-related matters.

WEEKLY TEACHER PROGRESS REPORTS

As a way of determining the ongoing progress of your students who are in the group for underachieving students, please complete the following items and either give this form to me or place it in my mailbox. A separate form should be used for each of your students who are in the group. You will receive this form every Friday for the next eight weeks.

Name of student _____

Answer yes or no.

_____ Over the past week, have you seen any signs of change or improvement in the attitude or behavior of this student?

_____ Is this student turning in all homework assignments? If the answer to this is no, how many assignments were not turned in this week? _____

_____ Is this student participating more in classroom activities?

_____ Do you see any change in the attitude of this student toward you?

_____ Progress noted. Rate the progress you are seeing in this student: 5 = tremendous, 4 = quite a bit, 3 = some, 2 = not much, 1 = none.

Comments:

_____

Your name: _____ Date _____

STATEMENT OF COMMITMENT

I, _____ , am making a commitment to _____

_____

as long as I am in this group. I am also committing myself to continue to do this after the group is over. I understand that a commitment is more than a promise. A promise is what I say I will do. A commitment is what I will really do.

Signed: _____

Date _____

GROUP EVALUATION

It is important to learn how effective this group counseling has been. Please answer each of the following questions with your honest opinion. You will not be asked to sign your name to this evaluation. Answer yes or no.

1. _____ Were the group sessions interesting?

2. _____ Has being in this group helped you?

3. _____ Have your grades improved since being in this group?

4. _____ Have you received help from your teachers?

5. _____ Have your parents been encouraging you to do better in school?

6. _____ If you feel the group has helped you, do you feel you will continue to make progress?

7. _____ Were you pleased with the group leaders?

8. _____ Were the group members helpful to you?

9. _____ Would you recommend this group to a friend who needs to improve school performance?

What did you like most about this group experience? _____

_____

If there was something you did not like about this group experience, what was it? _____

_____

If there are changes that you feel should be made the next time this topic is offered to a group, what are they?

_____

The group leaders should periodically check with teachers to determine the academic deficiencies of each member that need to be worked on in order for that student to be at or near grade level. Inquiries would be made to discover what could be done to help each member get the tutorial assistance that is needed. This is another opportunity for the faculty guidance committee to assist the counselor. At the four-week follow-up, the leaders would have checked with teachers to note progress. There would be an assessment of each member's current motivation and whether negative attitudes toward school persist. Members would be encouraged to bring up any problems they are having or to open up discussion on any topic that is relevant.

CHAPTER TEN

GROUP PLANS II

In this chapter the reader will see group plans and group activities that have been developed and used by practicing school counselors who are graduates of the school counseling program at the University of Maryland at College Park. The format and presentation will vary somewhat. A group plan is a reflection of the knowledge, creativity, insights, and experience a group leader has in developing topics to accomplish the stated objective. Group plans should constantly be modified for improvement.

GROUP PLAN FOR STRESS REDUCTION

Jennifer Watkinson

Forest Hill Elementary School, Forest Hill, Maryland

TOPIC: REDUCING STRESS
      Group level: Third through fifth grades
      Number of sessions planned: Seven
      Number of members: Six
      Time for each session: 30 to 40 minutes
      Location of sessions: Counselor's office

Prior to the beginning of Session 1, each group member would have had a screening interview. A parent letter should be sent home with each child and parental permission slips should have been returned (see Attachment 1).

SESSION 1
Purpose of Session 1
    1. To review the purpose of the group.
    2. To introduce group members to each other.
    3. To establish group rules.

Materials Needed
Sheets of construction paper
Pencils/crayons

Specific Strategies
1. Explain the purpose of the group.
2. Members will introduce themselves to the group stating (1) name, (2) name of homeroom teacher, (3) what they like to do after school.
3. Establish group rules. The group leader should suggest the important ones and the group can add to the list. Confidentiality should be emphasized. Write down the group rules on chart paper and have them posted in the room. They should be reviewed at each session.
4. Ten minute icebreaker. The group leader would have drawn a circle and titled it "My Crest." Give each member a copy of "My Crest." Say to the group, "This circle will become your personal crest. In the circle, write the words that best describe the kind of person you think you are. I will come around and help you spell any words that are difficult for you. Then using the crayons that I will provide, you can decorate your crest in some way. After you have finished, you will be asked to share your crest with the group and say the words that best describe you." Provide students with crayons and walk around the group helping them spell words. If it is felt necessary to provide the members with more structure in order to make their crest, the group leader can demonstrate what is being asked by saying words that best describe the group leader.
5. Have the members share their personal crest with the group.
6. Summarize the session.

SESSION 2
Purpose of Session 2
1. To review the last session.
2. To review the group rules.
3. To review the purpose of the group.
4. To define stress and how it affects our bodies.
5. To identify what the group members would like to know about stress.
6. To determine each member's stressors.

Materials Needed
Sheets of blank paper
Pencils
Stresssor location chart

Specific Strategies
1. Review the last session, the group rules, and the purpose of the group.
2. Open up a discussion of what stress is and how it affects us, and point out that everybody feels stress at times.
3. Give each member a sheet of paper and a pencil. Ask them to fold the paper in two so that there are two columns. Place the letter S on top of the first column and the letter W at the top of the second column. S represents what each member feels are personal *stressors*. The W column is *where* they experience the stressors. After defining stress and explaining that a stressor is anything or anyone who creates stress for a person, members

continued

Continued

of the group would list those things that they feel cause their stress and write them under the *S* column. The group would then be asked to indicate where each of their stressors occur, such as at home, in school, on the school bus, and so on and write this in the *W* column. For example, if someone writes "taking tests" in the *S* column, the person would write "school" under the *W* column.

If the group does not do so on their own, the group leader should make the connection as to how stress affects our bodies (e.g., stress can result in difficulty in sleeping or sleeping too much, changes in eating habits, forgetfulness, stomachaches, headaches, etc.). The stressor/location chart is an evaluative tool and should be reviewed by the group leader prior to every session. The group leader should collect the stressor/locator charts because they will be used in the third session and will be discussed again at the seventh session.

4. Summarize the session.

SESSION 3
Purpose of Session 3
1. To review the group rules.
2. To review what the members know about stress (see the stressor/location chart from previous session).
3. To identify specific stressors for the group members.

Materials Needed
Stress/location charts from Session 2
Sheets of construction paper
Sheets of paper
Pencils
Chalk and chalkboard

Specific Strategies
1. Review what was discussed in the previous session.
2. Ask one group member to review the group rules.
3. Ask members to tell what they know about stress. The group leader can ask members if they have anything else to add to their stressor/location chart.
4. Members will identify specific stressors. Prior to the group session, the group leader should have a poster board/chalkboard/overhead projector available so that the stressors identified by the group members can be written down. Ask the group members to tell the group what things make them feel stress (e.g., pressure, feeling overwhelmed). Create a list of potential stressors. Ask the group to indicate which of their stressors causes them to feel the most pressure and how they react when they are faced with that stressor.

   On a sheet of paper, ask the members to write down the single stressor that causes them the most pressure. Collect the papers and hand them back to the members at the next group session.
5. Summarize the session.

SESSION 4
Purpose of Session 4
1. To review the group rules.

2. To review the discussion from the last group and return the paper on which they stated the stressor that created the most pressure for them.
3. To expose the group to a relaxation technique. The group leader should obtain a quiet instrumental recording. Group members will listen to this quiet music for 10 minutes. They will then discuss how they feel after having listened to the music and offer their reactions to this relaxation technique.

Materials Needed
Audio tape of recorded quiet music
Audio tape player

Specific Strategies
1. Review the discussion from the last session.
2. Ask one member to review the group rules.
3. Say: "Today we are going to practice something that will help us to relax our muscles when we are feeling tense and overwhelmed by something that is stressful to us." Ask the members to tighten their muscles in their shoulders and backs. After 30 seconds, ask them to take a deep breath and release the tension in their muscles. Repeat this exercise a second time. Say, "One way we can help ourselves when we are feeling overwhelmed is to listen to calming music and allow ourselves to do nothing. We are going to try this relaxation technique right now. Put yourselves in a comfortable sitting position some-where in this room. You must separate from the other group members so that you are not distracted. You are not allowed to talk or get up while the music is playing. You are expected to close your eyes and just listen to the music. The music will play for 10 minutes. When the music stops I want you to join me back in the group. Are their any questions? (Answer any questions.) Now please find a place in the room away from the other group members." Give the members a minute or two to find a suitable place in the room. When all of the members are seated, play a recording of soft instrumental music. Stop the music after 10 minutes and ask the members to return to the group. When the members return to the group, ask "How do you feel?" Allow the members to respond. Other questions you may ask are:
   - Was it difficult or easy for you to listen to the music and not do anything else for 10 minutes? Why?
   - Is this something you could do at home to relax? Why?
   - Were you able to relax and only listen to the music or did you find yourself thinking about other things? Why?
   - Is this something you can do that will help you relax when you are faced with the stressor you wrote down on your paper?
4. Ask the members to identify other things that they can do to relax (e.g., go for a walk, ride a bike, read a book, write poetry, etc.).
5. Summarize the session.

SESSION 5
Purpose of Session 5
1. To review group rules.
2. To discuss the relaxation technique from the previous session.
3. To introduce and practice problem-solving strategies.

continued

Continued

Materials Needed
Basket containing six slips of paper on which are written stressful situations
Poster board showing a problem-solving model

Specific Strategies
1. Review the discussion from the previous session.
2. Ask a member to review the group rules.
3. Say: "The technique that we used last week allowed us to relax. There are times when relaxing will not take away the stress that we feel. Can you think of a situation when you might need to do more than just listen to relaxing music?" Some answers might be: when you are feeling overwhelmed because you've got a lot of homework to do, when you've gotten angry with your best friend, when you feel you are in trouble, and so on.
4. Say: "Today we are going to practice using problem solving in order to reduce our stress. The problem-solving model we are going to use is (1) first, identify the problem, (2) next, think of all possible solutions to the problem, (3) examine every possible solution by looking at the consequence of each solution, (4) choose a solution that seems to have the best consequence, and finally (5) make a commitment to do what needs to be done to solve the problem." (This model should be written on poster board and placed in full view of the group.)
5. Prior to the session, create stressful situations for the members to practice the problem-solving model. Write the stressful situations on small sheets of paper for the members to pull from a basket. Examples of problem situations involving stress would include studying for a test, being late for the school bus, being rejected by a classmate, hitting a baseball through a neighbor's window, or showing parents a bad report card.
6. Each member chooses a stressful situation from the basket and is asked to resolve the stressful problem by using the problem-solving model.
7. Remind the group there are two more sessions.
8. Summarize the session.

SESSION 6
Purpose of Session 6
1. To review the group rules.
2. To review the two stress reduction techniques, namely, listening to music and using the problem-solving model.
3. To practice using the problem-solving model.
4. To begin termination.

Materials Needed
Stressor/location lists used in the second session

Specific Strategies
1. Review the discussion from the previous session.
2. Ask a member to review the group rules if it is felt necessary.
3. Say: "During our last session we talked about and practiced two methods that can help us reduce our stress. One was relaxing by listening to soft music, the other was using a problem-solving model. You will recall that you once made a list of those things that you felt were stressors for you and where you have stress. Using this list of stressors, tell me

how you could use either soft music or the problem-solving technique to resolve the stressors on your list." Give members a copy of their stressor/location list.
4. Say: "Next week will be our last group session. I will be asking you to tell me what you have learned about stress and whether you have been able to reduce your stress. Think about what you have learned about stress."
5. Summarize the session.

SESSION 7
Purpose of Session 7
1. To review the previous sessions.
2. To evaluate the effectiveness of the group.
3. To ask members what they learned about stress and if they feel they have been able to reduce their stress.
4. To ask the members to think about having a short-term goal for themselves.
5. To discuss the possibility of having a follow-up in two or three weeks.

Materials Needed
Snacks or farewell souvenirs

Specific Strategies
1. Review the discussion from the previous session.
2. Ask the group to review the group rules, if necessary.
3. Ask each member to tell you what has been learned about stress. Write down their responses and distribute the list to them within a week.
4. Ask members to say what they will do in the near future to reduce the stress they feel when they are faced with pressure or a situation they find overwhelming.
5. Ask each member to name a short-term goal. Tell the group that you will be speaking with them individually in about two weeks to discuss what they are doing to reach their short-term goal. The group should be told that anyone who feels the need to meet sooner than two weeks should contact you.
6. Ask the group if they would like to have a follow-up meeting in a few weeks. If the group decides that it would like to meet again, arrange for this with letters to parents and contact with teachers.
7. Thank the group for their time and dedication. Provide a snack or farewell souvenir (e.g., pencil).

ATTACHMENT NUMBER 1
Initial Letter to Parents

Date _____

Dear Parents,

_____ has referred your child for membership in the stress reduction group that is being planned. The group will meet seven times, beginning _____ , for a 40-minute group session that will take place in the counselor's office. We will be discussing the skills that are needed to manage stress. These skills include understanding stress, identifying the stressors in your child's life, using quiet time to reduce stress, and acquiring problem-solving skills. So that your child will not miss the same class seven times, we will meet one week on Tuesday and the

continued

Continued

next week on Thursday. The time your child would be meeting is _____ on Tuesday and _____ on Thursday. About two weeks after the last session, I will arrange to meet with your child individually. At this follow-up session, I will review the skills that were learned during the seven weeks and allow your child to discuss how he or she is dealing with stressful situations. I will also monitor the progress your child is making toward reaching his or her short-term goals. Although each group session will involve spontaneous discussions among the group members, there are planned objectives for each session. They are as follows:

First Session: The group will introduce themselves and get to know the other members of the group.
Second Session: We will define stress and how it affects their lives.
Third Session: Members will identify the specific things in their lives that cause their stress.
Fourth Session: We will learn to use quiet time as a way of reducing stress.
Fifth Session: We will review the skills learned from previous group sessions and use problem-solving skills that are aimed at a further reduction of stress.
Sixth Session: We will practice these problem-solving skills.
Seventh Session: Each member of the group will develop short-term goals and reflect on the skills learned during the seven sessions.

Your child's participation is voluntary, but you must give your permission for your child to become a member of this group. Please sign the enclosed permission sheet and ask your child to return it to me _____ . It is necessary for me to have your signed permission prior to the first group session. You are encouraged to call me if you have questions. If you, or your child, wish to terminate membership in this group at any time, all you need to do is contact me.

_____ Counselor

Permission Sheet

I give my child, _____ , permission to become a member of the stress management group that is being assembled by the counselor at Forest Hill Elementary School. I have read and understand the statement that outlines the objectives of the seven sessions.

_____ (Parent/Guardian)   Date _____

GROUP PLAN FOR CHILDREN WITH ATTENTION PROBLEMS

Judy O'Rorke-Trigiani

Spring Hill Elementary School, Fairfax County Virginia Public Schools

Children who have been diagnosed as having ADD or ADHD can be expected to have difficulty with one or more of the basic learning tools, namely, reading, writing, or arithmetic.

The school counselor is not a specialist in doing remedial work in these areas. But in addition to academic deficiencies, many children who have attention disorders experience interpersonal and conduct problems for which individual or group counseling can be beneficial.

Group counseling with children who have attention deficit disorders should focus on the nonacademic behaviors that can have a serious impact on the child. These would include the child's relationship with peers, classroom conduct, and motivation to learn. Each group session would target a problematic area that is common to children with attention problems. One objective would be to determine that the child who has been diagnosed with an attention deficit has an understanding of the problem. It is important for the group leader to keep in mind that restlessness, easy distractability, and inattentive behaviors to varying degrees are part of the child's problems.

Parental involvement is desirable when working with children who have attention problems. Developing parent support groups, in conjunction with the school's psychologist, special education teacher, and nurse, can be helpful to parents. The assistance of these specialists in a parent group is an excellent way to inform parents how they can help their child.

What follows is an eight-session group plan for children who have ADD or ADHD that would be led by the school counselor with, or without, a co-leader.

Target population: Elementary school children (grade 3 and above) who have been diagnosed as having an attention deficit disorder with or without hyperactivity. Some of these children may be on a medication, others may not be medicated.

Number of sessions planned: 8
Number of members: 4 to 5
Time for each session: 30 minutes
Location of sessions: Counselor's office
Best group time: Early morning
Co-leadership: Recommended

Pre-group Preparation:
1. Carefully screen students for the group experience. Each student must be interested in becoming a member of the group and be willing to abide by rules.
2. Explain to the students that they will be expected to participate in the group discussions. They are asked to try to pay attention to what is being said by the group members. They should be told there will be group rules and they will have to abide by these rules. They should know the group will meet eight times for 30 minutes and that they will be working on friendship issues, classroom conduct, and ways to improve their grades. The students would be told that meeting times will be staggered and this will be explained, in detail, to them. They should also know that they are expected to attend every session and that confidentiality is very important. Confidentiality should be stressed at every session.
3. Assess the student's level of comfort in discussing ADD/ADHD.
4. Obtain parental permission.

SESSION 1
Purpose of Session 1: Orientation
1. To review group procedures and the expectations discussed in the pregroup session.

continued

Continued

2. To establish rules for the group.
3. To introduce the group members to each other.
4. To have members indicate their feelings about their academic subjects.
5. To encourage members to begin to develop academic goals.

Materials
Drawing paper and materials (e.g., pencils, crayons, erasers, etc.)
Chalk and chalkboard

Specific Strategies
1. Inform the group about the purpose of the group and the group leader's expectations of them as members of the group.
2. The group will decide on rules. The leader will suggest important rules and members can add rules they feel are necessary. Confidentiality and not interrupting a member who is talking should be emphasized.
3. Members will introduce themselves, stating their name, teacher, and one thing about themselves that makes them feel that they are an important person.
4. Members are asked to draw a picture of themselves, their family members, and an activity they enjoy doing. This drawing will be shared with the group.
5. Members will talk about the school subjects they find interesting and those they find difficult and begin to formulate their academic goals.
6. With the assistance of the group leader, the members will examine the similarities between themselves and other members of the group.
7. The group leader summarizes the session.

SESSION 2
Purpose of Session 2: What is ADD/ADHD?
1. To assess what the members currently know about ADD/ADHD.
2. To learn more about ADD and ADHD.

Materials
Lists of similarities from the first session
Large table covered with paper
Markers

Specific Strategies
1. The group leader will review what occurred in the first session.
2. The rules of the group will be reviewed.
3. The group will examine the similarities between members that the group generated from their drawings and personal introductions.
4. The group leader will cover a table with paper on which is written, "What is ADD/ADHD?" Members will be given a marker and instructed to list the things they know about ADD/ADHD on a portion of the paper.
5. Members will than share what they wrote about their knowledge of ADD/ADHD. The group leader will add to this list and correct misinformation.
6. The group leader will summarize the information obtained from the group and develop a definition of ADD/ADHD that the group can understand. (An excellent summary of

ADHD is available in *Putting on the Brakes* by Patricia O. Quinn and Judith M. Stern, New York. Magination Press, 1993.)
7. Summarize the session.

SESSION 3
Purpose of Session 3: The Impact of ADD/ADHD: Academic Concerns
1. To ascertain the impact of ADD/ADHD on academic achievement.
2. To discuss academic problems associated with ADD/ADHD.
3. To learn how members feel about their academic problems.
4. To ascertain what help each member may need in order to improve their academic performance. (In addition to what members say, information is obtained from the classroom teacher, resource teacher, and others who have contact with the child.)

Specific Strategies
1. Review the material from the previous session and reiterate the distinction between ADD and ADHD.
2. Review the group rules.
3. Ask group members to respond to the following questions:
   ■ Do you feel that your ADD or ADHD has affected your schoolwork?
   ■ If you do, how has it affected your schoolwork?
4. Ask members to specify the times when ADD/ADHD becomes a problem for them, their teachers, and their parents.
5. Summarize the session.

SESSION 4
Purpose of Session 4: The Impact of ADD/ADHD: Social Concerns
1. To review what was discussed in the previous session concerning the impact of ADD/ADHD on school performance.
2. To assess each member's experiences with friendship/social situations.
3. To begin to discuss good social skills.

Specific Strategies
1. Review the discussion from the previous session.
2. Review the group rules.
3. Ask members the following:
   ■ Do you feel that your ADD or ADHD has affected your peer relationships?
   ■ If so, how has it affected your relationships with peers?
4. Open up a discussion on social skills. Social skills are defined. The importance of developing good social skills is discussed. Members are asked to share their social problems.
5. Members will compare their social problems and begin to acquire insights into the reasons for their social problems.
6. There will be a discussion about positive and negative social skills and verbal and nonverbal communication. The group will develop lists of positive and negative social skills and ways that we communicate nonverbally. The group leader will make copies of these lists and distribute them to each member the next day.
7. As a homework assignment, members will be asked to identify one positive social skill and practice it during the forthcoming week. They will be asked to report to the group on how successful they were in working on that skill. There are a number of good books on the subject of social skills. The group leader should locate an appropriate book and

continued

Continued

read it to the group (e.g., *Feeling Left-out* by Kate Petty, Hallpauge, NY: Barrons Juveniles, (1991), or *Wilson Sat Alone* by Debra Hess, New York: Simon and Shuster, (1994).

6. Summarize the session.

SESSION 5
Purpose of Session 5: Acquiring Good Listening Skills
1. To review the important aspects of the previous session on social skills.
2. To demonstrate the importance of good listening skills.
3. To help members acquire better listening skills.

Materials Needed
Copies of good listening skills
A short story for practice in listening

Specific Strategies
1. Review the discussion from the previous session.
2. Review the group rules, if necessary.
3. The group will discuss the homework assignment and members will describe their experiences in working on one social skill.
4. The group will discuss why good listening is important and why it is necessary in academic and social situations.
5. The group will examine the consequences of not having good listening skills.
6. Good listening skills will be identified. They include (a) concentration, (b) focusing, (c) removal of distractions, (d) eliminating distracting thoughts, (e) eyes on the speaker, (f) a strong desire to hear what is being said, (g) understanding what the speaker is saying, (h) listening in order to remember, and (i) telling yourself that you are going to make a determined effort to listen carefully to what is being said. These points should be written and distributed to the members at the end of the session.
7. As an in-session activity, the group leader will read a short story to the group to evaluate their ability to listen. Questions about the story would be asked of individual group members. Correct responses should be praised.
8. Summarize the session.

SESSION 6
Purpose of Session 6: Problem-Solving
1. To discuss a model for problem solving.
2. To get practice in problem solving.

Materials Needed
List of problems for practice in problem solving
Problem solving model
Situation cards for practicing problem solving

Specific Strategies
1. Review the important points from the previous session on listening skills.

2. Discuss the reasons for doing problem solving. Members should be encouraged to do problem solving when it is possible rather than to expect others to solve their problems.
3. Develop a list of the kinds of problems that members will be expected to solve.
4. Ascertain the extent to which members are encouraged to problem solve at home.
5. Present a simple problem-solving model. It could be one suggesting that members
   - State the problem that needs to be resolved.
   - Think of all possible solutions.
   - Eliminate the choices that are not practical.
   - Decide on one solution and what needs to be done to accomplish it.
   - Make a commitment to do what needs to be done.
6. Have a group of situation cards available. Members draw a situation card from a box and, using the problem-solving model, show how they would solve the situation. Examples of situations would include
   - One of your classmates constantly taps his pencil when the class is taking a test. This bothers you. What would you do?
   - It is difficult for you to sit at your desk. What can you do?
   - One of your classmates frequently taps you on your shoulder when you are trying to work. This bothers you. What would you do?
   - At recess, you are usually by yourself. You would like to become a part of a small group that plays together. What would you do?
   - Your teacher often tells you to be quiet or asks you to sit in your seat. It is difficult for you to do these things. What would you do?
   - You didn't understand what the teacher just said to the class. What would you do?
   - The teacher just gave the class a homework assignment and you didn't understand what you are supposed to do. What would you do?
7. Remind the group that there are two more sessions.
8. Summarize the session.

SESSION 7
Purpose of Session 7: Coping Skills
1. To discuss why it is important to learn coping skills.
2. To be able to apply specific coping skills.

Materials Needed
Chalk and chalkboard
Sample coping situations

Specific Strategies
1. Review the problem-solving model discussed at the previous session.
2. Explain what it means to cope and why it is important to cope.
3. Explain the meaning of stress.
4. Explain what it means to adjust.
   Coping is how we respond to situations that involve stress.

   Stress is what we feel when we are upset or worried by things. It is stressful when you know you have to take a test or when you have to see your doctor or go to your dentist. It is stressful when you don't get invited to someone's birthday party or when you have done something your parents didn't approve of and feel that you will be punished. It is

continued

Continued

stressful when you are scolded by someone or feel rejected. When you are in a stressful situation it is important for you to know how to cope with that situation.

Adjustment is a way of coping. To adjust can mean to accept. If you adjust to being in school, this means you accept the rules of the school and the teacher. One of these rules is that you should not shout in the classroom. Another rule is that you are expected to be quiet when the teacher is talking. Rules of the school include not being late for school and not running in the halls. When you have accepted and obeyed all of the rules, you are showing that you have made an adjustment to being in school.

Ask: "How can you adjust to having an attention problem?"

There are good ways to cope, and ways that are not good. Ask the group if they can name good ways to cope and write them on the chalkboard. Good ways of coping would include problem-solving, telling yourself that you will adjust to the situation, doing what is expected of you, listening to what your teacher or parents tell you, maintaining control of yourself, trying to improve, understanding the reason for the problem, and setting goals. Ask the group if they can name ways that are not good ways to cope and write them on the chalkboard. Ways that are not good ways of coping would include having a temper tantrum, showing anger and aggression, crying, refusing to cooperate, blaming others instead of yourself, pouting, seeking revenge, giving up, avoiding the situation, having an "I don't care" attitude, expecting others to solve problems that you should be able to solve, and doing things that are illegal or harmful. Taking illegal drugs or stealing are examples of things that are illegal and can be harmful.

The group leader can pose situations that require coping and ask members to indicate how they would go about coping with the situation. For example, how would you cope with someone who won't play with you? How would you cope with someone who often teases you? How might you cope with your ADD/ADHD?

5. Remind the group that the next session is the last session.
6. Summarize the session.

SESSION 8
Purpose of Session 8: Review
1. To review the topics of the previous seven sessions.
2. To discuss the importance of having academic goals.

Materials Needed
An appropriate treat (healthy food or trinket)
Copies of an evaluation form

Specific Strategies
1. Review what was discussed in each of the previous sessions. This can be accomplished by asking the group to remember what was discussed.
2. Encourage each member to set academic goals. These goals would be shared with the group.
3. Ask members to indicate what things they would have to do in order to reach their goals.
4. Praise the group for cooperation within the group and give out an appropriate treat as a reward for the hard work.
5. Ask the group to evaluate the group experience.

GROUP PLAN FOR GRIEF/BEREAVEMENT

Heather Eig

Zadok Magruder High School, Rockville, Maryland

■ ■ ■ ■ ■

TOPIC: GRIEF/BEREAVEMENT
> Group level: High school (grades 9–12)
> Number of sessions planned: 8
> Number of members: 6 to 8
> Time for each session: One class period (50 minutes)
> Location of sessions: Conference room (guidance office or main office)
> A single facilitator/group leader (could be colead)

SESSION 1
Purpose of Session 1
1. To review the purpose of the group.
2. To introduce the group members to each other.
3. To introduce an icebreaker activity to relax the group.
4. To establish group rules.
5. To share reasons for participating in the group.

Have tissues, cups, and a pitcher of water available at all sessions.

Specific Strategies
1. Review the purpose of the group.
2. Students introduce themselves by stating (1) their name, (2) their grade, (3) the name of the person who died, (4) their relationship to that person, and (5) the cause of death.
3. Introduce the co-facilitator.
4. Ten-minute icebreaker activity: the candy dish. Pass around a candy dish and allow each member to take a handful of candy. Prior to eating the candy, each member is asked to share one piece of personal data for each piece of candy selected. Personal data may include (but is not limited to) personal interests, hobbies, sports interests, family constellation, travels, favorite musical groups, favorite places to eat, books enjoyed, and so on. (Note: If the group leader is aware that a group member is a diabetic or has an eating problem, food would not be used.)
5. Explain to the group the importance of having group rules and allow them to establish rules. Among the rules would be:
   a. Confidentiality. Anything said within the group may not be shared with others outside of the group. Group members are encouraged to share their grief with family, friends, teachers, and/or counselors. They are asked not to discuss the personal feelings of other group members with anyone. It is important that trust be created among members.
   b. All members are encouraged to participate in every session. This may be difficult for some members. The facilitator must be sensitive to those members who are not ready or willing to participate.

continued

Continued

    c. Group members are asked not to judge the way others are grieving or be critical of what members say. Everyone experiences different reactions to the loss of a loved one. There are no right or wrong ways to grieve.

    d. Refrain from using unacceptable language in group sessions.

Group members then begin to share their stories, experiences, feelings, and concerns. The facilitator encourages the flow of conversation and prevents domination of the session by one person. The facilitator attempts to tie related comments together (e.g., "several of you have commented that you felt angry at the person who died"). The facilitator should focus on similarities and differences in feelings, anger, frustrations, sadness, or specific concerns (e.g., being asked too many questions about details of the death, friends not understanding the grieving process, missing the lost loved one at holidays and special events, etc.).

6. Summarize the session.

SESSION 2
Purposes of Session 2
1. To review the summary of the first session.
2. To review the group rules.
3. To encourage the group to discuss topics related to the death of the loved one.

Specific Strategies
1. Review the summary from the first session.
2. Review the group rules.
3. Encourage members to guide the discussion. Each week the group will start with a weekly "check-in" of how the members handled their grief during the past week.
4. The facilitator opens up topics for discussion:
   - Were there any secrets surrounding the death (e.g., were details withheld to "protect" family members)? Did this result in anger, disappointment, or relief when the truth finally came out?
   - Has this experience brought about changes in relationships with friends, parents, siblings, other family members, peers, classmates, teachers, neighbors?
   - What are each member's current feelings? Have family expectations for the group member changed?
   - Has it been difficult to communicate with friends, family, and others?
   - Was gender a factor in dealing with grief (e.g., male versus female reactions to dealing with how grief was expressed, crying, "getting to the business of planning a funeral")?
5. Summarize the session.

SESSION 3
Purposes of Session 3
1. To continue to encourage group interaction.
2. To identify a particular hardship incurred by each member while grieving.
3. To identify the impact of loss on academic performance and attention span in a school setting.
4. To allow members to talk about the funeral arrangements or what happened at the funeral, if they so desire.

Specific Strategies
1. Review the summary of the second session.
2. Allow each member a few minutes to check-in with issues from the week (i.e., ups, downs, encounters, outlook, any new information).
3. Has the death resulted in personal hardships? If so, in what areas?
4. Continue discussing the impact of losing a loved one on school/academics (e.g., the ability to focus on schoolwork, concern over grades and making up missed work). Has there been a change in relationships with peers or teachers?
5. Ask members if they would like to talk about the funeral and their reactions. Talking about the funeral is strictly voluntary and no one should feel pressured to respond to this.
6. Compliment the group members on their efforts to share and encourage the members to become cohesive and work as a group.
7. Allow time for reflection on how the group experience may be benefiting each member.
8. Ask each member to bring in a picture of the lost loved one to share with the group. This is also a voluntary assignment, and members may choose not to bring in a picture. Say: "If you would care to bring a picture of your loved one for the group to see, you may do so next week. Whether or not you choose to bring in a picture is up to you."
9. Summarize the session.

SESSION 4
Purposes of Session 4
1. To continue encouraging the group to interact with each other.
2. To share pictures of the deceased with the group.
3. To discuss issues that may not have been addressed by anyone outside of the group.

Specific Strategies
1. Review the summary of the third session.
2. Conduct the weekly check-in with each member.
3. Let those members who have brought in pictures of their loved one show the pictures to the group. They can mention why this particular picture was selected.
4. Inquire if there are any issues that have yet to be discussed (e.g., how other members of the family are reacting to the loss, feeling guilty or responsible for the death).
5. Summarize the session.

SESSION 5
Purposes of Session 5
1. To continue to encourage group interaction.
2. To identify changes in family dynamics and relationships.

Specific Strategies
1. Review the summary of the fourth session.
2. Conduct the weekly check-in with each member.
3. Focus on changes that have occurred in relationships, family dynamics, and family members' roles after the death (e.g., "My sister is trying to act like my mom," or, "My aunt and uncle refuse to talk about my cousin. It's like he never lived.").
4. Ask members to recall one or two experiences with the deceased that stand out in their memories.
5. Summarize the session.

continued

Continued

SESSION 6
Purposes of Session 6
  1. To continue to encourage group interaction.
  2. To identify any awkward situations and discuss ways of dealing with these situations.
  3. To explore methods of grief and stress relief.

Specific Strategies
  1. Review the summary of the fifth session.
  2. Conduct the weekly check-in with each member.
  3. Revisit topics that need further discussion.
  4. Address new issues:
     - Communicating with others: feeling that friends "just can't understand what I'm going through" or feeling that "it's just not fair."
     - Changes in family dynamics since the death.
     - Media impact and privacy issues for the group member when the death has been the result of a murder or accident covered by the media.
     - Dealing with positive and negative ways of expressing grief. Positive ways would include talking about the deceased, reflecting on pleasant experiences with the deceased, realizing that grieving requires a certain time period after which grief is reduced but the memories of the deceased continue, and realizing that life goes on and time does make things easier to live with.
     - Religion. Utilizing personal religious beliefs as a source of strength.
     - Responding to grief with positive and negative coping forms of stress relief. Positive forms would include journal writing, jogging, aerobics, various team sports, fast walking, playing board games, singing, dancing, reading for pleasure, engaging in physical activities, and doing things that are enjoyable. Negative forms of coping would include taking medications not prescribed by a physician, using alcohol or illegal drugs, driving recklessly, not taking schoolwork seriously, expressing anger to family and friends, isolating oneself, excessive eating or refusal to eat, engaging in dangerous activities, and showing indifference and apathy to life.
  5. Summarize the session.

SESSION 7
Purposes of Session 7
  1. To check on how each member is feeling.
  2. To review coping strategies.

Specific Strategies
  1. Review the summary of the sixth session.
  2. Conduct the weekly check-in with each member.
  3. Review coping strategies.
  4. Discuss how each group member has benefited from being part of the group.
  5. Identify resources for additional support.
  6. Mention that next week is the last session.

SESSION 8
Purpose of Session 8
    1. To evaluate the grief/bereavement group counseling sessions.

Materials Needed
Copies of the evaluation form

Specific Strategies
    1. Review what topics were covered in the seven sessions.
    2. Allow the group members to reflect on their group experience.
    3. Complete paper-and-pencil evaluation (see below).
    4. Thank the group for cooperating.
    5. Serve light refreshments.
    6. Allow the group to determine if a follow-up group session is warranted.

EVALUATION OF THE GRIEF/BEREAVEMENT GROUP
(The group would be given sheets of paper on which to write their responses.)
       I would like you to evaluate the group of which you have been a member. Please answer each of the following questions.

    1. Were your expectations for this group met? If so, how? If not, why not?
    2. What are your feelings at the termination of this group?
    3. Would you like this group to continue? If so, why? If not, why not?
    4. What did you find to be the most difficult aspect of this group?
    5. What suggestions do you have that would improve future groups dealing with this topic?
    6. Overall, has this group been helpful to you? If so, in what way?

       Younger children who have experienced the loss of a loved one will often need group activities as part of the early sessions. The young child is often less vocal in the expression of grief. These activities are planned to encourage discussion and group interaction. Four such activities follow.

ACTIVITIES FOR A GRIEF/BEREAVEMENT GROUP

Leah A. Geiger

Green Holly Elementary School, Lexington Park, Maryland

       Grade level: 4 through 6
       Number of members: four to five

These activities are appropriate for younger students who have lost a loved one. The groups can have both boys and girls and should be small enough to enable the group to remember information about the person each of the group members is mourning. These activities can be used in conjunction with an eight-session group plan for grief/bereavement.

I have found that it is best when activity sheets and other materials being used in a session are on the conference table when the group members arrive. I give each member a manila folder and ask them to decorate it using crayons, stickers, glitter, glue, and other decorative materials. They put their work in this folder and take it home after the last session. I also ask them to draw a picture or bring in a photograph of their loved one to share with the group, if they wish.

Activity 1

At the first session the group members are asked to introduce themselves and talk about their deceased loved one to the group. They are asked to bring either a photograph or drawing of the person who has passed away to the second session. At the second session, I give them a sheet of paper on which I have drawn a wheel with eight spokes. I give them a small piece of two-sided tape and ask them to tape the photo or drawing of the deceased person to the middle of the wheel. On each of the spokes I ask them to write words that describe the deceased person. I am prepared to help them find appropriate words to choose. Some of the words I have seen used are *kind, loving, athletic, hard-working, good friend, funny, handsome, beautiful, generous, strong,* and *intelligent.* When finished, members share their work with the group.

Activity 2

Group members discuss a favorite memory they have of the deceased person. I create a sheet on which are listed the words *Who?* (Who are they talking about?), *Where?* (Where does the memory take place?), *When?* (When did the event happen?), *What?* (What are the details of the memory?), *How?* (How does the member feel about the memory?), and *Why?* (Why was this memory chosen?).

The memory is shared with the group. We then talk about the times we might need to use pleasant memories to feel better. (e.g., at certain holidays, birthdays, or when we are missing the person and feeling sad). This activity can be repeated at different group sessions and members can be asked to recall and share a different memory.

Activity 3

This activity focuses on helping the group members to go on with their lives in positive and productive ways. I encourage the group to think what they could do that might please the deceased person. I would start with, "If your loved one were alive, what kind of person would he or she want you to become? What would your loved one want you to do?" Answers to this would vary from "She'd want me to finish high school and go to college" or "He'd want me to be nicer to my brother and sister," to "To get better grades," and so on.

Group members often echo what other members have said. The group leader should encourage the members to add original things to what has already been said. This activity could result in a discussion of what each member needs to do in order to do what the deceased would want him or her to do. In essence, the members are defining goals they would like to achieve. This presents the group leader with an opportunity to help each member attain the goals through individual counseling.

Activity 4

In this activity the group makes a memory book. Begin by brainstorming the ways in which we can remember our lost loved one. This could involve writing about memories, using photographs, writing daily thoughts about the deceased, drawing pictures that depict specific scenes, writing down the comments made by members of the family, or writing a prayer, if this is consistent with family values. Then bring out supplies for making the memory book. (e.g., cardboard for the covers, a three-hole punch, ribbon, markers, glue, glitter, crayons, paint, etc.). Any sheets the member may have prepared during the eight sessions would be placed in the memory book. The member would first share the book with the group and later take the book home to share it with the family, who also may be grieving.

Icebreakers

Icebreakers can be used to begin groups at all grade levels. They are especially useful for use with introductory and primary groups but can be a way of relaxing intermediate and secondary groups as well. Icebreakers should be enjoyable activities involving all members of the group. They are intended to show the group that although the group has a serious purpose, the group experience can also be fun. Because group sessions meet for a short time, icebreakers should be planned to consume less than 10 minutes. They can be used at the first session and possibly once or twice again. With introductory and primary groups, an activity during the last 5 minutes of the session would also be appropriate as a reward and reinforcement for having had a good session. Developing an icebreaker challenges the counselor to be creative and innovative. After the group seems to be cohesive and is on-task, icebreakers can be eliminated. The types of icebreaker activities would vary. Most icebreakers involve a verbal response to some stimulus, yet a mild physical activity might also be appropriate. Knowing the group composition, the group leader may elect to use icebreakers that result in low to moderate activity. Whereas an icebreaker for an at-risk group in high school can be one that has moderate activity, an icebreaker for a grief/bereavement group should be one that is low-key, usually a personal introduction and a response to a stimulus question (e.g., "If you found a $100 bill on a sidewalk, what would you do with it?").

An icebreaker for an at-risk group could be one suggested by Ben Ouyang, a counselor at Walt Whitman High School in Bethesda, Maryland. He calls it the "Coin Game." Members are divided into two groups and are seated across from each other. Their hands are behind their backs. Each team has a coin (a quarter) that is passed from one person to another. The object is to not let the other side know where the coin is. As the coin is passed, the group leader counts to three. At the count of three, all members put their clenched fists on the table.

One member from each group will have the coin. Each person from the opposing team is then asked to guess the person who holds the coin. Oyang also reminds leaders to make sure to get the quarter back!

Colleen Ichniowski, the counselor at Page Elementary School in Silver Spring, Maryland, asks her group members to share a positive statement about something that happened to them in the last seven days. She will then ask each member of the group to share something positive observed about a group member during the last seven days. Ichniowski feels this is a helpful strategy because it allows children the opportunity to say or hear something positive about themselves. She also will ask children to rate themselves as to how they are feeling today, using a seven-point scale with 7 being the best.

Tracy Cass, who completed her training as a school counselor during the time this book was written, recommends what she calls "Guess the Fib." Group members are asked to make three statements about themselves, one of which is a fib. The group has to guess which statement was the fib. She feels this is always a popular game and has been impressed with the creative things the members are willing to share about themselves.

Mira Brancu, counselor at Perrywood Elementary School in Prince Georges County, Maryland, uses the "Unique Game" for children in grades 3 and above. For this game, the group leader puts a number of poker chips in front of each group member. If there are five members in the group, each child gets five poker chips. The members are asked to place the chips in any order they want, but having placed them, they are not to touch them again unless they are forced to surrender a chip. The group is first taught the meaning of the word *unique*. The first member begins by saying his or her name and one thing that he or she feels is special, or unique, about himself or herself. If another member has the same thing in common with the first member, the first member is required to give a chip to that member and a chip to all other members who have the same thing in common. The object is for the members to say something to the group about themselves that is so unique that no one else in the group can say that they share the same thing. Brancu demonstrates by saying, "My name is Ms. Brancu and I love to collect frogs. Does anyone in the group collect frogs? I see that two people have raised their hands, which means they also collect frogs. So, I will give one chip to Charlotte and one chip to Estelle. If I want to be sure to keep my chips, the next time it's my turn, I'll need to say something about myself that is even more unique or special than I said before."

At Francis Scott Key Middle School in Silver Spring, Maryland, Sue Tuttle, one of their counselors, will place a number of slips of paper in a hat or can. On the slips are such things as "my favorite food," "my favorite television program," "the sport I like best," "the class I like the most," "what I enjoy doing," "someone I would like to meet," or "a movie I could see again." Each group member takes a slip from the hat or can and responds to what is being asked. The slips should refer to positive preferences. Another icebreaker she uses is to ask the group members to name an animal that would be their "dream pet" and say why.

Rachael Herndon, a counselor with the Department of Alternative Programs in the Montgomery County Public School System in Maryland uses icebreakers for relaxation and communication with group members. One technique she uses for icebreakers is humor. She often begins a group by asking the members to share a joke or funny story. What the group perceives to be funny can reveal the developmental level of their humor. She feels that with adolescent groups, the school counselor can lose credibility if perceived as not having a sense of humor or of being "corny."

Group Games

It has been suggested that with introductory and primary groups, a game during the last 5 or 6 minutes can be a reward for having had a good group session. The group leader is cautioned not to allow the game to take up more than 5 or 6 minutes or to make the game the focal point of the group session. It goes without saying that the game selected must be one that can be played in a very short time. Teachers who reluctantly excuse students from class in order to participate in group counseling could be displeased if Curtis comes back from the group and excitedly announces that he won the game that was played in the group session. The thought that would probably cross the teacher's mind would be expressed as, "Hmmm, did I allow Curtis to miss part of a science group so that he could play games with the counselor?" This would not be good public relations for the counseling program and teachers and parents might question the purpose of group counseling. A game should not be the motivation for a student to affiliate or remain with a group. Games should be used as reinforcers, and ideally, the game should have some relationship to the group topic. Guessing games are easy to create and are not too time-consuming. If a session begins with an icebreaker, it would not be necessary to end it with a game. In the event the group did not have a good discussion, a game could be withheld.

Although games involving physical activity are enjoyable for members, this writer excludes them for reasons of safety and practical issues. The group leader is responsible in the event that a member is injured, and physical activities can result in aggressive behavior with youngsters who feel they need to win. For practical reasons, the writer also discourages the use of play media that can result in a member getting clothing soiled. Finger-painting is fun, but parents may not appreciate their child coming home with paint-spotted clothing. Sand play is also fun, but group leaders must remember that they would have to clean up a messy room so that the next child or group could come into a clean room.

Games can be an important adjunct to group counseling, especially when the group is comprised of introductory- and primary-level children. The games that are selected should be uncomplicated, fast moving, and fairly short.

CHAPTER ELEVEN

PROFESSIONAL ISSUES

The basic how-to-do-it of group counseling in schools has been presented. What remains is to examine the criteria for being a professional school counselor and group leader, ethical standards for group counseling in a school setting, a self-critique that counselors and group leaders can use to evaluate themselves, and the process of terminating group counseling.

THE PROFESSIONAL SCHOOL COUNSELOR

School counselors and group leaders are expected to be professional in their approach to students, teachers, parents, and administrators. All school counselors probably feel they are professional. The fact is, however, that many counselors who call themselves professional would fail to meet some of the criteria for being a professional. School counselors who share confidential information in the teacher's lounge for all to hear or those counselors who focus exclusively on guidance activities and are not involved in individual or group counseling are not meeting some of the criteria for being a professional school counselor. Professional school counselors are expected to place a high priority on counseling students who could benefit from counseling services. A professional school counselor should be able to meet the following criteria. They should

1. View themselves as being very knowledgeable about the field of counseling in general and specifically the role of the school counselor with the population and grade level they have been assigned.
2. Establish a reputation in the school as being a person whom students can turn to when they are experiencing academic, social, career, and certain personal problems.
3. Commit a portion of their day to seeing children who are in need of responsive counseling services. This would include developing sustaining relationships with students whose problems require several counseling sessions.
4. Be viewed by teachers as a person they would contact if they wanted to discuss a problem they feel their student is having.
5. Establish a liaison relationship between parents and the school.
6. Conduct themselves at all times in a manner that shows their respect for confidentiality and the dignity of their counselees.

7. Be able to apply the training that was acquired through their academic preparation and experiences to their practice of counseling.

8. Be able to formulate plans, develop strategies, and pursue counseling goals with counselees.

9. Feel comfortable using a variety of strategies and selecting the one that is appropriate for the counselee they are seeing.

10. Strive to move the counselee in the direction of needed improvement or change by means of a counseling strategy or group plan.

11. Be knowledgeable of professional trends and new information by staying current with research and by being actively involved in learning through continuing education.

12. Affiliate with national, state, and local professional counseling associations. Participation in these groups is an important professional activity.

13. Assist in promoting and implementing a comprehensive guidance and counseling program in a school.

14. Maintain accurate records for all counseling and guidance activities.

15. Make appropriate referrals in accordance with ethical standards.

16. Comply with the codes of ethical conduct as set forth by ACA, ASCA, and ASGW.

ETHICAL STANDARDS OF SCHOOL-BASED GROUP COUNSELING

Ethics essentially examines moral principles. It is concerned with what is right or wrong, proper or improper, in both professional and personal conduct. In counseling, ethics is also concerned with protecting the rights of the individual by defining the expectations and responsibilities of the counselor.

School counselors who are members of the American Counseling Association (ACA) or the American School Counselor Association (ASCA) have agreed to abide by the respective codes of ethical conduct as stated by these associations. Unfortunately, not all school counselors are members of these professional organizations. Even so, all school counselors have obtained certification from a state department of education, and inherent in this certification is the expectation that they will conduct themselves in an ethical manner. The reader should become very familiar with the *Ethical Standards for School Counselors* of ASCA, which cites fifteen responsibilities a school counselor has to students (see Appendix F), and ACA's *Ethical Standards for School Counselors* (see Appendix G). The reader is also encouraged to review the *Ethical Standards for Group Counselors* that has been established by the Association for Specialists in Group Work (ASGW), as shown in Appendix H.

Whether school counselors are involved in individual or group counseling, they are expected to practice ethical counseling. The rules that group leaders develop to govern the group will often cover some of these ethical principles, for example, the importance of confidentiality, protecting group members from verbal attacks, and the expectation that group members will share and communicate with each other. Other ethical principles have been covered in this text as part of the process of establishing counseling groups in schools, for example, the importance of conducting a screening interview, compliance with informed consent, obtaining written permission from parents, and the limits of confidentiality.

The ethical principles that follow are in addition to those stated in the codes of ethical conduct of the organizations just mentioned. They are termed "ethical principles" because they meet the criteria for conduct and behavior that is proper, based on practical and logical practices that protect both the group leader and group member. Ethical practices for school-based group counseling are related to the qualities inherent in effective group leadership and would include the following:

1. The decision to place a student in a group should be made on the basis of the benefits the student can derive with this form of counseling.
2. Counselors who lead groups must have received training for doing group counseling with a school-aged population and feel competent to lead a group.
3. Rules for the group must be developed and enforced by the group leader(s).
4. The rule of confidentiality that is imposed on the group also applies to the group leader, unless the duty to warn must be invoked.
5. Individuals who are not in the group should not be discussed by the group.
6. Parents or legal guardians are entitled to know how their child is progressing in the group, but the group leader is not expected to reveal specific comments made by their child or other members of the group.
7. Visitors should not be permitted to observe the group, including teachers, parents, and school administrators. If there is to be an exception to this rule, the entire group must have agreed to allow the exception prior to the visit.
8. The group leader is governed by the regulations and policies of the school system and the school. This would include the requirement to report any indication or suspicion of sexual or physical abuse, danger to self or others, and threats.
9. The group leader must be prepared to ask a member to leave the group if that member's actions or presence in any way endangers a member of the group.
10. When a group member elects to terminate membership in the group, the group leader has the responsibility to determine the reason for this decision and must notify the parents and appropriate teachers.
11. Professional conduct from the group leader is expected both inside and outside of school. *Professional* is not a label that applies to the counselor only within the school setting. What is said and what happens in the group, must stay in the group.
12. School counselors/group leaders are expected to conduct themselves in accordance with the codes of ethical conduct as established by the American Counseling Association, the American School Counseling Association, and the Association for Specialists in Group Work, regardless of membership in these associations.

A SELF-CRITIQUE FOR COUNSELORS

Evaluating how effective a group has been is usually done during the last group session. However, feedback obtained at the last session can only be useful for future groups, not the group that just concluded. In order to have constructive feedback for an ongoing group, it is necessary to collect data one or more times during the six- or eight-week sessions. It has previously been stated that one of the advantages of having co-leaders for a group is to strengthen the evaluation process. Meeting after each session, co-leaders are able to critique the current session in order to improve future sessions. Because most group counseling is done in elementary schools where co-leading is not common, the single group leader needs a way of evaluating each group session. A self-critique is one way to accomplish this objective. For a self-critique to be useful, the group leader must be honest and objective. Because the data being collected is only for the group leader's eyes, it should be easier for the group leader to evaluate himself or herself more honestly and objectively. An example of a self-critique for group counseling follows. Through responses to these questions, a group leader can get a picture of what happened in the most recent session and how effective the group leadership was.

Self-Critique for Group Counseling

1. Do I know the names of all the members?
2. Do the members seem to understand the objective of the group?
3. Were the group rules followed? If not, which rules are members having problems with?
4. Did I maintain control of the group throughout the session?
5. For the most part, did the group stay on task?
6. Did all members of the group participate? If not, which members need to be watched more carefully?
7. Does the group seem to be moving in the direction of the goal?
8. Was there sufficient spontaneity within the group?
9. Did I deal effectively with any problems that appeared today?
10. Did I summarize occasionally?
11. Did I prepare appropriate stimulus questions in advance?
12. Do I detect any member concerns? (e.g., a monopolizer, a silent member, an aggressive or hostile member, a bully, a disrupter, etc.)?
13. Does the group seem to be becoming cohesive?
14. Thus far, how pleased am I with this group? (Rate it on a seven-point scale with 7 being the highest rating.) If I have ranked it as a 4 or less, why am I not pleased and what can be done to improve the group?
15. Did this session give me any reason to change the plan for the next session?
16. Is there a need to consult with a colleague about any group problems?

A counselor can also develop a self-critique for classroom guidance presentations. The responsiveness of the class is a good indicator as to the effectiveness of the presentation. Likewise, if the classroom teacher remained in the room the entire time, the teacher's feedback should be constructive. Questions counselors could ask of themselves would be

1. Was I well prepared for presenting this topic?
2. Was the topic one that would be expected to hold the interest of the class?
3. What reactions did I observe or hear from the class?
4. Did I speak too fast, too slow, too loud, too softly?

5. Was my material organized?
6. Did I set appropriate and adequate rules for this class?
7. Was class participation satisfactory?
8. Did I verbally reinforce student participation?
9. Did the class seem to be restless? Bored?
10. Did I attempt to accomplish too much in the time that I had?
11. Was I speaking to the level of the class?
12. Was I noticeably nervous? Uncomfortable?
13. Do I know enough about the topic?
14. Did I answer the questions adequately?
15. Was this a difficult class to work with? If so, what made it difficult?
16. Was I able to maintain control of the class?
17. When I present this topic again, will I do anything different?
18. What did I learn from this presentation?
19. Is a follow-up appropriate?
20. On a seven-point scale, with 7 the highest, how would I rate my presentation?

A self-critique can also be used to evaluate individual counseling. Although a single counseling interview can be evaluated using a self-critique, it is best used when the counselor is involved in a sustained relationship with a counselee, consisting of four or more counseling sessions. Using a self-critique after each individual counseling session is almost guaranteed to improve the counselor's skills and can prevent unsuccessful counseling outcomes. What follows is the self-critique for individual counseling that the writer recommends to his counselor-trainees.

Self-Critique for Individual Counseling

During counseling, a counselor must be aware of many things. The counselor must actively listen to what is being said, process and remember what was heard, create the environment that is conducive for effective counseling, be aware of the counselee's nonverbal cues, be alert to the things the counselee does and does not do, respond appropriately to counseling leads, keep the counseling goals in mind, focus on the strategy that was selected, and feel comfortable with the counseling skills that are being used.

In order to be an effective counselor, counselors must learn to do at least seven things almost at the same time, namely, they must (1) listen, (2) reflect on what was said, (3) store what was heard in their memory, (4) associate what a counselee says with what the counselee had previously said, (5) recall information stored in their memory when it is necessary, (6) think, and (7) verbally respond. Even experienced counselors find that this can be a difficult task.

After each counseling session, write Yes or No to the following questions. The answers you give yourself should be used as a learning experience to help you become a more effective counselor. Be honest with yourself. In this interview, did I

1. _____ Seem to put the counselee at ease?
2. _____ Feel at ease myself?

3. _____ Practice active listening skills?

4. _____ Ask too many questions?

5. _____ Interrupt too often?

6. _____ Let the counselee ramble?

7. _____ Rush the counselee?

8. _____ Speak too fast?

9. _____ Maintain comfortable eye contact?

10. _____ Comprehend what was being said?

11. _____ Talk too much?

12. _____ Encourage discussion and/or dialogue?

13. _____ Use reflection effectively?

14. _____ Follow the counselee's leads effectively?

15. _____ Encourage the counselee to think?

16. _____ Stimulate or encourage the counselee to expand on his/her comments?

17. _____ Express a personal bias?

18. _____ Show respect to the counselee?

19. _____ Permit excessive digression from the issues?

20. _____ Overidentify with the counselee (countertransference)?

21. _____ Remain objective?

22. _____ Deal with silence effectively?

23. _____ Talk down to the counselee?

24. _____ Talk over the counselee's head?

25. _____ Encourage the counselee to acquire insights?

26. _____ Encourage the counselee to problem solve?

27. _____ Encourage the counselee to consider options in problem solving?

28. _____ Try to solve the counselee's problem?

29. _____ Obtain necessary information from the counselee?

30. _____ Move counseling in the direction of the goal or a subgoal?

31. _____ Carefully select the words I used?

32. _____ Allow the counselee adequate time to respond to what I asked or said?

33. _____ Stay on track most of the time?

34. _____ Summarize occasionally?

35. _____ Encourage the counselee to express feelings?

36. _____ Waste time on irrelevant issues/topics?

37. _____ Appear too judgmental?

38. _____ Confront the counselee when necessary?

39. _____ Avoid "playing god"?

40. _____ Make the interview/session meaningful for the counselee?

41. _____ Remember important things that I heard?

42. _____ Respond empathically when appropriate?

43. _____ Do or say something that could have jeopardized confidentiality?

44. _____ Handle myself in a professional manner?

45. _____ Accomplish something with the counselee (e.g., help my counselee acquire an insight)?

46. _____ Stay focused on what was being said?

47. _____ Gain a clearer picture of the counselee and what changes need to be made.
48. _____ Conduct myself ethically?
49. _____ Motivate the counselee to return?
50. _____ Overall, was I pleased with this interview/session?

Things I should work on:

_____   _____   _____

_____   _____   _____

TERMINATION

Planning for termination is a part of the group game plan. Because group counseling is usually time-limited, the number of remaining sessions is always known. The group leader should begin to remind the group of the remaining number of sessions at least two weeks prior to the final session. It must be presumed that although termination may be welcomed by some members, not all members want to see the group sessions end. Termination can be problematic for group members who have become comfortable with the group interaction and feel they are making progress toward their goal. Members can indicate through their words and actions that they are not ready to see the group end. This often happens in support groups and when a group has become cohesive. When, for example, a friendship group represents a welcomed opportunity to interact with peers and friendships have developed within the group as a result of the group experience, members may be reluctant to see it end. Although members of friendship groups are encouraged to continue peer interactions after the group ends, children are sometimes reluctant to extend themselves or find convenient times to meet. A friendship group offers members a built-in opportunity to interact with peers.

Termination can be traumatic for group members who have difficulty letting go of things. This is especially true for children who do not deal with change easily. Termination can also be a problem for members who needed several group sessions to feel safe enough to open up and talk freely in the group. For these members, it would seem that just when they were ready to be able to interact comfortably, the group sessions were coming to an end. Termination is not easy for group members who have become dependent upon the support they receive from the group. Even the nature of the topic can have implications for the way group members react to termination. Grief and divorce groups that have shared feelings and personal experiences and who have developed an empathic bond among themselves would be expected to have a more difficult time parting than would an anger-management or assertiveness group.

THE FINAL GROUP SESSION

The final group session is, after all, a farewell meeting. This is a time for review, reflection, and reminding the group of its accomplishments. For that last meeting, the group leader should have prepared a summary statement that informs the group of the attitudes and behaviors that were present when the group began, the topics that were discussed, what the homework assignments were, the progress it seems to have made with respect to movement toward the group goal, and what still needs to be accomplished. It is a way of saying to the group this is where we began, this is what we did, this is where we are, and this is what still needs to be done. A homework assignment for the last session, which would have been announced at the next-to-last-session, could be to ask the members to write down the things they will remember about their group experience. If the members agree to do the assignment, they could present their recollections at the last meeting.

Doing an evaluation of the group experience would be the last formal request to the members. The evaluation should be short and easy to complete. Yes or No responses would suffice. With older groups, one or two short-answer questions could be asked. Sharing the evaluations with teachers and administrators can be a form of patting oneself on the back; nevertheless, it represents a way to promote the counseling program to members of the faculty and support the value of group counseling. Ethically, if the group leader decides to share the evaluations, the names of the members should be removed.

Either the group leader or members of the group could raise the question of whether the group should try to meet for a follow-up in two to three weeks. This decision should be based on the unanimous agreement of the group. If the group decides to meet again, the group leader would be expected to inform the teachers, parents, and administrator of the decision. At the last group session, some groups have been known to request an extension to the number of group sessions. "Can't we meet for another week?" is the question. An extension is not the same as a follow-up since the follow-up occurs two or more weeks after termination. Extending the number of group sessions can start a precedent that the group leader may not want. It also entails a number of logistical variables, including offering an explanation to parents, teachers, and the administration. Although these arrangements can be made, this writer does not recommend that group sessions be extended unless it is to make up for a canceled session. A minigroup follow-up session would be preferred. A minigroup follow-up would involve one more session after a designated period of time has elapsed.

Prior to termination, the group leader might have some decisions to make. The group leader may have a valid reason for wanting to begin to see a member for individual counseling. Or, the group leader may feel the group experience has identified a group member for whom an out-of-school referral to a mental health professional would seem to be appropriate. There may even be times when the group leader wants to encourage a member to join a different group at a later time.

The final tasks of the group leader would be to thank the group members for their cooperation and participation and encourage them to continue to pursue the group's goal on their own. The group should be told that the ending of the group does not end the need to continue to work on the topic. Members should be encouraged to give themselves homework assignments and set subgoals. The group leader should stress that the number of weeks they met is too short a time for them to expect a complete solution to their problem. The group experience can only have provided them with a direction; now they must continue to achieve their objectives on their own.

Finally, in the last 5 to 10 minutes comes the "farewell party." This should consist of a treat in a relaxed atmosphere. If there are no available school funds for this purpose, the

PTA can be asked to provide a small amount of money for group counseling terminations. Within one or two weeks after termination, the group leader should make contact with the teachers of the members for their informal feedback.

WHERE IS COUNSELING GOING?

As we proceed into the twenty-first century, it is certain there will be gradual changes in the methods of teaching children. All phases of educating children will undergo modifications in order to accommodate the complexities of our pluralistic society. As the student population increases and becomes more diversified, the need for highly trained teachers will increase and greater demands will be placed on students to achieve scholastic excellence. As technology continues to advance and expectations for competency in the workplace increases, a strong emphasis will be placed on creative and innovative ideas for teaching. More will be expected from both teachers and students. Educators will continue to search for ways to improve instruction for all children. They will continue to struggle to find better ways to teach children who show resistance to learning.

Projecting school guidance and counseling programs into the future, this writer feels that major changes in both the training of school counselors and the quality of the services that are delivered in schools will be necessary if school counselors are to meet the needs of students in the twenty-first century. School counselors must be prepared to redefine their role and be willing to expand their professional scope. The school community must recognize the important contribution counselors can make and be supportive of counseling initiatives that encourage the development of new programs for all students. Counselor-educators must work more closely with school systems in order to be aware of the training that prospective counselors will be expected to have. What follows are those things this writer sees as needed changes and a realistic direction for the future of guidance and counseling programs in schools.

1. The title "guidance counselor" should be retired. What is needed are personnel trained in the field of guidance, and personnel who are trained to do counseling. They work together, but their tasks and focus are different. The terms *counselor* and *guidance specialist* would seem to be appropriate to describe these respective services.

2. Counseling in schools must emphasize working with the *total child*. The concept of total-child counseling involves identifying those things that enable children to acquire effective life skills. Helping children to achieve their academic potential is an example of one of these life skills. The ability to make and maintain friendships and the acquisition of socially acceptable behavior are other life skills. For students who are showing that they are experiencing success both academically and socially, total-child counseling would motivate them to maintain their current lifestyle and encourage them to make preparations for their future. For students who are not feeling successful in one or more dimensions of their lives, total-child counseling would seek to identify those things that could be having a negative impact on their ability to learn effective life skills. Total-child counseling encompasses the social, emotional, and environmental aspects of a child's life and attempts to help children become aware of the unmet needs that stand in the way of their satisfaction. Total-child counseling is a more comprehensive approach to counseling and usually involves parental input.

3. School counselors must be trained and prepared to do *clinical school counseling.* The parameters of clinical school counseling will need to be carefully defined. Clinical counseling from a school counselor is not expected to replace or duplicate psychotherapy as practiced by clinical psychologists, psychiatrists, or clinical social workers. However, school counselors will be expected to expand their services to provide more help to children and parents. Clinical counseling looks at the causes of behavior and seeks to help children acquire insights into themselves. Insight can bring about understanding, and understanding often leads to change. Ultimately, when a student's attitude and behavior is conducive to learning, teachers can be more effective, which enables schools to be more successful in fulfilling their mission. Clinical counseling would also encourage parents to become positive support systems for their children.

4. If clinical school counseling is to become a reality, counselor-trainees and practicing school counselors will need to receive additional didactic and practicum training. Counselor-training programs should be prepared to offer a three-year, 64-credit-hour program as a minimum. The focus should be on the internship skills that are needed for counseling the total child. This must also include working more closely with social service agencies, parents, parent groups, and the school community.

5. Counselor-education programs must be able to accommodate the changes that would prepare school counselors to do total-child counseling. Colleges and universities that offer less than a 64-credit-hour program will not be training counselors who will function effectively in the twenty-first century. School-counselor training programs, in addition to meeting the standards established by the Council for Accreditation of Counseling Related Educational Programs (CACREP), must have a faculty that feels competent to train clinical school counselors for total-child counseling. The curriculum should include child and adolescent psychology; abnormal psychology, with an emphasis on the child and adolescent disorders cited in the current DSM; crisis counseling; cross-cultural counseling; family counseling; crime and delinquency prevention; and medical aspects of disabilities. Inasmuch as schools have embraced the concept of inclusion, school counselors must have the knowledge and skills to work with the population of children who have special needs.

6. If schools are to attract top-level counselors, counselor training programs will need to recruit and admit outstanding counselor-trainees. Since a 64-credit-hour program will involve a three-year course of study, colleges should attempt to provide financial resources for paid internships to counselor-trainees. Funding for this could come from the colleges, local school systems, federal or state government, or special grants. Incentives for going into the counseling field are needed in order to attract the outstanding personnel that schools require.

7. As part of a continuing education program for teachers, and to keep parents informed, counselor education programs need to require counselor trainees to develop in-service programs for faculty and parents. These in-service programs should be planned in conjunction with other professionals, such as the school nurse, school psychologist, school social worker, a physician, a psychotherapist, or an attorney. A wide array of topics relevant to teachers and parents could be presented. In-service presentations for school faculty could include:

a. Identifying students who are using or dispensing illegal drugs.
b. Identifying students who are bullies or victims of a bully.
c. Information on sexually transmitted diseases.
d. Multicultural and diversity issues in the school.
e. Assessing intelligence through standardized testing.
f. Therapeutic treatment of specific emotional problems, such as depression, anxiety, oppositional defiant behavior, and phobias.
g. Planning effective consultations with parents.
h. Strategies for motivating students to learn.
i. The impact of divorce on a student's school performance.
j. Strategies for working with students who are underachieving.
k. Working with children who are at risk of dropping out of school.
l. Legal rights of children who are minors.

In-service presentations for parents could include some of the topics stated above, in addition to:

a. Parents as partners in educating a child.
b. Parenting with the resistant and defiant child.
c. The importance of parental consistency.
d. Education as an important value.
e. Essential health habits for school aged children.
f. Parent's and children's legal rights.
g. Examining effective punishment.
h. Necessary and unnecessary parental controls.
i. Career counseling: preparing for life after graduation.
j. When to consider medication for school-related problems.

Meeting either after school or early in the evening, these in-service meetings will give the guidance and counseling program increased visibility and can enhance the counselor's effectiveness. In middle, junior high, or high schools, in-service programs can be presented by the counseling staff. In-service programs aid in creating informed faculty and parents.

   8. Teachers and the pupil personal staff need to be encouraged to become more involved in guidance and counseling programs. This would include classroom teachers, resource teachers, special education teachers, school psychologists, school social workers, and all personnel who come in contact with students. An academic team concept that includes a school counselor is needed to ensure that the educational needs of the total child are being met. Although many school systems have educational management teams in place to discuss and resolve a student's issue, the school counselor may or may not have had contact with the child that is under discussion. The academic team should also meet regularly to discuss school issues unrelated to the specific problem of a student. Their agenda could deal with the school's handling of crisis issues, student decorum, specific concerns of teachers or parents, or student welfare issues. School counselors should be encouraged to work more closely with the school psychologist when the counselor feels that a consultation would be beneficial to a student. It is especially important for elementary school counselors to regularly confer with the school psychologist because there is usually only one counselor in the building and the input from a colleague can be invaluable. Increased contact with school personnel should bring about a greater respect for the guidance and counseling program.

9. There is need for a stronger emphasis on counseling in elementary schools. Every elementary school in the country must have one or more school counselors. Because elementary school counseling is directed at the prevention and identification of problems, it is difficult to understand why there has been resistance to elementary school counseling. In the long run, not having a strong elementary school counseling program is not cost-effective. Hiring elementary school counselors must become a high priority; it is justified even if it takes funds away from other school programs.

10. School counselors at all grade levels must be comfortable with and feel competent to work with children and parents who are from diverse ethnic and racial groups. Counselors will be required to understand concepts related to culturally diverse populations and to become familiar with the research on multicultural counseling. School counselors in the twenty-first century must be aware of cultural differences and be sensitive to the needs of all children. Multicultural counseling has to be emphasized in both the didactic and field experiences of counselor-education programs. Practicums and internships should reflect the knowledge and skills of a counselor who can effectively relate to a diverse population and engage in cross-cultural counseling. This may, at times, involve translators who can assist the counselor in communicating with students and parents.

11. The tragic events of September 11, 2001 have had a significant impact on schools and school-aged children. Acts of terrorism have removed our sense of security and invulnerability. It is not possible to say for certain that schools could not be targeted by a terrorist attack. The plane crashes at New York's World Trade Center and at the Pentagon, along with Anthrax scares and the random shootings we have seen in schools, have resulted in schools developing security and evacuation plans. School violence in all of its forms must be more carefully addressed and school counselors have a significant role to play if schools are to be regarded as a safe place to learn. School administrators and school faculties will need to become acutely aware of the danger signs to look for. Although no prevention plan can guarantee that there will not be violence in a school, it is important to identify students who are showing a propensity for antisocial and aggressive behavior.

Violence encompasses a wide range of behaviors. It can describe a student who pushes another student, a student who threatens another student, a student with a proclivity for hitting and fighting, a defiant student, or a student who carries a weapon to school. Bullying is a major precursor of violence in schools. The student who bullies will often carry threats into offensive and aggressive actions. The victim of bullying is also a potential danger to a school since they can reach a tolerance point and ultimately seek revenge on the bully as well as those who witnessed and failed to discourage the bullying. Since the victim usually lacks the courage and ability to extract revenge, a gun is often employed to give the victim courage and satisfaction. When a victim reaches a point of feeling that life has become intolerable, the victim can feel that killing is justified. For this reason, passive students who look harmless but are the victims of one or more bullies need to be identified. It is essential that bullying be stopped. Every person in the school community should feel responsible for reporting bullying incidents to a teacher, an administrator, or a school counselor. Although a zero tolerance policy for all forms of violence is necessary, it will not prevent violence from occurring. School campaigns against bullying can be effective.

Both bullies and victims should be referred to the school counselor to determine whether the problem can be handled within the school, or if an out of school referral is necessary. Most school counselors are in need of additional training in the areas of identification of violent students, methods for working with children who meet the criteria of being violent, and ethical and legal issues including student rights, determining when a referral is necessary, and deciding who should be contacted if a referral is made.

12. Non-counseling activities should not consume the bulk of a counselor's time. Middle school and high school counselors must be free of their non-counseling responsibilities so that they may devote their time to counseling students both individually and in groups. The practice of using school counselors primarily to develop class schedules for students and to make schedule changes throughout the school year discourages bright and talented counselor trainees from becoming secondary school counselors. Counselor trainees who have a strong desire to work with an adolescent population are often disappointed to learn that many high school counselors do very little counseling. When class scheduling is done by secretarial or the non-professional staff, counselors will be able to do the kind of work for which they have been trained and for which there is a strong need. Adolescents should know there are counselors in the building who are there to help them deal with academic, social, career, and personal issues. Secondary school counselors should be viewed as professionals who are committed to providing both counseling and guidance services.

13. If counselors are to be effective, the caseload of a school counselor should not be more than 300 to 1. Assuming that 10 percent of children will need individual assistance at some time during their school years, a 300 to 1 ratio means the school counselor could be seeing approximately 30 children individually on a sustained basis at some time during the school year. The fact that some elementary school counselors service two schools and could have a total caseload of up to 1,000 students is professionally unrealistic. A counselor who is forced to work with this number of students is rendered ineffective. The fact that some elementary schools do not have even one counselor is professionally unacceptable. A ratio of 250 to 1 is more acceptable, but for budgetary reasons this may not be realistic.

14. School counselors need to have the opportunity to receive clinical supervision. In most school systems, supervisors of guidance and counseling rarely get involved in case management or the professional and ethical issues inherent in counseling. They function as administrative supervisors. School counselors must have the opportunity to discuss counselee concerns with supervisors who have been trained to do clinical supervision.

15. Counselor education programs should work more closely with local school districts. The academician is often accused of being removed from the reality of what school counselors really do in schools, and are thought to be idealistic, not realistic, to the work of the school counselor. Counselor educators get a glimpse of what school counselors are doing when they visit schools in conjunction with supervising practicum and internship students who are engaged in their field experience. Counselor education programs and supervisors of guidance and counseling in schools should collaborate and share ideas about what can be done to make both counselor education and school counseling programs more effective. Counselor educators must be aware of what schools will expect of school counselors, as well as the problems counseling trainees will face. Public schools need to know that graduates of counselor education programs are prepared to function within the school system. A close collaboration, or partnership, between public schools and counselor education programs would make it easy for counselor educators to have a positive impact on a school's guidance and counseling program. Likewise, the public school's supervisor of guidance and counseling would have the opportunity to have an impact on the counselor education program whenever changes are recommended by either group.

Because public schools are used as the sites for the field experience of counselor trainees, it is important that counselor trainees receive a complete training experience in their assigned schools and that they are properly supervised. Instruction in the supervision of counselor trainees who are in a practicum or internship is one area in which counselor education programs can assist a school counselor who is functioning as a field supervisor. It is incumbent on counselor education programs to ensure that field supervisors have the fundamental skills needed for supervising counselor trainees. Developing a workshop on methods of supervision for field supervisors is one way this can be accomplished. Partnerships between universities and the public schools will encourage a professional relationship that benefits both institutions.

16. School principals need to become more aware of the training school counselors receive, how counselors define their role, and how best to utilize the counselors' skills. They also should have a clear understanding of what their role as administrators should be in a comprehensive guidance and counseling program. In the training of principals and teachers, the role of the school counselor is not usually discussed. Counselor training programs must begin to work more closely with the programs that prepare both teachers and school principals.

17. Parents must become more involved in the counseling process. With many of the problems that children present, counseling a child without some parental contact and cooperation will rarely be successful. Counselors will need to gain experience interacting with parents and be able to provide minimal services to dysfunctional families and parents who are in need of basic parenting skills. Minimal services implies that although school counselors are not expected to be family counselors, they should be able to identify family problems, discuss family concerns with parents, and make appropriate referrals to family agencies.

18. If school counselors are to work with parents, there are times when they will have to accommodate the work schedule of parents. Although highly involved parents usually find the time to see the school counselor during the school day, this may not always be possible. If counselors are meeting with parents about parenting skills or ways parents can help their child, or if they are meeting with small groups of parents, it may be necessary to be at the school at times other than the hours that children are in school. For this reason, the school counselor's hours should be flexible. Counselors who are working late afternoons or in the evenings should be able to have time off in a morning or afternoon so that their work week is not extended because of the services they provide.

19. Counselor-trainees should be required to receive personal counseling as a part of their training. There are at least three reasons why this is important: (1) It enables the counselor-trainee to have an experience that makes it possible to relate to what it feels like to be a counselee; (2) as counselees, counselor-trainees will observe and learn effective counseling skills firsthand from a counselor who could serve as a professional role model; (3) it will provide the counselor-trainee with an opportunity to identify and work out any personal problems that might interfere with his or her own counseling. Undoubtedly, there are practicing school counselors whose mental health would suggest that they should seek professional mental health services. There are also practicing school counselors who should probably not be school counselors. Requiring counselor-trainees to undergo counseling is both ethically and professionally correct. Advanced or doctoral-level counseling students, or doctoral-level clinical psychology students, could be used to provide counseling for the counselor-trainees. Counselor training could also be obtained through a college or university counseling center. A minimum number of individual counseling sessions could be required, but the exact number should be determined by the training counselor who is working with the counselor-trainee. In the event the counselor-trainer uncovers serious concerns relative to a trainee, appropriate professional and ethical actions would need to be taken. Universities that prepare school counselors have a moral and ethical responsibility to assure schools and society that their graduates are emotionally and mentally competent to work with a K–12 population.

20. School counselor recertification should be required every five years. Continuing education involving coursework, workshops, and supervision in both generic and school counseling should be implemented for all practicing school counselors. Continuing education should reflect professional training that is didactic, hands-on, research-based, and concerned with case management. The number of hours required and the responsibility for providing professional continuing-education opportunities could be determined by the state agency that certifies school counselors. Colleges and universities that offer approved counselor-training programs or a school system's in-service training programs could be used to satisfy this requirement if appropriate professional personnel are available.

21. Perhaps the greatest challenge confronting educational leaders is the need to improve conditions in the inner-city schools of our major cities. Urban education initiatives must focus on methods that will enable children to receive a quality education. Not only does the school environment have to become more conducive to learning but the standards of excellence in these schools also need to be raised. The issues that should be addressed include determining a relevant curriculum, making the commitment to elevate achievement scores, finding ways to improve attendance and social interactions, searching for competent teachers who have the passion to teach inner-city children, and imparting the value of education to all children.

School counselors have a critical role to play in urban education. They will need to acquire effective methods for empowering students not only to believe in their ability to succeed but also to take responsibility for doing what is necessary to become successful. Efforts to accomplish this objective must begin in the pre-kindergarten years. Elementary school counselors should be prepared to work with nursery school students and their parents in order to prevent negative and apathetic attitudes toward school from developing. School counselors will have to work closely with parents and form parent education groups. Group counseling with students will be a necessary component of an empowerment strategy. Career counseling needs to begin in the elementary school years. Students should be encouraged to begin making tentative plans and developing options for their lives in middle or junior high schools. The attitude that students bring into a high school is a valid predictor of the academic success the student will have in high school. It is important that students leave high school with a direction for their future.

Not many school counselors are trained or prepared to work with children from our inner-city schools. There is a need to initiate research on strategies that can be effective for these students and to begin to train urban school counselors who are motivated to accept the challenges that will greet them. Traditional approaches will have to be modified and new approaches must be developed if this large segment of our school-aged population is to be effectively integrated into society. Considerable attention is being directed at urban education initiatives. The school counselor must play a major role in these endeavors.

22. In order to accommodate increased diversity, school counselors in the twenty-first century should be encouraged to become bilingual. It is already common for students to enter our schools unable to speak or comprehend English. When their parents are also unable to communicate in English, it is difficult to help these students learn or adjust to their new school. If we are to keep pace with the changes that will occur in our society, schools should require students to become somewhat fluent in a second language. Colleges and universities could make a degree of fluency in a second language a mandatory requirement.

23. Counseling, as a behavioral science, will have to become more scientific. Research needs to be directed at counseling methods that can be used with students who pose the kinds of academic and social problems that have plagued schools for decades. Research-based treatment strategies are needed that can help schools and counselors deal more effectively with students who bully, are aggressive and sometimes violent, exhibit chronic conduct problems, have negative attitudes toward school, have weak interpersonal skills, are under-achieving or nonachieving, and who are at risk for dropping out of school without a career direction. There are many counseling theories, but no uniform, recommended, or standard treatment strategies for the many academic and behavior problems that are seen in schools. There is a need to learn what counseling approaches are most effective with specific problems. This knowledge would provide school counselors with a clear direction for an appropriate intervention through awareness of the skills that are needed to attack specific problems. It would also result in greater respect for the field of counseling by making counseling more scientific, school counselors more professional, and by leaving less to chance. Multiple task forces that focus on counseling strategies to use with specific problems would be welcomed. There is a need for ongoing research in all schools.

Perhaps this cannot be accomplished. It may not be possible to make counseling more scientific and to discover standard treatments that are effective for specific problems. There are many intervening variables that could make this an impossible task. One thing is certain, we will never know if it can be done until sincere efforts are undertaken.

24. Finally, the money issue. All schools need more money to operate effectively. Teachers and counselors need higher salaries; new schools need to be built and many schools are in need of remodeling. Some schools need money to buy books for students, and class size must be reduced to workable numbers. A strong comprehensive guidance and counseling program is not inexpensive. Caseloads must become more manageable, and for this to happen, more qualified counselors must be hired. The salary of new school counselors who complete a three-year, 64-credit hour graduate program, and those practicing counselors who take additional professional coursework to reach the 64-credit-hour minimum, should be commensurate with their training and responsibilities. School systems need to find a way to make counselors eleven-month employees. In order to accomplish the work that counselors need to do, school counselors should be able to use the summer months to prepare for the school year and do necessary follow-ups. This would include meeting with students who have been retained or those who did not do well academically, speaking with parents, visiting social service agencies, identifying and meeting with prospective employers of graduates, and talking with those mental health professionals who are used for referral purposes. The summer months could be used to develop student schedules and reduce the amount of time middle and high school counselors are forced to spend during the academic year changing schedules. As changes occur in the delivery of counseling services, more money will have to be set aside for the counseling program. Unless counseling programs are given a high priority in the school's budget, things cannot be expected to change. Investing money in a school counseling program is investing in the future leaders of our country.

School counseling is a growing field that is still evolving. Working with a school-aged population is very exciting and can be a gratifying experience. There is much that a school counselor can do to become a significant person in the present and future of a child. Group counseling, as a strategy, is an important part of this growing field. Yet, without a strong counseling program and effective group counselors, the impetus of group counseling is greatly reduced. We have come a long way since Frank Parsons . . . but we still have a long way to go.

EPILOGUE

It is generally acknowledged that one of the most serious national problems we face today is that of educating children in our public schools. Although this is not a new problem, in recent years it has become more evident that our educational system is in trouble. As the population of children seeking an education has increased, there has been a shortage of classrooms and trained teachers to accommodate the need. This has resulted in overcrowding and the hiring of teachers who do not always meet the standards that have been set by a school system. In recent years, educational eligibility has been extended to include children with special needs. This has resulted in a challenge to find ways to educate all children who can benefit from educational programs.

Money, personnel, instructional methods, and safety head the list of the problems faced by schools. Pressure is the common denominator underlying these problems. Federal directives and school systems in the twenty-first century are putting considerable pressure on students to achieve high scores on standardized tests. Administrators put pressure on teachers when test scores are not high. Parents voice concerns about the quality of education their children are receiving and put pressure on teachers to do better. Teachers are frustrated by uncooperative students who lack motivation to do their best and put pressure on children to learn. Despite efforts to deal with diversity issues, there is disparity in the test scores of students from growing minority populations. Drug problems, occasional shootings, the formation of gangs, and the need to have security officers in some schools have caused many parents and school-aged children to feel that schools are not a safe place to learn. It would seem that educators have yet to develop effective methods of educating and managing the increased number of children who live in our pluralistic society.

In order to deal with students who disrupt classrooms and create problems in a school, a significant part of a teacher's daily routine must be spent on discipline. Add to this the recent trend of violence that has occurred at all school levels and it is not difficult to realize that schools must examine new ways to identify, understand, and overcome these problems. Too many students are not achieving their academic potential. Too many students are dropping out of school and too many of these students may feel they have been pushed out of school. Too many students from diverse populations feel estranged from the school community. Too many teachers have become disenchanted with their chosen profession and have left teaching. Too many children who could and should do better in school are turned off to learning. Many parents no longer trust that schools will educate their children to reach their maximum academic potential.

Fundamentally, the mission of a school is to educate children. Figuratively speaking, education is the *product* that is being dispensed and teachers are, essentially, *dispensers* of the product. Students are the *consumers* of the product. When the consumers of the product fail to produce the results that are expected, that is, when students do not achieve their academic potential, school boards, administrators, parents, and state legislatures are critical of the dispenser of the product. The message has been that schools need to find better ways to market and deliver the product so that it is more stimulating, attractive, and beneficial to the consumer, who is, of course, the student. In other words, the thinking seems to be that if schools would evaluate themselves objectively, assess student competencies accurately, make needed changes in the curriculum, use state-of-the-art technology to upgrade instructional methods, test students more frequently, and insist on better teaching, more students will achieve their academic potential. This may be true.

Some students complain that what schools teach is not always relevant and often boring. This may also be true, at times. However, if this were true most of the time, what would explain the academic success that many school-aged children are experiencing and the high level of scholarship that can be seen in standardized achievement tests, SAT scores, and the number of merit scholars? The fact is many students *are* learning and their accomplishments can make an educational system feel proud of their efforts. Many students, on the other hand, are not succeeding in school. The number of low-achieving and underachieving students is significant, which means that many students are functioning below their academic potential. This is the population that is responsible for the national problem that is perplexing educators and our schools. This is the population whose negative attitudes toward schools and low test scores have loaded public schools with problems that have yet to be resolved. The comments made by this writer address this latter group.

What if equal responsibility for our educational crisis should be shared by the consumer of the product, namely, the student? What if a student's lack of motivation to learn is based on the *priorities* of the student, and that having *low academic priorities* is the best explanation for why standardized test scores are low and teachers' frustration high? Student apathy and indifference to school is usually related to priorities. What if the expectation of many students is that education should be less rigorous and more entertaining? What if many students view school primarily as a source of social interaction and its educative efforts are there to be tolerated? What if parental expectations are not always realistic and some parents have inadvertently programmed their children to place a low priority on formal education by abandoning some of their parental responsibilities? What if society has placed too many attractive distractions in front of impressionable youngsters? What if *student resistance to learning*, unrelated to the curriculum, teaching, or instructional methods, is the significant issue that has created and maintains the problem? What if the locus of the problem lies more in the attitude of the consumer than the ineptness of the dispenser? If these issues are valid in explaining the reasons for the problems faced by schools, then improved instructional methods or a stronger curriculum will not solve the problem.

The solution would seem to lie in sharing responsibility for the problem. Both the student and school system would need to clarify and understand their respective roles and strive to cooperate with each other in order to develop the changes that are needed. Educational reform should not be a one-way street. The burden for change should not lie exclusively with the educator. *Student reform* is long overdue.

Certainly, an educational curriculum needs constant reevaluation, and improvement must be an ever-present goal of education. Continuing education for teachers will always be needed to upgrade instructional methods and help weak teachers become stronger. But changes also seem to be needed in the attitude and behaviors of the student. Learning can be many things. It can be challenging, exciting, interesting, motivating, provocative, and can encourage students to think, reflect, understand, dream of goals, and formulate plans for the future. Sometimes learning can even be fun. Learning, however, is not fun the way going to a theme park, playing a sport, or "hanging out" with friends is fun. Aspects of learning can be fun, but learning is a discipline, a task, a responsibility. Learning should be considered hard work for most students regardless of how it is presented. If the attitude of students is to expect school to be fun and learning to be easy, the mind-set of students will not be conducive to meeting the standards set by educational systems and they will ultimately pose problems for a school. Education is both a philosophy and a value. The challenges educators face would seem to include finding ways to inculcate the value of education in all students and their parents, to develop an outstanding curriculum, to impart this curriculum effectively, to encourage parents to work cooperatively with the school, and to make education a high priority for students and their parents. School can be a major source of social interaction, extracurricular activities, and athletic competition, but the primary function of a school is to teach children and the primary goal for children who are in school should be to learn.

Yet the trouble schools are having should not be viewed solely as an educational problem; we are also facing a societal crisis. Schools are a microcosm of the society and reflect the values and attitudes of the culture. Significant changes in schools will not occur until changes appear in our social structure. A society that exploits violence and sex through the media is a breeding ground for violence and active sexuality in schools. An impatient culture that values speed and insists that everything be done quickly can result in children who are easily bored with routine and cannot be expected to spend the time needed to master concepts, regardless of their difficulty. A society in which family unity is not seen encourages young children to become autonomous too soon and to reject authority. And a society that only pays lip service to the impact that role models have on children should not be shocked when youngsters imitate the negative role models they see and hear. Today, professional athletes, musical groups, and actors probably command the highest adulation in our society. Although some athletes are positive role models, many are not. The changes that are needed must be across-the-board and would require an examination of our societal practices and what is tolerated in our culture. What society condemns should not be condoned. Schools cannot function independently of the society that governs them.

Unfortunately, school counseling has not made the significant impact that it could on helping children who are not academically achieving or who are having difficulty adjusting to the expectations of school. This is partly due to the inability of many counselors to function in accordance with the way their training defined their role. In many middle and high schools there is a serious discrepancy between the role that is assigned to the school counselor and the training the counselor received. It is unfortunate when middle and high school counselors must spend hundreds of hours scheduling classes for students instead of helping troubled students overcome the problems that prevent them from learning. We need more school counselors, especially at the elementary school level. We need more professional counselors at all levels who are allowed, expected, and understand *how* to counsel children. We need counselors who are well prepared and committed to help school-aged children become productive members of our society.

School counselors cannot solve the problems of schools. Nor should school counselors be expected to elevate standardized test scores by themselves. What they *can* do, however, is establish lines of communication with parents and attempt to impart to parents the value of an education and the role they must be prepared to assume in helping their child succeed academically. They *can* help students to overcome or reduce some of the barriers that prevent them from meeting their academic potential through individual and group counseling. They *can* work to improve the climate of a school for diverse groups of children. They *can* develop strategies directed at preventing and identifying student problems. They *can* encourage children to develop a more positive and realistic attitude toward themselves and the education they will need in the twenty-first century. They *can* assist students in the pursuit of educational and vocational goals. And they *can* work with teachers in a complementary and supportive way to develop a stronger team approach in dealing with the academic problems of students. School counselors are needed because schools are faced with problems that cannot be resolved solely by the efforts of teachers. If it is valid to assume that student apathy and indifference to learning underlies many of the problems faced by schools, then school counselors have a critical role to undertake in effecting some of the changes that are needed in the attitudes of many school-aged children. It is a challenge that must be met. A known but often forgotten fact is that today's school children are destined to become the adults who will serve our communities and lead our country.

Our educational system has been in trouble for many years. If there is ever to be a light at the end of the tunnel, it must come from a close examination of *all* of the components of the problem. This would include doing what is necessary to change the attitude of the student, improve the delivery of educational services, evaluate what society is doing that contributes to and maintains the problem, and then seek solutions.

School counseling is not a panacea, but it can be a valuable adjunct in meeting the needs of a child. A highly educated society might be the nearest thing to a panacea. An educated society could be the best means of reducing the problems of unemployment, crime, social inequities, and many other societal problems. As educators, school counselors have a critical role to play in shaping the future of our school-aged generation.

INDIVIDUAL COUNSELING MODEL FOR SCHOOL COUNSELORS

This is a model for working with children in a school setting. It can be used when the counselor feels that a student will be seen for multiple visits. It is best used for six or more sessions. Although usually only about 10 per cent of the counselor's caseload requires seeing a student that often, in some schools this might result in 50 or more youngsters needing a sustained counseling relationship during the school year.

The counseling strategy employed by a counselor should be determined by a number of factors, including (1) the nature of the problem, (2) the severity of the problem, (3) how long the problem has existed, (4) the motivation of the counselee to work toward change, (5) the ease or difficulty in establishing rapport, (6) the prognosis, (7) cooperation from teachers, (8) the need for parental involvement, (9) the counselor's available time, and (10) the comfort the counselor has with a particular strategy.

KEY POINTS WHEN DOING INDIVIDUAL COUNSELING

1. Be aware of logistical problems involved in scheduling times to see a student. When multiple appointments are planned, the times and days should be staggered so that one class is not repeatedly missed.

2. Counseling sessions should be considered almost "sacred" times. Interruptions should occur only for emergency reasons. No phone calls should be taken and interruptions should be discouraged. Counselees need your undivided attention and must feel that they are a high priority.

3. It is suggested that individual counseling sessions with children in kindergarten to grade 2 be about 20 to 30 minutes, grades 3 to 5 could be from 25 to 35 minutes, grades 6 to 8 could be from 35 to 40 minutes, and high school students could be a classroom period. The time of a counseling session can vary according to the interest of the child and your own judgment, but a counseling sessions should not exceed 45 minutes. Allow time for returning to class.

4. When seeing children who are in grades K and 1, be prepared to meet the child in the classroom and walk the child back to the classroom.

5. Be cautious when taking notes but always write a summary after the student leaves your office. Not only does this enable you to keep a record of what transpired in the session but it provides direction for the start of the next counseling session.

6. Remember that as a school counselor you are doing counseling, not psychotherapy. Although there are some similarities, there are significant differences. In general, the school counselor should

   ■ Attempt to establish rapport as quickly as possible.
   ■ Focus largely on present behavior.
   ■ Collect antecedent information only when this data is needed.
   ■ Determine a tentative goal.
   ■ Begin to formulate a strategy as soon as possible. The counselor should work from a game plan.
   ■ As early as deemed necessary, the counselee should know the reason that he or she is being seen for counseling.
   ■ Set and pursue subgoals that will lead to the reason the child is being seen.
   ■ Actively involve the counselee from the beginning.
   ■ Determine the motivation the counselee has for being in counseling and for undertaking change. Unless the counselee is motivated to attain the objective, counseling will not be effective. It may be necessary to work on motivation before dealing with the presenting problem.
   ■ Be sure to differentiate symptoms from the problem. Although the counselor may not be in a position to work with the problem directly and, therefore, must be content to deal with symptoms, it is important that the counselor never lose sight of what the problem is. The counselor needs to identify both the basic problem and the presenting problem.
   ■ Remember that you are dealing with a child whose behavior is expected to fall within the range of what could be termed "normal" or "expected." Should a counselor perceive that the child's behavior deviates from this expectation, a referral to an outside professional source would be necessary. School counselors must be aware of and respect their professional limitations.
   ■ Comply with the ethical standards of the American Counseling Association and the American School Counselors Association.
   ■ Always be prepared to consult with a colleague if a supervisor is not available and issues develop that suggest a second opinion is needed.
   ■ Use direct rather than nondirective methods when working with young children.
   ■ Use homework assignments when they seem to be appropriate and when there is a high level of probability that the counselee will carry out the assignment.
   ■ Anticipate counselee resistance and bring it out into the open when it is encountered.
   ■ Be aware of motivational differences between students who are self-referred and those who are referred by others.
   ■ Focus on helping the counselee gain insights when it is felt the counselee is capable of acquiring insight.

- Use interpretation in order to help a counselee become aware of explanations for behavior that had, heretofore, not been recognized. Interpretations often lead to insight.
- For change to occur, remember that three things must happen. First, counselees must want to change; second, counselees must be willing to do something to bring about the change; and third, counselees must feel that they have gotten something from the change that will motivate them to continue doing what is needed to bring about the change.
- Do the necessary homework in preparation for working with a student. This could mean checking the student's cumulative record, consulting with current and former teachers, talking with the school psychologist or nurse, checking IEPs, and/or making contact with parents.
- In order to get a good perspective of the counselee, it is often necessary to observe the counselee in a variety of situations. This could include seeing the student in the classroom, lunchroom, walking in the halls, at recess, or getting off the school bus.
- Pick up on all counselee leads. Open-ended responses to the comments of a counselee will yield more information than closed-ended responses (e.g., the answer to "When do you get angry?" is more important to the counselor than the question "Do you ever get angry?").
- Not be afraid of silence. Silence gives both the counselor and counselee time to think and reflect. The counselor should intervene when silence has lasted about 30 seconds.
- Encourage the counselee to do self-examination. (e.g., "Why do you think it has been difficult for you to make friends?" "When do you usually lose your temper?").
- The counselee's problem should be school-related or in some way have an impact on the student's school performance.
- Maintain confidentiality with the counselee unless there is a duty to warn. If what the counselee says gives the counselor a reason to feel there is probable danger to self or others, the counselor should not hesitate to contact parents and notify the principal. Confidentiality also applies to consultations with teachers and parents.
- When it is necessary to see parents, remember that the school counselor is not trained or expected to do family counseling. The counselor should be prepared to refer parents to an appropriate source when it is felt that parenting skills or family problems need to be resolved in order to help the counselee.
- Prepare the counselee for termination. Termination should not be done abruptly.
- Conduct oneself in a professional manner at all times.
- To the extent that it is possible, make an effort to leave problems at school when at home. This is very important to both the counselor and the counselor's family. It is also a preventative for counselor burnout.

A Brief Goal-Directed Counseling Model

PHASE	ACTIVITY INVOLVED	OBJECTIVES/OUTCOME	TIME INVOLVED

Initial	**ASSESSMENT**
	Reason for referral
	Symptomatic behaviors
	Brief history of problem
	Define the problem
	Determine motivation
	   for change
		Establish rapport
		Acquire initial impressions
		Prognosis/disposition
		Determine reference work
		   needed
		Formulate the initial
		   strategy
			1 visit

Exploration	**IDENTIFY/CLARIFY** Goals/subgoals Obstacles to overcome Problem-solving ability Current insights Readiness for change	Begin to know counselee Develop realistic goals Develop subgoals Determine the game plan Communicate/interact Initiate counseling process	2–3 visits

Counseling Process	**IDENTIFY SOLUTIONS**
	Examine consequences
	Increase motivation
	Examine solutions
	Pursue strategy, e.g.,
	   Role Play
	   Rehearse
	   Focus on positives
	Start problem solving
	Interpret behaviors
	Homework assignments
		Effect changes
		Direction to goals/subgoals
		Define objectives
		Working through problems
		Define first tasks
		Practice specific behaviors
		Acquire insights
		Encourage risk-taking
		Develop: Greater
		   awareness of self,
		   sensitivity, empathy
		Elevate self-esteem
			2–3 visits

Continuation	**REPORT AND DISCUSS**
	Behavior changes
	New insights
	New feelings
	Successes
	Nonsuccesses
	New subgoals
		Ascertain movement to
		   goals and subgoals
		Evaluate progress or
		   lack of progress
		Reinforce changes
			Weekly then
			biweekly

Kenneth R. Greenberg, Ph.D.

NEEDS ASSESSMENT SURVEY: PARENT EDITION

To: Parents of Students at Foster Middle School
From: Janet Dawes, Trudy Johnson, and Frank Williams
          Counselors at Foster Middle School
Re: The Group Counseling Program

The counselors at Foster Middle School are preparing to begin group counseling. Throughout the school year, a number of groups will be formed to benefit students through group interaction. As a parent, you can recommend that your child become a member of one of these groups. On the last page of this letter you will see eight topics that are frequently used in group counseling. Please indicate if you feel your child could profit from membership in one or more of these groups. Groups of five to seven students usually meet eight times during the semester. A group meeting lasts about 40 minutes. Group members would be excused from class but they are required to make up any missed work and they are expected to do all of their homework assignments.

Students find small group counseling to be very helpful. Meeting and talking with classmates about their concerns can be an important way to offer students support and encouragement. It is also a way to help them realize that other students have problems that are similar to theirs.

Your child has received a similar survey. The teachers at Foster Middle School have been asked to recommend students for small group counseling. All members who are selected to be in a group must have parental permission and you would be asked to sign a permission slip before your child can become a group member. Students are free to drop out of the group at any time. You would be notified if your child decides to leave the group.

One or two of the counselors in this school will be the group leaders. The room where the group will meet has yet to be determined. If your child is included in a group, you will receive all of the necessary details. If you have questions about the group counseling program, please do not hesitate to contact one of the counselors.

On the following page, please check the group topic that you feel would benefit your child. You may check more than one topic. Your child will be informed that you have suggested that he or she might want to consider becoming part of a particular group. Unfortunately, it may not be possible to include your child in the groups that are currently being formed. Since groups are limited to from five to seven students, your child may not be placed in the first groups, but be assured that your child will be included in an upcoming group. Also, children are not forced to be members of a group. They have to want to be in a group and be willing to abide by specific rules that will govern the group.

If you have more than one child at this school, please indicate the name of the child you are recommending after the description of the group.

Please remove the last sheet from this memo and return it to the counselors' office tomorrow or as soon as possible.

GROUP TOPICS BEING CONSIDERED

1. _____ A friendship group for students who are having a difficult time making friends.
2. _____ A bereavement or grief group for children who have recently experienced the loss of a loved one.
3. _____ A group for students whose parents are either separated or divorced and who are having a difficult time adjusting to the changes in the family.
4. _____ An anger-management group for students who seem to have difficulty controlling their temper or who get into trouble for doing or saying things.
5. _____ A stress-management group for students who have difficulty dealing with everyday pressures. This would include students who worry a lot, get upset easily, have frequent headaches, or who have other problems when they are upset.
6. _____ A self-esteem group for students who would like to feel better about themselves. This would include students who often put themselves down, feel they aren't as good as others, or seem to lack confidence in themselves.
7. _____ An academic group for students who are having problems studying or organizing their time and are not getting good grades.
8. _____ A group for children who have difficulty paying attention in class and may be easily distracted or overly restless.

You can return this survey by mailing it to the counseling office, by asking your child to bring it to school, or by dropping it off yourself at the counseling office in Room 110. But please return this survey tomorrow or as soon as possible since groups are in the process of being formed now.

Parent name _____ Phone _____

Child's name _____

Parent signature _____ Date _____

Thank you for your cooperation.

NEEDS ASSESSMENT SURVEY: FACULTY EDITION

To: Faculty of Foster Middle School
From: Counselors: Janet Dawes, Trudy Johnson, Frank Williams
Re: Identification of Student Needs

Your name: _____ Grade level _____

Subject taught: _____ Date _____

     We will soon be starting small group counseling in the school. We are seeking your help in identifying students whom you feel would benefit from a group counseling experience. The group would meet eight times for 40 minutes, and we would stagger and coordinate the time and days with your schedule. Students will be responsible for completing any missed work and all homework assignments.

     After the topic, please indicate the name(s) of your students whom you would recommend. Each named student would be interviewed to determine willingness and readiness to be in a group. The students and their parents have been given similar surveys to complete and return to us.

1. A friendship group for students who seem to be lacking in social skills.

_____ , _____ , _____

2. A bereavement/grief group for students who have recently experienced the death of a loved one.

_____ , _____ , _____

3. An anger-management group for students who have shown temper problems or who have been identified as being angry or rebellious.

_____ , _____ , _____

4. A stress-management group for students who do not deal with pressure well. This could include test anxiety or chronic problems that relate to stress.

_____ , _____ , _____

5. A self-esteem group for students whom you feel do not have good feelings about themselves. These students may be overly shy, passive, submissive, or quiet. They could also be compensating for their lack of self-esteem by showing a superior attitude or being a braggart.

    _____ , _____ , _____

6. An academic underachievement group for students who show a discrepancy between standardized test scores of ability and their achievement test scores.

    _____ , _____ , _____

7. A group for students who appear to be unmotivated to learn or who have a negative attitude toward school.

    _____ , _____ , _____

8. A group for students who have difficulty following instructions and whose problems could be related to an attention deficit disorder.

    _____ , _____ , _____

9. A group for students who seem to have problems organizing their schoolwork and are unprepared for class.

    _____ , _____ , _____

10. A group for students who are facing a parental divorce or separation and may be having a difficult time adjusting to their home environment.

    _____ , _____ , _____

Please return this survey to our office or put it in one of our mailboxes as soon as possible since we are ready to identify group members. If one of your students is selected to be in a group, you will be notified. Feel free to make comments at the bottom of this sheet.
    Thank you.

Comments/suggestions for other groups: _____

_____

_____

NEEDS ASSESSMENT SURVEY: STUDENT EDITION

To: Students of Foster Middle School
From: Ms. Smith, Ms. Johnson, and Mr. Williams
         Counselors at Foster Middle School
Re: Survey for Group Counseling

We are starting to form several small groups of students who have common concerns or problems. We would meet once a week for eight weeks this semester. If any of the topics listed below interest you, and you would like to be a member of a group, please check the topic or topics that interest you. If there is a topic you are interested in that we have not mentioned, you may write it in where it says "Other." When you have finished, fold these sheets in half and bring this survey to our office, Room 101. Or, you may ask one of your teachers to put it in our mailbox.

Name _____ Grade _____

Home Room Teacher's name _____

Today's date _____

        Read each of the following topics carefully. Put a check in front of the topic you might be interested in discussing as a member of a small group. You may put a check in front of more than one topic.

_____ I would like to have more friends.
_____ My parents are either divorced or they are getting divorced.
_____ I'd like to get better grades in school.
_____ Sometimes I get very angry and don't know how to stop being angry.
_____ I am upset because someone whom I loved has died.
_____ I am teased a lot and this makes me mad.
_____ I think that I am too shy.
_____ I don't like school.
_____ I am restless and have a hard time paying attention in class.
_____ I have trouble making decisions.

_____ I want to like myself more than I do now.
_____ I get into trouble a lot.
_____ I feel that I am under a lot of stress.
_____ I am not happy in this school.
_____ Someone in this school is bullying me.
_____ Other: Write in the topic you would like to discuss in a small group.

_____

_____

Please check one of the following statements.

1. _____   The topic or topics I have checked interest me and I may want to become a member of a small group dealing with that topic.

2. _____   I am not interested in becoming a member of a small group right now, but maybe later.

3. _____   I am not interested in becoming a member of a small group.

Please return this survey today since groups will be formed very soon.

SAMPLE TIME SHEET

To: _____

From: _____

Date _____

_____ arrived at my office at _____ and has been with me until _____ .

Thank you for allowing _____ to be excused from your class. If homework or other assignments have not been turned in, or if work has not been made up, please let me know.

CONTRACT OF MEMBER EXPECTATIONS

I, _____ , have heard and understand what is expected of group members, including the rules that my group will be using throughout our group sessions. I feel all of the rules are important, especially the rule about confidentiality, and I understand that breaking a rule can have serious consequences. I will do my best to be a good group member and I promise not to break any of the rules.

Signed _____ Date _____

ACA CODE OF ETHICS AND STANDARDS OF PRACTICE

PREAMBLE

The American Counseling Association is an educational, scientific, and professional organization whose members are dedicated to the enhancement of human development throughout the life-span. Association members recognize diversity in our society and embrace a cross-cultural approach in support of the worth, dignity, potential, and uniqueness of each individual.

The specification of a code of ethics enables the association to clarify to current and future members, and to those served by members, the nature of the ethical responsibilities held in common by its members. As the code of ethics of the association, this document establishes principles that define the ethical behavior of association members. All members of the American Counseling Association are required to adhere to the Code of Ethics and the Standards of Practice. The Code of Ethics will serve as the basis for processing ethical complaints initiated against members of the association.

SECTION A: THE COUNSELING RELATIONSHIP

A.1. Client Welfare

a. Primary Responsibility. The primary responsibility of counselors is to respect the dignity and to promote the welfare of clients.

b. Positive Growth and Development. Counselors encourage client growth and development in ways that foster the clients' interest and welfare; counselors avoid fostering dependent counseling relationships.

c. Counseling Plans. Counselors and their clients work jointly in devising integrated, individual counseling plans that offer reasonable promise of success and are consistent with abilities and circumstances of clients. Counselors and clients regularly review counseling plans to ensure their continued viability and effectiveness, respecting clients' freedom of choice. (See A.3.b.)

d. Family Involvement. Counselors recognize that families are usually important in clients' lives and strive to enlist family understanding and involvement as a positive resource, when appropriate.

e. Career and Employment Needs. Counselors work with their clients in considering employment in jobs and circumstances that are consistent with the clients' overall abilities, vocational limitations, physical restrictions, general temperament, interest and aptitude patterns, social skills, education, general qualifications, and other relevant characteristics and needs. Counselors neither place nor participate in placing clients in positions that will result in damaging the interest and the welfare of clients, employers, or the public.

A.2. Respecting Diversity

a. Nondiscrimination. Counselors do not condone or engage in discrimination based on age, color, culture, disability, ethnic group, gender, race, religion, sexual orientation, marital status, or socioeconomic status. (See C.5.a., C.5.b., and D.1.i.)

b. Respecting Differences. Counselors will actively attempt to understand the diverse cultural backgrounds of the clients with whom they work. This includes, but is not limited to, learning how the counselor's own cultural, ethnic, and racial identity impacts her or his values and beliefs about the counseling process. (See E.8. and F.2.i.)

A.3. Client Rights

a. Disclosure to Clients. When counseling is initiated, and throughout the counseling process as necessary, counselors inform clients of the purposes, goals, techniques, procedures, limitations, and potential risks and benefits of services to be performed, and other pertinent information. Counselors take steps to ensure that clients understand the implications of diagnosis, the intended use of tests and reports, fees, and billing arrangements. Clients have the right to expect confidentiality and to be provided with an explanation of its limitations, including supervision and/or treatment team professionals; to obtain clear information about their case records; to participate in the ongoing counseling plans; and to refuse any recommended services and be advised of the consequences of such refusal. (See E.5.a. and G.2.)

b. Freedom of Choice. Counselors offer clients the freedom to choose whether to enter into a counseling relationship and to determine which professional(s) will provide counseling. Restrictions that limit choices of clients are fully explained. (See A.1.c.)

c. Inability to Give Consent. When counseling minors or persons unable to give voluntary informed consent, counselors act in these clients' best interests. (See B.3.)

A.4. Clients Served by Others

If a client is receiving services from another mental health professional, counselors, with client consent, inform the professional persons already involved and develop clear agreements to avoid confusion and conflict for the client. (See C.6.c.)

A.5. Personal Needs and Values

a. Personal Needs. In the counseling relationship, counselors are aware of the intimacy and responsibilities inherent in the counseling relationship, maintain respect for clients, and avoid actions that seek to meet their personal needs at the expense of clients.

b. Personal Values. Counselors are aware of their own values, attitudes, beliefs, and behaviors and how these apply in a diverse society, and avoid imposing their values on clients. (See C.5.a.)

A.6. Dual Relationships

a. Avoid When Possible. Counselors are aware of their influential positions with respect to clients, and they avoid exploiting the trust and dependency of clients. Counselors make every effort to avoid dual relationships with clients that could impair professional judgment or increase the risk of harm to clients. (Examples of such relationships include, but are not limited to, familial, social, financial, business, or close personal relationships with clients.) When a dual relationship cannot be avoided, counselors take appropriate professional precautions such as informed consent, consultation, supervision, and documentation to ensure that judgment is not impaired and no exploitation occurs. (See F.1.b.)

b. Superior/Subordinate Relationships. Counselors do not accept as clients superiors or subordinates with whom they have administrative, supervisory, or evaluative relationships.

A.7. Sexual Intimacies With Clients

a. Current Clients. Counselors do not have any type of sexual intimacies with clients and do not counsel persons with whom they have had a sexual relationship.

b. Former Clients. Counselors do not engage in sexual intimacies with former clients within a minimum of 2 years after terminating the counseling relationship. Counselors who engage in such a relationship after 2 years following termination have the responsibility to examine and document thoroughly that such relations did not have an exploitative nature, based on factors such as duration of counseling, amount of time since counseling, termination circumstances, client's personal history and mental status, adverse impact on the client, and actions by the counselor suggesting a plan to initiate a sexual relationship with the client after termination.

A.8. Multiple Clients

When counselors agree to provide counseling services to two or more persons who have a relationship (such as husband and wife, or parents and children), counselors clarify at the outset which person or persons are clients and the nature of the relationships they will have with each involved person. If it becomes apparent that counselors may be called upon to perform potentially conflicting roles, they clarify, adjust, or withdraw from roles appropriately. (See B.2. and B.4.d.)

A.9. Group Work

a. Screening. Counselors screen prospective group counseling/therapy participants. To the extent possible, counselors select members whose needs and goals are compatible with goals of the group, who will not impede the group process, and whose well-being will not be jeopardized by the group experience.

b. Protecting Clients. In a group setting, counselors take reasonable precautions to protect clients from physical or psychological trauma.

A.10. Fees and Bartering (See D.3.a. and D.3.b.)

a. Advance Understanding. Counselors clearly explain to clients, prior to entering the counseling relationship, all financial arrangements related to professional services including the use of collection agencies or legal measures for nonpayment. (A.11.c.)

b. Establishing Fees. In establishing fees for professional counseling services, counselors consider the financial status of clients and locality. In the event that the established fee structure is inappropriate for a client, assistance is provided in attempting to find comparable services of acceptable cost. (See A.10.d., D.3.a., and D.3.b.)

c. Bartering Discouraged. Counselors ordinarily refrain from accepting goods or services from clients in return for counseling services because such arrangements create inherent potential for conflicts, exploitation, and distortion of the professional relationship. Counselors may participate in bartering only if the relationship is not exploitative, if the client requests it, if a clear written contract is established, and if such arrangements are an accepted practice among professionals in the community. (See A.6.a.)

d. Pro Bono Service. Counselors contribute to society by devoting a portion of their professional activity to services for which there is little or no financial return (pro bono).

A.11. Termination and Referral

a. Abandonment Prohibited. Counselors do not abandon or neglect clients in counseling. Counselors assist in making appropriate arrangements for the continuation of treatment, when necessary, during interruptions such as vacations, and following termination.

b. Inability to Assist Clients. If counselors determine an inability to be of professional assistance to clients, they avoid entering or immediately terminate a counseling relationship. Counselors are knowledgeable about referral resources and suggest appropriate alternatives. If clients decline the suggested referral, counselors should discontinue the relationship.

c. Appropriate Termination. Counselors terminate a counseling relationship, securing client agreement when possible, when it is reasonably clear that the client is no longer benefiting, when services are no longer required, when counseling no longer serves the client's needs or interests, when clients do not pay fees charged, or when agency or institution limits do not allow provision of further counseling services. (See A.10.b. and C.2.g.)

A.12. Computer Technology

a. Use of Computers. When computer applications are used in counseling services, counselors ensure that (1) the client is intellectually, emotionally, and physically capable of using the computer application; (2) the computer application is appropriate for the needs of the client; (3) the client understands the purpose and operation of the computer applications; and (4) a follow-up of client use of a computer application is provided to correct possible misconceptions, discover inappropriate use, and assess subsequent needs.

b. Explanation of Limitations. Counselors ensure that clients are provided information as a part of the counseling relationship that adequately explains the limitations of computer technology.

c. Access to Computer Applications. Counselors provide for equal access to computer applications in counseling services. (See A.2.a.)

SECTION B: CONFIDENTIALITY

B.1. Right to Privacy

a. Respect for Privacy. Counselors respect their clients right to privacy and avoid illegal and unwarranted disclosures of confidential information. (See A.3.a. and B.6.a.)

b. Client Waiver. The right to privacy may be waived by the client or his or her legally recognized representative.

c. Exceptions. The general requirement that counselors keep information confidential does not apply when disclosure is required to prevent clear and imminent danger to the client or others or when legal requirements demand that confidential information be revealed. Counselors consult with other professionals when in doubt as to the validity of an exception.

d. Contagious, Fatal Diseases. A counselor who receives information confirming that a client has a disease commonly known to be both communicable and fatal is justified in disclosing information to an identifiable third party, who by his or her relationship with the client is at a high risk of contracting the disease. Prior to making a disclosure the counselor should ascertain that the client has not already informed the third party about his or her disease and that the client is not intending to inform the third party in the immediate future. (See B.1.c and B.1.f.)

e. Court-Ordered Disclosure. When court ordered to release confidential information without a client's permission, counselors request to the court that the disclosure not be required due to potential harm to the client or counseling relationship. (See B.1.c.)

f. Minimal Disclosure. When circumstances require the disclosure of confidential information, only essential information is revealed. To the extent possible, clients are informed before confidential information is disclosed.

g. Explanation of Limitations. When counseling is initiated and throughout the counseling process as necessary, counselors inform clients of the limitations of confidentiality and identify foreseeable situations in which confidentiality must be breached. (See G.2.a.)

h. Subordinates. Counselors make every effort to ensure that privacy and confidentiality of clients are maintained by subordinates including employees, supervisees, clerical assistants, and volunteers. (See B.1.a.)

i. Treatment Teams. If client treatment will involve a continued review by a treatment team, the client will be informed of the team's existence and composition.

B.2. Groups and Families

a. Group Work. In group work, counselors clearly define confidentiality and the parameters for the specific group being entered, explain its importance, and discuss the difficulties related to confidentiality involved in group work. The fact that confidentiality cannot be guaranteed is clearly communicated to group members.

b. Family Counseling. In family counseling, information about one family member cannot be disclosed to another member without permission. Counselors protect the privacy rights of each family member. (See A.8., B.3., and B.4.d.)

B.3. Minor or Incompetent Clients

When counseling clients who are minors or individuals who are unable to give voluntary, informed consent, parents or guardians may be included in the counseling process as appropriate. Counselors act in the best interests of clients and take measures to safeguard confidentiality. (See A.3.c.)

B.4. Records

a. Requirement of Records. Counselors maintain records necessary for rendering professional services to their clients and as required by laws, regulations, or agency or institution procedures.

b. Confidentiality of Records. Counselors are responsible for securing the safety and confidentiality of any counseling records they create, maintain, transfer, or destroy, whether the records are written, taped, computerized, or stored in any other medium. (See B.1.a.)

c. Permission to Record or Observe. Counselors obtain permission from clients prior to electronically recording or observing sessions. (See A.3.a.)

d. Client Access. Counselors recognize that counseling records are kept for the benefit of clients, and therefore provide access to records and copies of records when requested by competent clients, unless the records contain information that may be misleading and detrimental to the client. In situations involving multiple clients, access to records is limited to those parts of records that do not include confidential information related to another client. (See A.8., B.1.a., and B.2.b.)

e. Disclosure or Transfer. Counselors obtain written permission from clients to disclose or transfer records to legitimate third parties unless exceptions to confidentiality exist as listed in Section B.1. Steps are taken to ensure that receivers of counseling records are sensitive to their confidential nature.

B.5. Research and Training

a. Data Disguise Required. Use of data derived from counseling relationships for purposes of training, research, or publication is confined to content that is disguised to ensure the anonymity of the individuals involved. (See B.1.g. and G.3.d.)

b. Agreement for Identification. Identification of a client in a presentation or publication is permissible only when the client has reviewed the material and has agreed to its presentation or publication. (See G.3.d.)

B.6. Consultation

a. Respect for Privacy. Information obtained in a consulting relationship is discussed for professional purposes only with persons clearly concerned with the case. Written and oral reports present data germane to the purposes of the consultation, and every effort is made to protect client identity and avoid undue invasion of privacy.

b. Cooperating Agencies. Before sharing information, counselors make efforts to ensure that there are defined policies in other agencies serving the counselor's clients that effectively protect the confidentiality of information.

SECTION C: PROFESSIONAL RESPONSIBILITY

C.1. Standards Knowledge

Counselors have a responsibility to read, understand, and follow the Code of Ethics and the Standards of Practice.

C.2. Professional Competence

a. Boundaries of Competence. Counselors practice only within the boundaries of their competence, based on their education, training, supervised experience, state and national professional credentials, and appropriate professional experience. Counselors will demonstrate a commitment to gain knowledge, personal awareness, sensitivity, and skills pertinent to working with a diverse client population.

b. New Specialty Areas of Practice. Counselors practice in specialty areas new to them only after appropriate education, training, and supervised experience. While developing skills in new specialty areas, counselors take steps to ensure the competence of their work and to protect others from possible harm.

   c. Qualified for Employment. Counselors accept employment only for positions for which they are qualified by education, training, supervised experience, state and national professional credentials, and appropriate professional experience. Counselors hire for professional counseling positions only individuals who are qualified and competent.

   d. Monitor Effectiveness. Counselors continually monitor their effectiveness as professionals and take steps to improve when necessary. Counselors in private practice take reasonable steps to seek out peer supervision to evaluate their efficacy as counselors.

   e. Ethical Issues Consultation. Counselors take reasonable steps to consult with other counselors or related professionals when they have questions regarding their ethical obligations or professional practice. (See H.1.)

   f. Continuing Education. Counselors recognize the need for continuing education to maintain a reasonable level of awareness of current scientific and professional information in their fields of vactivity. They take steps to maintain competence in the skills they use, are open to new procedures, and keep current with the diverse and/or special populations with whom they work.

   g. Impairment. Counselors refrain from offering or accepting professional services when their physical, mental, or emotional problems are likely to harm a client or others. They are alert to the signs of impairment, seek assistance for problems, and, if necessary, limit, suspend, or terminate their professional responsibilities. (See A.11.c.)

C.3. Advertising and Soliciting Clients

   a. Accurate Advertising. There are no restrictions on advertising by counselors except those that can be specifically justified to protect the public from deceptive practices. Counselors advertise or represent their services to the public by identifying their credentials in an accurate manner that is not false, misleading, deceptive, or fraudulent. Counselors may only advertise the highest degree earned which is in counseling or a closely related field from a college or university that was accredited when the degree was awarded by one of the regional accrediting bodies recognized by the Council on Postsecondary Accreditation.

   b. Testimonials. Counselors who use testimonials do not solicit them from clients or other persons who, because of their particular circumstances, may be vulnerable to undue influence.

   c. Statements by Others. Counselors make reasonable efforts to ensure that statements made by others about them or the profession of counseling are accurate.

   d. Recruiting Through Employment. Counselors do not use their places of employment or institutional affiliation to recruit or gain clients, supervisees, or consultees for their private practices. (See C.5.e.)

   e. Products and Training Advertisements. Counselors who develop products related to their profession or conduct workshops or training events ensure that the advertisements concerning these products or events are accurate and disclose adequate information for consumers to make informed choices.

   f. Promoting to Those Served. Counselors do not use counseling, teaching, training, or supervisory relationships to promote their products or training events in a manner that is deceptive or would exert undue influence on individuals who may be vulnerable. Counselors may adopt textbooks they have authored for instruction purposes.

   g. Professional Association Involvement. Counselors actively participate in local, state, and national associations that foster the development and improvement of counseling.

C.4. Credentials

   a. Credentials Claimed. Counselors claim or imply only professional credentials possessed and are responsible for correcting any known misrepresentations of their credentials by others. Professional credentials include graduate degrees in counseling or closely related mental health fields, accreditation of graduate programs, national voluntary certifications, government-issued certifications or licenses, ACA professional membership, or any other credential that might indicate to the public specialized knowledge or expertise in counseling.

   b. ACA Professional Membership. ACA professional members may announce to the public their membership status. Regular members may not announce their ACA membership in a manner that might imply they are credentialed counselors.

   c. Credential Guidelines. Counselors follow the guidelines for use of credentials that have been established by the entities that issue the credentials.

   d. Misrepresentation of Credentials. Counselors do not attribute more to their credentials than the credentials represent, and do not imply that other counselors are not qualified because they do not possess certain credentials.

   e. Doctoral Degrees From Other Fields. Counselors who hold a master's degree in counseling or a closely related mental health field, but hold a doctoral degree from other than counseling or a closely related field, do not use the title "Dr." in their practices and do not announce to the public in relation to their practice or status as a counselor that they hold a doctorate.

C.5. Public Responsibility

   a. Nondiscrimination. Counselors do not discriminate against clients, students, or supervisees in a manner that has a negative impact based on their age, color, culture, disability, ethnic group, gender, race, religion, sexual orientation, or socioeconomic status, or for any other reason. (See A.2.a.)

   b. Sexual Harassment. Counselors do not engage in sexual harassment. Sexual harassment is defined as sexual solicitation, physical advances, or verbal or nonverbal conduct that is sexual in nature, that occurs in connection with professional activities or roles, and that either (1) is unwelcome, is offensive, or creates a hostile workplace environment, and counselors know or are told this; or (2) is sufficiently severe or intense to be perceived as harassment to a reasonable person in the context. Sexual harassment can consist of a single intense or severe act or multiple persistent or pervasive acts.

   c. Reports to Third Parties. Counselors are accurate, honest, and unbiased in reporting their professional activities and judgments to appropriate third parties including courts, health insurance companies, those who are the recipients of evaluation reports, and others. (See B.1.g.)

d. Media Presentations. When counselors provide advice or comment by means of public lectures, demonstrations, radio or television programs, prerecorded tapes, printed articles, mailed material, or other media, they take reasonable precautions to ensure that (1) the statements are based on appropriate professional counseling literature and practice; (2) the statements are otherwise consistent with the Code of Ethics and the Standards of Practice; and (3) the recipients of the information are not encouraged to infer that a professional counseling relationship has been established. (See C.6.b.)

e. Unjustified Gains. Counselors do not use their professional positions to seek or receive unjustified personal gains, sexual favors, unfair advantage, or unearned goods or services. (See C.3.d.)

C.6. Responsibility to Other Professionals

a. Different Approaches. Counselors are respectful of approaches to professional counseling that differ from their own. Counselors know and take into account the traditions and practices of other professional groups with which they work.

b. Personal Public Statements. When making personal statements in a public context, counselors clarify that they are speaking from their personal perspectives and that they are not speaking on behalf of all counselors or the profession. (See C.5.d.)

c. Clients Served by Others. When counselors learn that their clients are in a professional relationship with another mental health professional, they request release from clients to inform the other professionals and strive to establish positive and collaborative professional relationships. (See A.4.)

SECTION D: RELATIONSHIPS WITH OTHER PROFESSIONALS

D.1. Relationships With Employers and Employees

a. Role Definition. Counselors define and describe for their employers and employees the parameters and levels of their professional roles.

b. Agreements. Counselors establish working agreements with supervisors, colleagues, and subordinates regarding counseling or clinical relationships, confidentiality, adherence to professional standards, distinction between public and private material, maintenance and dissemination of recorded information, work load, and accountability. Working agreements in each instance are specified and made known to those concerned.

c. Negative Conditions. Counselors alert their employers to conditions that may be potentially disruptive or damaging to the counselor's professional responsibilities or that may limit their effectiveness.

d. Evaluation. Counselors submit regularly to professional review and evaluation by their supervisor or the appropriate representative of the employer.

e. In-Service. Counselors are responsible for in-service development of self and staff.

f. Goals.Counselors inform their staff of goals and programs.

g. Practices. Counselors provide personnel and agency practices that respect and enhance the rights and welfare of each employee and recipient of agency services. Counselors strive to maintain the highest levels of professional services.

h. Personnel Selection and Assignment. Counselors select competent staff and assign responsibilities compatible with their skills and experiences.

i. Discrimination. Counselors, as either employers or employees, do not engage in or condone practices that are inhumane, illegal, or unjustifiable (such as considerations based on age, color, culture, disability, ethnic group, gender, race, religion, sexual orientation, or socioeconomic status) in hiring, promotion, or training. (See A.2.a. and C.5.b.)

j. Professional Conduct. Counselors have a responsibility both to clients and to the agency or institution within which services are performed to maintain high standards of professional conduct.

k. Exploitative Relationships. Counselors do not engage in exploitative relationships with individuals over whom they have supervisory, evaluative, or instructional control or authority.

l. Employer Policies. The acceptance of employment in an agency or institution implies that counselors are in agreement with its general policies and principles. Counselors strive to reach agreement with employers as to acceptable standards of conduct that allow for changes in institutional policy conducive to the growth and development of clients.

D.2. Consultation (See B.6.)

a. Consultation as an Option. Counselors may choose to consult with any other professionally competent persons about their clients. In choosing consultants, counselors avoid placing the consultant in a conflict of interest situation that would preclude the consultant being a proper party to the counselor's efforts to help the client. Should counselors be engaged in a work setting that compromises this consultation standard, they consult with other professionals whenever possible to consider justifiable alternatives.

b. Consultant Competency. Counselors are reasonably certain that they have or the organization represented has the necessary competencies and resources for giving the kind of consulting services needed and that appropriate referral resources are available.

c. Understanding With Clients. When providing consultation, counselors attempt to develop with their clients a clear understanding of problem definition, goals for change, and predicted consequences of interventions selected.

d. Consultant Goals. The consulting relationship is one in which client adaptability and growth toward self-direction are consistently encouraged and cultivated. (See A.1.b.)

D.3. Fees for Referral

a. Accepting Fees From Agency Clients. Counselors refuse a private fee or other remuneration for rendering services to persons who are entitled to such services through the counselor's employing agency or institution. The policies of a particular agency may make explicit provisions for agency clients to receive counseling services from members of its staff in private practice. In such instances, the clients must be informed of other options open to them should they seek private counseling services. (See A.10.a., A.11.b., and C.3.d.)

   b. Referral Fees. Counselors do not accept a referral fee from other professionals.

D.4. Subcontractor Arrangements

When counselors work as subcontractors for counseling services for a third party, they have a duty to inform clients of the limitations of confidentiality that the organization may place on counselors in providing counseling services to clients. The limits of such confidentiality ordinarily are discussed as part of the intake session. (See B.1.e. and B.1.f.)

SECTION E: EVALUATION, ASSESSMENT, AND INTERPRETATION

E.1. General

   a. Appraisal Techniques. The primary purpose of educational and psychological assessment is to provide measures that are objective and interpretable in either comparative or absolute terms. Counselors recognize the need to interpret the statements in this section as applying to the whole range of appraisal techniques, including test and nontest data.

   b. Client Welfare. Counselors promote the welfare and best interests of the client in the development, publication, and utilization of educational and psychological assessment techniques. They do not misuse assessment results and interpretations and take reasonable steps to prevent others from misusing the information these techniques provide. They respect the client's right to know the results, the interpretations made, and the bases for their conclusions and recommendations.

E.2. Competence to Use and Interpret Tests

   a. Limits of Competence. Counselors recognize the limits of their competence and perform only those testing and assessment services for which they have been trained. They are familiar with reliability, validity, related standardization, error of measurement, and proper application of any technique utilized. Counselors using computer-based test interpretations are trained in the construct being measured and the specific instrument being used prior to using this type of computer application. Counselors take reasonable measures to ensure the proper use of psychological assessment techniques by persons under their supervision.

   b. Appropriate Use. Counselors are responsible for the appropriate application, scoring, interpretation, and use of assessment instruments, whether they score and interpret such tests themselves or use computerized or other services.

c. Decisions Based on Results. Counselors responsible for decisions involving individuals or policies that are based on assessment results have a thorough understanding of educational and psychological measurement, including validation criteria, test research, and guidelines for test development and use.

d. Accurate Information. Counselors provide accurate information and avoid false claims or misconceptions when making statements about assessment instruments or techniques. Special efforts are made to avoid unwarranted connotations of such terms as IQ and grade equivalent scores. (See C.5.c.)

E.3. Informed Consent

a. Explanation to Clients. Prior to assessment, counselors explain the nature and purposes of assessment and the specific use of results in language the client (or other legally authorized person on behalf of the client) can understand, unless an explicit exception to this right has been agreed upon in advance. Regardless of whether scoring and interpretation are completed by counselors, by assistants, or by computer or other outside services, counselors take reasonable steps to ensure that appropriate explanations are given to the client.

b. Recipients of Results. The examinee's welfare, explicit understanding, and prior agreement determine the recipients of test results. Counselors include accurate and appropriate interpretations with any release of individual or group test results. (See B.1.a. and C.5.c.)

E.4. Release of Information to Competent Professionals

a. Misuse of Results. Counselors do not misuse assessment results, including test results and interpretations, and take reasonable steps to prevent the misuse of such by others. (See C.5.c.)

b. Release of Raw Data. Counselors ordinarily release data (e.g., protocols, counseling or interview notes, or questionnaires) in which the client is identified only with the consent of the client or the client's legal representative. Such data are usually released only to persons recognized by counselors as competent to interpret the data. (See B.1.a.)

E.5. Proper Diagnosis of Mental Disorders

a. Proper Diagnosis. Counselors take special care to provide proper diagnosis of mental disorders. Assessment techniques (including personal interview) used to determine client care (e.g., locus of treatment, type of treatment, or recommended follow-up) are carefully selected and appropriately used. (See A.3.a. and C.5.c.)

b. Cultural Sensitivity. Counselors recognize that culture affects the manner in which clients' problems are defined. Clients' socioeconomic and cultural experience is considered when diagnosing mental disorders.

E.6. Test Selection

    a. Appropriateness of Instruments. Counselors carefully consider the validity, reliability, psychometric limitations, and appropriateness of instruments when selecting tests for use in a given situation or with a particular client.

    b. Culturally Diverse Populations. Counselors are cautious when selecting tests for culturally diverse populations to avoid inappropriateness of testing that may be outside of socialized behavioral or cognitive patterns.

E.7. Conditions of Test Administration

    a. Administration Conditions. Counselors administer tests under the same conditions that were established in their standardization. When tests are not administered under standard conditions or when unusual behavior or irregularities occur during the testing session, those conditions are noted in interpretation, and the results may be designated as invalid or of questionable validity.

    b. Computer Administration. Counselors are responsible for ensuring that administration programs function properly to provide clients with accurate results when a computer or other electronic methods are used for test administration. (See A.12.b.)

    c. Unsupervised Test Taking. Counselors do not permit unsupervised or inadequately supervised use of tests or assessments unless the tests or assessments are designed, intended, and validated for self-administration and/or scoring.

    d. Disclosure of Favorable Conditions. Prior to test administration, conditions that produce most favorable test results are made known to the examinee.

E.8. Diversity in Testing

Counselors are cautious in using assessment techniques, making evaluations, and interpreting the performance of populations not represented in the norm group on which an instrument was standardized. They recognize the effects of age, color, culture, disability, ethnic group, gender, race, religion, sexual orientation, and socioeconomic status on test administration and interpretation and place test results in proper perspective with other relevant factors. (See A.2.a.)

E.9. Test Scoring and Interpretation

    a. Reporting Reservations. In reporting assessment results, counselors indicate any reservations that exist regarding validity or reliability because of the circumstances of the assessment or the inappropriateness of the norms for the person tested.

    b. Research Instruments. Counselors exercise caution when interpreting the results of research instruments possessing insufficient technical data to support respondent results. The specific purposes for the use of such instruments are stated explicitly to the examinee.

    c. Testing Services. Counselors who provide test scoring and test interpretation services to support the assessment process confirm the validity of such interpretations. They accurately describe the purpose, norms, validity, reliability, and applications of the procedures and any special qualifications applicable to their use. The public offering of an automated test interpretations service is considered a professional-to-professional consultation. The formal responsibility of the consultant is to the consultee, but the ultimate and overriding responsibility is to the client.

E.10. Test Security

Counselors maintain the integrity and security of tests and other assessment techniques consistent with legal and contractual obligations. Counselors do not appropriate, reproduce, or modify published tests or parts thereof without acknowledgment and permission from the publisher.

E.11. Obsolete Tests and Outdated Test Results

Counselors do not use data or test results that are obsolete or outdated for the current purpose. Counselors make every effort to prevent the misuse of obsolete measures and test data by others.

E.12. Test Construction

Counselors use established scientific procedures, relevant standards, and current professional knowledge for test design in the development, publication, and utilization of educational and psychological assessment techniques.

SECTION F: TEACHING, TRAINING, AND SUPERVISION

F.1. Counselor Educators and Trainers

a. Educators as Teachers and Practitioners. Counselors who are responsible for developing, implementing, and supervising educational programs are skilled as teachers and practitioners. They are knowledgeable regarding the ethical, legal, and regulatory aspects of the profession, are skilled in applying that knowledge, and make students and supervisees aware of their responsibilities. Counselors conduct counselor education and training programs in an ethical manner and serve as role models for professional behavior. Counselor educators should make an effort to infuse material related to human diversity into all courses and/or workshops that are designed to promote the development of professional counselors.

b. Relationship Boundaries With Students and Supervisees. Counselors clearly define and maintain ethical, professional, and social relationship boundaries with their students and supervisees. They are aware of the differential in power that exists and the student's or supervisee's possible incomprehension of that power differential. Counselors explain to students and supervisees the potential for the relationship to become exploitative.

c. Sexual Relationships. Counselors do not engage in sexual relationships with students or supervisees and do not subject them to sexual harassment. (See A.6. and C.5.b)

d. Contributions to Research. Counselors give credit to students or supervisees for their contributions to research and scholarly projects. Credit is given through co-authorship, acknowledgment, footnote statement, or other appropriate means, in accordance with such contributions. (See G.4.b. and G.4.c.)

e. Close Relatives. Counselors do not accept close relatives as students or supervisees.

f. Supervision Preparation. Counselors who offer clinical supervision services are adequately prepared in supervision methods and techniques. Counselors who are doctoral students serving as practicum or internship supervisors to master's level students are adequately prepared and supervised by the training program.

g. Responsibility for Services to Clients. Counselors who supervise the counseling services of others take reasonable measures to ensure that counseling services provided to clients are professional.

h. Endorsement. Counselors do not endorse students or supervisees for certification, licensure, employment, or completion of an academic or training program if they believe students or supervisees are not qualified for the endorsement. Counselors take reasonable steps to assist students or supervisees who are not qualified for endorsement to become qualified.

F.2. Counselor Education and Training Programs

a. Orientation. Prior to admission, counselors orient prospective students to the counselor education or training program's expectations, including but not limited to the following: (1) the type and level of skill acquisition required for successful completion of the training; (2) subject matter to be covered; (3) basis for evaluation; (4) training components that encourage self-growth or self-disclosure as part of the training process; (5) the type of supervision settings and requirements of the sites for required clinical field experiences; (6) student and supervisee evaluation and dismissal policies and procedures; and (7) up-to-date employment prospects for graduates.

b. Integration of Study and Practice. Counselors establish counselor education and training programs that integrate academic study and supervised practice.

c. Evaluation. Counselors clearly state to students and supervisees, in advance of training, the levels of competency expected, appraisal methods, and timing of evaluations for both didactic and experiential components. Counselors provide students and supervisees with periodic performance appraisal and evaluation feedback throughout the training program.

d. Teaching Ethics. Counselors make students and supervisees aware of the ethical responsibilities and standards of the profession and the students' and supervisees' ethical responsibilities to the profession. (See C.1. and F.3.e.)

e. Peer Relationships. When students or supervisees are assigned to lead counseling groups or provide clinical supervision for their peers, counselors take steps to ensure that students and supervisees placed in these roles do not have personal or adverse relationships with peers and that they understand they have the same ethical obligations as counselor educators, trainers, and supervisors. Counselors make every effort to ensure that the rights of peers are not compromised when students or supervisees are assigned to lead counseling groups or provide clinical supervision.

f. Varied Theoretical Positions. Counselors present varied theoretical positions so that students and supervisees may make comparisons and have opportunities to develop their own positions. Counselors provide information concerning the scientific bases of professional practice. (See C.6.a.)

g. Field Placements. Counselors develop clear policies within their training program regarding field placement and other clinical experiences. Counselors provide clearly stated roles and responsibilities for the student or supervisee, the site supervisor, and the program supervisor. They confirm that site supervisors are qualified to provide supervision and are informed of their professional and ethical responsibilities in this role.

h. Dual Relationships as Supervisors. Counselors avoid dual relationships such as performing the role of site supervisor and training program supervisor in the student's or supervisee's training program. Counselors do not accept any form of professional services, fees, commissions, reimbursement, or remuneration from a site for student or supervisee placement.

i. Diversity in Programs. Counselors are responsive to their institution's and program's recruitment and retention needs for training program administrators, faculty, and students with diverse backgrounds and special needs. (See A.2.a.)

F.3. Students and Supervisees

a. Limitations. Counselors, through ongoing evaluation and appraisal, are aware of the academic and personal limitations of students and supervisees that might impede performance. Counselors assist students and supervisees in securing remedial assistance when needed, and dismiss from the training program supervisees who are unable to provide competent service due to academic or personal limitations. Counselors seek professional consultation and document their decision to dismiss or refer students or supervisees for assistance. Counselors ensure that students and supervisees have recourse to address decisions made to require them to seek assistance or to dismiss them.

b. Self-Growth Experiences. Counselors use professional judgement when designing training experiences conducted by the counselors themselves that require student and supervisee self-growth or self-disclosure. Safeguards are provided so that students and supervisees are aware of the ramifications their self-disclosure may have on counselors whose primary role as teacher, trainer, or supervisor requires acting on ethical obligations to the profession. Evaluative components of experiential training experiences explicitly delineate predetermined academic standards that are separate and do not depend on the student's level of self-disclosure. (See A.6.)

c. Counseling for Students and Supervisees. If students or supervisees request counseling, supervisors or counselor educators provide them with acceptable referrals. Supervisors or counselor educators do not serve as counselor to students or supervisees over whom they hold administrative, teaching, or evaluative roles, unless this is a brief role associated with a training experience. (See A.6.b.)

d. Clients of Students and Supervisees. Counselors make every effort to ensure that the clients at field placements are aware of the services rendered and the qualifications of the students and supervisees rendering those services. Clients receive professional disclosure information and are informed of the limits of confidentiality. Client permission is obtained in order for the students and supervisees to use any information concerning the counseling relationship in the training process. (See B.1.e.)

e. Standards for Students and Supervisees. Students and supervisees preparing to become counselors adhere to the Code of Ethics and the Standards of Practice. Students and supervisees have the same obligations to clients as those required of counselors. (See H.1.)

SECTION G: RESEARCH AND PUBLICATION

G.1. Research Responsibilities

a. Use of Human Subjects. Counselors plan, design, conduct, and report research in a manner consistent with pertinent ethical principles, federal and state laws, host institutional regulations, and scientific standards governing research with human subjects. Counselors design and conduct research that reflects cultural sensitivity appropriateness.

b. Deviation From Standard Practices. Counselors seek consultation and observe stringent safeguards to protect the rights of research participants when a research problem suggests a deviation from standard acceptable practices. (See B.6.)

c. Precautions to Avoid Injury. Counselors who conduct research with human subjects are responsible for the subjects' welfare throughout the experiment and take reasonable precautions to avoid causing injurious psychological, physical, or social effects to their subjects.

d. Principal Researcher Responsibility. The ultimate responsibility for ethical research practice lies with the principal researcher. All others involved in the research activities share ethical obligations and full responsibility for their own actions.

e. Minimal Interference. Counselors take reasonable precautions to avoid causing disruptions in subjects' lives due to participation in research.

f. Diversity. Counselors are sensitive to diversity and research issues with special populations. They seek consultation when appropriate. (See A.2.a. and B.6.)

G.2. Informed Consent

a. Topics Disclosed. In obtaining informed consent for research, counselors use language that is understandable to research participants and that (1) accurately explains the purpose and procedures to be followed; (2) identifies any procedures that are experimental or relatively untried; (3) describes the attendant discomforts and risks; (4) describes the benefits or changes in individuals or organizations that might be reasonably expected; (5) discloses appropriate alternative procedures that would be advantageous for subjects; (6) offers to answer any inquiries concerning the procedures; (7) describes any limitations on confidentiality; and (8) instructs that subjects are free to withdraw their consent and to discontinue participation in the project at any time. (See B.1.f.)

b. Deception. Counselors do not conduct research involving deception unless alternative procedures are not feasible and the prospective value of the research justifies the deception. When the methodological requirements of a study necessitate concealment or deception, the investigator is required to explain clearly the reasons for this action as soon as possible.

c. Voluntary Participation. Participation in research is typically voluntary and without any penalty for refusal to participate. Involuntary participation is appropriate only when it can be demonstrated that participation will have no harmful effects on subjects and is essential to the investigation.

d. Confidentiality of Information. Information obtained about research participants during the course of an investigation is confidential. When the possibility exists that others may obtain access to such information, ethical research practice requires that the possibility, together with the plans for protecting confidentiality, be explained to participants as a part of the procedure for obtaining informed consent. (See B.1.e.)

e. Persons Incapable of Giving Informed Consent. When a person is incapable of giving informed consent, counselors provide an appropriate explanation, obtain agreement for participation, and obtain appropriate consent from a legally authorized person.

f. Commitments to Participants. Counselors take reasonable measures to honor all commitments to research participants.

g. Explanations After Data Collection. After data are collected, counselors provide participants with full clarification of the nature of the study to remove any misconceptions. Where scientific or human values justify delaying or withholding information, counselors take reasonable measures to avoid causing harm.

h. Agreements to Cooperate. Counselors who agree to cooperate with another individual in research or publication incur an obligation to cooperate as promised in terms of punctuality of performance and with regard to the completeness and accuracy of the information required.

i. Informed Consent for Sponsors. In the pursuit of research, counselors give sponsors, institutions, and publication channels the same respect and opportunity for giving informed consent that they accord to individual research participants. Counselors are aware of their obligation to future research workers and ensure that host institutions are given feedback information and proper acknowledgment.

G.3. Reporting Results

a. Information Affecting Outcome. When reporting research results, counselors explicitly mention all variables and conditions known to the investigator that may have affected the outcome of a study or the interpretation of data.

b. Accurate Results. Counselors plan, conduct, and report research accurately and in a manner that minimizes the possibility that results will be misleading. They provide thorough discussions of the limitations of their data and alternative hypotheses. Counselors do not engage in fraudulent research, distort data, misrepresent data, or deliberately bias their results.

    c. Obligation to Report Unfavorable Results. Counselors communicate to other counselors the results of any research judged to be of professional value. Results that reflect unfavorably on institutions, programs, services, prevailing opinions, or vested interests are not withheld.

    d. Identity of Subjects. Counselors who supply data, aid in the research of another person, report research results, or make original data available take due care to disguise the identity of respective subjects in the absence of specific authorization from the subjects to do otherwise. (See B.1.g. and B.5.a.)

    e. Replication Studies. Counselors are obligated to make available sufficient original research data to qualified professionals who may wish to replicate the study.

G.4. Publication

    a. Recognition of Others. When conducting and reporting research, counselors are familiar with and give recognition to previous work on the topic, observe copyright laws, and give full credit to those to whom credit is due. (See F.1.d. and G.4.c.)

    b. Contributors. Counselors give credit through joint authorship, acknowledgment, footnote statements, or other appropriate means to those who have contributed significantly to research or concept development in accordance with such contributions. The principal contributor is listed first and minor technical or professional contributions are acknowledged in notes or introductory statements.

    c. Student Research. For an article that is substantially based on a student's dissertation or thesis, the student is listed as the principal author. (See F.1.d. and G.4.a.)

    d. Duplicate Submission. Counselors submit manuscripts for consideration to only one journal at a time. Manuscripts that are published in whole or in substantial part in another journal or published work are not submitted for publication without acknowledgment and permission from the previous publication.

    e. Professional Review. Counselors who review material submitted for publication, research, or other scholarly purposes respect the confidentiality and proprietary rights of those who submitted it.

SECTION H: RESOLVING ETHICAL ISSUES

H.1. Knowledge of Standards

Counselors are familiar with the Code of Ethics and the Standards of Practice and other applicable ethics codes from other professional organizations of which they are member, or from certification and licensure bodies. Lack of knowledge or misunderstanding of an ethical responsibility is not a defense against a charge of unethical conduct. (See F.3.e.)

H.2. Suspected Violations

    a. Ethical Behavior Expected. Counselors expect professional associates to adhere to the Code of Ethics. When counselors possess reasonable cause that raises doubts as to whether a counselor is acting in an ethical manner, they take appropriate action. (See H.2.d. and H.2.e.)

b. Consultation. When uncertain as to whether a particular situation or course of action may be in violation of the Code of Ethics, counselors consult with other counselors who are knowledgeable about ethics, with colleagues, or with appropriate authorities.

c. Organization Conflicts. If the demands of an organization with which counselors are affiliated pose a conflict with the Code of Ethics, counselors specify the nature of such conflicts and express to their supervisors or other responsible officials their commitment to the Code of Ethics. When possible, counselors work toward change within the organization to allow full adherence to the Code of Ethics.

d. Informal Resolution. When counselors have reasonable cause to believe that another counselor is violating an ethical standard, they attempt to first resolve the issue informally with the other counselor if feasible, providing that such action does not violate confidentiality rights that may be involved.

e. Reporting Suspected Violations. When an informal resolution is not appropriate or feasible, counselors, upon reasonable cause, take action such as reporting the suspected ethical violation to state or national ethics committees, unless this action conflicts with confidentiality rights that cannot be resolved.

f. Unwarranted Complaints. Counselors do not initiate, participate in, or encourage the filing of ethics complaints that are unwarranted or intend to harm a counselor rather than to protect clients or the public.

H.3. Cooperation With Ethics Committees

Counselors assist in the process of enforcing the Code of Ethics. Counselors cooperate with investigations, proceedings, and requirements of the ACA Ethics Committee or ethics committees of other duly constituted associations or boards having jurisdiction over those charged with a violation. Counselors are familiar with the ACA Policies and Procedures and use it as a reference in assisting the enforcement of the Code of Ethics.

ACA STANDARDS OF PRACTICE

All members of the American Counseling Association (ACA) are required to adhere to the Standards of Practice and the Code of Ethics. The Standards of Practice represent minimal behavioral statements of the Code of Ethics. Members should refer to the applicable section of the Code of Ethics for further interpretation and amplification of the applicable Standard of Practice.

SECTION A: THE COUNSELING RELATIONSHIP

Standard of Practice One (SP-1): Nondiscrimination. Counselors respect diversity and must not discriminate against clients because of age, color, culture, disability, ethnic group, gender, race, religion, sexual orientation, marital status, or socioeconomic status. (See A.2.a.)

Standard of Practice Two (SP-2): Disclosure to Clients. Counselors must adequately inform clients, preferably in writing, regarding the counseling process and counseling relationship at or before the time it begins and throughout the relationship. (See A.3.a.)

Standard of Practice Three (SP-3): Dual Relationships. Counselors must make every effort to avoid dual relationships with clients that could impair their professional judgment or increase the risk of harm to clients. When a dual relationship cannot be avoided, counselors must take appropriate steps to ensure that judgment is not impaired and that no exploitation occurs. (See A.6.a. and A.6.b.)

Standard of Practice Four (SP-4): Sexual Intimacies With Clients. Counselors must not engage in any type of sexual intimacies with current clients and must not engage in sexual intimacies with former clients within a minimum of 2 years after terminating the counseling relationship. Counselors who engage in such relationship after 2 years following termination have the responsibility to examine and document thoroughly that such relations did not have an exploitative nature.

Standard of Practice Five (SP-5): Protecting Clients During Group Work. Counselors must take steps to protect clients from physical or psychological trauma resulting from interactions during group work. (See A.9.b.)

Standard of Practice Six (SP-6): Advance Understanding of Fees. Counselors must explain to clients, prior to their entering the counseling relationship, financial arrangements related to professional services. (See A.10. a.–d. and A.11.c.)

Standard of Practice Seven (SP-7): Termination. Counselors must assist in making appropriate arrangements for the continuation of treatment of clients, when necessary, following termination of counseling relationships. (See A.11.a.)

Standard of Practice Eight (SP-8): Inability to Assist Clients. Counselors must avoid entering or immediately terminate a counseling relationship if it is determined that they are unable to be of professional assistance to a client. The counselor may assist in making an appropriate referral for the client. (See A.11.b.)

Section B: Confidentiality

Standard of Practice Nine (SP-9): Confidentiality Requirement. Counselors must keep information related to counseling services confidential unless disclosure is in the best interest of clients, is required for the welfare of others, or is required by law. When disclosure is required, only information that is essential is revealed and the client is informed of such disclosure. (See B.1.a.–f.)

Standard of Practice Ten (SP-10): Confidentiality Requirements for Subordinates. Counselors must take measures to ensure that privacy and confidentiality of clients are maintained by subordinates. (See B.1.h.)

Standard of Practice Eleven (SP-11): Confidentiality in Group Work. Counselors must clearly communicate to group members that confidentiality cannot be guaranteed in group work. (See B.2.a.)

Standard of Practice Twelve (SP-12): Confidentiality in Family Counseling. Counselors must not disclose information about one family member in counseling to another family member without prior consent. (See B.2.b.)

Standard of Practice Thirteen (SP-13): Confidentiality of Records. Counselors must maintain appropriate confidentiality in creating, storing, accessing, transferring, and disposing of counseling records. (See B.4.b.)

Standard of Practice Fourteen (SP-14): Permission to Record or Observe. Counselors must obtain prior consent from clients in order to record electronically or observe sessions. (See B.4.c.)

Standard of Practice Fifteen (SP-15): Disclosure or Transfer of Records. Counselors must obtain client consent to disclose or transfer records to third parties, unless exceptions listed in SP-9 exist. (See B.4.e.)

Standard of Practice Sixteen (SP-16): Data Disguise Required. Counselors must disguise the identity of the client when using data for training, research, or publication. (See B.5.a.)

Section C: Professional Responsibility

Standard of Practice Seventeen (SP-17): Boundaries of Competence. Counselors must practice only within the boundaries of their competence. (See C.2.a.)

Standard of Practice Eighteen (SP-18): Continuing Education. Counselors must engage in continuing education to maintain their professional competence. (See C.2.f.)

Standard of Practice Nineteen (SP-19): Impairment of Professionals. Counselors must refrain from offering professional services when their personal problems or conflicts may cause harm to a client or others. (See C.2.g.)

Standard of Practice Twenty (SP-20): Accurate Advertising. Counselors must accurately represent their credentials and services when advertising. (See C.3.a.)

Standard of Practice Twenty-One (SP-21): Recruiting Through Employment. Counselors must not use their place of employment or institutional affiliation to recruit clients for their private practices. (See C.3.d.)

Standard of Practice Twenty-Two (SP-22): Credentials Claimed. Counselors must claim or imply only professional credentials possessed and must correct any known misrepresentations of their credentials by others. (See C.4.a.)

Standard of Practice Twenty-Three (SP-23): Sexual Harassment. Counselors must not engage in sexual harassment. (See C.5.b.)

Standard of Practice Twenty-Four (SP-24): Unjustified Gains. Counselors must not use their professional positions to seek or receive unjustified personal gains, sexual favors, unfair advantage, or unearned goods or services. (See C.5.e.)

Standard of Practice Twenty-Five (SP-25): Clients Served by Others. With the consent of the client, counselors must inform other mental health professionals serving the same client that a counseling relationship between the counselor and client exists. (See C.6.c.)

Standard of Practice Twenty-Six (SP-26): Negative Employment Conditions. Counselors must alert their employers to institutional policy or conditions that may be potentially disruptive or damaging to the counselor's professional responsibilities, or that may limit their effectiveness or deny clients' rights. (See D.1.c.)

Standard of Practice Twenty-Seven (SP-27): Personnel Selection and Assignment. Counselors must select competent staff and must assign responsibilities compatible with staff skills and experiences. (See D.1.h.)

Standard of Practice Twenty-Eight (SP-28): Exploitative Relationships With Subordinates. Counselors must not engage in exploitative relationships with individuals over whom they have supervisory, evaluative, or instructional control or authority. (See D.1.k.)

Section D: Relationship With Other Professionals

Standard of Practice Twenty-Nine (SP-29): Accepting Fees From Agency Clients. Counselors must not accept fees or other remuneration for consultation with persons entitled to such services through the counselor's employing agency or institution. (See D.3.a.)

Standard of Practice Thirty (SP-30): Referral Fees. Counselors must not accept referral fees. (See D.3.b.)

Section E: Evaluation, Assesment and Interpretation

Standard of Practice Thirty-One (SP-31): Limits of Competence. Counselors must perform only testing and assessment services for which they are competent. Counselors must not allow the use of psychological assessment techniques by unqualified persons under their supervision. (See E.2.a.)

Standard of Practice Thirty-Two (SP-32): Appropriate Use of Assessment Instruments. Counselors must use assessment instruments in the manner for which they were intended. (See E.2.b.)

Standard of Practice Thirty-Three (SP-33): Assessment Explanations to Clients. Counselors must provide explanations to clients prior to assessment about the nature and purposes of assessment and the specific uses of results. (See E.3.a.)

Standard of Practice Thirty-Four (SP-34): Recipients of Test Results. Counselors must ensure that accurate and appropriate interpretations accompany any release of testing and assessment information. (See E.3.b.)

Standard of Practice Thirty-Five (SP-35): Obsolete Tests and Outdated Test Results. Counselors must not base their assessment or intervention decisions or recommendations on data or test results that are obsolete or outdated for the current purpose. (See E.11.)

Section F: Teaching, Training, and Supervision

Standard of Practice Thirty-Six (SP-36): Sexual Relationships With Students or Supervisees. Counselors must not engage in sexual relationships with their students and supervisees. (See F.1.c.)

Standard of Practice Thirty-Seven (SP-37): Credit for Contributions to Research. Counselors must give credit to students or supervisees for their contributions to research and scholarly projects. (See F.1.d.)

Standard of Practice Thirty-Eight (SP-38): Supervision Preparation. Counselors who offer clinical supervision services must be trained and prepared in supervision methods and techniques. (See F.1.f.)

Standard of Practice Thirty-Nine (SP-39): Evaluation Information. Counselors must clearly state to students and supervisees in advance of training the levels of competency expected, appraisal methods, and timing of evaluations. Counselors must provide students and supervisees with periodic performance appraisal and evaluation feedback throughout the training program. (See F.2.c.)

Standard of Practice Forty (SP-40): Peer Relationships in Training. Counselors must make every effort to ensure that the rights of peers are not violated when students and supervisees are assigned to lead counseling groups or provide clinical supervision. (See F.2.e.)

Standard of Practice Forty-One (SP-41): Limitations of Students and Supervisees. Counselors must assist students and supervisees in securing remedial assistance, when needed, and must dismiss from the training program students and supervisees who are unable to provide competent service due to academic or personal limitations. (See F.3.a.)

Standard of Practice Forty-Two (SP-42): Self-Growth Experiences. Counselors who conduct experiences for students or supervisees that include self-growth or self-disclosure must inform participants of counselors' ethical obligations to the profession and must not grade participants based on their nonacademic performance. (See F.3.b.)

Standard of Practice Forty-Three (SP-43): Standards for Students and Supervisees. Students and supervisees preparing to become counselors must adhere to the Code of Ethics and the Standards of Practice of counselors. (See F.3.e.)

Section G: Research and Publication

Standard of Practice Forty-Four (SP-44): Precautions to Avoid Injury in Research. Counselors must avoid causing physical, social, or psychological harm or injury to subjects in research. (See G.1.c.)

Standard of Practice Forty-Five (SP-45): Confidentiality of Research Information. Counselors must keep confidential information obtained about research participants. (See G.2.d.)

Standard of Practice Forty-Six (SP-46): Information Affecting Research Outcome. Counselors must report all variables and conditions known to the investigator that may have affected research data or outcomes. (See G.3.a.)

Standard of Practice Forty-Seven (SP-47): Accurate Research Results. Counselors must not distort or misrepresent research data, nor fabricate or intentionally bias research results. (See G.3.b.)

Standard of Practice Forty-Eight (SP-48): Publication Contributors. Counselors must give appropriate credit to those who have contributed to research. (See G.4.a. and G.4.b.)

Section H: Resolving Ethical Issues

Standard of Practice Forty-Nine (SP-49): Ethical Behavior Expected. Counselors must take appropriate action when they possess reasonable cause that raises doubts as to whether counselors or other mental health professionals are acting in an ethical manner. (See H.2.a.)

Standard of Practice Fifty (SP-50): Unwarranted Complaints. Counselors must not initiate, participate in, or encourage the filing of ethics complaints that are unwarranted or intended to harm a mental health professional rather than to protect clients or the public. (See H.2.f.)

Standard of Practice Fifty-One (SP-51): Cooperation With Ethics Committees. Counselors must cooperate with investigations, proceedings, and requirements of the ACA Ethics Committee or ethics committees of other duly constituted associations or boards having jurisdiction over those charged with a violation. (See H.3.)

REFERENCES

The following documents are available to counselors as resources to guide them in their practices. These resources are not a part of the Code of Ethics and the Standards of Practice.

American Association for Counseling and Development/Association for Measurement and Evaluation in Counseling and Development. (1989). *The responsibilities of users of standardized tests (rev.).* Washington, DC: Author.

American Counseling Association. (1988) (Note: This is ACA's previous edition of its ethics code). *Ethical standards.* Alexandria, VA: Author.

American Psychological Association. (1985). *Standards for educational and psychological testing (rev.).* Washington, DC: Author.

Joint Committee on Testing Practices. (1988). *Code of fair testing practices in education.* Washington, DC: Author.

National Board for Certified Counselors. (1989). *National Board for Certified Counselors code of ethics.* Alexandria, VA: Author.

Prediger, D. J. (Ed.). (1993, March). *Multicultural assessment standards.* Alexandria, VA: Association for Assessment in Counseling.

ETHICAL GUIDELINES FOR GROUP COUNSELORS

ASSOCIATION FOR SPECIALISTS IN GROUP WORK (ASGW)

PREAMBLE

One characteristic of any professional group is the possession of a body of knowledge, skills, and voluntarily self-professed standards for ethical practice. A Code of Ethics consists of those standards that have been formally and publicly acknowledged by the members of a profession to serve as the guidelines for professional conduct, discharge of duties, and the resolution of moral dilemmas. By this document, the Association for Specialists in Group Work (ASGW) has identified the standards of conduct appropriate for ethical behavior among its members.

The association for Specialists in Group Work recognizes the basic commitment of its members to the Ethical Standards of its parent organization, the American Association for Counseling and Development (AACD) and nothing in this document shall be construed to supplant that code. These standards are intended to complement the AACD standards in the area of group work by clarifying the nature of ethical responsibility of the counselor in the group setting and by stimulating a greater concern for competent group leadership.

The group counselor is expected to be a professional agent and to take the processes of ethical responsibility seriously. ASGW views "ethical process" as being integral to group work and views group counselors as "ethical agents." Group counselors, by their very nature in being responsible and responsive to their group members, necessarily embrace a certain potential for ethical vulnerability. It is incumbent upon group counselors to give considerable attention to the intent and context of their actions because the attempts of counselors to influence human behavior through group work always have ethical implications.

The following ethical guidelines have been developed to encourage ethical behavior of group counselors. These guidelines are written for students and practitioners, and are meant to stimulate reflection, self-examination, and discussion of issues and practices. They address the group counselor's responsibility for providing information about group work to clients and the group counselor's responsibility for providing group counseling services to clients. A final section discusses the group counselor's responsibility for safeguarding ethical practice and procedures for reporting unethical behavior. Group counselors are expected to make known these standards to group members.

ETHICAL GUIDELINES

1. *Orientation and Providing Information:* Group counselors adequately prepare prospective or new group members by providing as much information about the existing or proposed group as necessary.
   - Minimally, information related to each of the following areas should be provided.
   a. Entrance procedures, time parameters of the group experience, group participation expectations, methods of payment (where appropriate), and termination procedures are explained by the group counselor as appropriate to the level of maturity of group members and the nature and purpose(s) of the group.
   b. Group counselors have available for distribution, a professional disclosure statement that includes information on the group counselor's qualifications and group services that can be provided, particularly as related to the nature and purpose(s) of the specific group.
   c. Group counselors communicate the role expectations, rights, and responsibilities of group members and group counselor(s).
   d. The group goals are stated as concisely as possible by the group counselor including "whose" goal it is (the group counselor's, the institution's, the parent's, the law's, society's, etc.) and the role of group members in influencing or determining the group's goals(s).
   e. Group counselors explore with group members the risks of potential life changes that may occur because of the group experience and help members explore their readiness to face these possibilities.
   f. Group members are informed by the group counselor of unusual or experimental procedures that might be expected in their group experience.
   g. Group counselors explain, as realistically as possible, what services can and cannot be provided within the particular group structure offered.
   h. Group counselors emphasize the need to promote full psychological functioning and presence among group members. They inquire from prospective group members whether they are using any kind of drug or medication that may affect functioning in the group. They do not permit any use of alcohol and/or illegal drugs during group sessions and they discourage the use of alcohol and/or drugs (legal or illegal) prior to group meetings which may affect the physical or emotional presence of the member or other group members.
   i. Group counselors inquire from prospective group members whether they have ever been a client in counseling or psychotherapy. If a prospective group member is already in a counseling relationship with another professional person, the group counselor advises the prospective group member to notify the other professional of their participation in the group.

j. Group counselors clearly inform group members about the policies pertaining to the group counselor's willingness to consult with them between group sessions.

k. In establishing fees for group counseling services, group counselors consider the financial status and the locality of prospective group members. Group members are not charged fees for group sessions where the group counselor is not present and the policy of charging for sessions missed by a group member is clearly communicated. Fees for participating as a group member are contracted between group counselor and group member for a specified period of time. Group counselors do not increase fees for group counseling services until the existing contracted fee structure has expired. In the event that the established fee structure is inappropriate for a prospective member, group counselors assist in finding comparable services of acceptable costs.

2. *Screening of Members:* The group counselor screens prospective group members (when appropriate to their theoretical orientation). Insofar as possible, the counselor selects group members whose needs and goals are compatible with the goals of the group, who will not impede the group process, and whose well-being will not be jeopardized by the group experience. An orientation to the group (i.e., ASGW Ethical Guideline #1) is included during the screening process.

■ Screening may be accomplished in one or more ways, such as the following:

a. Group interview of prospective group members,

b. Interview as part of a team staffing, and

c. Completion of a written questionnaire by prospective group members.

3. *Confidentiality:* Group counselors protect members by defining clearly what confidentiality means, why it is important, and the difficulties involved in enforcement.

a. Group counselors take steps to protect members by defining confidentiality and the limits of confidentiality (i.e., when a group member's condition indicates that there is clear and imminent danger to the member, others, or physical property, the group counselor takes reasonable personal action and/or informs responsible authorities).

b. Group counselors stress the importance of confidentiality and set a norm of confidentiality regarding all group participants' disclosures. The importance of maintaining confidentiality is emphasized before the group begins and at various times in the group. The fact that confidentiality cannot be guaranteed is clearly stated.

c. Members are made aware of the difficulties involved in enforcing and ensuring confidentiality in a group setting. The counselor provides examples of how confidentiality can non-maliciously be broken to increase members' awareness, and help to lessen the likelihood that this breach of confidence will occur. Group counselors inform group members about the potential consequences of intentionally breaching confidentiality.

d. Group counselors can only ensure confidentiality on their part and not on the part of the members.

e. Group counselors video or audio tape a group session only with the prior consent and the members' knowledge of how the tape will be used.

    f. When working with minors, the group counselor specifies the limits of confidentiality.

    g. Participants in a mandatory group are made aware of any reporting procedures required of the group counselor.

    h. Group counselors store or dispose of group member records (written, audio, video, etc.) in ways that maintain confidentiality.

4. *Voluntary/Involuntary Participation:* Group counselors inform members whether participation is voluntary or involuntary.

    a. Group counselors take steps to ensure informed consent procedures in both voluntary and involuntary groups.

    b. When working with minors in a group, counselors are expected to follow the procedures specified by the institution in which they are practicing.

    c. With involuntary groups, every attempt is made to enlist the cooperation of the members and their continuance in the group on a voluntary basis.

    d. Group counselors do not certify that group treatment has been received by members who merely attend sessions, but did not meet the defined group expectations. Group members are informed about the consequences for failing to participate in a group.

5. *Leaving a Group:* Provisions are made to assist a group member to terminate in an effective way.

    a. Procedures to be followed for a group member who chooses to exit a group prematurely are discussed by the counselor with all group members either before the group begins, during a prescreening interview, or during the initial group session.

    b. In the case of legally mandated group counseling, group counselors inform members of the possible consequences for premature self-termination.

    c. Ideally, both the group counselor and the member can work cooperatively to determine the degree to which a group experience is productive or counterproductive for that individual.

    d. Members ultimately have a right to discontinue membership in the group, at a designated time, if the predetermined trial period proves to be unsatisfactory.

    e. Members have the right to exit a group, but it is important that they be made aware of the importance of informing the counselor and the group members prior to deciding to leave. The counselor discusses the possible risks of leaving the group prematurely with a member who is considering this option.

    f. Before leaving a group, the group counselor encourages members (if appropriate) to discuss their reason for wanting to discontinue membership in the group. Counselors intervene if other members use undue pressure to force a member to remain in the group.

6. *Coercion and Pressure:* Group counselors protect member rights against physical threats, intimidation, coercion, and undue peer pressure insofar as is reasonably possible.

    a. It is essential to differentiate between "therapeutic pressure" that is part of any group and "undue pressure," which is not therapeutic.

    b. The purpose of a group is to help participants find their own answer, not to pressure them into doing what the group thinks is appropriate.

    c. Counselors exert care not to coerce participants to change in directions which they clearly state they do not choose.

    d. Counselors have a responsibility to intervene when others use undue pressure or attempt to persuade members against their will.

    e. Counselors intervene when any member attempts to act out aggression in a physical way that might harm another member or themselves.

    f. Counselors intervene when a member is verbally abusive or inappropriately confrontive to another member.

7. *Imposing Counselor Values:* Group counselors develop an awareness of their own values and needs and the potential impact they have on the interventions likely to be made.

    a. Although group counselors take care to avoid imposing their values on members, it is appropriate that they expose their own beliefs, decisions, needs, and values, when concealing them would create problems for the members.

    b. There are values implicit in any group, and these are made clear to potential members before they join the group. (Examples of certain values include: expressing feelings, being direct and honest, sharing personal material with others, learning how to trust, improving interpersonal communication, and deciding for oneself.)

    c. Personal and professional needs of group counselors are not met at the members' expense.

    d. Group counselors avoid using the group for their own therapy.

    e. Group counselors are aware of their own values and assumptions and how these apply to a multicultural context.

    f. Group counselors take steps to increase their awareness of ways that their personal reactions to members might inhibit the group process and they monitor their countertransference. Through an awareness of the impact of stereotyping and discrimination (i.e., biases based on age, disability, ethnicity, gender, race, religion, or sexual preference), group counselors guard the individual rights and personal dignity of all group members.

8. *Equitable Treatment:* Group counselors make every reasonable effort to treat each member individually and equally.

    a. Group counselors recognize and respect differences (e.g., cultural, racial, religious, lifestyle, age, disability, gender) among group members.

    b. Group counselors maintain an awareness of their behavior toward individual group members and are alert to the potential detrimental effects of favoritism or partiality toward any particular group member to the exclusion or detriment of any other member(s). It is likely that group counselors will favor some members over others, yet all group members deserve to be treated equally.

    c. Group counselors ensure equitable use of group time for each member by inviting silent members to become involved, acknowledging nonverbal attempts to communicate, and discouraging rambling and monopolizing of time by members.

d. If a large group is planned, counselors consider enlisting another qualified professional to serve as a co-leader for the group sessions.

9. *Dual Relationships:* Group counselors avoid dual relationships with group members that might impair their objectivity and professional judgment, as well as those which are likely to compromise a group member's ability to participate fully in the group.

    a. Group counselors do not misuse their professional role and power as group leader to advance personal or social contacts with members throughout the duration of the group.

    b. Group counselors do not use their professional relationship with group members to further their own interest either during the group or after the termination of the group.

    c. Sexual intimacies between group counselors and members are unethical.

    d. Group counselors do not barter (exchange) professional services with group members for services.

    e. Group counselors do not admit their own family members, relatives, employees, or personal friends as members to their groups.

    f. Group counselors discuss with group members the potential detrimental effects of group members engaging in intimate inter-member relationships outside of the group.

    g. Students who participate in a group as a partial course requirement for a group course are not evaluated for an academic grade based upon their degree of participation as a member in a group. Instructors of group counseling courses take steps to minimize the possible negative impact on students when they participate in a group course by separating course grades from participation in the group and by allowing students to decide what issues to explore and when to stop.

    h. It is inappropriate to solicit members from a class (or institutional affiliation) for one's private counseling or therapeutic groups.

10. *Use of Techniques:* Group counselors do not attempt any technique unless trained in its use or under supervision by a counselor familiar with the intervention.

    a. Group counselors are able to articulate a theoretical orientation that guides their practice, and they are able to provide a rationale for their interventions.

    b. Depending upon the type of intervention, group counselors have training commensurate with the potential impact of a technique.

    c. Group counselors are aware of the necessity to modify their techniques to fit the unique needs of various cultural and ethnic groups.

    d. Group counselors assist members in translating in-group learnings to daily life.

11. *Goal Development:* Group counselors make every effort to assist members in developing their personal goals.

    a. Group counselors use their skills to assist members in making their goals specific so that others present in the group will understand the nature of the goals.

    b. Throughout the course of a group, group counselors assist members in assessing the degree to which personal goals are being met, and assist in revising any goals when it is appropriate.

    c. Group counselors help members clarify the degree to which the goals can be met within the context of a particular group.

12. *Consultation:* Group counselors develop and explain policies about between-sessions consultation to group members.
    a. Group counselors take care to make certain that members to do not use between-session consultations to avoid dealing with issues pertaining to the group that would be dealt with best in the group.
    b. Group counselors urge members to bring the issues discussed during between-session consultations into the group if they pertain to the group.
    c. Group counselors seek out consultations and/or supervision regarding ethical concerns or when encountering difficulties which interfere with their effective functioning as group leaders.
    d. Group counselors seek appropriate professional assistance for their own personal problems or conflicts that are likely to impair their professional judgment and work performance.
    e. Group counselors discuss their group cases only for professional consultation and educational purposes.
    f. Group counselors inform members about policies regarding whether consultations will be held confidential.
13. *Termination from the Group:* Depending upon the purpose of the participation in the group, counselors promote termination of members from the group in the most efficient period of time.
    a. Group counselors maintain a constant awareness of the progress made by each member and periodically invite the group members to explore and reevaluate their experiences in the group. It is the responsibility of group counselors to help promote the independence of members from the group in a timely manner.
14. *Evaluation and Follow-up:* Group counselors make every attempt to engage in ongoing assessment and to design follow-up procedures for their groups.
    a. Group counselors recognize the importance of ongoing assessment of a group, and they assist members in evaluating their own progress.
    b. Group counselors conduct evaluation of the total group experience at the final meeting (or before termination), as well as ongoing evaluation.
    c. Group counselors monitor their own behavior and become aware of what they are modeling in the group.
    d. Follow-up procedures might take the form of personal contact, telephone contact, or written contact.
    e. Follow-up meetings might be with individuals, or groups, or both to determine the degree to which: (i) members have reached their goals, (ii) the group had a positive or negative effect on the participants, (iii) members could profit from some type of referral, and (iv) as information for possible modifications of future groups. If there is no follow-up meeting, provisions are made available for individual follow-up meetings to any member who needs or requests such a contact.
15. *Referrals:* If the needs of a particular member cannot be met within the type of group being offered, the group counselor suggests other appropriate professional referrals.
    a. Group counselors are knowledgeable of local community resources for assisting group members regarding professional referrals.
    b. Group counselors help members seek further professional assistance, if needed.

16. *Professional Development:* Group counselors recognize that professional growth is a continuous, ongoing, developmental process throughout their careers.
   a. Group counselors maintain and upgrade their knowledge and skill competencies through educational activities, clinical experiences, and participation in professional development activities.
   b. Group counselors keep abreast of research findings and new developments as applied to groups.

SAFEGUARDING ETHICAL PRACTICE AND PROCEDURES FOR REPORTING UNETHICAL BEHAVIOR

The preceding remarks have been advanced as guidelines which are generally representative of ethical and professional group practice. They have not been proposed as rigidly defined prescriptions. However, practitioners who are thought to be grossly unresponsive to the ethical concerns addressed in this document may be subject to a review of their practices by the AACD Ethics Committee and ASGW peers.

- For consultation and/or questions regarding these ASGW Ethical Guidelines or group ethical dilemmas, you may contact the Chairperson of the ASGW Ethics Committee. The name, address and telephone number of the current ASGW Ethics Committee Chairperson may be acquired by telephone from the AACD office in Alexandria, Virginia at (703) 823-9800.
- If a group counselor's behavior is suspected as being unethical, the following procedures are to be followed:
   a. Collect more information and investigate further to confirm the unethical practice as determined by the ASGW Ethical Guidelines.
   b. Confront the individual with the apparent violation of ethical guidelines for the purposes of protecting the safety of any clients and to help the group counselor correct any inappropriate behaviors. If satisfactory resolution is not reached through this contact then:
   c. A complaint should be made in writing, including the specific facts and dates of the alleged violation and all relevant supporting data. The complaint should be included in an envelope marked "CONFIDENTIAL" to ensure confidentiality for both the accuser(s) and the alleged violator(s) and forwarded to all of the following sources:
1. The name and address of the Chairperson of the state Counselor Licensure Board for the respective state, if in existence.
2. The Ethics Committee, c/o The President, American Association for Counseling and Development, 5999 Stevenson Avenue, Alexandria, Virginia 22304.
3. The name and address of all private credentialing agencies that the alleged violator maintains credentials or holds professional membership. Some of these include the following:

National Board for Certified Counselors, Inc., 5999 Stevenson Avenue, Alexandria, Virginia 22304

National Council for Credentialing of Career Counselors, c/o NBCC, 5999 Stevenson Avenue, Alexandria, Virginia 22304

National Academy for Certified Clinical Mental Health Counselors, 5999 Stevenson Avenue, Alexandria, Virginia 22304

Commission on Rehabilitation Counselor Certification, 162 North State Street, Suite 317, Chicago, Illinois 60601

American Association for Marriage and Family Therapy, 1717 K Street, N.W., Suite 407, Washington, DC 20006

American Psychological Association, 1200 Seventeenth Street, N.W., Washington, DC 20036

American Group Psychotherapy Association, Inc., 25 East 21st Street, 6th Floor, New York, New York 10010

Approved by the Association for Specialists in Group Work (ASGW) Executive Board, June 1, 1989

ETHICAL STANDARDS FOR SCHOOL COUNSELORS

AMERICAN SCHOOL COUNSELOR ASSOCIATION (ASCA)

PREAMBLE

The American School Counselor Association (ASCA) is a professional organization whose members have a unique and distinctive preparation, grounded in the behavioral sciences, with training in clinical skills adapted to the school setting. The school counselor assists in the growth and development of each individual and uses his/her specialized skills to ensure that the rights of the counselee are properly protected within the structure of the school program. School counselors subscribe to the following basic tenets of the counseling process from which professional responsibilities are derived.

1. Each person has the right to respect and dignity as a unique human being and to counseling services without prejudice as to person, character, belief or practice.
2. Each person has the right to self-direction and self-development.
3. Each person has the right of choice and the responsibility for decisions reached.
4. Each person has the right to privacy and thereby the right to expect the counselor–client relationship to comply with all laws, policies, and ethical standards pertaining to confidentiality.

In this document, the American School Counselor Association has specified the principles of ethical behavior necessary to maintain and regulate high standards of integrity and leadership among its members. The Association recognizes the basic commitment of its members to the *Ethical Standards* of its parent organization, the American Association of Counseling and Development [Note: In July 1992, and after publication of these standards, the name of the association was changed to the American Counseling Association] and nothing in this document shall be construed to supplant the code. The *Ethical Standards for School Counselors* was developed to complement the AACD standards by clarifying the nature of ethical responsibilities for present and future counselors in the school setting. The purposes of this document are to:

1. Serve as a guide for the ethical practices of all professional school counselors regardless of level, area, population served, or membership in this Association.
2. Provide benchmarks for both self-appraisal and peer evaluations regarding counselor responsibilities to students, parents, colleagues and professional associates, school and community, self, and the counseling profession.
3. Inform those served by the school counselor of acceptable counselor practices and expected professional deportment.

A. RESPONSIBILITIES TO STUDENTS

The school counselor:

1. Has a primary obligation and loyalty to the student, who is to be treated with respect as a unique individual, whether assisted individually or in a group setting.
2. Is concerned with the total needs of the student (educational, vocational, personal and social) and encourages the maximum growth and development of each counselee.
3. Informs the counselee of the purposes, goals, techniques, and rules of procedure under which she/he may receive counseling assistance at or before the time when the counseling relationship is entered. Prior notice includes confidentiality issues such as the possible necessity for consulting with other professionals, privileged communication, and legal or authoritative restraints. The meaning and limits of confidentiality are clearly defined to counselees.
4. Refrains from consciously encouraging the counselee's acceptance of values, lifestyles, plans, decisions, and beliefs that represents only the counselor's personal orientation.
5. Is responsible for keeping abreast of laws relating to students and strives to ensure that the rights of students are adequately provided for and protected.
6. Avoids dual relationships which might impair his/her objectivity and/or increase the risk of harm to the client (e.g., counseling one's family members, close friends or associates). If a dual relationship is unavoidable, the counselor is responsible for taking action to eliminate or reduce the potential for harm. Such safeguards might include informed consent, consultation, supervision and documentation.
7. Makes appropriate referrals when professional assistance can no longer be adequately provided to the counselee. Appropriate referral requires knowledge about available resources.
8. Protects the confidentiality of student records and releases personal data only according to prescribed laws and school policies. Student information maintained through electronic data storage methods is treated with the same care as traditional student records.

9. Protects the confidentiality of information received in the counseling relationship as specified by law and ethical standards. Such information is only to be revealed to others with the informed consent of the counselee and consistent with the obligations of the counselor as a professional person.

    In a group setting the counselor sets a norm of confidentiality and stresses its importance, yet clearly states that confidentiality in group counseling cannot be guaranteed.

10. Informs the appropriate authorities when the counselee's condition indicates a clear and imminent danger to the counselee or others. This is to be done after careful deliberation and, where possible, after consultation with other professionals. The counselor informs the counselee of actions to be taken so as to minimize confusion and clarify expectations.

11. Screens prospective group members and maintains an awareness of participants' compatibility throughout the life of the group, especially when the group emphasis is on self-disclosure and self-understanding. The counselor takes reasonable precautions to protect members from physical and/or psychological harm resulting from interaction within the group.

12. Provides explanations of the nature, purposes, and results of tests in language that is understandable to the client(s).

13. Adheres to relevant standards regarding the selection, administration, and interpretation of assessment techniques. The counselor recognizes that computer-based testing programs require specific training in administration, scoring and interpretation which may differ from that required in more traditional assessments.

14. Promotes the benefits of appropriate computer applications and clarifies the limitations of computer technology. The counselor ensures that (1) computer applications are appropriate for the individual needs of the counselee, (2) the counselee understands how to use the applications, and (3) follow-up counseling assistance is provided. Members of underrepresented groups are assured of equal access to computer technologies and the absence of discriminatory information and values within computer applications.

15. Has unique ethical responsibilities in working with peer programs. In general, the school counselor is responsible for the welfare of the students participating in peer programs under his/her direction. School counselors who function in training and supervisory capacities are referred to the preparation and supervision standards of professional associations.

B. RESPONSIBILITIES TO PARENTS

The school counselor:

1. Respects the inherent rights and responsibilities of parents for their children and endeavors to establish a cooperative relationship with parents to facilitate the maximum development of the counselee.

2. Informs parents of the counselor's role, with emphasis on the confidential nature of the counseling relationship between the counselor and counselee.
3. Provides parents with accurate, comprehensive and relevant information in an objective and caring manner, as appropriate and consistent with ethical responsibilities to the counselee.
4. Treats information received from parents in a confidential and appropriate manner.
5. Shares information about a counselee only with those persons properly authorized to receive such information.
6. Adheres to laws and local guidelines when assisting parents experiencing family difficulties which interfere with the counselee's effectiveness and welfare.
7. Is sensitive to changes in the family and recognizes that all parents, custodial and noncustodial, are vested with certain rights and responsibilities for the welfare of their children by virtue of their position and according to law.

C. RESPONSIBILITIES TO COLLEAGUES AND PROFESSIONAL ASSOCIATES

The school counselor:

1. Establishes and maintains a cooperative relationship with faculty, staff, and administration to facilitate the provision of optimal guidance and counseling programs and services.
2. Promotes awareness and adherence to appropriate guidelines regarding confidentiality, the distinction between public and private information, and staff consultation.
3. Treats colleagues with respect, courtesy, fairness, and good faith. The qualifications, views, and findings of colleagues are represented accurately and fairly to enhance the image of competent professionals.
4. Provides professional personnel with accurate, objective, concise and meaningful data necessary to adequately evaluate, counsel, and assist the counselee.
5. Is aware of and fully utilizes related professions and organizations to whom the counselee may be referred.

D. RESPONSIBILITIES TO THE SCHOOL AND COMMUNITY

The school counselor:

1. Supports and protects the educational program against any infringement not in the best interests of students.
2. Informs appropriate officials of conditions that may be potentially disruptive or damaging to the school's mission, personnel and property.
3. Delineates and promotes the counselor's role and function in meeting the needs of those served. The counselor will notify appropriate school officials of conditions which may limit or curtail their effectiveness in providing programs and services.

4. Assist in the development of (1) curricular and environmental conditions appropriate for the school and community, (2) educational procedures and programs to meet student needs, and (3) a systematic evaluation process for guidance and counseling programs, services and personnel. The counselor is guided by findings of the evaluation data in planning programs and services.

5. Actively cooperates and collaborates with agencies, organizations, and individuals in the school and community in the best interest of counselees and without regard to personal reward or remuneration.

E. RESPONSIBILITIES TO SELF

The school counselor:

1. Functions within the boundaries of individual professional competence and accepts responsibility for the consequences of his/her actions.

2. Is aware of the potential effects of her/his own personal characteristics on services to clients.

3. Monitors personal functioning and effectiveness and refrains from any activity likely to lead to inadequate professional services or harm to a client.

4. Recognizes that differences in clients relating to age, gender, race, religion, sexual orientation, socioeconomic and ethnic backgrounds may require specific training to ensure competent services.

5. Strives through personal initiatives to maintain professional competence and keeps abreast of innovations and trends in the profession. Professional and personal growth is continuous and ongoing throughout the counselor's career.

F. RESPONSIBILITIES TO THE PROFESSION

The school counselor:

1. Conducts herself/himself in such a manner as to bring credit to self and the profession.

2. Conducts appropriate research and reports findings in a manner consistent with acceptable educational and psychological research practices. When using client data for research, statistical or program planning purposes, the counselor ensures protections of the identity of the individual client(s).

3. Actively participates in local, state, and national associations which foster the development and improvement of school counseling.

4. Adheres to ethical standards of the profession, other official policy statements pertaining to counseling, and relevant statutes established by federal, state and local governments.

5. Clearly distinguishes between statements and actions made as a private individual and as a representative of the school counseling profession.

6. Contributes to the development of the profession through the sharing of skills, ideas and expertise with colleagues.

G. MAINTENANCE OF STANDARDS

Ethical behavior among professional school counselors, association members and nonmembers, is expected at all times. When there exists serious doubt as to the ethical behavior of colleagues, or if counselors are forced to work in situations or abide by policies which do not reflect the standards as outlined in these *Ethical Standards for School Counselors* or the AACD *Ethical Standards,* the counselor is obligated to take appropriate action to rectify the condition. The following procedures may serve as a guide:

1. If feasible, the counselor should consult with a professional colleague to confidentially discuss the nature of the complaint to see if she/he views the situation as an ethical violation.
2. Whenever possible, the counselor should directly approach the colleague whose behavior is in question to discuss the complaint and seek resolution.
3. If resolution is not forthcoming at the personal level, the counselor shall utilize the channels established within the school and/or school district. This may include both informal and formal procedures.
4. If the matter still remains unresolved, referral for review and appropriate action should be made to the Ethics Committees in the following sequence:
   - local counselor association
   - state counselor association
   - national counselor association
5. The ASCA Ethics Committee functions in an educative and consultative capacity and does not adjudicate complaints of ethical misconduct. Therefore, at the national level, complaints should be submitted in writing to the ACA Ethics Committee for review and appropriate action. The procedure for submitting complaints may be obtained by writing the ACA Ethics Committee, c/o The Executive Director, American Counseling Association, 5999 Stevenson Avenue, Alexandria, VA 22304.

H. RESOURCES

School counselors are responsible for being aware of, and acting in accord with, the standards and positions of the counseling profession as represented in official documents as those listed below.

Code of Ethics (1989). National Board for Certified Counselors. Alexandria VA.

Code of Ethics for Peer Helping Professionals (1989). National Peer Helpers Association. Glendale, CA.

Ethical Guidelines for Group Counselors (1989). Association for Specialists in Group Work. Alexandria, VA.

Ethical Standards (1988). American Association for Counseling and Development. Alexandria, VA.

Position Statement: The School Counselor and Confidentiality (1986). American School Counseling Association. Alexandria, VA.

Confidentiality (1986). American School Counselor Association. Alexandria, VA.

Position Statement: The School Counselor and Peer Facilitation (1984). American School Counseling Association. Alexandria, VA.

Position Statement: The School Counselor and Student Rights (1982). American School Counselor Association. Alexandria, VA.

Ethical Standards for School Counselors was adopted by the ASCA Delegate Assembly March 19, 1984. This revision was approved by the ASCA Delegate Assembly, March 27, 1992.